SELECTED LETTERS
ON POLITICS AND SOCIETY

Alexis de Tocqueville

SELECTED LETTERS
ON POLITICS AND SOCIETY

Edited by Roger Boesche

Translated by James Toupin

and Roger Boesche

University of California Press
Berkeley Los Angeles London

University of California Press
Berkeley and Los Angeles, California
University of California Press, Ltd.
London, England
© 1985 by
The Regents of the University of California
Printed in the United States of America
1 2 3 4 5 6 7 8 9

Library of Congress Cataloging in Publication Data
Tocqueville, Alexis de, 1805–1859.
  Selected letters on politics and society.
  Includes index.
  1. Tocqueville, Alexis de, 1805–1859. 2. Historians—
France—Correspondence. 3. Statesmen—France—Corres-
pondence. I. Boesche, Roger. II. Title.
DC255.T6A4 1985   944.07'092'4   84-2524
ISBN 0-520-05047-9

To our parents

CONTENTS

ACKNOWLEDGMENTS

We would like to thank some of the people who assisted us with this project. Claude Forteau read early pieces of our translation, and her encouragement and suggestions were very helpful throughout this undertaking. Ruth Benz read almost all of our draft with great care; for such errors as may remain, we have only ourselves to blame for not taking enough advantage of her willing and very capable aid. Ed and Ruth Mickle performed the herculean task of typing our entire first draft. Later, Ann Manning of Occidental College graciously and meticulously repeated this effort one and a half times; we thank Ann not only for her nimble fingers but also for her quick eye in spotting typographical errors. As for Amanda Reynolds Boesche, we remain amazed that she could put up with the intensity and frequent weariness of two Tocquevilleians at their work, and we thank her for all her support.

The John Randolph and Dora Haynes Foundation twice decided it had confidence in this project, and we hope the results are worthy of its financial contributions and expectations. In addition, Occidental College's strong commitment to supporting scholarship was indispensable, and we are grateful for the countless ways that institution offered financial assistance and encouragement.

Every student of Tocqueville owes a debt to the pioneers of Tocqueville scholarship. While we cannot mention all of them, we must thank G. W. Pierson for his part in furthering the Yale University Tocqueville Manuscripts Collection at the Beinecke Rare Book and Manuscript Library, from which we obtained key letters. The debt we have incurred to J. P. Mayer, André Jardin, and the countless other editors of the Commission nationale in Paris that is compiling and editing the definitive edition of Tocqueville's works in conjunction with Editions Gallimard is impossible to measure and hence impossible to repay. Without borrowing from these efforts, no modern Tocqueville scholar can proceed intelligently. Finally, we would like to thank Alexis de Tocqueville and Gustave de Beaumont—who saw one of us to his doctorate and the other to a law degree—and whom we have come to know and like very much. We hope this translation is worthy of their efforts and their friendship.

INTRODUCTION

Despite widespread admiration for his remarkable insights into American politics and for his analysis of French society before the Revolution of 1789, Alexis de Tocqueville remains an anomalous figure to most readers. He is known principally for his great work *Democracy in America,* the analysis of American society that he wrote after he toured the United States in 1831–1832 with his friend Gustave de Beaumont, ostensibly to study American penitentiaries. Occasionally. *The Old Regime and the French Revolution* and his *Recollections* about the 1848 Revolution and its aftermath appear on college reading lists. As a scholar, however, he fits no modern category neatly. As a political scientist who wrote an enduring analysis of American politics, the nineteenth century's finest French historian, a precursor of the modern sociologist, and a practical politician elected to the Chamber of Deputies and appointed foreign minister of France, Tocqueville offers something for everyone. Yet it is difficult to assimilate all these parts into a whole.

This volume of selected letters offers a more complete picture of Tocqueville than previously available. The first English translation of a broad selection of his letters to appear in this century, it has been made possible both by the ongoing publication, since the early 1950s, of Tocqueville's complete works in the definitive French edition under the direction of J. P. Mayer and also by the 1972 German publication of letters to his local election manager. To supplement these sources, we have also drawn upon the Tocqueville collection at Yale University and the nineteenth-century publication of some of Tocqueville's letters.[1]

In this volume we have tried to offer an overview of Tocqueville's political ideas and his political life. We trace Tocqueville from his adolescent fascination with England through his early days as a lawyer, his journey to North America, his writing of *Democracy in America,* his frustrating career as an opposition politician in the Chamber of Deputies, his immediate reactions to the 1848 Revolution, and, finally, his renewed political writing during his forced retirement from politics under Louis Napoleon's Second Empire. Although his letters from North America are extremely important and his long letters to Chabrol and Kergorlay give a fine sense of his first impressions and reactions to American democracy, we have not overemphasized this part of his life. As a result, our selection covers his entire life and necessarily pays more attention to the French political and intellectual worlds in which he circulated. After all, his primary concern was always France. "Although I very rarely spoke of France in [*Democracy in America*], I did not write one

---

1. The definitive French edition of Tocqueville's works currently being published under the direction of J. P. Mayer is *Oeuvres complètes* (Paris: Gallimard, 1951–); hereafter referred to as *Oeuvres* (M). See also Alexis de Tocqueville, *Alexis de Tocqueville als Abgeordneter: Briefe an seinen Wahlagenten Paul Clamorgan, 1837–1851* (Hamburg: Ernst Hauswedell & Co., 1972); and *Oeuvres complètes d'Alexis de Tocqueville* (Paris: Michel Lévy Frères, 1860–1866), published under the direction of his friend Gustave de Beaumont; hereafter referred to as *Oeuvres* (B). For a complete listing of the origin of each letter, see Appendix C.

page of it without thinking about her" (Letter 53). Tocqueville always regarded himself as both a political actor and a scholar, but in each capacity he concerned himself primarily with adapting democratic institutions to the political culture of France. Although these letters focus on the political side of Tocqueville's life, they unavoidably characterize him as an individual. His letters are especially important in this regard because although there are sketches of his life and detailed studies of his journey to North America, there is no complete and detailed biography.[2] His correspondence therefore permits an insight into how Tocqueville's analyses of politics and society sprang, at least in part, from his personal temperament and aspirations. Four sentiments thread their way through the letters: first, the anxieties of his personal life and his reliance on close friendship; second, the concerns he held in common with participants in the contemporary French Romantic movement; third, his simultaneous disenchantment with and love for his country; and, fourth, the importance of religion in his personal life and in his political convictions.[3]

2. Recent biographies tend to be good but too short whereas turn-of-the-century biographies tend to be tedious and tainted by an urge to claim Tocqueville for the Catholic church. For the former, see J. P. Mayer, *Alexis de Tocqueville: A Biographical Study in Political Science* (Gloucester, Mass.: Peter Smith, 1966); and also Edward Gargan, *De Tocqueville* (New York: Hillary House Publishers, 1965). For the latter, see Antoine Redier, *Comme disait M. de Tocqueville* (Paris: Librairie Académique Perrin, 1925).

There are two excellent and detailed studies of Tocqueville's journey to America and his completion of *Democracy in America*. See George Wilson Pierson, *Tocqueville and Beaumont in America* (New York: Oxford University Press, 1938); and James T. Schleifer, *The Making of Tocqueville's "Democracy in America"* (Chapel Hill: University of North Carolina Press, 1980).

3. Readers who wish a comprehensive study of Tocqueville's thought might profitably consult one or more of the following: Jack Lively, *The Social and Political Thought of Alexis de Tocqueville* (Oxford: Clarendon Press, 1962); Marvin Zetterbaum, *Tocqueville and the Problem of Democracy* (Stanford: Stanford University Press, 1967); Raymond Aron, *Main Currents in Sociological Thought,* I, *Montesquieu, Comte, Marx, Tocqueville,* trans. Richard Howard and Helen Weaver (Garden City, N.Y.: Doubleday, 1968); R. Pierre Marcel, *Essai politique sur Alexis de Tocqueville* (Paris: Librairie Félix Alcan, 1910); Maxime Leroy, *Histoire des idées sociales en France,* II, *De Babeuf à Tocqueville* (Paris:

Personal Life: Anxiety, Unhappiness, Friendship

One characteristic that emerges from Tocqueville's letters might surprise some readers. Whether in the United States or in Algeria, in the Chamber of Deputies or behind the barricades of 1848, Tocqueville seemed calm and self-confident; yet when in the first letter he confesses to "moments of despair," we discover that Tocqueville was unhappy and tormented by a mind that, as he once said, regularly preyed upon itself.[4] In one letter to his brother he admits that the same anxiety and impatience that drives him to significant accomplishment also torments him "without cause" and makes him "suffer greatly" (Letter 39). Late in his life he acknowledges to Beaumont that he has never found the way to happiness: "In my youth, I used to have a disordered mind in a fairly healthy body. Now, my mind is nearly healed, but its envelope does not lend itself any more to what is asked of it. I did not know how to be happy then; I cannot be so now" (Letter 86). Occasionally, Tocqueville seems even desperate; he confides to his lifelong friend Kergorlay that "there are moments when I think my reason is

Gallimard, 1950); Hugh Brogan, *Tocqueville* (London: Fontana, 1973); Seymour Drescher, *Tocqueville and England* (Cambridge, Mass.: Harvard University Press, 1964); Jean-Claude Lamberti, *Tocqueville et les deux démocraties* (Paris: Presses Universitaires de France, 1983); Xavier de la Fournière, *Alexis de Tocqueville: Un monarchiste indépendant* (Paris: Librairie Académique Perrin, 1981); Roger Boesche, "The Prison: Tocqueville's Model for Despotism," *Western Political Quarterly* XXXIII (December 1980): 550–563; Roger Boesche, "The Strange Liberalism of Alexis de Tocqueville," *History of Political Thought* II (Winter 1981):495–524; Roger Boesche, "Why Could Tocqueville Predict So Well?" *Political Theory* XI (February 1983):79–103; Georges Lefèbvre, "A propos de Tocqueville," *Annales historiques de la révolution française* XXVII (October–December 1955):313–323; Harold Laski, "Alexis de Tocqueville and Democracy," in *The Social and Political Ideas of Some Representative Thinkers of the Victorian Age,* ed. F. J. C. Hearnshaw, pp. 100–115 (London: George Harrap & Co., 1933).

4. Below, Letter 1; Alexis de Tocqueville and Nassau William Senior, *Correspondence and Conversations of Alexis de Tocqueville with Nassau William Senior,* 2 vols. in 1, ed. M. C. M. Simpson, trans. Mrs. M. C. M. Simpson (New York: Augustus M. Kelley, 1968), 1:125; hereafter referred to as *Correspondence . . . Senior.*

going," and to Beaumont he declares that "there are certain moments when I am so tormented and so little master of myself."[5] His frustration at finding happiness may very well have reinforced his political pessimism and disenchantment.

These feelings apparently led Tocqueville to regard life much like the Stoic who was taught to expect disappointment. Life, he says at one point, is neither a pleasure nor a sorrow, but simply a serious task that it is our duty to carry out with dignity and propriety. "Life is therefore neither an excellent nor a very bad thing, but, allow me the expression, a *mediocre* thing partaking of both. One must neither expect too much from it, nor fear too much, but attempt to see it as it is, without disgust or enthusiasm, like an inevitable fact . . . which it is above all a matter of making endurable" (Letter 10).

In a well-known passage, Tocqueville says that he lives constantly with the ideas of Pascal, Montesquieu, and Rousseau.[6] For any nineteenth-century French political thinker, the latter two authors seem obvious choices, but readers of Tocqueville's published works might wonder about the private significance of Pascal. Having observed his anxiety and his inability to find peace of mind, we can understand his fondness for Pascal more readily. Pascal, however, suggested that most people attempt to escape from anxiety and doubt by diversion, and yet in his letters Tocqueville rarely mentions what we would call diversions. In reading anyone's letters, it is important to detect what topics an author either omits or seldom mentions, and Tocqueville omits nearly all discussion of anything that might divert his mind from anxiety or entertain him—meals with friends, parties, the theater, recreation, vacations for pleasure, finance, hobbies, gambling, light read-

5. Below, Letter 23; Tocqueville, *Oeuvres* (M), VIII, pt. 1, *Correspondance d'Alexis de Tocqueville et de Gustave de Beaumont*, p. 499; hereafter referred to as *Correspondance . . . Beaumont*.

6. Tocqueville, *Oeuvres* (M), XIII, pt. 1, *Correspondance d'Alexis de Tocqueville et de Louis de Kergorlay*, p. 418; hereafter referred to as *Correspondance . . . Kergorlay*.

ing, and sporting activities. Even if he engaged in some of these activities to a limited extent, he apparently had only three important "diversions": his intellectual work, political action, and the pleasures of friendship.

Although Tocqueville came to recognize that his fame would rest not on his ultimately unsuccessful political efforts, but on his writing, his writing did not itself lessen his anxiety and bring happiness. He wrote Beaumont that he dreaded six months of winter with only his scholarly work to occupy his mind and distract him, and even after great acclaim for both volumes of *Democracy in America,* he wrote his brother that his undreamed-of success could not give him "complete happiness" because "I have lived enough to know that there is not a single good thing in this world the enjoyment of which can hold me and satisfy me."[7] By contrast, he was more excited by political action. "There is no happiness comparable to political success, when your own excitement is justified by the magnitude of the questions at issue, and is doubled and redoubled by the sympathy of your supporters."[8] Yet he was frustrated by his ineffectiveness in politics and by his distaste for all the political alternatives that seemed available to France in his lifetime.

Not only the seriousness of political issues but also the prospect of working closely with friends drew Tocqueville to politics. In the last analysis, friendship seemed to bring Tocqueville most of the happiness of which he was capable. To be sure, friendship was politically important to Tocqueville because friends acting in common—in associations and groups—might mitigate the threat of centralized government. Yet from beginning to end these letters tell a story of the intrinsic importance of friendship, friendship as an end in itself. His statement that "it is only in a father or a wife that true and continual sympathy can be found," because "all other friendships are

7. Tocqueville, *Oeuvres* (M), VIII, pt. 3, *Correspondance . . . Beaumont,* pp. 153–154; below, Letter 39.

8. Tocqueville, *Correspondence . . . Senior,* 2:206–207.

only incomplete and ineffective sentiments compared to that" (Letter 94), is an aberration from his lifelong conviction of the importance of friendship in personal and political affairs. To be sure, friendship caused Tocqueville pain. His deep friendship with Louis de Kergorlay gradually faded as Kergorlay withdrew from the practical world to keep his royalist principles pure, refused or was unable to undertake intellectual endeavors of which Tocqueville thought him capable, and eventually turned to what Tocqueville regarded as the distasteful world of commerce. Tocqueville and Beaumont hurt each other keenly in their quarrel in 1844, a quarrel that arose from political differences and misunderstandings,[9] and their friendship seemed to lack intensity until the 1848 Revolution brought them back together.

Nevertheless, friendship was inestimably important to Tocqueville. At twenty-two he wrote to Kergorlay of how deeply he felt "the value of the friendship that unites us. Let us hold onto that feeling with all our might, my dear Louis: it alone in this world is firm and stable" (Letter 4). With Beaumont, who traveled with him to the United States and Algeria and nursed him through a serious illness on each journey, this sentiment only deepened. In 1855 Tocqueville reminisced about the previous twenty-five years and, despite melancholy and nostalgia, concluded on a happy note. "In order to complete cheering myself up again, I considered that I had kept to this day the same friend with whom I hunted parrots in Memphis, and that time had only managed to strengthen the ties of confidence and friendship that existed between us then" (Letter 82). The last, very sad letter of this volume, in which Tocqueville desperately asks Beaumont to come to his aid while he is sick, again testifies to the strength of their friendship. It is a moving end for anyone who has read their long exchange of letters.

9. Letter 47; and Beaumont's reply, Letter 48.

Tocqueville and French Romanticism

Tocqueville cannot be labeled a Romantic because he reminds one more readily of realists such as Balzac and Stendhal than Romantics such as Jules Michelet and Alphonse de Lamartine (see n. 18, p. 166). Nevertheless, his anxiety and disquiet remind any student of French intellectual history of the disenchantment of so many of his Romantic contemporaries, typified by the melancholy of Lamartine's *Méditations poétiques* (1820) and the emptiness expressed by François Chateaubriand's famous character René. His letters thus startle us by locating Tocqueville—who scoffed at sad-eyed Romantics and preferred Bishop Bossuet to Alfred de Musset—in his own restless Romantic generation. Not only did he reenact Sir Walter Scott in one letter for the benefit of his fiancée Mary Mottley (Letter 16), but several themes characteristic of French Romanticism recur throughout his letters.

First, we discover that Tocqueville, who often seems in his published writings so calm and judiciously analytical, longed for adventure, political action, and even the accomplishment of great deeds. At nineteen, he wrote to Kergorlay about stealing away to see England and about their dream *"to roam about for the rest of time"* (Letter 2). Just three years later he lamented that studying law was transforming him into a machine, a man with one narrow specialization, incapable of great intellectual understanding and unable to undertake any great deeds (Letter 3). To those who see Tocqueville as a bookish man, uncomfortable outside his study stuffed with ancient authors, it is surprising how often this wish for great political action appears in his letters. In 1835 he confided his wish that providence would present him with a chance to accomplish something grand, allowing him to quench an "internal flame" that was trying to drive him to action (Letter 23). In the midst of the 1848 Revolution, he announced to Beaumont with apparent satisfaction: "Perhaps a moment will come in which the action we will undertake can be glorious"

(Letter 56). He embraced the principles of 1789, disliked Napoleon's authoritarian tendencies, but regarded him as the most extraordinary man to have appeared in the world for centuries, and even found the English conquest of southern China in the Opium War a great deed on behalf of progress, even if it entailed "the enslavement of four parts of the world by the fifth" (Letter 36; see also Letters 43 and 51).

Tocqueville's aristocratic background and an affinity with his Romantic generation made it impossible for him to adapt to his era and enjoy a comparatively quiet life devoted to commerce and the accumulation of wealth. In 1853, Beaumont found himself in some economic difficulty, and Tocqueville suggested with great reluctance that Beaumont, just for a few years, might join an industrial enterprise to augment his income; but he quickly added: "Surely, I would not want, even from the point of view of your well-intended interest in your children, to see you devote your life to increasing your fortune, as poor Louis [de Kergorlay] seems bent on doing" (Letter 73). Despite an occasional longing for a quiet middle-class life of financial security, Tocqueville found such a life personally impossible and intellectually distasteful. In one letter he declared that he would rather sail for China, enlist as a soldier, or gamble his life away than live like a "potato," his description of the way ordinary middle-class people lived (Letter 18). To John Stuart Mill, Tocqueville blustered about France preserving its military and national glory by standing firm in a quarrel with England, rather than backing down cowardly and consoling itself by building railroads (Letter 40). Without question he felt out of place in the commercial world that surrounded him, and his longing for adventure or glory was more appropriate either to an idealized aristocratic ethic of previous centuries or to the discontent of some Romantics. "There are moments when I fear becoming mad in the manner of Don Quixote. My mind is completely crammed with a heroism that is hardly of our time, and I fall very flat when I come out of these dreams and find myself face to face with reality" (Letter 31).

Tocqueville shared another characteristic with his Romantic generation: he admired strong passions, and, despite all his enormous debts to the French Enlightenment, he occasionally distrusted excessive reasoning. "Reason," he suggested, "has always been for me like a cage that keeps me from acting, but not from gnashing my teeth behind the bars" (Letter 42). By contrast, he applauded strong passions that led anyone to care strongly about almost anything.

The further away I am from youth, the more regardful, I will say almost respectful, I am of passions. I like them when they are good, and I am not even very certain of detesting them when they are bad. . . . What we meet least in our day are passions, true and solid passions that bind up and lead life. We no longer know how to want, or love, or hate. Doubt and philanthropy make us incapable of all things, of great evil as well as great good. . . . (Letter 41)

Less than a year before his death, he repeated this sentiment, lamenting that people had no strong feelings, neither a powerful love nor a powerful hatred, but only hoped for a quick profit at the stock exchange (Letter 103).

If Tocqueville felt out of place, it was partly because he felt acutely that he was living in a transitional period of history. This too was characteristic of French Romanticism. Musset suggested: "Everything that was is no more; everything that will be is not yet. Look no further for the secret of our troubles."[10] Similarly, Saint-Simon wrote of "wavering between an order of things which has been destroyed and cannot be restored, and another order which is coming but not yet consolidated."[11] Too late for the glories of the Revolution and Napoleon's empire and too soon for what some thought might be a golden future, so many of this Romantic generation felt condemned to live in an age of transition, an age of political

10. Harry Levin, *The Gates of Horn: A Study of Five French Realists* (New York: Oxford University Press, 1963), pp. 79–80.
11. Henri de Saint-Simon, *Social Organization: The Science of Man and Other Writings,* trans. and ed. Felix Markham (New York: Harper & Row, 1964), p. 60.

decadence on the one hand and cultural immaturity on the other. Whereas Tocqueville also articulated this feeling, he turned the sense of living in an age of transition into an advantage. He believed that living in this transitional period allowed him to analyze the strengths and weaknesses of both aristocracy and democracy. In a well-known letter to Henry Reeve, he argued this most clearly: "Aristocracy was already dead when I started life and democracy did not yet exist; so my instinct could lead me blindly neither toward one nor toward the other. . . . In a word, I was so thoroughly in equilibrium between the past and the future that I felt naturally and instinctively attracted toward neither the one nor the other, and I did not need to make great efforts to cast calm glances on both sides" (Letter 28). Late in his life he described this transition as "the prevalence of the bourgeois classes and the industrial element over the aristocratic classes and landed property," and he wondered whether the future would judge this to be a change for the better (Letter 72). Whatever the future might bring and while he hoped for freedom, he feared a new despotism; he also felt strongly, like so many of his Romantic generation, that he must make the best of a transitional era that offered both political and cultural sterility.

Disenchantment with His Age

For much of his life, Tocqueville was an active politician, but this political life always left him with a bitter taste of exasperation. Tocqueville was a member of the Chamber of Deputies from 1839 to 1848 during the July Monarchy, but in the parliamentary politics of this time, one was completely ineffective unless one sided either with Guizot (see n. 44, p. 128), who defended the status quo, or with Thiers (see n. 43, p. 128), who led an opposition with only a program for ambition, not effective reform. As Tocqueville said to Pierre-Paul Royer-Collard, Guizot and Thiers were both "fundamentally antipathetical to

my way of feeling and thinking. I despise them" (Letter 42).
Thiers especially drew his anger: "What I love, he hates or
ridicules; what he loves, I fear or despise" (Letter 50). In
another letter he lamented that "in other times and with other
men, I could have done better. But will the times improve?
And will the men we see, will they be replaced by better or at
least by *worse*? I would be disappointed about this last change
for the country, but not for myself. Because the true nightmare
of our period is in not perceiving before oneself anything either
to love or to hate, but only to despise" (Letter 42).

Tocqueville tried to remain an independent member of the
Chamber of Deputies, he associated himself with the left opposition to Guizot, he attempted to form his own opposition, and
he tried to separate Barrot (see n. 9, p. 159) from Thiers with
the hope that Barrot would provide an effective alternative.
Always his efforts proved futile. Despite serious misgivings
about the 1848 Revolution, he breathed a secret and grateful
sigh of relief to Beaumont that at least the sterile debates of
Guizot, Thiers, and the July Monarchy were over: "We will
assuredly see worse, but at least we will not see this again and
that itself is something" (Letter 56). Yet when the events of the
1848 Revolution had run their course, when Louis Napoleon
first had been elected president and eventually declared himself
emperor by force of arms, Tocqueville found himself even
more discouraged. Louis Napoleon, whom Tocqueville once
described as "the poorest usurper who will ever present himself
before a great nation" (Letter 64), ultimately managed to provide order and stimulate industry—and in Tocqueville's opinion, the citizens of France adopted a "taste for servitude" (Letter 87). In the end, Tocqueville tried to escape from his era
through his scholarly work and by reading books from the past.
"We are surrounded by the best books that have been published
in the principal languages of Europe. I have admitted nothing
into this library but what is excellent: it is enough to tell you that
it is not very voluminous, and above all that the nineteenth
century does not occupy a very great place" (Letter 91).

One can find two basic reasons for Tocqueville's disenchantment. First, France had lost its confidence, no longer attempted great achievements in politics and intellectual matters, and busied itself with what Tocqueville called a nearly "universal pettiness" (Letter 29). Whereas the preceding century displayed enormous pride and lofty, idealistic goals, the France of his time seemed humbled and incapable even of minor improvement. "After having believed ourselves capable of transforming ourselves, we believe ourselves incapable of reforming ourselves . . . we believed ourselves capable of everything, today we believe ourselves capable of nothing" (Letter 78). France had become a tired nation with no energy for accomplishment, and Tocqueville was quite willing to call it "boring" (Letter 91). Even worse, Tocqueville thought France was losing its position as the intellectual center of the world, and he suggested that if Pascal or Bossuet visited the nineteenth century, they would conclude sadly that France was "receding into semibarbarism."[12]

If the brilliant talkers and writers [of the seventeenth and eighteenth centuries] were to return to life, I do not believe that gas, or steam, or chloroform, or electric telegraph, would so much astonish them as the dullness of modern society.[13]

France, he wrote Beaumont, was becoming "covetous and frivolous"; everyone was obsessed either with making money or with "insane" ways to spend it.[14]

The second reason for Tocqueville's disenchantment was more political. In an early letter, he complained of a widespread "indifference" to "all the ideas that can stir society" because "everyone is focusing more and more on individual interest" (Letter 14). Gradually, the people of France had come to regard politics with indifference because they saw politics as only "a game in which each person seeks only to win," as only a drama in which the actors care not about the outcome of the produc-

12. Tocqueville, *Correspondence . . . Senior,* 1:140–141.
13. Ibid., 2:85.
14. Tocqueville, *Oeuvres* (M), VIII, pt. 3, *Correspondance . . . Beaumont,* p. 469.

tion but about the success and applause for their individual roles (Letter 50). Tocqueville began "to wonder if there really are principles" in the political world or if people professed principles only so long as it served their self-interest (Letter 29). In short, he despaired because the people of France had withdrawn from politics and embraced apathy, and the political leaders of France had no use for a politics of principle but instead regarded politics as an investment for increasing one's personal and material self-interest.

Tocqueville did not, however, blame the French people. Instead, he blamed an acquisitive ethic and an ethic of self-interest that had accompanied the middle class in its rise to power. In his view, the middle class had no wish for great accomplishment but sought only to satisfy people with "material enjoyments and small pleasures" (Letter 40). Tocqueville portrayed the bourgeoisie under the July Monarchy as "the most selfish and grasping of plutocracies," one which "treated government like a private business," and he regarded the middle class as no more than a new, corrupt, and vulgar aristocracy.[15] In one letter, written late in his life, he even dreamed of a new revolution guided by the "enlightened" classes and fueled with the energy of the French people (Letter 100).

Despite his disenchantment, Tocqueville rarely lost hope for the future, and he bristled at others who criticized France. Using the principle that what an author omits from his letters is frequently as important as what he includes, we discover how French Tocqueville really was because he rarely referred to foreign authors. While he occasionally discusses classical authors such as Plutarch and Machiavelli, one seeks in vain for more than a mention of writers whom modern readers might consider great English and German political thinkers, for example, Locke, Hume, Smith, Burke, Bentham, Kant, Fichte, and Hegel. Despite his well-known claim that England was

15. Tocqueville, *Correspondence . . . Senior,* 1:134; Tocqueville, *Recollections,* trans. George Lawrence (Garden City, N.Y.: Doubleday, 1971), p. 6; below, Letter 52.

his second country, despite his visits to England and Germany, Tocqueville—like so many French thinkers—assumed that Paris was the intellectual capital of the world. In his own intellectual cosmology, French writers were at the center of the universe whereas English and German writers were distant satellites.

His affection for his own country led Tocqueville to a lifelong ambivalence toward England. He admired England occasionally but criticized it frequently. At nineteen, he showed his French prejudices by boasting to Kergorlay that they would catch "sight of those English pigs who are always pictured to us as being so strong and so prosperous" (Letter 2). Although it may have required a bit of self-deception on his part, he regarded the United States and France as partners leading the world to democracy. England, by contrast, had mired itself in aristocracy. From England he wrote: "The aristocratic spirit appears to me to have descended into all classes. . . . In short, I do not recognize our America here in any point" (Letter 15). Nearly a quarter of a century later, despite admiring the class cooperation in England and bemoaning France's class conflict, he still concluded that "the aristocracy [seems] to be more solidly in place than ever" and England left "government in the hands of a very small number of families" (Letter 97). As the controlling force in 1844–1845 of a newspaper called *Le Commerce*, Tocqueville put his position (and his hopes) more bluntly:

Nowhere has an aristocracy dug deeper roots than in England. Nowhere has the principle of equality received such a complete acceptance as in France. . . . The great interest in France is thus to substitute everywhere free institutions for despotic ones. . . . This is not the interest of England.[16]

When Nassau William Senior took exception to Tocqueville's claim that the rich of England treated the poor unfairly, Tocqueville defended himself: "I will believe, until I have proof

---

16. *Le Commerce*, September 6, 1844, and January 21, 1845. For a more detailed discussion of Tocqueville's views in *Le Commerce*, see Roger Boesche, "Tocqueville and *Le Commerce*: A Newspaper Expressing His Unusual Liberalism," *Journal of the History of Ideas* XLIV (April-June 1983): 277–292.

to the contrary, that in England the rich have little by little drawn to themselves almost all the advantages that the state of society furnishes to men" (Letter 20). In an 1855 letter he seemed to take delight at the sight of England floundering with a "mediocre and soft government" (Letter 83).

Curiously, because of his conviction about France's intellectual decline, Tocqueville seemed incapable of defending France, even when he wanted to, against the charge that it produced no great intellectual works. When Arthur de Gobineau made the charge, Tocqueville could only cite Lamartine and the marvelously mediocre Scribe in defense of French literary talents (Letter 103). It is not that Tocqueville was unfamiliar with French literary figures. With the two notable exceptions of Baudelaire and Flaubert, Tocqueville mentioned, in one context or another, probably every major French writer of his time: Balzac, Béranger, Chateaubriand, Dumas, Gautier, Hugo, Lamartine, Musset, Sainte-Beuve, Sand, Scribe, and Sue—and he almost certainly knew of Stendhal.[17] Why was Tocqueville unable to defend nineteenth-century France's most impressive literary record? Perhaps, because he omitted all serious discussion of literature, this very political man had no real desire to make a careful study of contemporary literature. Or perhaps his own disenchantment with his age would not allow him to admit the quality of the French literary achievements of his day.

The Importance of Religion

Although he displayed occasional hostility to organized religion, in his letters Tocqueville leaves no doubt that he was a

17. When Tocqueville controlled the newspaper *Le Commerce* in 1844–1845, it reviewed most of the authors listed above. See also *Oeuvres* (M), VI, pt. 1, *Correspondance anglaise: Correspondance d'Alexis de Tocqueville avec Henry Reeve et John Stuart Mill,* p. 320, where he demonstrated his familiarity with French literature in a critique he undertook for Mill; R. Virtanen, "Tocqueville and the Romantics," *Symposium* XIII (Spring 1959): 167–185. Finally, because both Tocqueville and Stendhal were close friends with the literary critic Jean-Jacques Ampère, it is likely Tocqueville was familiar with Stendhal's work.

very religious man who relied upon religious values in both his personal and intellectual life. In an early letter, for example, he acknowledged that he had great anxiety and doubt about whether the world offered any certain truths: "That was the unhappiest time of my life; I can only compare myself to a man who, seized by dizziness, believes that he feels the floor tremble under his feet and sees the walls that surround him move; even today, I recall that period with a feeling of horror. I can say that then I fought with doubt hand to hand, and that it is rare to do so with more despair" (Letter 10). In another letter he seemed to project his own doubt on others. Protestants of the United States, he wrote Kergorlay, have a wide range of beliefs from which to choose, but "such a spectacle cannot fail to throw the mind of a thinking Protestant into inextricable doubt," and as a result Tocqueville thought more and more Americans would throw themselves into the authoritative arms of the Catholic church (Letter 8). One must wonder if his own religious dilemmas did not influence his analysis of religion in the United States, and one must wonder if, despite his distrust of the Catholic church, Tocqueville did not like the comfortable certainty offered by Catholicism.

One searches in vain in Tocqueville's published writings for any systematic discussion of the philosophical basis for his personal ethical positions. His letters reveal, however, that he relied on Christianity for his most basic ethical assumptions. Tocqueville's friend Gobineau was among the first racial theorists of the nineteenth century, but Tocqueville objected vehemently to his friend's views, partly on the grounds that Gobineau's theory defied all Christian belief: "Christianity certainly tended to make all men brothers and equals. Your doctrine makes all of them cousins at most, the common father of whom is only in heaven; here below there are only conquerors and conquered, masters and slaves by right of birth, and this is so true that your doctrines are approved, cited, commented on by whom? By the owners of slaves. . . ." (Letter 92). At one time Tocqueville considered writing a work on the moral philosophy of the previous several centuries, but he never made the study in any thoroughness perhaps because he remained convinced that despite all the philosophical arguments of modern philosophers, none of them had added significantly to the doctrines of Christianity. As he said in an 1843 letter to Gobineau:

> What is there really new in the works or in the discoveries of the modern moral philosophers? . . . Did they really establish new foundations, or even new explanations, for human duties? . . . Through all the darkness all I think I can recognize is this: to me it is Christianity that seems to have accomplished the revolution—you may prefer the word *change*—in all the ideas that concern duties and rights; ideas which, after all, are the basic matter of all moral knowledge. . . . Thus Christianity put in grand evidence the equality, the unity, the fraternity of all men.[18]

Tocqueville had little use for philosophical speculation; indeed he called such speculation a "voluntary torment that man has consented to inflict on himself" (Letter 10). Once again his letters are revealing for what they omit. The reader will find no mention of natural rights theories, Kantian categorical imperatives, or English Utilitarianism because Tocqueville's ethical assumptions apparently originated in his Catholic education and in some notion of political duty. However much he had misgivings about the Catholic church and about the aristocratic class into which he was born, his convictions about morality, which one can trace to these two traditions, remained remarkably constant and largely unexplored.

If religion played an important role in his private life, it was no less present in his intellectual life. Tocqueville never offered a comprehensive theory of history, and he certainly never tried to outline laws of historical development. For this reason he regarded the future as disturbingly undetermined, with possibilities either for great democratic freedom or a qualitatively new democratic despotism. Nevertheless, with some help from lectures by Guizot, he argued that there was one discernible

---

18. Alexis de Tocqueville, *The European Revolution and Correspondence with Gobineau*, trans. John Lukacs (Gloucester, Mass.: Peter Smith, 1968), pp. 190f.

tendency in European historical development, and that, of course, was the tendency to ever-increasing equality. Although he occasionally gave this march of history an economic, political, or class analysis, he made his public argument by relying on the designs of God. Every reader of *Democracy in America* knows that Tocqueville suggested that "Providence" was pushing Europe irresistibly toward equality. He may have phrased his argument in this way because it was an easier and more palatable argument to make to his audience,[19] far easier than Guizot's class analysis, but I think he also did it from conviction, as if he had never emerged from under the sway of Bossuet's arguments about God guiding history. In a letter to Kergorlay, he said: "I cannot believe that God has been pushing two or three million men for several centuries toward equality of conditions in order to have them end in the despotism of Tiberius and Claudius" (Letter 19). When he found himself exasperated with Gobineau, having argued against the merits of Gobineau's doctrine and against its practical effects, he suggested that God did not put us on earth to end up in the passive servitude depicted by Gobineau: "You will permit me to have less confidence in you than in the bounty and justice of God" (Letter 92).

Finally, however, Tocqueville's Christian beliefs remained indelibly political. On a number of occasions he indicated that he always wanted to reconcile political liberty with Christianity, and on one trip to England, he apparently found this happy combination: "It made me see a perfect accord between the religious world and the political world, private virtues and public virtues, Christianity and liberty" (Letter 96). Too many Christians, Tocqueville argued, believed their duties to be over when they maintained private faith and even carried out acts of private charity. But Tocqueville was part of a family with a political tradition; his father held political office and his great-grandfather, Lamoignon de Malesherbes, was one of the most

---

19. See Zetterbaum, *Tocqueville and the Problem of Democracy,* ch. 1.

remarkable men of the Old Regime, the royal official who allowed publication of *L'Encyclopédie* and who represented Louis XVI at his trial for treason. As a consequence, Tocqueville's upbringing taught him that religion should support political duty and political participation, as well as private virtue. In one letter he recalled that his grandmother reminded her son that religion demanded private morality and public duty, charity to one's neighbor and participation in the affairs of one's nation (Letter 90).

Tocqueville's letters show him to have been a man passionately devoted to the application of his highest personal convictions in the public realm. They show that his most private concerns—his anxiety, his disenchantment, his wish for adventure and political glory, his religious convictions—impinged upon his political ideas and political actions. When we know the man better, we find him no less political.

Roger Boesche
Occidental College
Los Angeles

A NOTE ON THE EDITION

When one sets out to select only about one hundred letters from over a dozen volumes of letters between Tocqueville and his correspondents, one must have some criteria in mind. Accordingly, the letters in this volume have been selected with the intention of shedding light on the political ideas and concerns one finds in Tocqueville's most famous published works, thus showing how those ideas and concerns developed and how they were reflected in his own active political life. The letters selected fall into one or more of the following categories: (1) letters in which Tocqueville speculates about political problems in France and about his hopes for the emergence of stable democratic mores and institutions throughout Europe; (2) letters that disclose Tocqueville's opinions about the major political actors and events of the July Monarchy, the Second Republic, and the Second Empire; (3) letters that reveal his own political aspirations, motivations, and frustrations—especially passages that illuminate his own political actions and what he tried to accomplish in the Chamber of Deputies during the July Monarchy and later in the two assemblies of the Second Republic; (4) letters in which he analyzes other political thinkers such as Plato, Plutarch, and Machiavelli; (5) letters in which he examines the ways in which he both researches and writes about political matters; and, finally, (6) those letters that demonstrate the nature of Tocqueville's closest friendships because for Tocqueville friendship was both one of life's enduring pleasures and also a political virtue. Of course, no selection of letters can escape the charge of subjectivity, but these choices comprise at least one representative sample of Tocqueville's letters about political concerns.

In translating, we have tried to keep intact the frameworks of the sentences Tocqueville created, unlike translators of our author's work in the last century who were too frequently willing to break an inconvenient sentence into two or three to suit their literary or even political tastes. Within the limitation of such a rule, we have tried to make our English as satisfying to read as his French. This does not mean that the translated letters will everywhere show the mark of a great style. Tocqueville occasionally wrote badly, which will be easy to detect in his early letters and in the hurried notes he wrote during the frantic days of 1848, and we have not in general presumed to smooth over what our author left rough. More generally, however, Tocqueville wrote a clear and incisive prose. We hope that we have not too often or too drastically let our prose styles worsen his and that where his language is elegant and powerful, as it often is, the readers of this volume will be able to detect his effect through the inevitable distortion of our renderings.

We have not tried to assure that every French conceptual term is translated into the same English word every time it appears, although we have striven for consistency within letters. Tocqueville's letters were sprinkled with semicolons, as was much of the writing of his day in English and in French. In this edition, punctuation is somewhat simplified so that contemporary readers will not be distracted by it.

Since it is our hope that readers of this volume will not be limited to specialists in Tocqueville studies or French history, we have provided fairly extensive editorial assistance. The letters are divided into sections reflecting stages of Tocqueville's literary and political career, and interpretive introductions precede each section. The footnotes provide historical background, which many readers may need in order to follow the course of Tocqueville's life and political career.

The notes also identify the more important people to whom Tocqueville refers in his letters. The editor has endeavored to identify all those people who appear important in understanding Tocqueville's character and thought. Many people remain unidentified. These tend to fall into one or more of the following categories: (1) people so obscure that one cannot find any information identifying them; (2) acquaintances mentioned once in passing and hence judged to be unimportant for the purposes of this book; (3) people about whom all that is known is what is implied in the text, for example, that an acquaintance is a member of the Chamber of Deputies; and (4) people so famous that it was thought unnecessary to identify them, for example, Rousseau. Although deciding which people to identify entails an element of subjectivity, it is probably less of a subjective process than the selection of the letters themselves. In general, the reader will find that those people who are important for understanding the context of Tocqueville's letters have been identified.

Biographical sketches of Tocqueville's correspondents appear separately in Appendix A. Appendix B gives parallel chronologies of his life and political events of the time, and Appendix C lists our sources for the letters, sources useful for information on the period and bibliographical information on Tocqueville's works mentioned in the text.

James Toupin
Roger Boesche

The Letters

One

YOUTH AND THE JOURNEY TO NORTH AMERICA (1823–1832)

Tocqueville's early letters reveal both the personality of the man and his earliest political and religious concerns. In the opening letter, written when he was only seventeen, he discloses his lasting conviction that one must endure and act within a harsh world always to be characterized by some degree of "injustice and deceit." Part of the harshness of this world emerges from an inability to find peace of mind. Toward the close of this first letter, Tocqueville confides, as he will do so often, that if his mind is not busily occupied with work, it has a tendency to torment him with anxiety and doubt. (See also Letters 39 and 86.) Similarly, in a powerful letter written from America to Charles Stoffels, Tocqueville asserts his lifelong belief that one can bear life more easily and accomplish greater things only if one learns not to expect a great quantity of happiness: "Life is neither a pleasure nor a sorrow; it is a serious affair with which we are charged, and toward which our duty is to acquit ourselves as well as possible" (Letter 10). The one abiding source of satisfaction and strength, Tocqueville repeats again and again, is the tie of friendship, for "it alone in this world is firm and stable" (Letter 4).

Nevertheless, if Tocqueville accepts the ancient Stoic dictum that one should learn to expect disappointment, he certainly does not advocate Stoic resignation to the limitations of the world. We see, for example, his excitement at the prospect of a teenage adventure, that is, a delightful dash from the authority of his father and a secret whirlwind trip to see the wonders of London. Later, as he joins the legal profession, he confesses his fear that he is being transformed into a "law machine" and hence "incapable of judging a great movement" and "of guiding a great undertaking" (Letter 3). Soon after, we read letters written while he is undertaking a real adventure in North America, an adventure complete with a long sea voyage, hazardous travel from New York to Quebec to New Orleans, and at least two very dangerous moments.

In the letters from North America, we find his early religious, moral, and aristocratic principles clashing openly with an irresistible admiration for so much of American democracy. Although the aristocrat Tocqueville questions the poor manners, the vulgar commercial spirit, the instability of desires, and the lack of an enlightened, ruling elite, nevertheless he is attracted to the piety, morality, independence, self-reliance, and respect for law that he discovers. In fact, he admits that he must fight his admiration for the country: "The principles of government are so simple, the consequences are deduced from them with so perfect a regularity, that the mind is subjugated and carried away if it does not take care" (Letter 8). In particular, he admires two characteristics. First, Tocqueville admires the lack of centralized government, and he shudders when he remembers that the French Ministry of Interior had 1,200 employees. By contrast, he reports that in the United States: "In spite of anxiously searching for the government, one can find it nowhere" (Letter 9). Second, Tocqueville marvels that in a land of such freedom and abundance, "private interest is never contrary to the general interest, which is certainly not the case in Europe" (Letter 6),

Certainly Tocqueville finds fault with the United States. For one thing, this spirit of self-interest appears crass to Tocqueville's aristocratic mind, and he suggests that Americans judge the value of anything only by asking, "How much money will it bring in?" (Letter 6). We find a more chilling example of Tocqueville's criticism in a marvelously written letter to his mother, composed while steaming down an icy Mississippi River. Here Tocqueville displays his indignation at the United States' treatment of the great Indian nations. The Spanish, he says, used to hunt the Indians with dogs and guns, but "the Americans . . . more humane, more moderate, more respectful of law and legality . . . are profoundly more destructive" (Letter 12). With its sarcasm, its irony, and an intentionally ambiguous use of the word *savage,* Tocqueville's letter reminds one of Montaigne's satirical essay "Of Cannibals."

1. *To Eugène Stoffels*[1]

Amiens, September 16, 1823

I was, my dear Stoffels, as indignant as you were at the actions the council took toward you. I see no reason for such measures, and I understand your initial anger. But, my dear friend, you must put yourself above all that. Two awards for excellence and three others answer the behavior of these gentlemen better than all the speeches in the world. Why give up? Why despair? Undoubtedly there is injustice and deceit in this world, but were you waiting for this proof in order to be persuaded? Certainly not. One has to live, therefore, with one's enemies, since one cannot have everyone for a friend, to take men for what they are, to be content with the virtues one finds in them, to endeavor to see that their vices do you the least possible harm, to restrict oneself to a certain circle of intimate friends, outside of that to expect only coldness and

1. The reader can find sketches of each of Tocqueville's correspondents in Appendix A.

indifference hidden or open, and to keep oneself on one's guard. And then, after all, my dear friend, I have seen you listen more than once to the voice of conscience rather than that of the world. Your conscience cannot reproach you with anything. All right! You are above everything. What distressed me most in what you told me was that I feared that this delay might impede the trip from Paris. But you reassure me. I already have in mind a little trip to the sea. We are going to stay at Amiens for a few days at my father's house, and from there it is only a step to the coast.

Until then, my dear friend, try to occupy yourself vigorously—hunt, dance, rouse yourself in fact. Substitute as much activity of the body as possible for that of the soul. The first can tire the machine, but never use it up. The second, especially at our age, cannot be in motion without turning on itself, and producing moments of despair which, although without real cause, are nonetheless painful. I myself unhappily know something of this. . . .[2]

2. To Louis de Kergorlay

Amiens, 1824

Your letter, my dear friend, made me laugh with all my heart, especially in the coolness, so worthy of us, with which you put in the margin: *to roam about for the rest of time.* That paints us in a single stroke. Besides, I do not approve much of the last plan. It seems to me that we are leaving things too much to chance and that at the end of the trip, we might have seen very little. Moreover, we would have to give up the sea, and I confess that I am extremely attached to it. Of all the world's spectacles, the sea is the one that most impressed me and inspired me in my childhood, and I am anxious to see

2. The gaps in this letter, and all subsequent letters, are almost always the result of Beaumont's editing for the first publication (1860–1866) of Tocqueville's letters.

what effect it will have on me now. Of the two other plans, I believe your mother's is the most reasonable, because both the trip there and the return are beautiful.

I am informed here . . . Rouen and Le Havre are the . . . that people are most glad to have seen. What attracted me to our first plan was something I had learned about Valenciennes, where, it is said, there are coal mines 1,200 feet beneath the earth. Edouard has been there; by contrast flat plains like Brie tire me terribly. Besides, you will find at our place, especially at Bébé's,[3] a very fine map of France. Only do not tell him why you. . . . I do not have the least means. . . . Having nothing to do here, I have formed a plan of the utmost extravagance, which has only the more charm for that. Although the voyage would last only a week, it would cost as much as two weeks. But the results would be magnificent. The plan would be to go straight to London; we would go by public coach to Calais; there we would take the . . . hours would lead us . . . up to London by going up the Thames, past the two files of ships that line its banks and through all the riches of England that are there. We would stay in London two days. Williams assures me that, with the detailed directions he could give us, that would be enough time to see London; and on the third day we would set foot again in France. This is a magnificent plan; what a shame that it is hardly practical. First, it would be necessary to do this as we have done our marionette shows and other things, that is to say secretly—waiting to tell him about it afterward, when we speak of it as if it had been a sudden resolution that seized us at the seashore. I have already told Father that I would be going with you to Calais and to Lille. It is not only that; the great, the capital difficulty, is that one has to have a passport

3. The childhood nickname for Tocqueville's tutor, the Abbé Lesueur, the very pious Catholic priest who had been charged with the early education of Tocqueville's father, his two older brothers, and Tocqueville himself. The moral influence of the abbé was evidently profound, and Tocqueville always remembered him with gratitude and fondness.

abroad. I cannot get one here. If you could get one in Paris, that would be excellent. If it were for yourself and a servant, that would be better still . . . perfectly with Williams's English passport, who is the same height as I am and has the same description. Once we are in England, there is no further need for a passport; it is only for leaving and returning to France. We might well get ourselves arrested, and that is where the extravagance lies. But one surely must risk something. Besides, we always have the recourse of starting a dispute. I confess that I would be satisfied, one could not be more so, to do fifteen leagues by sea with you and to . . . the sight of those English pigs who are always pictured to us as being so strong and so prosperous. I . . . this moment am sending the total of what a trip of three weeks will cost, and I am adding to it the list Williams has attached.

I saw, in the little trips I made to Metz, that it was impossible to feed a horse for less than thirty sous a day; for a man's lunch and dinner 25 sous, for his bed 10 sous. That is the least; in towns that are a little larger, one has to add more. That, together with what is given to the servant, makes what one has to estimate for the life . . .

horse	5 fr.
———	90
to carry forward	180
carry forward	180
In that, I do not count the cost of horses	90
Unforeseen expenses	10
	280

VOYAGE TO ENGLAND

———	3.00
From Calais to London	25
Living expenses	5
2 days in London	10
A guide	12
The tour	3.10

Saint Paul's	1.10
Steamboat	25
Living expenses	5
From Calais to Amiens	25
Unforeseen expenses	10
	149
	298.[4]

3. To Louis de Kergorlay

Versailles, July 23, 1827

. . . You ask me how I am finding my new position. That is not something I can answer in a single word; I cannot say it is either good or bad, because it is a little of both, and the only way to get through it is to separate the two. Let us look first at the bad: to begin with, I thought I was rather strong in law, and I was grossly deceiving myself. I was about as knowledgeable about law as a person who has just left college is about science. I have unformed materials in my head, and that is all. Having to apply them, I become dazed, and my insufficiency makes me despair. I am definitely the weakest one here, and although the store of pride within me, as it is within everyone else, tells me that after I have worked as much as my colleagues, I will be as good as they are, I still feel frazzled. In general, I have a need to excel that will torment me cruelly all my life. At present I have another fault. I am finding it difficult to become used to speaking in public; I grope for my words and I pay too much attention to my ideas. All about me I see people who reason badly and who speak well; that continually throws me into despair. It seems to me that I am above them, but whenever I make an appearance, I feel beneath them. And nonetheless Paris contains many talents that I perceive . . . perspective.

There you have part of the bad. Let us look at the good.

---

4. These totals make no sense because of gaps in the letter.

I am no longer bored. No one can conceive, without having experienced it, what it is to turn one's attention seriously to one's subject, and ultimately one cannot help being interested in this work. So law, which disgusts me in theory, no longer produces the same effect on me in practice. All my faculties are marshaled to find a solution or an approach; I feel my mind acting with all its power, and the result of that is the same satisfaction that I have felt in my heart when I was in love and when, I was saying, I felt myself alive. In the second place, my companions offer me more support than I at first had thought they would. They show me an affection and good fellowship that are very agreeable. I believe that I have already succeeded in establishing my character among them and in curing them of their preconceptions about me, because I noticed, from the first moment, that the ideal being they had fashioned of me before my arrival corresponded, to whom can I say? To Victor, for example. I confused them from the start with my appearance of being a good fellow and especially by setting myself . . . to work. In examining them up close, I have found among them one or two young men who are truly honorable and full of good sentiments and conscientiousness. This discovery has made me overcome the disgust that the *legal* developments and mores naturally inspire.

In short, my dear friend, I am beginning to think that I will adopt the spirit of my profession. That is the important point. I still experience cruel moments in which I take stock of myself and in which I bitterly regret not having taken another route; but in general I am concentrating on it so much, I am living so outside of all society and of all affections of the heart, that I am beginning to fear that with time I will become a law machine like most of my fellows, specialized people if ever there were any, as incapable of judging a great movement and of guiding a great undertaking as they are well fitted to deducing a series of axioms and to finding analogies and antonyms. I would rather burn my books than reach that point! Who however can foresee the effects of daily influence, and who can say that he will not submit to the common rule? The second fear is that by dint of proceeding [toward] . . . a goal, I would see only that in life, that this ambition toward which you know I have always had a certain leaning, would take hold of me completely, absorbing all other passions, and if, as is only too possible, this ambition could be satisfied, it would make me miserable.

4. To Louis de Kergorlay

Versailles, March 27, 1828

I thank you with all my heart for your letter, my dear friend, I have never felt more deeply than while reading it the value of the friendship that unites us. Let us hold onto that feeling with all our might, my dear Louis: it alone in this world is firm and stable. As long as we can support ourselves on each other with confidence this way, we will never be weak; and if one of us falls, he will at least soon be lifted up again. You might have noticed in me, during our childhood, a singular effect of the false experience that one finds too early in books. I distrusted all generous sentiments. I surrendered myself to them only with a sort of regret, as if to something that is brilliant, but which, by its nature, is not lasting. Thus it was with that beautiful passion of friendship, the ideal of which seemed to be capable of being conceived only by the exalted imagination of early youth. On the contrary, the more that I advanced in life, the more I believed that friendship, as I conceived it, can indeed exist and conserve its character forever, not undoubtedly among all men, but among some. It cannot arise at all ages; but once it does arise, I do not see why age should weaken it or even make it change its nature, especially for those who, understanding all of its value, watch over it unceasingly and do not allow to alter what alone sustains it, confidence in great as well as in small things. In this respect, my dear friend, we must always be on our guard. In

that, I admit, I am more sure of myself than of you. There are
parts of your soul in which I have never been able to penetrate, and your discretion, which can only increase, has often
hurt me, all the more as, since it rests on an estimable basis
and on theoretically true principles, I could not reproach you
for it. There is, among others, a conversation that I absolutely
must have with you one of these days. . . .

5. Gustave de Beaumont to Tocqueville[5]

Sing Sing, June 6, 1831

I the undersigned, well qualified in politeness and courtesy,
and candid friend of Mr. Alexis de Tocqueville, that is to say
quicker to tell him of his faults than to speak to him of his
good qualities, certify the following facts:

The said Alexis, formerly reproachable for a rather cold and
too reserved air in society, for too much indifference toward
people who did not please him, and for a silent and calm attitude, unduly bordering on dignity, has effected a complete
reform in his manners; today he is seen to be affable and gra-
cious toward everyone, amiable with old as well as with
young women, and taking on the responsibility for keeping a
gathering alive even for those whose appearance displeases
him. Is an example necessary? On June 5, in an overwhelming
heat, we were at Sing Sing in the drawing room of a *respectable* woman (more respectable, perhaps, than the one of whom
Brantôme spoke and of whom des Essarts reminded us on
the eve of our departure); this lady, who numbers about 45
springs, has a passion for music, an unfortunate passion if ever
there was one. To our misfortune she sits down to the piano;
she begins an infernal music, which she continues for two
deadly hours, singing, crying, howling as if she had been pos-

5. We include this letter from Beaumont to Tocqueville because it illustrates
so succinctly the friendship between the two men and also because it reveals the
often underestimated sense of humor that passed between them.

sessed by a demon. Unfaithful to my habits, I was in a corner, succumbing to boredom, without the strength to dissemble. What was Alexis doing at this moment. Seated near the piano, his face smiling, he was approving, applauding each tirade, and pouring the *balm of satisfaction* into the soul of our virtuosa, who was eager for praise without measure. He truly appeared to be enjoying himself and the expression of happiness was painted on his face! And yet this woman was ugly, old, and a detestable musician!!! Behold the man! *Ab uno disce omnes!*[6]

I owe so many salutary reforms to the said Alexis, I receive so many services from him every day, that I would very much like to be able to say that I have rendered him a single one by pushing him to correct any little fault that he had; but since I had not spoken of it again to him since our departure from Le Havre, I am forced to recognize that paternal advice has produced more effect on him than mine. Be that as it may, I certify that this account conforms to the truth, and since I am in the process of giving certifications, I attest that the said Alexis is the best friend one could find in the world; and, this friend being mine, I am very glad I have him.

Made and given at Sing Sing, June 6, 1831.

6. To Ernest de Chabrol

New York, June 9, 1831

Thank you very much, my dear friend, for the letters you have already written and for the care you are taking in transmitting my neighbors'. I assure you that this packet is not the one I receive with the least pleasure. I would like to reward the true service that you are rendering me at this time by writing some description that could interest you, but up to this point my ideas are in such a state of confusion, and I am

6. "From one he learns all!"

noticing so many things all at once, that I do not know how
to go about telling you something.

I do not mean to say that I have an embarrassment of
riches; I am quite simply dazed by all I see and hear, and I do
not know how to choose what might be of interest. Still, one
has to say something; otherwise it would not be worth the
trouble to go so far.

Imagine, my dear friend, if you can, a society formed of all
the nations of the world: English, French, Germans . . .
people having different languages, beliefs, opinions: in a
word, a society without roots, without memories, without
prejudices, without routines, without common ideas, without
a national character, yet a hundred times happier than our
own; more virtuous? I doubt it. That is the starting point:
What serves as the link among such diverse elements? What
makes all of this into one people? Interest. That is the secret.
The private interest that breaks through at each moment, the
interest that, moreover, appears openly and even proclaims itself as a social theory.

In this, we are quite far from the ancient republics, it must
be admitted, and nonetheless this people is republican, and I
do not doubt that it will be so for a long time yet. And for
this people a republic is the best of governments.

I can explain this phenomenon only by thinking that America finds itself, for the present, in a physical situation so fortunate, that private interest is never contrary to the general interest, which is certainly not the case in Europe.

What generally inclines men to disturb the state? On the
one hand, the desire to gain power; on the other, the difficulty
of creating a happy existence for themselves by ordinary
means.

Here, there is no public power, and, to tell the truth, there
is no need for it. The territorial divisions are so limited; the
states have no enemies, consequently no armies, no taxation,
no central government; the executive power is nothing; it
confers neither money nor power. As long as things remain

this way, who will want to torment his life in order to attain power?

Now, looking at the other part of my assertion, one arrives at the same conclusion; because, if political careers are more or less closed, a thousand, ten thousand others are open to human activity. The whole world here seems a malleable material that man turns and fashions to his liking. An immense field, of which the smallest part has yet been traversed, is here open to industry. There is no man who cannot reasonably expect to attain the comforts of life: there is none who does not know that with love of work, his future is certain.

Thus, in this fortunate country, nothing attracts the restlessness of the human spirit toward political passions; everything, on the contrary, draws it toward activity that poses no danger to the state. I would wish that all of those who, in the name of America, dream of a republic for France, could come see for themselves what it is like here.

This last reason that I just gave you, to my mind the prime reason, explains equally well the only two outstanding characteristics that distinguish this people: its industrial spirit and the instability of its character.

Nothing is easier than becoming rich in America; naturally, the human spirit, which needs a dominant passion, in the end turns all its thoughts toward gain. As a result, at first sight this people seems to be a company of merchants joined together for trade, and as one digs deeper into the national character of the Americans, one sees that they have sought the value of everything in this world only in the answer to this single question: how much money will it bring in?

As for the instability of character, it breaks through in a thousand places; an American takes up, quits and takes up again ten trades in his lifetime; he changes his residence ceaselessly and continually forms new enterprises. Less than any other man in the world he fears jeopardizing a fortune once he has acquired it, because he knows with what ease he can acquire a new one.

Besides, change seems to him the natural state of man, and how could it be otherwise? Everything is ceaselessly astir around him—laws, opinions, public officials, fortunes—the earth itself here changes its face every day. In the midst of the universal movement that surrounds him, the American could not stay still.

One must not look here either for that family spirit, or for those ancient traditions of honor and virtue, that distinguish so eminently several of our old societies of Europe. A people that seems to live only to enrich itself could not be a virtuous people in the strict meaning of the word; but it is *well ordered.* All of the trifles that cling to idle riches it does not have: its habits are regular, there is little or no time to devote to women, and they seem to be valued only as mothers of families and managers of households. Mores are pure; this is incontestable. The *roué* of Europe is absolutely unknown in America; the passion for making a fortune carries away and dominates all others.

You are sensing that everything I am telling you is approximate. I have been in this country such a very short time. But I have already had a multitude of opportunities for educating myself. My father undoubtedly told you that we had been received here with the utmost in good will. Not only have we encountered the greatest support among the people in office, but all the private homes have been opened to us and, if we have anything to complain about, it is the multitude of social obligations that the eagerness of our hosts imposes on us.

Living this way from morning to night with men belonging to all classes of society, speaking the language badly, but understanding it well enough so that little escapes us, having moreover an inordinate desire to understand, we are well enough placed to learn quickly. However, take all that I have just told you as only first impressions, which one day I will perhaps modify.

I would rather not as a rule stop with the general ideas that I just stated to you, but I do not know what details to introduce; I would rather that you posed me questions. Then, I would try my best to respond.

I read in the newspapers that Carné[7] had finally arrived in Paris. Do you not think that he is buying this promotion rather dear? Into what category will his old and his new political friends place him now? I also saw that Hardoin, in his summary of the conspiracy of the month of December, had been furiously applauded. In truth, I cannot imagine that; is this one also beginning to bend at the knees?

I think that you were perfectly right to refuse to be the king's attorney; it is still necessary to keep in the shadows.

Farewell, my dear friend, I love you and embrace you with all my heart.

7. *To Eugène Stoffels*

New York, June 28, 1831

Just now we are very far away from one another, my good friend, and nonetheless, despite the distance, our hearts bring us closer. For myself, I feel just as much as, perhaps more than in France, that we are tied for life and that, in whatever may happen, we can count on all the friendship and all the help that one man can give another.

Who told us, my dear Stoffels, when we were in college, then when we were doing the law, finally when I occupied a permanent post and you a quiet and assured position, that a political tempest should force us to put a quarter of the diameter of the globe between us, and who knows yet what the future has in store for us? We are now, at least I am, thrown onto a boundless sea; God only knows where and when I will

7. Louis-Marcien, Count de Carné (1804–1876), was a devout Catholic who served in the Ministry of Foreign Affairs during the Restoration and in the Chamber of Deputies from 1839 to 1847 under the July Monarchy. He was a prolific journalist, political analyst, and historian, writing several books on political institutions in nineteenth-century France and England.

land. Still, I would be far from complaining if I were alone, but parents, friends, a family composed in part of people old or sick, that is what alarms my imagination and makes me regard the future with fear.

You know that we set sail April 2, after midnight. At first the weather was favorable to us; we seemed to be gliding on the ocean. I cannot tell you how imposing the solitude of the mid-Atlantic is. During the first days a great number of birds follow the ship; the sea is full of fish that play on the surface; finally, not an hour passes that someone does not point out a sail on the horizon. Soon all that becomes more rare; at last the birds, the fish, the ships disappear. Above, below, around you, there reigns a profound solitude and a complete silence. The vessel you are on then quite truly forms your universe. You know that I like such a spectacle well enough, but renewed unceasingly, reproducing itself every day, it ultimately weighs on the soul and oppresses it.

At the approach of the Newfoundland bank, the sea began to glisten. I believe that this effect is produced by the millions of little phosphorescent animals that toss about in its waters. Be that as it may, nothing is more extraordinary. I remember one night especially: the weather was very stormy; our ship, blown by a violent wind, cleaved the sea while casting up on both sides an enormous mass of foam; this foam seemed made of fire; one would have said that the vessel was crossing one of those blast furnaces, such as I saw at Hayeuche, where the ore is molten; it left behind it a long blazing trail.

The night was perfectly dark; only with difficulty could the rigging of the ship be seen standing out against the sky. It was a scene of inexpressible beauty.

We experienced, some days from there, very violent gusts of wind, but without danger. Our vessel was too large to fear them. We had left the coast thirty-five days when the first cry of *land* was heard. The coasts of America that we had in sight are low and barren. I imagine that they did not entice the Europeans who first visited them three centuries ago.

We thought we were in port, when a storm from the south-
west forced us to repair very rapidly from the vicinity of New
York. Because we lacked wood and sugar, because the bread
was about to be used up, and because we had a certain number of sick people, it was decided to give up the plan of land-
ing in New York. Instead, we reached a little port located
sixty leagues further north called *Newport.*

I assure you that there is a certain pleasure in treading on
the earth again after having crossed the great moat that separates Europe from America. The next day we boarded a
steamboat, which transported us here in eighteen hours.[8]
These are immense machines much larger than a house, in
which five hundred, six hundred and up to a thousand persons
are gathered together in vast saloons, have beds and a good
table at their disposal, and thus cover quite tranquilly, without
suspecting it, their three or four leagues an hour.

New York is located in one of the most admirable sites I
know, with an immense port, at the mouth of a river, which
war vessels can sail up for thirty leagues. It is the key to
northern America. Through it each year arrive thousands of
foreigners who will populate the wilderness of the west, and
all the manufactured items of Europe which then stream rapidly toward the interior of the land. Likewise, its population,
which was only twenty thousand souls fifty years ago, is today two hundred and thirty thousand. It is a clean city built of
brick, of marble, but without noteworthy public monuments.
In short, it does not resemble in the least our principal cities in
Europe.

We have been admirably received here. In general, the
French are liked here. Moreover our mission gave us special
title to kindness. Authorities and private citizens therefore
concurred in giving us the most flattering reception. All the
public documents were placed at our disposal. All the information we requested was instantly furnished to us. . . .

8. Tocqueville and Beaumont arrived in New York on May 10, 1831.

You understand that I cannot yet have a fully developed opinion of this people. At first sight, it presents, like all others, a mixture of vices and virtues that is rather difficult to classify and that does not form a single picture. Mores here are very pure. The bond of marriage in particular is more sacred here than anywhere else in the world. Respect for religion is pushed to the point of scrupulousness. No one, for example, would be permitted to go on a hunt, to dance, or even to play an instrument on Sunday. Even a foreigner is not free on this point.

I have seen streets blocked off before churches at the hour of holy services. These are republicans who hardly resemble our liberals in France at all. There are millions of other differences in ideas, material condition, mores, but I do not have time to point them out.

That is the good side. The bad is the immoderate desire to make a fortune and to do it quickly, the perpetual instability of desires, the continual need for change, the absolute absence of old traditions and old mores, the commercial and mercantile spirit that is applied to everything, even to what least admits of it. Such at least is the external appearance of New York. . . .

We are leaving tomorrow to plunge into the interior. We will sail up the North River[9] to Albany. From there we will go see Niagara Falls. After having visited the Indian tribes that live near Lake Erie, we will return through Canada to Boston and finally to New York, from which we will leave again for a new tour.

The news from France that has come by several steamers seems to me to be of a reassuring nature. If the Ministry of Périer holds firm, I think that it will make itself master of the field at least for a moment.[10] Because once the terror of the

9. The Hudson River, which was called the North River in the early nineteenth century.

10. Casimir-Pierre Périer (1777–1832) served in the French army in Italy in 1798–1801, founded a bank with his brother, and by the Restoration was one

Republic is forgotten, I greatly fear that the spirit of opposition will unwittingly throw the nation into the arms of the republicans.

When this letter reaches you, the results of the general elections will undoubtedly be known. If, as I very much hope, they are favorable for moderation, we have some chance for tranquility for some time (especially if the royalists of the west are willing to keep themselves quiet).

I hope that the revolutionary fervor that seemed to be agitating Metz is beginning to calm down. I keenly hope this is the case both for the public and particularly for you, my dear friend, whose fate very keenly concerns me and of whom I think very often.

8. *To Louis de Kergorlay*

Yonkers, June 29, 1831,
20 miles from New York

I am beginning my letter here, my dear friend, but I do not know when or where I will finish it. I have not written you earlier because I have not had anything in particular to tell you; I dislike talking of France from so far away. You would have nearly forgotten the events to which my letter referred by the time it reached you; the things I would be discussing would have changed ten times in the interim. On the other

---

of the most important bankers in France. He had a genius for speculation and, at least some alleged, profiteering. He was elected to the Chamber of Deputies in 1817 and under the Restoration was among the moderate opposition of the left.

After the 1830 Revolution, Périer served first as president of the Chamber of Deputies in 1830 and then in 1831–1832 as president of the Council of Ministers (effectively prime minister) and as minister of the interior. He was a dominating and conservative man who believed in the Charter of 1814 but felt that any further steps toward extending freedoms would result in anarchy. Attacked from both left and right, he brought order to France and put down demonstrations in Paris and an insurrection in Lyons. He died of cholera in 1832.

hand, before talking to you about this country, I wanted to
know it a little better than I did when I had first arrived. I see
that I have not gained much by waiting. The people of every
foreign country have a certain external appearance that one
perceives at first glance and retains very readily. When one
wants to penetrate a little further, one finds real difficulties
that were not expected, one proceeds with a discouraging
slowness, and doubts seem to grow the more one progresses.
I feel at this moment that my head is a chaos into which a
throng of contradicting notions are pell-mell making their
way. I am wearing myself out looking for some perfectly
clear and conclusive points, and not finding any. In this state
of mind, it is both agreeable and useful for me to be writing
you. Maybe my ideas will untangle themselves a little under
the obligation of explaining them; moreover, were I to find
only hollow musings and doubts, I would still send them to
you without any qualms. One of the advantages of our friendship is that we know each other so perfectly and we are so
sure of our truthfulness toward each other that we can express
to each other the *beginnings* of opinions without fearing inter-
pretations; we are quite sure that the mind of the one who is
writing is exactly in the position in which it reveals itself to
be, neither more nor less.

You ask me in your last letter if there are *beliefs* here. I do
not know what precise sense you attach to that word; what
strikes me is that the immense majority of people are united in
regard to certain *common opinions*. So far, that is what I have
envied most about America. To begin with, I have not yet
been able to overhear in a conversation with anyone, no matter to what rank in society they belong, the idea that a republic is not the best possible government, and that a people does
not have the right to give itself whatever government it
pleases. The great majority understands republican principles
in the most democratic sense, although among some one can
see a certain aristocratic tendency piercing through that I will
try to explain to you below. But that a republic is a good

government, that it is natural for human societies, no one seems to doubt—priests, magistrates, businessmen, artisans. That is an opinion that is so general and so little discussed, even in a country where freedom of speech is unlimited, that one could almost call it a belief. There is a second idea that seems to me to be of the same character; the immense majority has *faith* in human wisdom and good sense, faith in the doctrine of human perfectibility. That is another point that finds little or no contradiction. That the majority can be fooled once, no one denies, but people think that necessarily in the long run the majority is right, that it is not only the sole legal judge of its interests but also the surest and most infallible judge. The result of this idea is that enlightenment must be diffused widely among the people, that one cannot enlighten the people too much. You know how many times in France we have been anxious (we and a thousand others) to know if it is to be desirable or fearful for education to penetrate through all the ranks of society. This question, which is so difficult for France to resolve, does not even seem to present itself here. I have already posed this question a hundred times to the most reflective men; I have seen, by the way they have answered it, that it has never given them pause, and to them even stating the question had something shocking and absurd about it. Enlightenment, they say, is the sole guarantee we have against the mistakes of the multitude.

There you have, my dear friend, what I will call the *beliefs* of this country. They believe, in good faith, in the excellence of the government that rules them, they believe in the wisdom of the masses, provided that they are enlightened, and they do not seem to suspect that there is some education that can never be shared by the masses and that nonetheless can be necessary for governing a state.

As for what we generally understand by *beliefs,* ancient mores, ancient traditions, the power of memories, I have not seen any trace of these up to now. I even doubt that religious opinions have as great a power as one thinks at first sight.

The state of religion among this people is perhaps the most curious thing to examine here. I will try to tell you what I know about this when I again pick up my letter, which I now have to interrupt, perhaps for several days.

Calwell, 45 miles from New York

My mind has been so stirred up since this morning by the beginning of my letter that I feel I have to take it up again without knowing just what I am going to say to you. I was speaking to you above about religion: one is struck on arriving here by the practical exactitude that accompanies the practice of religion. Sunday is observed Judaically, and I have seen streets blocked off in front of churches during the holy services. The law commands these things imperiously, and opinion, much stronger than the law, compels everyone to appear at church and to abstain from all amusements. Nevertheless, either I am badly mistaken or there is a great store of doubt and indifference hidden underneath these external forms. Political passion is not mixed, as it is in our country, with irreligion, but even so religion does not have any more power. It is a very strong impulse that was given in days gone by and which now is expiring day by day. Faith is evidently inert; enter the churches (I mean the Protestant ones) and you hear them speak of morality; of dogma not a word, nothing that could in any way shock a neighbor, nothing that could reveal the hint of dissidence. The human spirit loves to plunge itself into abstractions of dogma, discussions which are especially appropriate to a religious doctrine, whenever a belief has seized it strongly; the Americans themselves were formerly like that. This so-called tolerance, which, in my opinion, is nothing but a huge indifference, is pushed so far that in public establishments like prisons, the homes for juvenile delinquents . . . seven or eight ministers of different sects come to preach successively to the same inmates. But, I was saying, how those men and those children who belong to one sect find themselves listening to the ministry of another. The infal-

lible response is this: the different preachers, because they occupy themselves only with treating the platitudes of morality,
cannot do harm to one another. Besides, it is evident that
here, generally speaking, religion does not move people deeply; in France those who believe demonstrate their belief by
sacrifices of time, effort, and wealth. One senses that they are
acting under the sway of a passion that dominates them and
for which they have become agents. It is true that alongside
these people one finds the kinds of brutes who hold in horror
the very name of religion and who do not very easily even
distinguish good from evil. Neither of these groups seems to
exist here among the bulk of Protestants. People follow a religion the way our fathers took a medicine in the month of
May—if it does not do any good, people seem to say, at least
it cannot do any harm, and, besides, it is proper to conform
to the general rule. How could it be otherwise? The reformers
of the 16th century made the same compromise in religious
matters that people in our time are striving to make in political matters. They said: this principle is bad in regard to this
consequence, but apart from that we find it good and it is
necessary to judge it so with us, and vice versa. But ardent
and logical minds were encountered who could not stand to
stop halfway; as a result, an immense field was opened to the
human spirit and I assure you that it has taken advantage of
that. It is an incredible thing to see the infinite subdivisions
into which the sects have been divided in America. One might
say they are circles successively drawn around the same point;
each new one is a little more distant than the last. The Catholic faith is the immobile point from which each new sect
distances itself a little more, while drawing nearer to pure
deism. You feel that such a spectacle cannot fail to throw the
mind of a thinking Protestant into inextricable doubt, and that
indeed is the sentiment I think I see visibly ruling in the
depths of almost everyone's soul. It seems clear to me that the
reformed religion is a kind of compromise, a sort of *representative monarchy* in matters of religion which can well fill an era,

serve as the passage from one state to another, but which cannot constitute a definitive state itself and which is approaching
its end. By what will it be replaced? Here is where my doubt
begins: this country presents as the solution to this question,
which is after all a *human* question, very precious information,
because the religious and irreligious instincts which can exist
in man develop here in perfect liberty. I would like to have
you see this curious spectacle; you would encounter here the
struggle between two principles which divide the political
world elsewhere. Protestants of all persuasions—Anglicans,
Lutherans, Calvinists, Presbyterians, Anabaptists, Quakers,
and a hundred other Christian sects—this is the core of the
population. This church-going and indifferent population,
which lives day to day, becomes used to a *milieu* which is
hardly satisfying, but which is tranquil, and in which the *pro-
prieties* are satisfied. They live and die in compromises, without ever concerning themselves with reaching the depths of
things; they no longer recruit anyone. Above them is to be
found a fistful of Catholics, who are making use of the tolerance of their ancient adversaries, but who are staying basically
as intolerant as they have always been, as intolerant in a word
as people who *believe*. For them there is only truth in a single
point; on any line one side or another of this point: eternal
damnation. They live in the midst of civil society, but they
forbid themselves any relationship with the religious societies
that surround them. It even seems to me that their dogma on
liberty of conscience is pretty much the same as in Europe,
and I am not sure that they would not be persecuting if they
found themselves to be the strongest. These people are in general poor, but full of zeal, their priests are completely devoted
to the religion of sacrifice they have embraced; they are not in
effect businessmen of religion, as are the Protestant ministers.
Everything I have observed to date leads me to think that Catholics are increasing in number in a prodigious manner. Many
Europeans who are arriving strengthen their ranks; but conversions are numerous. New England and the Mississippi

Basin are beginning to fill up with them. It is evident that all
the naturally religious minds among the Protestants, serious
and complete minds, which the uncertainties of Protestantism
tire and which at the same time deeply feel the need for a
religion, are abandoning the despair of seeking the truth and
are throwing themselves anew under the empire of *authority*.
Their reason is a burden that weighs on them and which they
sacrifice with joy; they become Catholics. Catholicism, moreover, seizes the senses and the soul deeply and is better suited
to the people than reformed religion; thus the greatest number
of converts belongs to the working classes of the society. That
is one of the ends of the chain; now we will pass to the other
end. On the borders of Protestantism is a sect which is Christian only in name; these are the *Unitarians*. Among the Unitarians, which is to say among those who deny the Trinity
and recognize only one God, there are some who see in Jesus
Christ only an angel, others a prophet, finally others a philosopher like Socrates. These are pure deists; they speak of the
Bible, because they do not want to shock opinion too
strongly, as it is still completely *Christian*. They have a service
on Sunday; I have been to one. There they read verses of
Dryden or other English poets on the existence of God and
the immortality of the soul. A speech on some point of morality is made, and the service is over. This sect is gaining
proselytes in almost the same proportion as Catholicism, but
it recruits in the upper ranks of society. It is growing rich,
like Catholicism, from the losses of Protestantism. It is evident that the Protestants, whose spirit is cold and logical, *debating* classes, men whose habits are intellectual and scientific,
are seizing the opportunity to embrace a completely philosophical sect that allows them to profess, almost publicly,
pure deism. This sect, moreover, does not resemble the Saint-
Simonians of France in any way. Independently of the point
of departure, which is completely different, the Unitarians
mix nothing puffed up or *buffoonish* with their doctrine and
worship. On the contrary, they aim as much as possible at

becoming reconciled in appearance with the Christian sects; therefore no kind of ridicule attaches to them; no party spirit either impels them or stops them. Their ways are naturally grave, and their forms simple. Thus you see: Protestantism, a mixture of authority and reason, is battered at the same time by the two absolute principles of *reason* and *authority*. Anyone who wants to look for it can see this spectacle to some extent everywhere; but here it is quite striking. It is apparent here, because in America no power of fact or opinion hinders the march of human intelligence or passions on this point; they follow their natural bent. At a time that does not seem to me very far away, it seems certain that the two extremes will find themselves face to face. What will be the final result then? Here I am absolutely lost in uncertainty, and I no longer see the clear path. Can deism ever be suitable for all classes of a people? Especially for those who have the most need to have the bridle of religion? That is what I cannot convince myself of. I confess that what I see here disposes me more than I ever was before to believing that what is called natural religion could suffice for the superior classes of society, provided that the belief in the two or three great truths that it teaches is real and that something of an external religion mixes and ostensibly unites men in the public profession of these truths. By contrast, the people either will become what they once were and still are in all parts of the world, or they will see in this natural religion only the absence of any belief in the afterlife and they will fall steadily into the single doctrine of self-interest.

But to return to the current state of minds in America, one must not take what I have just said in too absolute a sense. I spoke to you of a *disposition* and not of accomplished facts. It is evident that there still remains here a larger foundation for Christian religion than in any other country in the world, to my knowledge, and I do not doubt that this disposition of minds still has influence on the political regime. It gives a moral and regular shape to ideas; it stops the deviations of the spirit of innovation; above all it makes very rare the disposition of the soul, so common among us, that compels people to rush over all obstacles *per fas et nefas*[11] toward the goal they have chosen. It is certain that a party, however it might desire to obtain a result, would still feel obliged to proceed toward it only by methods that have an appearance of morality and that do not openly shock religious beliefs, which are always more or less moral, even when they are false.

But do you not wonder at the misery of our nature? One religion works powerfully on the will, it dominates the imagination, it gives rise to real and profound beliefs; but it divides the human race into the fortunate and the damned, creates divisions on earth that should exist only in the other life, the child of intolerance and fanaticism. The other preaches tolerance, attaches itself to reason, in effect its symbol; it obtains no power, it is an inert work, without strength and almost without life. That is enough on that subject, to which my imagination is constantly dragging me back and which in the end would drive me mad if I often examined it deeply. Besides, it seems to me I still have a lot of other things to tell you.

Do you know what is striking me most vividly about political matters in this country? It is the effect of the laws on estates. At the time of the American Revolution, political equality existed among the colonials, but not equality of wealth. The English had brought here their primogeniture laws, according to the terms of which the oldest took three-quarters of the father's wealth all to himself. As a result, the country had been filled with vast territorial domains passing from father to son, perpetuating riches within families. So, and here I am only following the accounts of the Americans themselves, there was no class of nobles, but a class of great landowners, living a simple but intellectual enough life, having a certain tone, certain elevated manners, attached to the

11. "By fair means or foul."

spirit of family to the point of honor. . . . A certain number
of these families took England's side and consequently were
the cause of the revolution. Now, that was all less than sixty
years ago. The laws concerning estates were changed; equal
division succeeded the right of primogeniture. A change
which has something magical about it has resulted from that.
Estates were broken up and passed into other hands, the
family spirit was lost, the aristocratic tendency, which had
marked the first period of the republic, was replaced by a
democratic tendency which is irresistible and which no one
can have the least hope of fighting. Now the division of properties is immense, the rapidity with which they change hands
surpasses anything I could have imagined. I saw several members of these old families I have been telling you about. It is
easy to perceive in the depths of their hearts great discontent
against the new order of things. They regret the passage of
patronage, the family spirit, the elevated mores, in a word—
aristocracy. But they submit themselves to a fact that henceforth is irreparable. They acknowledge that they are no longer
anything but a single unit in the state. But they submit to this
necessity in good enough grace, because if they are no longer
favored more than others, at least their old position has not
become a mark of exclusion. Their family having taken part
in the revolution, they themselves never having done more
than struggle indirectly against the extension of democracy,
public opinion has never systematically declared itself against
them. I have heard it said in Europe that there was an aristocratic tendency in America. Those who say that are mistaken;
this is one of the things that I would affirm most readily.
Democracy is, on the contrary, either in full march in certain
states or in its fullest imaginable extension in others. It is in
the mores, in the laws, in the opinion of the majority. Those
who are opposed to it hide themselves and are reduced to taking its very colors in order to advance. In New York, only
vagrants are deprived of electoral rights. The effects of a
democratic government are visible elsewhere; that is, in a per-

petual instability in men and in laws, an external equality
pushed to its farthest point, a tone of manners and a uni-
formly common turn of ideas. One cannot doubt that the law
concerning estates is one of the principal causes of this complete triumph of democratic principles. The Americans recognize this themselves, either because they complain about it
or because they rejoice in it; it is the law of succession that
makes us what we are, it is the foundation of our republic—
this is what we hear every day. This has made me reflect seriously if it is true that the equal division of estates leads, in a
more or less rapid but infallible course, to the destruction of
families and of the family spirit and to the complete annihila-
tion of aristocratic principles (which now seems evident to
me). Does it not forcibly result from this, that all peoples
among whom such a civil law has been established are proceeding rapidly either to absolute government or to a republic;
and that the attempts that are being made to stop definitively
on one or the other of these two routes are chimerical? Applying those ideas to France, I cannot keep from thinking that the
charter of Louis XVIII was necessarily a temporary creation; it
had introduced aristocratic principles into the political laws
and left in the civil laws such an active democratic principle
that it was bound to destroy rather quickly the bases of the
edifice it had raised. Charles X's faults undoubtedly greatly
accelerated the movement, but we were proceeding along
without him. We ourselves are moving, my dear friend, toward a democracy without limits. I am not saying that this is
a good thing; what I see in this country convinces me, on the
contrary, that France will come to terms with it badly; but we
are being pushed toward it by an irresistible force. All the
efforts that will be made to stop this movement will only provide pauses, since there is no human force that can change the
law concerning estates and with this law our families will disappear, estates will pass into other hands, riches will tend
more and more to be equalized, the higher class dissolving
itself into the middle and the middle becoming immense and

imposing its equality on all. To refuse to embrace these consequences seems to me a weakness, and I am forcibly led to think that the Bourbons, instead of seeking to reinforce the aristocratic principle, which is dying among us, should have worked with all their power to give to democracy the interests of order and stability. In my opinion, the communal and departmental system should have attracted their attention from the outset. Instead of living day to day, with Napoleon's communal institutions, they should have hastened to modify them, to initiate the inhabitants little by little into their affairs, to interest them in the times, to create local interests and above all to found, if possible, *those habits and those legal ideas* that are, in my opinion, the only possible counterweight to democracy. Perhaps then they would have rendered the movement that is taking place less dangerous for them and for the state. In a word, from now on democracy seems to me a fact that a government can have the pretension of *regulating,* but of stopping, no. It is not without difficulty, I assure you, that I have surrendered to this idea; what I see in this country does not prove to me that, even in the most favorable circumstances, and they have existed here, the government of the multitude is an excellent thing. It is generally agreed that in the first days of the republic, the men of state, the members of the chambers, were much more distinguished than they are today. They almost all belonged to the class of proprietors, of which I spoke to you above. Now the people no longer have *so fortunate a hand.* Their choices in general fall on those who flatter its passions and put themselves within its reach. This effect of democracy, together with the extreme instability in all things, with the absolute lack that one notices here of any spirit of continuation and duration, convinces me more every day that the most rational government is not that in which *all* the interested parties take part, but that which the most enlightened and most moral classes of the society direct. It cannot be concealed, however, that as a whole this country presents an admirable spectacle. It impresses me, I tell you frankly, with the superiority of free governments over all others. I feel more convinced than ever that all peoples are not made to enjoy such government to the same extent, but I am also more than ever disposed to think that it is regrettable that this is so. A universal satisfaction with the existing government prevails here, to an extent you cannot imagine. These people incontestably are situated higher on the moral scale than among us; each man has a sense of his independent position and his individual dignity that does not always make his bearing very agreeable, but which definitely leads him to respect himself and to respect others. I especially admire two things here: the first is the extreme respect people have for the law; alone and without public force, it commands in an irresistible way. I believe, in truth, that the principal cause of this is that they make it themselves and can change it. One is always seeing thieves who have violated all the laws of their countries scrupulously obeying those they make themselves. I believe that something similar is happening in the spirit of the people everywhere. The second thing that I envy in the people here is the ease with which it does without government. Every man here considers himself interested in public security and in the exercise of laws. Instead of counting on the police, he counts only on himself. It follows, in short, that without its ever appearing, public force is everywhere. It is a truly incredible thing to see, I assure you, how this people keeps itself in order by the sole sentiment that it has no safeguard against itself except within itself.

You see that I am giving you the most thorough account I can of all the impressions I am receiving. In short, they are more favorable to America than they were during the first days after my arrival. There is in the picture a throng of defective details, but the ensemble seizes the imagination. I understand especially that it acts in an irresistible way on logical and superficial minds, a combination that is not rare. The principles of government are so simple, the consequences are deduced from them with so perfect a regularity, that the mind is subjugated and carried away if it does not take care. It is necessary to take stock of oneself, to struggle against the current in order to perceive that these institutions which are so simple and so logical would not suit a great nation that needs a strong internal government and fixed foreign policy; that it is not durable by its nature; that it requires, within the people that confers it on itself, a long habit of liberty and of a body of *true* enlightenment which can be acquired only rarely and in the long run. And after all that is said, one comes back again to thinking that it is nonetheless a good thing and that it is regrettable that the moral and physical constitution of man prohibits him from obtaining it everywhere and forever.

I would very much like you to answer me about all this if you have the time to do it and if you are inclined to occupy yourself with theoretical matters. Up to now we have not been discussing, although we have been communicating with one another. I have not yet received an answer to the first letter I wrote you. In the midst of all the theories with which I am amusing my imagination here, the memory of France is becoming like a worm that is consuming me. It manages to surprise me by day in the midst of our work, by night when I wake up. I devour the newspapers and the private letters when they come. The latest news greatly upsets me; I thought I saw very serious indications of agitation in the west. You know that I have never believed an insurrection would succeed; I would die, then, of anxiety if I learned it was taking place. We stayed almost two months in New York; now we have gone a little distance from there, but in such a way that we can always be back there in a week. Every five or six days, ships depart for Europe; so, I am in a position to do what suits me best. I now hold more than ever the opinion I expressed to you on my departure. As long as Louis Philippe is there, my hands are tied; but whoever his replacement may be, I am going to withdraw from public functions and I will regain control of my conduct and my actions.

Farewell, my dear friend; my uncertainty about how you

are doing is one of the most difficult things to bear. A tone
of sadness and a disgust with men dominated your last letter
and that caused me pain; no day goes by that I do not desire
to be with you and to share completely all your good or bad
fortune. Farewell once again; I embrace you from the bottom
of my heart. Keep this letter. It will be interesting for me
later on.

9. To Ernest de Chabrol

Hartford, October 7, 1831

I have not yet received the letters of August 20, my
dear friend. Consequently, I have nothing to say about what
is happening in France, but I want to speak to you about
myself.

Our stay in Boston was very useful for us; we discovered a
great many distinguished men and precious documents there,
but we are noticing again and again that the greatest obstacle
to learning is not knowing.

On a multitude of points, we do not know what to ask,
because we do not know what exists in France and because,
without comparisons to make, the mind does not know how
to proceed. It is therefore absolutely necessary for our friends
in France to furnish us part of what we lack, if we are to
gather some useful ideas here.

What is most striking to everyone who travels in this country, whether or not one bothers to reflect, is the spectacle of a
society marching along all alone, without guide or support,
by the sole fact of the cooperation of individual wills. In spite
of anxiously searching for the government, one can find it
nowhere, and the truth is that it does not, so to speak, exist at
all.

You appreciate that to understand such a state of things, one
must take apart the body social with great care, to examine
each unit separately and then to see into what sphere of action

these units need to go for the whole to form a nation. In order to make such a study fruitful, one would have had to reflect much more than I have on the principles that in general govern the administration of a people. But this is a subject to which I have never applied myself, not having had the time to do so.

I would at least like to know what *in fact* is the situation in France. The government, as I told you just now, is so small a thing here that I cannot conceive how it is so large in France. The Ministry of the Interior's 1,200 employees seem to me inexplicable. I know that you have never been any more occupied with administrative matters than I have, so I am not asking you about general principles, but perhaps you could obtain some precise practical information.

I would like to know what is the division of labor in the Ministry, or rather the Ministries, of the Interior (because today there are two), and, as much as possible, with what they are concerned. Perhaps there are some printed documents on the subject, in which case it would be necessary to send them to me, not by mail, but by commercial transport. Perhaps there is a rule describing the various functions. I would like to take apart the word *centralization,* which, by virtue of its vague immensity, wearies the mind without leading it to anything.

I declare, my dear friend, that if such a request were made to me, I would not know how to satisfy it; even you may find it impossible. However, you know so many people, and you have lived so long with the powers of the earth that I do not despair (*adjurante amicitia*)[12] that you will succeed. Try to send me something positive; do not fear details. If you can obtain them, you will be doing me a great service.

If I have the time, I will send with this letter a letter for Blosseville;[13] I intend to address to him some questions on

12. "While swearing friendship."

13. Ernest, Viscount de Blosseville (1799–1886), was an ambassador to Spain under the Restoration before he served as an assistant to the prefects of

administrative tribunals, a machine that is absolutely unknown in this country. I hope that he will answer me.

The misfortune in our position here is being obliged to busy ourselves with so many things at once. When an idea comes to us, if we do not set it down at once on paper, we are almost sure never to see it again.

If, when we speak to a particular man, we do not know right away the most useful questions to pose to him, the opportunity is lost. We never have the time to make a man come around to an idea by an indirect route. It is necessary to seize on the run a multitude of things that would require a detailed examination and to pass from one object to another with a speed of which I had no idea. So I am not perfectly sure that I will not go mad before returning to France. My brain here is in a continual ferment.

This type of life nonetheless has its charms. There is no life that draws a man more completely outside of himself, and you know that the great point of this life is to forget as much as possible that one exists. I imagine that people malign the ministers who are out of office when it is said that they are dying of ambition. I believe that they are dying above all of inaction. A minister becomes a complete stranger to himself while he is a minister; he then can never grow used to having to live all the time in his own company. He is like an old bachelor who gets married.

Farewell, my dear friend, I love you and embrace you with all my heart.

Try to obtain *something* from Carné for me; I have been wanting for a century to write him and ask him myself, but I do not have the time. I think that we know each other well enough not to stand on ceremony. Therefore, ask him very earnestly to write me. He has a very broad theoretical mind

---

Versailles from 1827 to 1832, one of whom was Tocqueville's father. He also was a journalist and historian; his most important historical work for Tocqueville's purposes was *Histoire des colonies de l'Angleterre dans l'Australie* (1831). He once more became involved in politics under the Second Empire.

and great practical knowledge. I would regard it as good fortune if he were willing to send me some ideas and ask me some questions.

Carry off this business; I place a great deal of value on it.

10. *To Charles Stoffels*[14]

Philadelphia, October 22, 1831

I have been wanting, my dear Charles, to write you for quite a long time now, but I am carried away in a current of affairs that, without keeping me from thinking about good friends like you, deprives me of the leisure to speak to them. I very much hope, however, that my negligence in responding will not cause you to interrupt the correspondence; your letters always give me great pleasure: and, indeed, you do not have the same excuse I do for not writing.

I see by the tenor of your last letter that you were sad, dejected, prey to a thousand doubts. This melancholic disposition will have undoubtedly disappeared by the time I write this letter. However, I want to speak to you of it, because I know that your train of thought very often carries you toward that painful state of the soul, of which I can speak about all the better since I have experienced it many times myself.

You live, my dear friend, if I am not mistaken, in a world of chimeras. I am not holding it against you; I have lived amidst them a long time myself; and despite all my efforts I still find myself repeatedly drawn back to them. In the first stage of youth, one sees all of life before one, like an ensemble complete with misfortunes or troubles, which may become your lot. I believe it is not at all like that; one hopes or fears too much. There are almost no men who have been continuously unhappy; there are not any who are continuously

14. When Beaumont edited this letter, he eliminated Stoffels's last name, probably because of the sensitive nature of the letter.

happy. Life is therefore neither an excellent nor a very bad thing, but, allow me the expression, a *mediocre* thing partaking of both. One must neither expect too much from it, nor fear too much, but attempt to see it as it is, without disgust or enthusiasm, like an inevitable fact, which one has not produced, which one will not cause to stop, and which it is above all a matter of making endurable. Do not believe I have come to consider existence from this point of view without great internal conflicts, nor that I hold on to it always. Like you, like all men, I feel within me an ardent passion that carries me away toward limitless happiness, and makes me consider the absence of that happiness to be the greatest misfortune. . . . But that, you can be sure, is a foolish passion that must be fought. The feeling is not manly and cannot produce anything that is. Life is neither a pleasure nor a sorrow; it is a serious affair with which we are charged, and toward which our duty is to acquit ourselves as well as possible. I assure you, my dear friend, that whenever I have managed to view it in this way, I have drawn great internal strength from this thought. I have found in myself more tranquility for the future, more courage to bear the pains, the worries, the monotony, the vulgarity of the present, fewer immoderate desires for whatever there might be. I have felt that I was less apt to be discouraged and that, not expecting too much, I was much more easily satisfied with reality.

There is yet another chimera of youth against which it is very important to take precautions. When I first began to reflect, I believed that the world was full of demonstrated truths; that it was only a matter of looking carefully in order to see them. But when I sought to apply myself to considering the objects, I perceived nothing but inextricable doubts. I cannot express to you, my dear Charles, the horrible state into which this discovery threw me. That was the unhappiest time of my life; I can only compare myself to a man who, seized by dizziness, believes that he feels the floor tremble under his

feet and sees the walls that surround him move; even today,
I recall that period with a feeling of horror. I can say that then
I fought with doubt hand to hand, and that it is rare to do so
with more despair. Well! I ultimately convinced myself that
the search for absolute, *demonstrable* truth, like the quest for
perfect happiness, was an effort directed toward the impossible. It is not that there are not some truths that merit man's
complete conviction, but be sure they are very few in number. Concerning the immense majority of points that it is important for us to know, we have only probabilities, almosts.
To despair of its being so is to despair of being a man, for
that is one of the most inflexible laws of our nature. Does it
follow that man must never act because he is never sure of
anything? Certainly that is not my doctrine. When I have a
decision to make, I weigh the pros and the cons with great
care, and instead of despairing at not being able to arrive at
complete conviction, I proceed toward the goal that seems
most probable to me, and I proceed toward it as though I did
not doubt at all. I act this way, because experience has taught
me that on the whole it is better to risk entering quickly and
vigorously onto a bad path than to remain in uncertainty or
act weakly.

Thus, one must resign oneself to arriving only very rarely
at demonstrated truth. But, whatever one does, you tell me,
the doubt on which one risks oneself is always a painful state.
Undoubtedly: I consider this doubt to be one of the greatest
miseries of our nature; I place it immediately after illnesses
and death, but precisely because I hold this opinion of it, I
cannot imagine that so many men inflict it on themselves gra-
tuitously and uselessly. That is why I have always considered
metaphysics and all the purely theoretical sciences, which
serve for nothing in the reality of life, to be voluntary torment
that man has consented to inflict on himself. . . . I am at the
end of my page, I must finish. I hope that you are not vexed
at my sending you a lecture, rather than a description of
America. Farewell.

11. To Hippolyte de Tocqueville

Cincinnati, December 4, 1831

I found on arriving here, my dear friend, a letter from you that brought me great pleasure. When you wrote me, you were proceeding quite like Emilie[15] and were going to leave Paris to return to Nacqueville. I was afraid that instead of that you were taking a long trip, the usefulness of which was not readily apparent to me. The newspapers of October 16 informed us of the rejection of the Reform Bill.[16] The English aristocracy in this has taken a very rash step; it seems to me that it has placed itself in the same position as did Charles X after he chose his ministry on August 7th.[17] It is entering into a vicious circle from which I do not see how it can

15. Emilie de Belisle (1805–1870), wife of Hippolyte.

16. By 1830 England had experienced considerable agitation for some kind of Reform Bill, with radicals hoping for a new political world and middle-class reformers seeking changes that would create a Parliament more receptive to their interests. The Whig cabinet under the leadership of Lord Grey passed the First Reform Bill in March 1831 by one vote, but it was eventually defeated by opposition amendments and committee squabbling. After dissolving Parliament, the Whigs won a more substantial majority in the ensuing elections, and in September 1831 the Second Reform Bill passed the House of Commons easily. The House of Lords defeated the Second Reform Bill on October 8, 1831, and Tocqueville is referring to this event.

The famous Reform Bill that finally passed both houses in April 1832 after much public agitation was hardly democratic. This Reform Bill gave the middle classes a greater share in government, redistributed seats to provide for greater representation of industrial areas, kept property qualifications that excluded the working classes and lower-middle classes from voting, and ended with a House of Commons, which, despite an extended franchise, represented property and not the entire English population and which still disproportionately represented the landed interests. Despite its conservative nature, the Reform Bill of 1832 did extend the franchise, did demonstrate that the English Parliament was capable of slow but significant change, did bring the new commercial classes into Parliament, and perhaps did forestall a real revolution.

17. On August 6, 1829, Charles X dismissed Martignac, who had been a moderate trying to balance the liberal opposition and the extreme right. Two days later, on August 8, Charles X named a new ministry headed by the Prince de Polignac and including General Bourmont, who had deserted Napoleon in battle, and La Bourdonnaye, who was a bigot of the extreme right. Eventually this unpopular and uncompromising right-wing Ministry attacked the authority of the Charter of 1814, tried to undermine the Chamber of Deputies, tried

emerge. Perhaps it has resources that a foreigner cannot know.

You know well that, although far away from France, I often think about what is happening there. It is the subject of nearly all my thoughts. And I admit that after having exhausted my brain trying to divine the fortunes that the future has in store for us, I ordinarily fall into complete doubt about everything. The clearest fact is that we are living in a time of transition, but whether we are going toward liberty or marching toward despotism, God alone knows precisely with what we will have to content ourselves on this point.

I avow that nonetheless I still hope more than I fear. It seems to me that in the midst of our chaos I perceive one incontestable fact. This is that for forty years we have made immense progress in the practical understanding of the ideas of liberty. Nations, like private people, need to acquire an education before they know how to behave. That our education advances, I cannot doubt. There are riots in the largest towns, but the mass of the population peacefully obeys the laws and yet the government is of no value. Do you think it would have happened like that forty years ago? We are harvesting the fruit of fifteen years of liberty which the Restoration allowed us to enjoy. Are you not struck to see the extreme left protesting that it only wants to proceed by legal means and at the same time to hear the royalists declare that it is necessary to appeal to public opinion, that this alone can give strength to the throne, that it is this public opinion above all that has to be won? Amidst all the miseries of the present time and amidst the attack of high fever that the July Revolution gave us, do you not find in all this reasons for hope that we will finally arrive at a social state that is settled? I do not know if we are made to be free, but it is certainly the case that we are infinitely less incapable of being free than we were forty

---

to alter the electoral system to deprive the wealthy bourgeoisie of the vote, challenged the rights of the press, and thereby helped to provoke the July Revolution of 1830.

years ago. If the Restoration had lasted ten years more, I believe we would have been saved; the habit of legality and constitutional forms would have completely become part of the mores. But how could things now be put back in their place; could a second restoration take place? I see many obstacles to it. Unquestionably, the greatest of all is in the personnel of the royalist party that would triumph. You will never be able to make the active portion of the royalist party understand that there are concessions that have to be made without which there can be no hope of governing; that for legitimate monarchy to be durable, it must be national and it must make an alliance with the ideas of liberty or let itself be broken by them. If the Bourbons ever regain the throne, they will want to make a show of strength and will fall again. Perhaps there exists in France the wherewithal to create a strong government on the basis of military glory, but not a strong government solely on the basis of its title. This title may well help it sustain itself if it is able, but not rid it of its own faults.

In any case, it seems to me that the royalists' conduct is well conceived. I am delighted to see them placing themselves on the field of legality, to see them working to win the majority and not making the minority triumph by force. That bodes well. If they had always acted this way, they would have spared themselves as well as France from great misfortune. Besides, in adopting in this way what is reasonable in the ideas of liberty, they are tacitly committing themselves in the sight of all to honor these ideas if they ever become the masters. Many of them are convincing themselves, unwittingly, with their own words. In appealing to the public, they are acquiring the habit of associating themselves with all the free and constitutional habits that they had never had. It is this spectacle that reassures me a little about the future. I hope that, after a great deal of jarring, we will succeed in saving ourselves from anarchy and despotism.

This has been a long string of political balderdash, my dear friend. The fact is that on such an immense subject one

cannot say anything in a letter that makes common
sense.

Happily, I hope that in less than five months I will be able
to talk to you about all this in person. Now all I have to do is
end my letter, but not without embracing you with all my
heart.

12. *To Louise-Madeleine-Marguerite Le Pelletier de Rosanbo,
Countess de Tocqueville*

> December 25, 1831,
> on the Mississippi

Finally, finally, my dear mama, the signal is given; and here
we are descending the Mississippi with all the swiftness that
steam and current together can give to a vessel. We were beginning to despair of ever getting out of the wilderness in
which we were confined. If you wish to go to the trouble of
examining the map, you will see that our position was not
cheerful. Before us, the Mississippi half-frozen over and no
boat for descending the river; above our heads, a Russian sky
pure and ice cold. One could retrace one's steps, you say.
That last recourse escaped us. During our stay in Memphis,
the Tennessee had frozen over, so that wagons were no longer
crossing it. So we found ourselves in the middle of a triangle
formed by the Mississippi, the Tennessee, and by impenetrable wilderness to the south, as isolated as on a rock in the
ocean, living in a little world made deliberately for us, without newspapers, without news of the rest of mankind, with
the prospect of a long winter. We spent a week this way. The
anxiety aside, those days, nonetheless, were spent in a quite
pleasant way. We were living with good people, who did
everything possible to make us feel comfortable. Within
twenty paces from our house began the most admirable forest,
even beneath the snow, the most sublime and most pictur-
esque place in the world. We had guns, powder, and shot

without limit. Some miles from the village lived an Indian nation (the Chickasaws); once on their lands, we always discovered some of them who asked no more than to hunt with us. Hunting and warfare are the sole occupations, and the sole pleasures, of the Indians. One would have to go too far to find real game in quantity. But we killed, on the other hand, a host of pretty birds unknown in France: this hardly raised us in the esteem of our allies, but had the merit of amusing us thoroughly. And so I killed red, blue, yellow birds, not to forget the most brilliant parrots I have ever seen. And so our time passed, lightly with regard to the present; but the future did not leave us calm. Finally, one fine day, a little smoke was seen on the Mississippi, on the limits of the horizon; the cloud drew near little by little, and there emerged from it, neither a giant nor a dwarf as in fairy tales, but a huge steamboat, coming from New Orleans, and which, after parading before us for a quarter of an hour, as if to leave us in uncertainty as to whether it would stop or continue on its route, after spouting like a whale, finally headed toward us, broke through the ice with its huge framework and was tied to the bank. The entire population of our universe made its way to the riverside, which, as you know, then formed one of the furthest frontiers of our empire. The whole city of Memphis was in a flutter; no bells were rung because there are no bells, but people cried out hurrah! and the newcomers alighted on the bank in the manner of Christopher Columbus. We were not yet saved, however; the boat's destination was to go up the Mississippi to Louisville, and our purpose was to go to New Orleans. We happily had about fifteen companions in adversity who desired no more than we did to make their winter quarters in Memphis. So we made a general *push* on the captain. What was he going to do up the reaches of the Mississippi? He was certainly going to be stopped by the ice. The Tennessee, the Missouri, the Ohio were closed. There was not one of us who did not affirm having ascertained as much by his own eyes. He certainly would be stopped, damaged, smashed perhaps by the ice. As for us, we were speaking only in his interest. That goes without saying: in his own interest properly understood. . . . Love of our fellow man gave so much warmth to the speeches that at last we began to shake up our man. I am nevertheless of the conviction that he would not have turned in his tracks, without a fortunate event, to which we owe our not becoming citizens of Memphis. As we were thus debating on the bank, an infernal music resounded in the forest; it was a noise composed of drums, the neighing of horses, the barking of dogs. Finally a great troop of Indians, elderly people, women, children, baggage, all conducted by a European and heading toward the capital of our triangle. These Indians were the Chactas (or Choctaws),[18] after the Indian pronunciation; with regard to this, I will tell you that M. de Chateaubriand was a little like La Fontaine's ape; he did not take the name of a port for the name of a man: but he gave to a man the name of a powerful nation in the south of America. Be that as it may, you undoubtedly wish to know why these Indians had arrived there, and how they could be of use to us; patience, I beg you, now that I have time and paper, I want nothing to hurry me. You will thus know that the Americans of the United States, rational and unprejudiced people, moreover, great philanthropists, supposed, like the Spanish, that God had given them the new world and its inhabitants as complete property.

They have discovered, moreover, that, as it was proved (listen to this well) that a square mile could support ten times more civilized men than savage men, reason indicated that wherever civilized men could settle, it was necessary that the savages cede the place. You see what a fine thing logic is. Consequently, when the Indians begin to find themselves a little too near their brothers the whites, the President of the United States sends them a messenger, who represents to

18. The forced westward emigration of Indian nations from their lands, journeys known as the "trail of tears," accelerated with Andrew Jackson's election to the presidency in 1828.

them that in their interest, properly understood, it would be good to draw back ever so little toward the West. The lands they have inhabited for centuries belong to them, undoubtedly: no one refuses them this incontestable right; but these lands, after all, are uncultivated wilderness, woods, swamps, truly poor property. On the other side of the Mississippi, by contrast, are magnificent regions, where the game has never been troubled by the noise of the pioneer's axe, where the Europeans will *never* reach. They are separated from it by more than a hundred leagues. Add to that gifts of inestimable price, ready to reward their compliance; casks of brandy, glass necklaces, pendant earrings and mirrors; all supported by the insinuation that if they refuse, people will perhaps see themselves as constrained to force them to move. What to do? The poor Indians take their old parents in their arms; the women load their children on their shoulders; the nation finally puts itself on the march, carrying with it its greatest riches. It abandons forever the soil on which, perhaps for a thousand years, its fathers have lived, in order to go settle in a wilderness where the whites will not leave them ten years in peace. Do you observe the results of a high civilization? The Spanish, truly brutal, loose their dogs on the Indians as on ferocious beasts; they kill, burn, massacre, pillage the new world as one would a city taken by assault, without pity as without discrimination. But one cannot destroy everything; fury has a limit. The rest of the Indian population ultimately becomes mixed with its conquerors, takes on their mores, their religion; it reigns today in several provinces over those who formerly conquered it. The Americans of the United States, more humane, more moderate, more respectful of law and legality, never bloodthirsty, are profoundly more destructive, and it is impossible to doubt that within a hundred years there will remain in North America, not a single nation, not even a single man belonging to the most remarkable of the Indian races. . . .

But I no longer know at all where I am in my story. It had

to do, I think, with the Choctaws. The Choctaws formed a powerful nation that inhabited the frontier of the state of Alabama and that of Georgia. After long negotiations, they finally managed, this year, to persuade them to leave their country and to emigrate to the right bank of the Mississippi. Six to seven thousand Indians have already crossed the great river; those who arrived in Memphis came there with the aim of following their compatriots. The agent of the American government who accompanied them and was charged with paying for their passage, knowing that a steamboat had just arrived, hurried down to the bank. The price he offered for transporting the Indians sixty leagues down river managed to settle the shaken mind of the captain; the signal to depart was given. The prow was turned toward the south and we cheerfully climbed the ladder down which descended the poor passengers who, instead of going to Louisville, saw themselves forced to await the thaw in Memphis. So goes the world.

But we had not yet left; there was still the matter of embarking our exiled tribe, its horses and its dogs. Here began a scene which was something truly lamentable. The Indians came forward toward the shore with a despondent air; they first made the horses go, several of which, little accustomed to the forms of civilized life, took fright and threw themselves into the Mississippi, from which they could be pulled out only with difficulty. Then came the men, who, following their usual custom, carried nothing except their weapons; then the women, carrying their children attached to their backs or wrapped up in the blankets that covered them; they were, moreover, overburdened with loads that contained all their riches. Finally the old people were led on. There was among them a woman of a hundred and ten years of age. I have never seen a more frightening figure. She was naked, with the exception of a blanket that allowed one to see, in a thousand places, the most emaciated body that one can imagine. She was escorted by two or three generations of grandchildren. To leave her country at that age to go seek her fate in a strange

land, what misery! There was, amidst the old people, a young
girl who had broken her arm a week before; for want of care,
the arm was frostbitten below the fracture. She nonetheless
had to follow the common march. When all had gone by, the
dogs advanced toward the bank; but they refused to enter the
boat and took to making frightful howls. Their masters had to
lead them by force.

There was, in the whole of this spectacle, an air of ruin and
destruction, something that savored of a farewell that was final and with no return; no one could witness this without
being sick at heart; the Indians were calm, but somber and
taciturn. There was one of them who knew English and of
whom I asked why the Choctaws were leaving their
country—"To be free," he answered—I could never draw
anything else out of him. We will deposit them tomorrow in
the solitudes of Arkansas. It has to be confessed that this is a
singular accident, that made us come to Memphis to witness
the expulsion, one might say the dissolution, of one of the
most celebrated and most ancient American nations.

But this is enough on the savages. It is time to return to
civilized people. Only one word more on the Mississippi,
which, in truth, hardly merits being preoccupied with it. It is
a great river, yellow, rolling rather gently in the deepest solitudes, in the midst of forests that it inundates in the spring
and fertilizes with its mud. Not a hill is seen on the horizon,
but woods, then woods, and still more woods: reeds,
creepers; a perfect silence; no vestige of man, not even the
smoke of an Indian camp.

[Tocqueville and Beaumont left the United States on February
20, 1832.]

Two

POLITICAL SPECULATION, *Democracy in America,* AND ELECTION TO THE CHAMBER OF DEPUTIES (1832–1839)

The first letter of this section opens with Tocqueville admitting to Beaumont that he has been stricken with writer's paralysis and hence finds himself unable to begin writing his share of the report on prisons in the United States. In vain does he close his eyes and "wait for the spirit of the penitentiary system to appear" (Letter 13). One can only surmise at the many possible reasons for this paralysis: his longing to write, not about American prisons, but about American democracy, his accelerating romance with Mary Mottley, and his undeniable wish all throughout the 1830s *both* to write about politics and to act politically.

In regard to the latter point, one can see from the letters in this section that Tocqueville's wish to become a political participant has often been underestimated. He bitterly criticizes Stoffels's avowed "*political atheism*" because this attitude of indifference fosters the growth of petty self-interest, the decline of virtue and national purpose, and a strange "apoplectic torpor" that could lead to national ruin (Letter 14). Without question, these letters reveal that Tocqueville, while writing *Democracy in America,* felt smothered and constricted by what he once called the grasping plutocracy of the July Monarchy, and he exhibits a somewhat aristocratic longing for some political action or adventure. After spending six weeks in the countryside, he writes Kergorlay:

I feel very strongly that it would be easier for me to leave for China, to enlist as a soldier, or to gamble my life in I know not what hazardous and poorly conceived venture, than to condemn myself to leading the life of a potato, like the decent people I have just seen. (Letter 18)

A year later, he confides to Kergorlay that he longs to accomplish "good and grand things" and thus to quench an "internal flame" that torments him (Letter 23). Finally, with a tone of despair he asks Royer-Collard if there had ever been a moment in history when men of "great passions" reigned, when men of vision and principle dominated politics rather than men driven only by "miserable day-to-day interests" (Letter 29).

While these letters certainly demonstrate a wish for "grand" political action, they demonstrate something else as well. Tocqueville longs for a political world guided, at least some of the time, by questions of morality and political principle. He tells Stoffels that the moral world and the political world must not be rigidly separated, and he suggests to Royer-Collard that Machiavelli knew the difference between "virtue and vice," but, "like so many people of our day," Machiavelli concerned himself with what was "profitable" rather than with what was right (Letters 14 and 26). Convinced that the middle-class society of the July Monarchy cultivated "almost universal pettiness," Tocqueville sees a political world in which men have no fixed principles but rather vacillate according to their interests (Letter 29). To Beaumont, he laments: "I cannot tell you, my dear friend, the disgust I feel in watching the public men of our day traffic, according to the smallest interests of the moment, in things as serious and sacred to my eyes as principles" (Letter

32). As a result, Tocqueville thinks that the parliamentary squabbles among Molé (see n. 42, p. 128), Guizot, and Thiers constitute a shabby spectacle because under the pretense of important political debate, one can find almost no political substance: each seeks only personal power and will quickly sacrifice political conviction to attain this goal.

There is one other probable reason for Tocqueville's temporary inability to write. His journey to North America had produced a clash between his aristocratic heritage and a new fascination with American democracy. In attempting to resolve this clash, Tocqueville's mind must have exhibited a fascinating and fruitful turmoil. Ultimately, in a famous letter to Reeve, Tocqueville pictures himself as attached neither to aristocracy nor to democracy, as respectful of both but fully satisfied with neither. Born after aristocracy had been destroyed and before democracy had emerged, Tocqueville says he can view both with dispassionate eyes (Letter 28). Still, Tocqueville's neutrality does not emerge quite so clearly in his letters. Of course, one might accept his own convenient argument that since democracy is inevitable, one can only labor to eliminate its dangers and correct its imperfections. But why then does he so obviously criticize aristocratic England, telling Senior, for example, that the rich of England sacrifice the poor and monopolize almost all the good things of life? (Letter 20). And why does he confess to Mill: "I love liberty by taste, equality by instinct and reason"? (Letter 22). Even when Tocqueville tells his conservative friend Stoffels that he prefers "hereditary monarchy," he proceeds to advocate decentralization of government and "extensive" popular political participation (Letter 27). One cannot deny, of course, that Tocqueville had criticisms and reservations concerning the emerging middle-class democracy. Nevertheless, many of his aristocratic contemporaries accepted the argument that such a democracy was inevitable and simply resigned themselves to this development. By contrast, these letters make clear that Tocqueville embraced the democratic movement more eagerly and longed to take part in extending its benefits and in guiding it in an acceptable direction.

13. *To Gustave de Beaumont*

Paris, April 4, 1832

I am writing you, my dear friend, only to prove to you that, as of now, nine o'clock in the morning, the 4th of the present month, I am not dead; something you would tend (and not be *tempted*)[1] to believe, if you were to read in today's newspaper that since yesterday there have been 315 new patients of which 50 plus are in our district.[2] Up till now our district is the most favored of all on this point.

I was telling you, then, that I would not have written you except to let you know this trifle. In fact, I have almost nothing more to tell you. I am beginning to think that I definitely was stricken with imbecility during the last month I spent in America. We thought it was an attack, but the complaint is assuming more every day the character of a chronic illness. I am still where you left me. In this time of public calamity and under the pressure which we are beginning to feel to produce our report, I can think of nothing but of . . . I leave it to you to choose the word that should follow. I believe, God forgive me, that I have just made a line of poetry. The fact remains that I think I am more than ever a human machine.[3] You would laugh with all your might if you saw the way I direct my intellectual efforts each morning. I get up and at once sink into the immense easy chair my father was imprudent enough to give me; on one side, I place a chair and on the chair a

---

1. Fr. = "tenté (et non *tempté*)."
2. Tocqueville refers here to a recent outbreak of cholera.
3. Fr. = "l'homme-machine"; a well-known French phrase because it was the title of Julien Offray de La Mettrie's famous book *L'Homme machine* published in 1747.

writing stand. On my knees, I have a notebook, a thick notebook with paper, and very near a pile of old books. Thus
prepared, I lean back into my easy chair and my eyes half-
closed, I wait for the spirit of the penitentiary system to appear to me.[4] I have finally tired of this way *of working,* because
I have observed that I was thinking about everything except
prisons. I decided that, it was necessary whatever the cost, to
get out of this culpable inertia: so I took your letter and I read
it twice without taking a breath. But, having noticed that
coming to the end, I could not remember the first word of
what it contained, I prepared a large piece of paper on the top
of which I wrote in large and legible letters: *What I have to do
before Beaumont's return.* Following that a numbered list; it goes
up to number 11; I am very glad to tell you that.

This first piece of work done, I felt the holy ardor begin to
come to me and I immediately began working on number
one, very determined not to invert the order for fear of getting confused. So it is that Richmond and Baltimore have already passed in review. But why the devil, as long as you are
setting about to write, do you give so few details? You tell
me: examine this, and when I turn to your letter (which is
always in front of me on the table) nothing indicates to me
what you want me to examine. I feel overwhelmed by the
responsibility you leave me. I would even so have been capable of following your instructions word for word, but if you
abandon me to myself, I am a lost man. The fact is that I
sincerely hope, for the honor of the penitentiary system of
America, that in the last week you have been feeling more in
the mood than I.

I almost forgot to speak to you about the only thing even a
bit interesting that I have to tell you. Two days ago, I spent

4. Tocqueville and Beaumont are trying to write a book-length report on
the penitentiary system in the United States and its relation to France, the
ostensible reason for their trip to North America. This report was published in
Paris in 1833 under the title *Du système pénitentiaire aux Etats-Unis et son application en France.*

the morning chatting with cousin D['Aunay].[5] He received me, as is his custom, with open arms, even more than ever. There was in his manner a certain something that announced that the trip had the same effect on him that it had on so many others. I brought him, besides, the American documents we had promised him, and for which he seemed very grateful (I established firmly that it was only a loan). We then talked, with our feet on the andiron, for more than an hour. He first spoke to me about our position; he strongly advised me that we not be in a hurry, seeming to attach a keen interest to the success of the memoir; he gave me a great deal of advice about its editing, some of which, I think, is very good and all of which was received by me as such. I do not have time to explain it all to you. His system broadly would be to be positive and practical in regard to America, more general and more doubtful in regard to France: "You are both very young," he told me, "you have a great future before you; do not tie yourselves to an idea in such a way as to fall irrevocably with it." There is something there to reflect about. But I am too pressed at the moment to tell you everything those words in fact suggested to me. My instinct is that he is right. We or rather he then tackled politics. I wish you could have been there, my dear friend. It was the most curious scene I have seen in a long time. If you had heard him speak en masse of the state of France, of the administration, of the Chambers, of the one who has been put at our head, and even of the *glorious* July Revolution, you would have been stupified by the road minds have taken in the last year. One conversation like that teaches one more about revolutions than all the histories of the world. You would have smiled inwardly on seeing

5. Louis-Honoré-Félix Le Pelletier d'Aunay (1782–1855), one of Tocqueville's cousins. Le Pelletier d'Aunay was a prefect under the Empire, a member of the Chamber of Deputies from 1827 to 1848, and a representative to the Constituent Assembly in the Second Republic. He was very influential in helping Tocqueville and Beaumont secure an officially sanctioned mission, i.e., the study of prisons, for their journey to America.

with what admirable facility these coryphées of liberalism of 1828, these makers of 1830, easily sabre the first principles of civil liberty that we others, old royalists, would not abandon at any price.[6] In truth, the political world is a dirty arena.

April 6. I am adding a word to my letter from Saint-Germain, where I have come to pass a few hours with Edouard.[7] We would like to lure my mother here and establish all of us there during the peak of the epidemic. But it is very doubtful that we will manage to persuade my mother. In any case, my dear friend, I advise you strongly to return to Paris only when the cholera has begun to pass its apogee. It is growing now, and God knows when it will stop. Nothing is pressing us, that is what Dau assured me again the other day. Besides, with your instructions, I will easily be able to do everything preparatory. What I can tell you is that, being in Paris, I am staying here and am even very calm, but that I would not come here without being forced to, if I were outside. Upon which, farewell, I embrace you with all my heart. Do not fail to remember me to your parents. As for mine, you know they have regarded you as part of the family for a long time.

14. To Eugène Stoffels

Paris, January 12, 1833

I was beginning, my dear friend, to be seriously angry with you when I received your letter. . . .

6. Tocqueville is probably referring to policies followed by King Louis Philippe, his prime minister Casimir Périer, and their supporters. Whereas the liberals of 1828 and the makers of the 1830 Revolution had promised freedom of the press, freedom of association, and an end to hereditary privilege, by 1832 they had harassed newspapers, suppressed political associations, and justified a new rule of privilege composed now of the wealthiest of the bourgeoisie and the landlords.

7. Edouard, Viscount de Tocqueville (1800–1874), the younger of Tocqueville's two older brothers. His oldest brother was Hippolyte, Count de Tocqueville (1797–1877). Although Tocqueville himself was technically a baron, he refused to acknowledge or permit the use of the title. Despite the fact that

You speak of what you call *your political atheism,* and you
ask me if I share it. On this we must understand each other.
Are you disgusted only with parties or also with the ideas
they exploit? In the first case, you know that such has always
more or less been my way of thinking. But when it comes to
the second, I am no longer your man in the least. There is
now an obvious tendency to treat with indifference all the
ideas that can stir society, whether they are right or wrong,
noble or base. Everyone seems to agree in considering the
government of his country *sicut res inter alios acta.*[8] Everyone is
focusing more and more on individual interest. It is only those
who want power for themselves, and not strength and glory
for their homeland, who rejoice at the sight of such a symptom. One does not have to read very far into the future to
reckon on the tranquility that will be bought at such a price.
It is not a healthy and virile repose. It is a sort of apoplectic
torpor that, if it lasts a long time, will lead us inevitably to
great misfortune. No, certainly, I do not laugh at political beliefs; I do not consider them things indifferent in themselves,
which men turn over at their will. I laugh bitterly when I see
the monstrous misuse that is made of them every day, but I
laugh the way I do when I see virtue and religion made to
serve dishonest goals, without respecting virtue and religion
any the less for that. I struggle with all my might against this
bastard wisdom, this fatal indifference to which the energy of
so many beautiful souls is being lost in our day. I am trying
not to construct two worlds: the one moral, in which I am
still enthusiastic for what is beautiful and good; the other political, in which I lie down flat on my face in order to smell
more at my leisure the dung on which we walk. I am trying
not to imitate in another fashion the great lords of old, who
held that it was honest to deceive a woman, but that one
could not without infamy fail in one's word toward a man. I

Tocqueville was the youngest, by agreement with his brothers he lived at the
ancestral château at Tocqueville.

8. "As one thing that is done among others."

am seeking not to divide what is indivisible. There you have, my good friend, a long tirade at the end of which my lack of paper forces me to end my letter. . . .

15. To Gustave de Beaumont

London, August 13, 1833

Here I have finally arrived in England,[9] my dear friend; it was not without difficulty, I assure you; first I had to make my way to Guernsey in a yacht on which the proprietor had offered me a place. There I found a steamboat which delivered me in ten hours to a little town on the southern coast of England called Weymouth, from which I finally managed to reach London. I arrived in this city last Saturday, the 10th. It would be difficult for me to tell you anything about the impression that I have felt since I set foot in this immense metropolis. It is a continual dizziness and a profound feeling of my nullity. We were a great deal in America, we are hardly anything in Paris, but I assure you that it is necessary to go to below zero and to use what mathematicians call negative numbers to compute what I am here. This comes from two causes: first from the immensity of this city, which exceeds all that Paris could make one imagine, and from the multitude of different celebrities who meet here; secondly from the position the aristocracy occupies, something of which it seems to me I had no idea. The position that fortune joined to birth gives here appears to me to be still a million feet above all the rest. You are aware that I cannot yet speak of the spirit of the English people: what I can say, what strikes me most up to the present in its mores, is their aristocratic exterior. The aristocratic spirit appears to me to have descended into all classes; *every marquis wants to have pages,* make no mistake about it. In short, I do not recognize our America here in any point.

9. Tocqueville visited England for five weeks in August and September 1833.

Be that as it may, I am wandering on the surface of London like a gnat on a haystack. I have already seen some people, but it is very difficult to meet with them, because the distances are prodigious. Moreover, a worse season could not be chosen. Nearly everyone has already left for the country, and I have too little time before me. Whatever you said about it, it is not a reasonable thing to do, to come to spend six weeks in a country like England, unless, however, it is to see again acquaintances that have already been made. It will take me at least ten days before I am able to become acquainted with anyone and consequently before I am in a position to make any substantial observations; it has already been 10 days since I left France; judge by that what I can do. Nevertheless, I assure you I am not lacking in courage and that I am still moving around as much as I can. But, I am no longer in America here. I am experiencing moreover a great aptitude for listening and being understood.

But let us speak of our business. In Cherbourg I received the letter in which you asked me for a power of attorney, at the moment I was making my way on board the yacht; I ran at once to a notary and the next day the agent must have sent you the document. I confess that the announcement of the thousand écus made me very happy, as I hardly expected it. This truly places us in a very agreeable position.

Yesterday I received from you a long letter in which you speak to me about the project of establishing a review. This project very much strikes my fancy, as you can believe, and henceforth you can count on the 1,000 francs, the first result of the cooperation. However, I have one objection to make. You know the extreme difficulty I have in writing unless I have reflected on the subject I wish to deal with. It follows that it is almost impossible for me to write on two matters at once. Now, you know how deeply I am immersed in America.[10] Until this work is finished, you will only be able

10. Tocqueville of course refers to his work *Democracy in America*.

to expect a little intellectual cooperation from me. Once this time has passed, I am yours. There is one thing of capital importance in the establishment of a review, which is the choice of men. Rest assured that complete success is there. I find Blosseville and above all Chabrol very weak champions. They are hardly good for anything, as you said yourself, except for their names and their money. It is absolutely necessary to have truly intellectual recruits along with them or the enterprise is scarcely practicable, since nothing is more difficult to make succeed than a serious review. The difficulty of choosing collaborators is increased further by this consideration, that we must try to take them along a line of opinion analogous to our own. I am not speaking of the doctrines of legitimacy, but of the doctrines of order and of liberty. The idea of cornering Montalembert[11] seems to me very good; he is a man whose reputation is already made and whose social position is elevated. The difficulty is in approaching him. There still must be other talented men whom one could have. Perhaps one could accept less than 1,000 francs per share. Do not lose sight either of the new review that is coming out just now, headed by M. Fix. Perhaps it is to be feared as a competitor; its editors must not lack know-how, because I have seen their review announced in a very becoming manner in the English journals.

I repeat that for my part I am going to do all that I can here to gather together ideas and materials. But my stay is too short and the season is too unfavorable to be able to succeed at anything great. All the people whom I can reach treat me with distinction, but the difficulty is in meeting with them. Mr. Prior just came to see me. He invited me to dinner next Sunday with the archbishop of Dublin. Write me as soon as you

11. Charles de Montalembert (1810–1870), a follower of the progressive and democratic Catholic reformer Félicité de Lamennais. Together they founded the journal *L'Avenir* in April 1830. During the July Monarchy, Montalembert led the liberal Catholic movement in its attempt to secure for Catholics the right of establishing secondary schools.

can. Try to set my mind in motion; you know that that is the
point. I slumber willingly and put myself into complete activity only when I see clearly the goal toward which I want to
lead. The most difficult thing here is to know how to limit
one's curiosity to some one thing; the multitude of interesting
objects (intellectually speaking) crushes one. It is in this choice
that I need to be directed. I see clearly on the whole what
would be most useful for us to study, which would be the
advance that human industry is taking in England; the manner
in which the government encourages it; the degree of liberty
industry enjoys; the manner in which it creates all by itself so
many marvels. I see this well as a whole. But when I come to
examine my ideas, I find them so vague, that I do not know
how to pose the questions I want to ask; I therefore need for
your practical spirit to give me a shove; but hurry, because
time flies. The expenses in this country, besides, surpass my
expectations. To exist somewhat suitably in London it is impossible for me to spend less than 12 or 15 francs per day.
I am only speaking of lodging, drinking, and eating, which I
am still doing as cheaply as possible. Imagine how unforeseen
expenses mount up in a city where one has to pay for everything.

Farewell, my good friend, I embrace you with the best in
my heart.

16. To Mary Mottley[12]

Warwick, August 26, 1833

. . . I came out of Warwick castle in a state of intellectual
excitement; and although night was coming on, not knowing
what to do in modern Warwick, a place altogether prosaic and
unworthy of me at such a moment (note that I had dined), I

12. Mary Mottley (1799–1864), later Tocqueville's wife and referred to
throughout these letters as *Marie*. Although she was English, she was living in
Versailles with her aunt, Mrs. Belam, when she first met Tocqueville in 1828.

hired a horse to the great amazement of my host, who nonetheless in the end delivered over his mount to me with all the
deference and all the respect that people show in England to
those who appear to have the means to commit follies. Thus
I mounted the horse and headed for the ruins of Kenilworth
castle,[13] which are six or seven miles from Warwick. Imagine
to yourself an Italian night: not a breath of wind; a sky without a cloud, the moon at its full; add to that a horse ardent
and light afoot, all the centuries of chivalry in my head and
something of the fire of youth circulating in my veins; and
you will understand that I did not, so to speak, touch the
earth. I arrived at the village of Kenilworth but everyone had
already gone to bed; but I shouted so loudly at the door of
one of the last huts, that a young woman (very pretty, so far
as the moon and my eyes could allow me to judge) at last put
her face to the window. The difficulty was making her understand that I wanted to go to the ruins of the castle at that
unseemly hour. The ruins were in the fields a mile from the
village. She finally understood me, however, and pointed out
the way with a good will that perhaps proved her desire *to get
rid of me*,[14] but for which I thanked her nonetheless. There I
was, then, in the fields, opening gates, jumping over ditches
and in quest of the castle of Dudley. At the end of a half-hour
I finally discovered it at the top of a hill, and I was soon
within its walls; there I dismounted, I tied my horse to a gate,
and I penetrated into the midst of the ruins: it was, in truth, a
grand and solemn spectacle. There reigned in the middle of
this wild an inexpressible silence and an air of desolation. I
entered into the rooms of this magnificent manor. The upper
floors were destroyed, I perceived the sky above my head; but
the walls still existed; and the moon, while penetrating from
all sides through the gothic windows that adorn the walls, cast

13. Tocqueville is referring to Sir Walter Scott's novel *Kenilworth*. This
entire letter constitutes an interesting contrast to Tocqueville's own claims that
he remained uninfluenced by romanticism.

14. Tocqueville uses the English phrase.

upon them a sepulchral glow in accord with the ensemble of objects. Was I not, indeed, there in the domains of Death? After having visited the ruins in all directions and made beneath my feet echoes resound that probably have been mute for many years, I went back to the center; there I sat down on a rock and I fell into a sort of somnambulism, during which it seemed that my soul was being swept away into the past with an inexpressible force. But guess a little, I ask you, on what point, in the innumerable centuries that were flowing by, my imagination was going to perch? I made vain efforts to replace in these high walls, covered with ivy and falling into ruin, great personages that the sixteenth century had seen, when Elizabeth led her brilliant court there. It was neither Raleigh, nor Cecil, nor any of the great historical figures of the epoch that the destroyed towers of Kenilworth had the power to revive in my eyes, but Amy Robsart, that delightful creature from the genius of Walter Scott. The image of that woman, so charming and so unfortunate, appeared to me attached to each of the stones of the immense edifice; and at times it seemed to me I heard resound from the top of the walls that last cry she let out while falling into the precipice prepared for her. I think I would have stayed there all night, if my horse, kicking the gate, had not reminded me of returning. I left and retraced my steps. I enjoyed the profound calm that surrounded me on all sides; I admired the singular power that genius has to give to its fictions even more reality than the real. Why be astonished by that, after all? Does what no longer lives have some appreciable advantage over what has never been? They both exist only by the will of those who occupy themselves with them. If the fictitious being is more engaging than the real being, why would it occupy thought less? All the while philosophizing in this way, I found myself back in Warwick, after one of the evenings most replete with memories that I have ever had in my life. That impression was not of long duration; the smoke from the coal that I smelled on awaking, and the rain that was soon falling, soon

recalled me to the real world, and I saw once more that poetry is encountered only by chance in this life; but that the
essence of existence is only vile prose.

17. To Louis de Kergorlay

Monday evening [Paris, November 11, 1833]

I received your letter yesterday, my dear friend; I have been
meaning to write you for a long time, but I kept putting it off
day to day, always having something pressing to do, because
I am working as hard as I can on my America, and it is going
very well. At least my morale is good. One other thing that
has kept me from writing you is the fact that I have absolutely
nothing new to tell you. The day of your departure, I was in
the communications office; they explained to me that it was
necessary to write c/o Algiers to the office of *Le Moniteur* to
obtain our subscription; but they could not understand why
we had still not received any response and it is much more
surprising now. The agents of the communications office told
me that they were going to write again, and they will let me
know what they learn; since then I have not heard anything
more. I cannot believe that our name has anything to do with
this matter. A journal is by its nature a public matter, and it
would be too stupid to refuse to accept our subscription; especially when we can satisfy our curiosity in every reading room
in Paris. The blame is due rather to the agents of the communications office. I saw a little article in *Le Journal des Débats* recently that led one to think that land is beginning to sell rapidly in the Metidja plain and that soon it is possible that prices
will rise considerably. It is very possible that this article was
circulated by the colonists with the aim of bringing about what
they claim is already the case. Nonetheless, the thing is not
altogether unlikely. For, on the other hand, Lamoricière's[15]

15. Juchault de Lamoricière (1806–1865) was an important military figure in
Northern Africa from the 1830 capture of Algiers to 1848. Lamoricière

inexplicable silence continues and God knows now when he
will break this silence. I think that as soon as you have six
weeks to yourself, it will be a matter of going there in person.
Without that we will never be finished of this, and we will
only come to a decision when it is too late to get any advantage out of doing so.

I have absolutely nothing new to tell you about my situation. My life is regulated like that of a monk. From morning
to dinner my existence is *completely intellectual,* and at night I
go to Marie's house. And I enjoy with extreme pleasure the
happiness of finding once again a very tender and very sweet
intimacy and long fireside chats with which I am never bored.
The next day I begin again, and so on with a surprising regularity, because my books and Marie form exactly my entire
existence since my return from England. It is difficult for me
to live for others and others for me. This way of making the
time flow by is singularly sweet. But this life lacks one thing
which a man cannot do without: a future. If I had to die in a
year, I would be very happy with the present and as content
as can be about this situation, with an end coming into view;
but like all other men, I see before me in my imagination a
long string of years and once the book that I am writing is
published and youth has floated away, I do not know what I
will do with these years. This thought exhausts me and often
brings me great distress; but I ward it off as much as I can,
I confess, and the ease with which I begin to live day to day,
enables me to understand the state of mind in which I have
seen many people in my life and which, up to now, was an
impenetrable mystery to me. Several years ago, I could only
have wondered how men could let themselves be dragged
backward into the future without having even a strong desire

---

was appointed to the rank of general in 1844, but the crowning moment of his
career occurred in 1847 when he accepted the surrender of the elusive, charis-
matic Arab leader Abd-el-Kader. Tocqueville's acquaintance with the general
was no doubt facilitated by the general's very old friendship with Kergorlay.

to turn their heads. Here I am, however, exactly what they are. This present monotonous sweetness lulls my soul and softens it to an extraordinary degree, and it is truly rare for me to think more than a week into the future. Whether that is a regrettable or fortunate state, I cannot say. But it exists.

Besides, I persist in thinking that despite the extraordinary and fortunately quite rare annoyances your soul has experienced, all things considered you are in an infinitely better position than I. You have before you a multitude of possible combinations for happiness, and I have very few. If we were both carried off today by a cannon shot, my existence would be considered more valuable than yours; but I am almost sure that you will have your revenge, provided the cannon shot is held off. Without speaking of the material obstacles in my position, I have used up nearly all the sentiments which are the true foundations of what is very improperly called *happiness* in this world. Of all the sweet emotions that can stir the heart, there is only *one* that I do not know. I have never experienced, although I understand it very well and although my imagination presents it to me very vividly, the interest that one's children and the mother of one's children must inspire in a man. So, that is the sole plank of safety I see in the future, and if by misfortune, M. should not become a mother, I would entirely despair of my existence.[16] In place of that, my dear friend, you have in your hand the most beautiful portion of existence still nearly intact. What you experienced two years ago, and especially what you still feel is a sort of sickly irritability in the soul. It is in part the result of the halfway unsociable life you lead. I am sure that there are many similar passions in the cloister. I do not doubt that this painful dream that disturbs you will disappear easily before the realities of love. You think that you are hardly made for feeling these sweet sentiments now, and I am convinced that you are mis-

16. Tocqueville and his wife, Marie, were unable to have children.

taken. And I believe that I know you better than you know yourself. Like all other men you have the unhappy chance of meeting a woman you cannot love or who lacks what is necessary to appreciate you.

Like you, I am feeling more and more what you tell me about the pleasures of the conscience. I too believe that these are the most real and the most profound. There is only one great goal in this world, one which merits the efforts of man: that is the good of humanity. There are people who work to do good for men while despising them and others while loving them. One always encounters in the services that the first renders something incomplete, coarse, and haughty, which creates neither conviction nor gratitude. I would much rather be in the latter group, but often I cannot. I love man in general, but I am constantly encountering so many individuals who repel me by the baseness of their souls! My daily efforts tend to ensure that I will be invaded by a universal contempt for my fellow men. I often succeed, at my expense, in investigating minutely and with a pitiless analysis, the motives for my actions. Often I find in them many calculations of personal interest, which do not in the least appear to the eyes of others or which escape my own. I sometimes discover that I am doing evil out of a good principle. And, still most often, viewing myself from the point of view of someone who is indifferent or an adversary, I feel severe but unjust judgments being directed toward me. In all this, I discover reasons for mistrusting my own capacity for insight and, in judging other men, for attacking their intelligence more than their heart. I believe that it is nearly impossible for one to be really of service to them by judging them as one is tempted to do at first sight; and I would rather descend a little in my own estimation, than let them fall to the very bottom.

Farewell. I embrace you with all my heart. Come for a short visit soon.

18. To Louis de Kergorlay

Paris, September 21, 1834

I only received your letter two days ago, my dear friend; while it was going to Beaumont, I was coming back to Paris.

The first thing with which I occupied myself was finding you a *Moniteur*. I was at several people's homes and finally at Dumont's (at Palais-Royal), the same, I believe, who had agreed and then refused to let you subscribe to *Le Moniteur*. He first made a lot of trouble; but I spoke to him of Dentu, who, I said, would answer to him for me. That seemed to reach him, and he consented to lend me the volume of *Le Moniteur* that I wanted for eight francs a month. He will re-place the volumes as I have need of new ones. I said that I would think it over some more. Are these terms agreeable to you? If so, which volume of *Le Moniteur* do you want to have? I think that if you decide, as I believe you will, to take advantage of Dumont's offer, you would do well to come to Paris yourself to find the volume you need, so you can take it carefully to Fosseuse. A complete collection of *Le Moniteur* costs 1,500 to 2,000 francs, and there is no need to make one-self liable to pay that amount. Besides, this little trip would give us a chance to see each other and chat.

There is the pasture, my dear friend; you either have to take advantage of it or if not of this, of another. You must not remain in your status quo. Get out of that, whatever it costs, or you will lose the energy you need to find someone who understands your projects for intellectual occupations. What does that matter? Do you not know yourself? Do you not know the natural bent of your tastes and your habits? And as for success, who has ever known anything about that before having succeeded? On that point the whole universe has noth-ing certain to teach you. What you know, which is not to be doubted, is that you are at the age of strength and of action; that political events impede you from exercising and applying this strength in public offices; that your nature refuses to bow to the petty cares of private existence; and that nonetheless it is necessary at any price to direct the activity of your mind toward something, under penalty of falling even beneath the level of those who are successfully occupied with their affairs. I just spent six weeks in the country, which I have not done since I was nine years old. I saw what people do there. I experienced there something analogous to what I feel upon seeing a very *devout* person: an extreme longing to think and to feel that way, while at the same time it is obvious that for me this is impossible. I do not know what I will become; but I feel very strongly that it would be easier for me to leave for China, to enlist as a soldier, or to gamble my life in I know not what hazardous and poorly conceived venture, than to condemn myself to leading the life of a potato, like the decent people I have just seen. . . .

I am not writing you anything more today, because I hope to see you again soon. I will have to talk to you about a plan for a review that we have formed—Beaumont and I and two or three others. Perhaps you could give us a hand. Farewell, I embrace you with all my heart. Thank you for having spoken to Genton about me. His letter is full of generous compliments, to such an extent that I believe he is mistaken about me!

19. To Louis de Kergorlay

January 1835

I am as deeply convinced as one can be of anything in this world that we are being carried away irresistibly by our laws and our mores toward an almost complete equality of conditions. Once conditions are equal, I confess that I no longer see any intermediaries between a democratic government (and by this word I do not mean a republic, but a state of society in which everyone more or less would take part in public affairs) and the government of one person ruling without any control.

I do not for an instant doubt that with time we will arrive at either one or the other. Now, I do not want the latter; if an absolute government were ever to establish itself in a country that is democratic in its social state and demoralized as France is, one cannot conceive what the limits of the tyranny would be; we have already seen fine specimens of this regime under Bonaparte and if Louis Philippe were free, he would enable us to see much more perfect ones still. Therefore only the first choice remains. I hardly like it any better than the latter, but nevertheless I do prefer it to the latter, and besides, if I fail in attaining the former, I am certain that the other will always be there. Thus, of two evils I choose the lesser.

But isn't it very difficult to establish a democratic government among us? Of course. So, if I had the choice, I would not attempt it. Is it impossible to succeed? I doubt this greatly, because independent of the political reasons I do not have time to elaborate, I cannot believe that God has been pushing two or three million men for several centuries toward equality of conditions in order to have them end in the despotism of Tiberius and Claudius. This would not truly be the problem. Why He is carrying us along this way toward democracy, I do not know; but embarked on a vessel I did not construct, I look for the means to reach the nearest port. Is it perilous to attempt such an enterprise? Show me something that would be more perilous than staying still and a route that would be less dangerous to follow, and I will confess that I am wrong. In our day, society seems to me in the same situation as a man who is wounded in the arm; gangrene has set in and it is spreading. He is doubtless very upset about amputating the arm, and the operation may be fatal, but is it not better to live one-armed than to die with two? You see I am writing in a hurry, I am throwing my ideas at you rather than explaining them. But you will pardon me because of the multitude of things with which I am occupied just now.

There is the way I see things; it remains to be known if I

ought to make this view public and in what form I should reveal it.

I am not by nature quarrelsome: when an opinion I do not share seems to me indifferent or when I am not sure of the contrary view, I keep silent. So it is that I have sometimes lived a year with people who were totally surprised at the end of that time to see me start unhesitatingly along a path from which they thought I was very far. It is not without having carefully reflected that I decided to write the book I am just now publishing.[17] I do not hide from myself what is annoying in my position: it is bound to attract active sympathy from no one. Some will find that at bottom I do not like democracy and that I am severe toward it; others will think that I favor its development imprudently. It would be most fortunate for me if the book were not read, and that is a piece of good fortune that may perhaps come to pass. I know all that, but this is my response: nearly ten years ago I was already thinking about part of the things I have just now set forth. I was in America only to become clear on this point. The penitentiary system was a pretext: I took it as a passport that would let me enter thoroughly into the United States. In that country, in which I encountered a thousand things beyond my expectation, I perceived several things about questions that I had often put to myself. I discovered facts that seemed useful to know. I did not go there with the idea of writing a book, but the idea for a book came to me there. I said to myself that each man should account to society for his thoughts, as well as for his physical energy. When one sees one's fellows in danger, one's duty is to go to their aid; strong men do much, the weak little, but being weak is no reason for folding one's arms and refusing one's cooperation. I therefore told myself: if what you are going to publish is not worth anything, it will not be noticed, my vanity will suffer, and that is all. If there is

17. The first part (2 vols.) of Tocqueville's *Democracy in America* appeared in January 1835.

something useful in my book, the danger that I am going to run personally by publishing it is in no way an argument for keeping myself from doing it.

Now, have I used the most suitable form for exhibiting my ideas? You tell me, my dear friend, that I am wrong in laying myself open to discovery from the first words. There is a great deal of truth and accuracy in this observation. I am determined to do it this way for two reasons: it would have been impossible to place in the rest of the work the body of ideas that forms the introduction, and moreover I did not want people to be unaware of the foundation of my thinking. . . .

20. To Nassau William Senior

Paris, February 21, 1835

My dear M. Senior, I thank you very much for the kind and obliging letter you have just written me. Your approbation is one for which I have most aspired, and I am proud to have attained it. How I wish this book were put within the grasp of a great number of your compatriots, and that they generally formed the opinion of it that you personally seem to have conceived! Its success here greatly surpasses my expectations. But I will not be satisfied if it does not extend to a country that I regard as my second intellectual homeland.

I come to your criticisms, which have given me almost as much pleasure as your praises, because they proved to me with what attention you read the work, and because there are several of which I intend to avail myself for the second edition.

You tell me with great justification concerning a note on page 77 that the support of the poor is not a mark that a government is democratic, and then I have cited America on this point only to give French readers an example of the expenditures in which a democracy likes to indulge. All governments can be pushed, for different reasons, to support the poor at the expense of the state, but democratic government is inclined by *nature* to act in this way.

I had said, page 115, that in English legislation *the good*[18] *of the poor had ultimately been sacrificed to that of the rich.* You attack me on this point, on which you are surely a very competent judge. You will nonetheless permit me not to share your opinion. At first it seems to me that you give to the expression *the good*[19] *of the poor* a restricted meaning that I did not give to it: you translate it by the word *wealth,*[20] which applies in particular to riches. I had wished to speak, myself, of all the things that can concur in the well-being of life: consideration, political rights, ease of obtaining justice, pleasures of the mind, and a thousand other things that contribute indirectly to happiness. I will believe, until I have proof to the contrary, that in England the rich have little by little drawn to themselves almost all the advantages that the state of society furnishes to men. In taking the question in the restricted sense that you give to it, and in admitting that the poor man temporarily makes more from cultivating the land of another rather than his own, do you think that there are not political, moral, intellectual benefits attached to the possession of the earth, and which more than compensate, and above all in a permanent manner, for the disadvantage that you point out? I know besides that I touch there one of the greatest questions of our times and the one on which we are probably the most profoundly in disagreement. We will soon have, I hope, the leisure to talk about it. While waiting, I cannot refrain from telling you that I have not been satisfied with the way in which M. MacCulloch,[21] to whose talents I otherwise pay

18. Fr. = "le bien."
19. Fr. = "le bien."
20. Tocqueville uses the English word *wealth.*
21. The Scottish political economist John Ramsay MacCulloch (1789–1864). Tocqueville is probably referring to MacCulloch's *Principles of Political Economy* (1825).

homage, has treated this question. I was surprised to see him
cite us, us other Frenchmen, in support of his arguments in
favor of the nondivision of landed property, and maintain that
material well-being was diminishing in France in proportion
as inheritances were being divided: which I am convinced is
up to now *materially false*. Such an opinion would find no
echo among us, even among those who attack the law of succession as impolitic and dangerous in the long run. Even they
recognize that for the time being the progress of the people
along the road of well-being and of civilization is continuous
and rapid and that, in this respect, the France of today already
no longer resembles the France of twenty years ago. Besides,
I repeat, such questions cannot be dealt with by letter. It is
necessary to reserve them for long conversations. Regards.

21. *To Eugène Stoffels*

Paris, February 21, 1835

. . . To return to the principal subject of your letters, I will
tell you, my dear friend, that the impression my book produced on you, although stronger in one sense than I would
like, neither surprises nor alarms me. Here is the political goal
of the work:

I wanted to show what a democratic people was in our day,
and through this rigorously exact picture, I intended to produce a double effect on the minds of the men of my time.

To those who have worked out an ideal democracy, a
glowing dream, that they believe can easily be realized, I undertook to show that they had covered the picture with false
colors; that the democratic government they advocate, if it
furnishes real benefits to the men who sustain it, does not
have the elevated characteristics that their imagination gives it;
that this government, moreover, can be maintained only by
means of certain conditions of enlightenment, of private morality, of beliefs that we do not have, and which it is necessary

to work to obtain before drawing from them the political consequences.

To men for whom the word *democracy* is synonymous with upheaval, anarchy, spoliation, murders, I tried to show that democracy could manage to govern society while respecting fortunes, recognizing rights, securing liberty, honoring beliefs; that if democractic government developed less than some other governments certain beautiful faculties of the human soul, it had beautiful and grand sides; and that perhaps, after all, the will of God was to diffuse a mediocre happiness on the totality of men, and not to concentrate a large amount of felicity on some and allow only a small number to approach perfection. I intended to demonstrate to them that, whatever their opinion might be in this regard, there was no longer time to deliberate; that society was every day proceeding and dragging them along with it toward equality of conditions; that it only remained to choose between evils henceforth inevitable; that the question was not knowing if one could obtain aristocracy or democracy, but if one would have a democratic society proceeding without poetry and without grandeur, but with order and morality, or a democratic society disordered and depraved delivered over to frenzied furors, or bent under a yoke heavier than all those that have weighed on men since the fall of the Roman Empire.

I wanted to diminish the ardor of the former, and, without discouraging them, show them the only road to take.

I sought to diminish the terrors of the latter and to bend their will to the idea of an inevitable future, so that, the ones having less ardor and the others offering less resistance, society could advance more peacefuly toward the necessary fulfillment of its destiny. There is the mother-idea of the work, the idea which links all the others in a single web, and which you should have perceived more clearly than you did. What is more, up to now only very few men understand it. I please many people of conflicting opinions, not because they understand me, but because they find in my work, by considering it only from a single side, arguments favorable to their passion of the moment. But I have confidence in the future, and I hope that a day will come when everyone will see clearly what only some perceive today. . . .

As for the material success of the book, it continues. . . .

What you tell me about your summer arrangements, my dear friend, makes me very much fear not being able to visit you again this summer. Beaumont and I are counting on going to England within a month. . . .

22. *To John Stuart Mill*

Saturday evening [June 1835]

I received your letter two evenings ago, my dear Monsieur Mill: I was hoping to reply to it yesterday, but several circumstances prevented me from doing so. I will not tell you that your letter, as to form, would do honor to a Frenchman and that few Frenchmen know how to handle their own language as you handle ours; I will not speak to you of all that, because we are not in the habit of exchanging compliments and because I have besides too much for which to thank you concerning the very *substance* of your thoughts. Nothing could flatter me more than the opinion you express of me in this letter. I fear only, I say this sincerely, that it is exaggerated.[22] I love liberty by taste, equality by instinct and reason. These two passions, which so many pretend to have, I am convinced that I really feel in myself, and that I am prepared to make great sacrifices for them. Such are the only advantages I recognize in myself. They result even more from the absence of certain common vices than from the possession of some rare qualities.

22. When the first part of Tocqueville's *Democracy in America* appeared in 1835, it received enormous praise. Mill added his voice to this praise in a review printed in the *London and Westminster Review;* and in a letter to Tocqueville dated June 11, 1835, Mill again complimented Tocqueville and asked him to write an article for this journal.

To return to the principal subject of your letter, I will say I am prolonging my stay in England,[23] and I feel more disposed to take the role in your review that its principal contributors believe suitable to assign to me; and I will explain frankly what is disposing me more every day to come to this decision.

I admit to you that I arrived in this country with rather great prejudices against the democratic party. I was comparing it to what occupies an analogous position in France, and this comparison was not favorable to it. You know France well enough to know that one of our greatest miseries is to watch democratic ideas, the only ones that have any future in our modern societies, being exploited by such a large number of men who do not understand them and whose efforts only serve to remove from the cause of Democracy many good minds who of themselves would tend toward it. A French democrat is, in general, a man who wants to place the exclusive direction of society not in the hands of all of the people, but in the hands of a certain portion of the people and who, to arrive at this result, understands only the use of material force; unfortunately, there would be many other traits yet to add to this portrait. But those are the principal ones.

All that I see of English democrats leads me on the contrary to think that if their views are often narrow and exclusive, at least theirs is the true goal that friends of Democracy must take. Their final object seems to me to be, in reality, to put the majority of citizens in a fit state for governing and to make it capable of governing. Faithful to their principles, they do not claim to force the people to be happy in the way that they judge most suitable, but they want to see to it that the people are in a fit state to discern it, and, discerning it, to conform to it. I am myself a democrat in this sense. To lead

23. Tocqueville and Beaumont visited England from April to August 1835; during July and August of this stay, they visited Ireland.

modern societies by degrees to this point seems to me to be the only way to save them from barbarism or slavery. All the energy and will that I possess will always be at the service of such a cause, represented as it is in this country by enlightened and honest men. You know that I am not exaggerating the final result of the great Democratic Revolution that is taking place at this moment in the world; I do not regard it in the same light as the Israelites saw the Promised Land. But, on the whole, I believe it to be useful and necessary, and I work toward it resolutely, without hesitation, without enthusiasm and, I hope, without weakness.

There would be a great many other things to say on this subject. But I am writing you on the run now and am again putting off saying everything that escapes me now until a time when we can talk at liberty. I asked you to indicate to me what you wanted to have from me in your *Review,* because I have not seen clearly enough what I could do in it.[24] Your letter does not dispel my doubts, but does incline me to apply my mind to dissipating them. I positively promise you I will do this, as soon as I am in a position to think seriously about something. Ponder this yourself and let me know what ideas you have. Meanwhile, believe in the feelings of esteem and friendship that I have confessed to you.

P.S. Could we, my dear Monsieur Mill, dine tomorrow at 5 o'clock? Here is why I am making this request of you. An important matter forces me to leave tomorrow evening at 7 o'clock for France, where, moreover, I will only stay two or three days, not going farther than Boulogne. I would be very happy to be able, before getting into the carriage, to have the time to pass two hours with you.

---

24. Tocqueville eventually wrote an essay, translated by Mill, entitled "Political and Social Condition of France," and published it in the *London and Westminster Review* of April 1836. Tocqueville returned to this subject of France before the revolution in his *The Old Regime and the French Revolution,* published in 1856.

23. *To Louis de Kergorlay*

Dublin, July 6, 1835

I have found on arriving here, my good friend, two letters from you, the one of June 18 and the other of July 1st. I was beginning to wonder at your silence and to worry, but not to complain about it, because we have never known such touchiness in our friendship. Not seeing any letters arrive, I thought perhaps you had already undertaken your great journey.[25] You see that our minds are linked despite the distance that separates us, and that one mind cannot feel itself preoccupied with an object without the other experiencing a sort of repercussion. I wanted to write you about it yesterday from Liverpool. I put it off only in the hope of finding letters from you here.

The idea of this great journey distresses me a great deal: it worries me; but, after all, I do not know whether, in your place, I would not do just as you are doing. That is my last word. It would take too long to develop everything those last lines contain, but you will understand them easily. I would never advise you to undertake so long and so dangerous a journey; my mind is not set enough on its utility; it inclines toward the negative rather than toward the affirmative. But if you settle on it, my heart will follow you without sorrow and without regret. May God go with you, my good and dear friend, and let us see each other again in happier times! The longer I live, the more I perceive life from the point of view that I used to think only resulted from youthful enthusiasm: as a thing of mediocre worth that is only of value insofar as one uses it to do one's duty, to serve men, and to take one's position among them. Stricken by internal afflictions that at this moment embitter my existence, I find in these thoughts a resilience that revives my soul. You share these thoughts, my dear friend; you have done so all our life. They have thrived

25. Kergorlay took a voyage a year later to Germany, but Tocqueville is probably referring to another trip that Kergorlay planned but did not take.

unceasingly in the course of our friendship. We have in some way blended them amidst the sweetest sentiments that intimacy has ever created between two men. Whatever happens to you, my dear friend, be sure that my entire soul is with you. Be sure that, however different our manner of *thinking* might be about this or that subject, we will always be united in the manner of *feeling;* be sure that a noble emotion, a generous and disinterested resolution of yours will always thrill me, and that if I myself have the good fortune of meeting with such resolutions on my way, whatever the result may be, I will always believe that in giving myself over to them I am doing something you approve. How small, cold, and sad life would become if, beside this everyday world so full of egoism and cowardice, the human spirit could not construct another in which disinterestedness, courage, in a word, virtue, could breathe at ease! But the elements of that world can be found only at the heart of a few souls like yours.

I have nothing new to tell you about myself. I am still agitated in the most painful way. I want to return to Paris and I fear doing so. My mind passes from one resolution to another with a childish rapidity. The future presents itself with twenty different faces, and I cannot settle on any of them. At the end of the day, I am no longer thinking about anything, but I am feeling a kind of numbness that is perhaps more painful than sorrow. I was in Boulogne, although it was not my intention to go there nor Marie's desire to see me do so. My will power was lifted from the assault. The trip, besides, produced good effects, at least for a time. Marie saw with her own eyes with what warmth I love her. This notion at once absorbed all others; she became easy to accompany again, content and happy. I saw that she doubted even me. For sadness makes people unjust and mistrustful. For myself, I was calmed by seeing the momentary tranquility my presence caused. I had been frightened, on my arrival, by the disorder of her ideas, and almost as much by the disorder of my own, for I confide to you that there are moments when I think my reason is going. . . . I had no idea of the violence of passions . . . the only experience that I am having at this moment. She makes me tolerant of many men and actions that I would have condemned without remission several years ago. Oh! How I wish that Providence would present me with an opportunity to use, in order to accomplish good and grand things, whatever dangers Providence might attach to them, this internal flame I feel within me that does not know where to find what feeds it. There are so many people who ask of Providence only for wrongly acquired power, and shameful riches, and who obtain them.

You see, my dear friend, I am letting my pen run on. But I am coming back to you. I hope that I am going to receive a new letter from you soon. For the next two weeks, it will be necessary to write me in Dublin, then in London. If you undertake your great voyage, which I still hope does not happen, write me unceasingly. Promise me that you will let me know very exactly everything that happens to you, especially what is bad. It is bad news that has to be sent on quickly. Good news always has time to arrive. Farewell, my good friend. I embrace you from the depth of my heart. If I cannot find you again when I arrive in Paris, I would at least want to find a letter there from you in which you tell me completely about the point of view you are adopting, the actions of my family and those of Marie since my departure. This is an appraisal from you that I prize greatly. Farewell once again, my dear Louis.

24. *To Gustave de Beaumont*

Baugy, November 15, 1835

My dear friend, I duly sent to *your* Lydia the decree you had charged me with conveying to her, not without having laughed heartily under my breath at the way it was phrased.

Besides, I do not think that she will be fooled by your hypocritical sorrow; you added to the horror of your perfidy without hiding it and I expect to learn any day now that you have been torn to pieces like Orpheus, if I am not mistaken, since I am a little muddled on mythology.

I discovered on returning here a very warm bed, in which I was very tenderly received.[26] Since then I have passed my time very agreeably, but I am doing absolutely nothing, which is beginning to weigh on me. I therefore long to be settled in my home and to take up a routine again. Nevertheless, my current idleness can be excused, if it must be, whereas the one in which I *am sure* you are immersed can only excite indignation. You have all the time in the world for working, and I will wager that you are doing nothing. Nevertheless, I do not mind telling you, however audacious it may be, that today we have come to November 15, a time at which cold-blooded animals fall asleep, but at which man awakens and flares up with new ardor. Think about that and write me. When I do not receive any letter from you, it is a bad sign. Then you have few good things to say. The other day, chatting with that ox, Buloz, I expressed an idea that is coming back to me just now and that I want you to hear. I am not sure it is new, but I believe it is right. What is taking place at this moment in England, I told him, presents a singularly curious spectacle. The previous revolutions that the English have undergone were essentially English in *substance* and in *form*. The ideas that gave birth to them circulated only in England; the form in which these ideas clothed themselves was unknown to the continent; the means that were used in order to make them victorious were the product of mores, habits, laws, practices different or contrary to the mores, the habits, and laws of the rest of Europe (all of that up to a certain point). Those previous revolutions in England thus were an object of great curiosity to the philosophers, but it

26. Tocqueville married Mary Mottley on October 26, 1835.

was difficult for them to give rise to a popular book among us. It is no longer so today: today it is the European revolution that is being continued among the English, but it is being continued there by taking wholly English forms. The twofold reason that must arouse curiosity: if the ideas that shake England had nothing in common with those that disturb us, what would be said about England would hardly interest us more than what is recounted about China; if the English revolutionaries did nothing but imitate our own, as all of France's continental neighbors have done, interest would exist but it would be feeble; one is keenly interested only in what on the one hand touches you and on the other is in some way new and original. Now, the English have indeed taken our ideas, but they have poured them into their own mold, and they seek to make them triumph and to apply them in their own manner. They are European in substance, English only in form.

There you have what I said to Buloz, who listened while fastening his fish eye on me, in which I could not find the least reflection of my idea, which made me think that what I was saying was something old that I was merely putting new clothes on without suspecting it. Be that as it may, as you are working on the part about England,[27] I wanted to tell you about this.

I must leave you. Farewell, my dear friend, I embrace you. I hope that you do not forget to go to my upholsterer's. If he says to you that the frames of my armchairs have not yet been sent to him by the man who was supposed to do so, you will have to send Jacques to this latter's home, armed with a thundering letter. They were promised to me for the 17th of last month.

---

27. Beaumont published *Marie, ou l'esclavage aux Etats-Unis: Tableau des moeurs américaines* in 1835, but Tocqueville is probably referring here to the research Beaumont was doubtlessly doing for his finest book, *L'Irlande sociale, politique, et religieuse,* eventually published in 1839.

25. To Claude-François de Corcelle

Berne, July 27, 1836

I am traveling here, my dear friend, much more as a lover of beautiful nature than as a philosopher. However, when I find myself accidentally forced to read a newspaper or to have a reasonable conversation, I try to understand what I am being taught. I thus already, in my capacity as an American, have conceived a very superb disdain for the federal constitution of Switzerland, which I unceremoniously call a league and not a federation.

A government of this nature is surely the weakest, the most powerless, the most maladroit, and the most incapable of leading peoples anywhere except to anarchy. I am already struck also with how little political life prevails in the population. The kingdom of England is a hundred times more republican than this republic. Others would say that this results from the differences in the races. But that is an argument that I will never admit except at the last extremity, and when there remains absolutely nothing to say. I would rather find the reason for this in a little-known fact, or at least one ignored by me until now: it is that communal liberty is a very recent fact in most of the cantons of Switzerland.

The bourgeoisie of the towns were governing the countryside as the royal power does in France. It was a little bourgeois centralization that, like our centralization, would not tolerate someone sticking one's nose in its affairs.

Enough about politics. If Quincy Adams's speech is still in your hands, please save it for me. Believe in my tender and very sincere friendship.

26. To Pierre-Paul Royer-Collard

Baden, August 25, 1836

I do not want, Monsieur, to delay any longer in taking advantage of the permission you have given me to write to you.

I would even have done so much earlier, if anything had happened to me that merited being reported to you. From that you will conclude that, since I am finally writing, it is because I have something very important to tell you. Nothing of the sort is the case, however. I am writing because I hope to obtain news from you, and also because you have let me become used to talking freely with you, and because I am very steadfast in habits of that sort.

I had come to Switzerland for a vacation. But I soon converted it into a trip made for reasons of health. Madame de Tocqueville was somewhat unwell in Berne; we were strongly urged to go take the baths at Baden, and we finally decided to do so. It is from there that I am writing you. Imagine, if you will, a fairly deep ravine, on which hang three or four houses inhabited by bathers; at the bottom, a torrent that rolls very loudly over the stones, and toward which on all sides rush little rivers of hot water, which are forced to pass through conduits and finally emerge from faucets; surround all of that with a tepid and slighly sulfurous atmosphere, and you have a rather exact picture of the place. You must already pity me, and I confess I would consider myself pitiable, if, on leaving Paris, I had not thrown at random on the bottom of my trunk a certain number of books that I am rediscovering here with pleasure.

It would be difficult to judge the tastes of their owner from a report of their titles. The first is Machiavelli. This is a rather good book to have at the present time; so, I am tempted to display it with a little ostentation. But I would confess the other two to you: the second is *Histoire des variations*,[28] and the third *The Complete Works* of Plato. What encourages me to make this confession is a memory which stays with me of the first visit I had the pleasure of making to you. I remember

28. Written by Bishop Bossuet in 1688. The full title is *Histoire des variations des églises protestantes*. Here Bossuet links Protestant individualism to social and political disunity, defends the absolutism of Louis XIV, and sketches a very influential theory arguing that world history is guided by providential design.

that, having by accident seen a book that was open on your desk, I thought I saw it was in Greek. That instantly made me feel I had entered a world other than the one which is disturbed by all the violent and transitory passions of our epoch. What struck me further was to see that you read this Greek in Greek, whereas I, alas, would have been reduced to reading in translation. But, to return to my three authors, at first I gathered them together willy-nilly on the same shelf; then, I started reading them, not lightly and without stopping, as I had already done, but with reflection and deliberateness, as the occasion allowed. I began with Machiavelli. I first read *The Prince,* then *The History of Florence.* I would have a lot to tell you about the impressions which this reading made on me, a lot of opinions to submit in order to be enlightened by yours. But I fear it would bore you. I cannot however resist the desire to tell you *in broad terms* what I think.

What struck me above all in the book *The Prince* is that it was, taken as a whole, a superficial work, despite the very profound thoughts that are to be found in it from time to time. I will try to explain: there is in *The Prince* a great display of villainy; the art of crime in political matters is learnedly professed there; it is a very complicated contraption in which cunning, deceit, lying, and intrigue form the springs. But to what will all that lead in the end? As I see it, the student of Machiavelli would be constantly encumbered in his own ruses; while trying to fortify himself on one side, he always opens himself somewhere else. He is never so adroit that he is not seen to be cunning, and his treasons are never so hidden that he does not finally come across as a traitor. If the author knows the weaknesses and vices of men well, he does not seem to suspect that, after all, at the core of the human heart there exists a vague, but powerful, sentiment of justice, which, sooner or later, will come to light, and that, if it is common to see a known villain succeed for a while, it is very rare to see him execute anything great or, above all, durable. In short, Machiavelli's *Prince* works so learnedly and laboriously at becoming a great criminal that I think that it would be less difficult still to get out of the affair simply by being honest.

For myself, I imagine that if Machiavelli had undertaken to teach men the art of mixing together the doses of deceit and rectitude, of truth and errors, which can the most surely lead to success; if he had taught them how to husband trickery, violence, and intrigue with great care, in order to make use of them only in extreme cases, instead of squandering them at every turn; if he had told them how to go about cloaking their vices in feigned virtues and, if it were possible, in true virtues, in such a way that contemporaries would remain in suspense and posterity undecided; if, in a word, he had shown them the means by which to accomplish their culpable designs by the least evil means possible, I think he would have shown proof of genius as perverse, but really more profound than in writing *The Prince.*

Moreover, I cannot understand how there has ever been the least doubt about Machiavelli's morality. After *The Prince,* I read *The History of Florence,* which seemed to me the work of a great writer and often of a great man of politics; I found the same man there that I had seen before. The author of *The Prince* and that of *The History of Florence* seem to me to be one and the same individual. There is only the difference of subject between them. One finds in both works the same indifference for justice or injustice; the same adoration for adroitness, whatever might be the means it employs; the same profound esteem for those who succeed. What is equally singular in these two works is that the author also shows himself able to understand virtue and vice, without that knowledge influencing either his judgments or his actions in any way. In one as in the other, one senses that Machiavelli, like so many people of our day, is endowed with a nature so flexible and so *free* of all principles that he would be capable of doing anything, even good, if the thing became profitable.

From *The History of Florence,* I went to that of the *Variations* by Bossuet. The distance was great. I had never looked at this work so closely, and I cannot tell you how I admired its content, and, even more perhaps, its form. It is truly a magnificent and powerful arrangement. But I want to stop here. I would have had infinite pleasure in reporting to you my impressions, I dare not say my opinions, of Plato. But I am already ashamed of having spoken to you for so long of things, which, since you know them so well yourself, can hardly interest you. Please forgive me for this long letter on account of the sentiments that made me write, and, among these sentiments, you will find the respectful affection that I have pledged to you for life.

Will you please present my esteem to Madame Royer, whose kind reception I have not forgotten.

P.S. I would be very happy if I could have some news from you on my return. I will be in Paris about September 15; I will stay there a week, after which I will go bury myself in the country to work there and *to escape* from Paris for two or three months. I hope that, if you have the occasion to see M. the Prince de T[alleyrand][29] and Madame the Duchess de D[ino],[30] you will be so good as to offer them my respectful esteem.

27. *To Eugène Stoffels*

Tocqueville, October 5, 1836

I found your letter of August 18th on passing through Geneva. Everything you tell me does not touch me, because I

29. Charles Maurice de Talleyrand, prince of Benevento (1754–1838), one of the most remarkable participants and survivors in the politics of some of France's most turbulent decades. Technically a bishop, he was elected to the Estates General and joined the Revolution in 1789. Under Napoleon he proved to be an able foreign minister, and during the Restoration he briefly advised Louis XVIII but was soon dismissed. Finally, he took part in the replacement of Charles X and became King Louis Philippe's special ambassador to London.

30. Talleyrand's niece.

adopt it all as my opinion. It is obvious that we are fighting each other in the dark without seeing each other clearly. I was rather heated in the reasoning of my discussions with you, and you took that for the sign that I was impetuously carried away by my own ideas toward immediate action: nothing of the kind is true. You represent to me with good reason that revolutions are great evils and rarely serve in the education of a people, that a prolonged agitation is indeed regrettable and that respect for law arises only from stability of the laws. . . . All things that I believe deeply. I do not think that in France there is a man who is less revolutionary than I, nor one who has a more profound hatred for what is called the revolutionary spirit (a spirit which, parenthetically, is very easily combined with the love of an absolute government). What am I then? And what do I want? Let us distinguish, in order to understand each other better, between the end and the means. What is the end? What I want is not a republic, but a hereditary monarchy. I would even prefer it to be legitimate rather than elected like the one we have, because it would be stronger, especially externally. What I want is a central government energetic in its own sphere of action. Energy from the central government is even more necessary among a democratic people in whom the social force is more diffused than in an aristocracy. Besides our situation in Europe lays down an imperative law for us in what should be a thing of choice. But I wish that this central power had a clearly delineated sphere, that it were involved with what is a necessary part of its functions and not with everything in general, and that it were forever subordinated, in its tendency, to public opinion and to the legislative power that represents this public opinion. I believe that the central power can be invested with very great prerogatives, can be energetic and powerful in its sphere, and that at the same time provincial liberties can be well developed. I think that a government of this kind can exist, and that at the same time the majority of the nation itself can be involved with its own affairs, that political life can be spread almost everywhere, the direct or indirect exercise of political rights can be quite extensive. I wish that the general principles of government were liberal, that the largest possible part were left to the action of individuals, to personal initiative. I believe that all these things are compatible; even more, I am profoundly convinced that there will never be order and tranquility except when they are successfully combined.

As for the means: with all those who admit that we must make our way gradually toward this goal, I am very much in accord. I am the first to admit that it is necessary to proceed slowly, with precaution, with legality. My conviction is that our current institutions are sufficient for reaching the result I have in view. Far, then, from wanting people to violate the laws, I profess an almost superstitious respect for the laws. But I wish that the laws would tend little and gradually toward the goal I have just indicated, instead of making powerless and dangerous efforts to turn back. I wish that the government would itself prepare mores and practices so that people would do without it in many cases in which its intervention is still necessary or invoked without necessity. I wish that citizens were introduced into public life to the extent that they are believed capable of being useful in it, instead of seeking to keep them away from it at all costs. I wish finally that people knew where they wanted to go, and that they advanced toward it prudently instead of proceeding aimlessly as they have been doing almost constantly for twenty years. What else will I tell you, my dear friend? One could speak all day on the text without doing anything else but enlarging upon it. You must understand my thought without my having to dilute it or to explain it by a thousand examples. . . . In short, I conceive clearly the ideal of a government that is not at all revolutionary or agitated beyond measure, and one which I believe possible to give to our country. But on the other hand, I understand as well as anyone that such a government (which is moreover only the extension of the one we have), in order to become established, requires mores, habits, laws that do not yet exist, and which can only be introduced slowly and with great precautions. . . .

28. *To Henry Reeve*

Paris, March 22, 1837

Receiving your letter gave me great pleasure, my dear Reeve; you gave me good news of yourself and of your translation; I take great interest in both; I even think I am sufficiently unselfish to prefer the prosperity of the former to that of the latter. Both are doing well, thank heavens. I had previously received Sir Robert Peel's speech and the tract of *An American Citizen;* I think I owe them to you. Please keep me up-to-date on such publications, if more appear. Independently of the serious interest I take in the opinions others may hold of me, it delights me to see the different features that are given to me according to the political passions of the person who cites me. It is a collection of portraits that I like to assemble. To the present day, I have not yet found one of them that completely looked like me. They absolutely want to make me a party man and I am not that in the least; they assign to me passions and I have only opinions, or rather I have only one passion, the love of liberty and human dignity. All forms of government are in my eyes only more or less perfect ways of satisfying this holy and legitimate passion of man. They alternately give me democratic or aristocratic prejudices; I perhaps would have had one set of prejudices or the other, if I had been born in another century and in another country. But the chance of birth has made me very comfortable defending both. I came into the world at the end of a long Revolution, which, after having destroyed the old state, had created nothing durable. Aristocracy was already dead when I started life and democracy did not yet exist, so my instinct could lead me blindly neither toward one nor toward the other. I was living in a country that for forty years had tried a little of everything without settling definitely on anything; therefore I was not susceptible to political illusions. Belonging to the old aristocracy of my homeland, I had neither hatred nor natural jealousy against the aristocracy, and that aristocracy being destroyed, I did not have any natural love for it either, since one only attaches oneself strongly to what is living. I was near enough to it to know it well, far enough away to judge it without passion. I would say as much about the democratic element. No family memory, no personal interest gave me a natural and necessary bent toward democracy. But for my part I had not received any injury from it; I had no particular motive for either loving or hating it, independent of those that my reason furnished me. In a word, I was so thoroughly in equilibrium betweeen the past and the future that I felt naturally and instinctively attracted toward neither the one nor the other, and I did not need to make great efforts to cast calm glances on both sides.

But that is enough about me; let us speak about the principal purpose of your letter. You want to know when you will be able to have the initial pages of the two new books. I do not think I will be ready to have it printed before the month of December.[31] I am not even interested in doing it earlier. What is of importance to a literary work is that it not appear in the summer, but once winter starts the month does not matter.

With regard to the difficulty that Gosselin[32] may cause concerning the pages, I very much hope that we will remove it. You know what makes him so fearful on the subject. The counterfeiters of Brussels went to the point of *stealing* the Lamartine proofs in his printing house. You have perhaps heard tell of this affair. Be that as it may, I expect that we will manage to accomplish what we want.

31. Tocqueville did not, in fact, publish the last part (2 vols.) of *Democracy in America* until 1840.

32. Charles Gosselin, publisher of both parts of *Democracy in America,* as well as books by Beaumont and Alphonse de Lamartine.

You make me hope in your letter that we will see you as well as Madame your mother in Paris this year. I do not need to tell you the pleasure you will give to my wife and myself by following through with this plan.

Farewell, my dear Reeve, please accept the assurance of my very sincere friendship.

P.S. Please give respectful regards to your mother. If you have the chance to remember me to Lord Lansdowne,[33] do not fail to do so.

29. To Pierre-Paul Royer-Collard

Tocqueville, August 20, 1837

I would be very happy, Monsieur, if my letters gave you a little of the satisfaction that yours give me. But that cannot be. Because, for me, your correspondence is not only agreeable, it is useful and, to use a word that expresses my thought well, it is healthy. I find in everything you say pure and elevated inspiration, a manly taste for the great and the just that confirms me in my good resolves and would divert me, if need be, from the bad ones. I place myself, in reading what you write, back on the track of the honest thoughts that come to me from time to time out of all order or sequence. It seems to me that I rediscover them clearer and more distinct in your words than in mine and that the form that you give them makes me devoted to them. Such impressions would be salutary in any time, but they are particularly so in ours. I

33. Lord Lansdowne (1780–1843) was a Whig politician in Prime Minister Melbourne's cabinet. When Tocqueville visited England in 1833, he often found it difficult to meet the people with whom he wished to talk. Upon returning to England in 1835, he discovered that he was regarded as one of the century's preeminent political philosophers, as the nineteenth century's Montesquieu. Naturally, he found that he was welcome in English intellectual circles that had heretofore been remote. Through his friend Henry Reeve, Tocqueville met Lord Lansdowne, and when dining at the Lansdowne house, Tocqueville met Lord Granville, George and Harriet Grote, Prime Minister Melbourne, and many others. See Seymour Drescher, *Tocqueville and England* (Cambridge, Mass.: Harvard University Press, 1964).

confess that, after having spent a few months in Paris, I am always tempted, returning home, to wonder if there really are principles and if it is good to follow these principles. When I consider the sorry intrigues to which our society is delivered in our day, the despicable charlatans who exploit it, the almost universal pettiness that reigns over it and above all the astonishing absence of disinterestedness and even of personal interest, taken on a large scale, that is to be noticed in it, I sometimes wonder if what I take for an accident might not be the general rule. Is what we see before us, then, the natural bearing and the eternal condition of humanity? Is the man of our day at his full height? Has there never been a political world in which, I do not say virtue, but great passions have reigned and which was led by considerations other than miserable day-to-day interests? You have spanned, Monsieur, the most agitated half-century of our history; were these things that were so beautiful, so horrible, so singular, which you have witnessed, done by men similar to those we see today quarreling with each other over power? Is it the meeting of so much pettiness and misery that has produced this grandeur and this brilliance? Or are we rather, in fact, stricken by an exceptional, accidental and consequently transitory malady? I have thought so for a very long time and I would like to think so still, because it would be very discouraging to have to struggle endlessly and without rest in the midst of what we see about us. While waiting for the change to occur, I like to form for myself alongside the greater society, a small, ideal city, peopled with men whom I like and whom I respect and to live there. I do not have to tell you, Monsieur, that you are among them, nor what place you hold there.

I am speaking to you of my ideas, because, of my actions, I have absolutely nothing to tell you. I am doing nothing outside, and my life wanders with great tranquility from my study to my garden. I work as much as I can and hardly advance. I need you to tell me again in order to console me in my slowness, that the time does not matter in the least and that one ought to dream of doing something well and not quickly. The subject is so difficult that it drives me to despair. I find it difficult to deal with ideas that have not yet been treated by anyone, but even much more difficult to restate completely, reasonably, and with some novelty a large number of things that have already been glimpsed or roughly portrayed by others. In a picture as vast as the one I have undertaken to paint, parts are necessarily encountered that are not new; I cannot omit them without doing harm to the overall view, and it is a laborious and often thankless task to deal with them. In short, however, I hope not to do worse than the first time.

It seems that the dissolution of the Chamber has definitely stopped for this year. For my part I was very vexed by it. I have not yet had time to take sufficient root in this part of the country to hope to be named to the Chamber and, if by chance I were, I would not be able to finish my book, and, what is more serious, in the current state of minds, I do not see clearly what good I could do in the Chamber. Thus the political career, which nevertheless I ultimately want to try, is either closing before me for a long time or opening badly. But one has to make the best of this, as of all the evils about which there is nothing one can do.

To return to my work, which, after all, is my great concern, you cannot conceive how the desire to put the last touches on my work keeps me in constant agitation, because it contradicts another desire in me that is no less lively, which is to let nothing imperfect escape; so I am thus very slow and very irritated with my slowness, in which I ever persist. It is hardly reasonable, I know, to want so much to finish. But I am so constructed that the moment I let my mind become entirely devoted to a subject, I cannot rest until the moment it is dealt with. The confused ideas to which my mind gives birth are like an unbearable burden until I have specified them and set them down with some sureness on paper. Had I eternity before me, it would be the same, and I could not keep

myself every day from making efforts as desperate as if I were
going to have to stop the next day. Scold me, Monsieur, I
beg you, and tell me quite plainly that I am wrong.

Monsieur and Madame de Beaumont just came to us from
England in very good health. It is a long time since the old
manor house of Tocqueville has seen so many people gathered
together and so content to find themselves together again. M.
de B. is relating, as far as I can judge, admirable materials on
England and above all on Ireland. I have great hope for his
book. He saw the English elections, which were very turbulent and fundamentally not very impassioned. Many blows
were dealt there, but few real political emotions were to be
seen. In short, the conservative reaction seems to be more
and more pronounced in England proper. But Ireland is more
subjected to O'Connell[34] and more difficult to handle than
ever. B. believes that the reformist majority will be the same
as in the past in Parliament, by 20 to 40 votes.[35] The
Whigs are losing in England and in Scotland and are winning
in Ireland.

Many apologies, Monsieur, for the interminable length of
my letter. Once I start writing you, I do not know how to
stop. Madame de Tocqueville and I send our regards to Madame Royer. Please accept for yourself, Monsieur, the expression of my lively and respectful affection. I hope that you will
be so good as not to forget me at Valençay and to perceive
all that my lack of paper does not permit me to express.

34. Daniel O'Connell (1775–1847), leader of the Catholic emancipation
movement, was elected to Parliament in 1828; he was allowed to sit in Parliament only after the Wellington government, more fearful of Irish agitation than
Tory reaction, passed the 1829 Catholic Emancipation Bill allowing Catholics,
if they met property qualifications, to hold office and to vote.

35. Tocqueville here refers to the second Melbourne government, which in
1837 favored a more conciliatory policy toward Ireland, including some relief
for the poor and more participation in local government by wealthier Catholics. Melbourne was opposed by the Conservatives (such as the moderately
conservative Robert Peel), as well as the Irish members of Parliament who
regarded his reforms as insufficient.

30. To Gustave de Beaumont

Tocqueville, November 12, 1837

I have just received your letter of the 8th, my dear friend;
you were surprised by my loss.[36] I confess that I was surprised
by it myself. I did not know this region, and my friends reck-
oned on a majority of 80 votes. I told you what caused the
loss. The intrigues of the agents of the administration on the
one hand, on the other hand the blindly democratic passions
of the lower class, and finally the money of my adversary. We
have no idea, my dear friend, what the power of money is
when it is not joined to nobility and has the hatred of nobility
for an auxiliary. For three days all the cabarets of Valognes
were filled at M. Le Marois's expense, and the peasant electors
who came to vote for me were led to the voting half-drunk
with cries: "*No noblemen!*" It is not that all my adversaries did
not recognize that I had neither the opinions nor the prejudices of the nobility. But in the heads of these coarse men it
was something like the instinctive repugnance Americans have
for men of color. The *mind* has struggled for some time
against this impression, but the *beast* finally got the better of
it. Besides, as I informed you, all the consolations that a vanquished man could have, I have had. I had 207 votes, and the
first day I fell short of a majority by only 15 votes. The upper
class and, what is more valuable, the middle class were for me
almost en masse. Never had so fierce an election been seen in
the region. I was only concerned with moderating my supporters. Thus, I was beaten, but I was not disheartened for an
instant. And now that I see the composition of the new
Chamber, not only am I not angry at having failed, but I
would be in despair at not having failed, and now even if

36. On November 4, 1837, Tocqueville sought to represent his home district of Valognes (near Cherbourg) in the Chamber of Deputies, but he lost.
With the electorate under the July Monarchy so drastically restricted (about
200,000 in a nation of 33 million), Tocqueville might well have accepted the
help of Molé, the prime minister and a relation of Tocqueville's, but he did not
wish to compromise his ability to achieve independence within the legislature.

someone offered me some fine door by which to enter the Palais-Bourbon, I would refuse to knock on it.

Now let us speak of you: I must confess that I first felt a lively surge of joy in seeing that you were not named.[37] I can say that to you because you know my motives well. I felt an even greater one, seeing that you had lost by only 10 votes. I dare say that in the face of the difficulties of your position and with the state of the country as it is at this moment, that is an unhoped for result. Your next election seems to me as sure as anything in this world can be. The reaction will come, be sure of that, and we with it. I have received your letter to the electors concerning the newspaper's attack. I have savored and admired this morsel very much. It must do you infinite honor. You have never done anything better.

Now, my dear friend, I would be content, very content, I assure you, if I were sure that you were so yourself. Some words in your letter make me fear that at bottom you were a little vexed with me and accused me of having dragged you along into an ill-conceived maneuver. You must tell me what you are thinking about that. As for me, I persist in believing that we did all that there was to do and that we achieved a great result, even though we fell short of the principal result. But perhaps I am mistaken, and I ask you to have it out with me clearly on this point. You know that I have always known how to hear the truth, especially from you who have so often told me such useful things.

We are free at last, my dear friend, and I cannot tell you how joyfully and with what ardor I am rushing back to my studies and my work.[38] We will spend, if you wish it, happy and useful years. The future is ours, believe me. Never have I been so convinced. You are retiring to La Grange in order to work, something of which I approve all the more as I myself am going to Baugy for the same purpose. But I am going to

37. Beaumont also lost this first attempt to enter the Chamber of Deputies.

38. One might well wonder what would have happened to the second part of *Democracy in America* if Tocqueville had been elected in 1837.

make you the same recommendation I am making myself.
Let us not be in such a rush. You frighten me in saying
that you want to return to Paris with your book completed.
Who is forcing you to announce it before next winter? And
why finish it before announcing it? Consider this to be your
great battle. So work, I entreat you, with energy, but with
deliberateness.

I will leave Valognes the 19th or the 20th. If you can, write
me there between now and then; you will give me great
pleasure. If you lack the time, try to see at least that I find a
letter from you at my home in Paris. If, as I think, you will
not be in Paris when I pass through, I will try to slip away
one day in order to see you at La Grange, while my wife goes
to Chamarande. Thus we are going to see each other again
soon, and I am thinking about this with great pleasure, because from now on, we will be more *inseparable* than ever. For
my part and from the bottom of my heart, I swear to you
that it is more agreeable to have succumbed honorably with
you than to have triumphed alone.

Be assured of my great affection. My regards to Madame de
Beaumont.[39]

31. To Gustave de Beaumont

Baugy, March 21, 1838

Although I have absolutely nothing new to tell you, my
dear friend, I nevertheless want to write you in order to give
you my news and receive some from you, because this complete solitude is beginning to weigh on me.

I came back here the day I left you, and I started to work
again like a wild man until my brain would not perform any
further service, which is my present state. For the moment I
am filled more with agitation than with ideas, and I have no

39. Beaumont had married Clémentine de Lafayette, granddaughter of the
famous general, in June 1836.

alternative but to stop for two or three days, so that I will not have to stop for many more. I am angry to see myself brought back to earth this way when I was at the height of my impetus, and I am reflecting in the most philosophical way, but I will not communicate these reflections to you, since you are quite well and would consequently not be equal to my theories. Do not go thinking me ill, from this long discourse. I am not ill, but tired. It would be best for me to rest, and rest is unbearable to me, so that I have this illness and in the bargain the impatience of illness. But in two days things will no longer appear this way to me. Thus, if you want to respond to this item in my letter, hurry. What keeps me so impatient is the sight of how little I have done for the three months I have been working like a wretch. If I had put this much time and this much effort into the first work, it would only now be making its appearance. Am I wrong or right to turn my thoughts over again and again in my head this way before setting them to paper? In truth, I just do not know. You will judge it, my dear Aristarchus,[40] before all others. Within the next eight months, I very much hope to pass through your mill, just as you will pass through mine, if you do not mind.

Unable to do anything better, for several days I have been reading some old books that I brought here with me, among others Plutarch, whom I confess, to my great shame, to have scarcely opened until now. I at first read one of his lives rather inattentively, then another less nonchalantly; now I find a singular charm in this reading. What a great devil of a world was this ancient world! Plutarch, who, in his gossiping, shows the small sides of it better than anyone else, makes the great appear by the same sally. He succeeds and makes people move who had always seemed to me more or less contrived; he

40. Tocqueville is probably referring to Aristarchus of Samothrace (second century B.C.), who was head of the Alexandrian Library, a famous scientist of the ancient world, and a commentator and critic of Homer, Hesiod, Pindar, and others. His name has often been used, by Cicero and others, to exemplify the scrupulous and complete critic.

makes men of them, only a little higher than nature, and, reduced to men, they strike you much more than when you
only saw in them immobile colossi and imaginary giants. This
reading has captured my imagination so well that there are
moments when I fear becoming mad in the manner of Don
Quixote. My mind is completely crammed with a heroism
that is hardly of our time, and I fall very flat when I come out
of these dreams and find myself face to face with reality. But
it is no less on that account fine reading, and I recommend it
to you if by chance you should come upon the time and the
taste for reading.

But when will this time come, and when will we be able to
take advantage of it in order to read together? I truly fear that
we will lose touch with each other little by little. True communication is not reestablished with conversations such as
those we have had three times in four months. A lot of time
is needed to become familiar with someone else's actions and
thoughts again, and I do not know now when we will have
the time. You come back at the end of May, and we leave at
the beginning of June. That makes another meeting shortened
and consequently wasted, since we will only meet to wish
each other good day.

I hope that after your excursion to Paris you have resumed
work with a new energy. Nevertheless, I would doubt that
you were the same Beaumont you were ten years ago. Because then you needed more than a week to grow tired of
doing nothing. The moment you gave ground, you always
made a great retreat, then returned very resolutely to the
charge. Now, time is hurrying you, so I suppose you went
back to work as soon as you arrived at La Grange. But is the
work going as well? Isn't your verve cooling off? Let me
know. You know how interested I am in your work. I long
to read it all at once, because I have never been able to
understand a book well that is explained to me by word of
mouth. I become tangled in the details of my draft when I
undertake to make one, nor do I judge someone else's draft
except when I have it before me. We will have to do this

reciprocally and read each other's works almost without stopping.

Farewell, my dear friend, give my household's regards to Madame de Beaumont and believe in my old friendship.

P.S. Remember me to M. and Mme. de Puzy. Have you been happy with your stay in Paris?

32. To Gustave de Beaumont

Baugy, April 22, 1838

Today I have a little time to myself, my dear friend, and I want to take advantage of it to talk with you. It seems to me that I have hardly any ideas, but ideas are not absolutely necessary in order to speak or even to write. I will begin with what is most agreeable: I received, about a week ago, a letter from Corcelle, who was coming from La Grange. He informed me that you read him several portions of your work, with which he was struck; I do not need to tell you that this part of his letter, which is very long and detailed, gave me tremendous pleasure. Corcelle, who is only a mediocre worker, is a good judge of the works of others. His opinion on this point has considerable weight in my eyes, and, since one is only half-content when one rejoices alone, I wanted to inform you of my satisfaction. Corcelle added that you seemed perfectly happy, as did your kind little wife. He maintains that we were right to rejoice in your marriage. We do not doubt that, but we always like to hear it said.

We will finally be returning to Paris shortly. I will be there the 1st day of May at the latest. Marie will return, I think some days before me, in order to set up our little establishment. I have a great need finally to tear myself away from my work. I am tired both physically and mentally, or rather my state of mind is reacting on my body. My health, which has been excellent all winter, has been completely unsteady for three weeks. Here I am not only absorbed by my work, but by a thousand other ideas which come to me endlessly, either as I read or without any occasion at all. Because my head has never worked more than in this solitude. It has been some years since I have read as much and thought as much about what I was reading as I have during these four months devoted to *Democracy*. I am putting at this moment the finishing stroke on the *penultimate* chapter. But what will be the shape of the last? Into how many little chapters will it be divided? I still do not know anything about this. The only thing that I understand is that before undertaking it, I will have to marshal my strength in order to finish by one last effort. I am already frightened by this decisive chapter, and I believe I will need several months to do it. I will only undertake it at Tocqueville.

I will tell you nothing about politics, which I am observing from so far away. All that I can say is that the administration's enemies will ultimately, if this continues, make me one of its partisans. Never in France has ambition for positions appeared more disgustingly out in the open than, especially, in the conduct of the Doctrinaires.[41] Those men irritate my nerves with their moral peevishness and their shabby actions.

41. The name *Doctrinaire* originated under the Restoration and was applied to a number of eminent and intellectual political figures who sought to find political ground between the ultra-royalists, who longed to restore the Old Regime, and the republicans, who believed in the principles of 1789. The Doctrinaires—sometimes called constitutional royalists—supported conservative government by an aristocracy of wealth, increasing the powers of the clergy within limitations, and strong central government under the principles of the Charter of 1814. The Doctrinaires consistently opposed the left, but when Charles X attempted to suppress the Charter, they led the opposition.

Under the July Monarchy, the Doctrinaires really had no consistent doctrine, nor was the group entirely identifiable and homogeneous. About all they could promise was a period of stability and prosperity generated by a limited suffrage. Royer-Collard and later Guizot were the outstanding Doctrinaires under the Restoration. Under the July Monarchy, one could include such men as de Broglie, Rémusat, and Guizot.

To overthrow the administration[42] in order to see M. Thiers[43] or M. Guizot[44] come to office, in truth this would make dupes of the sincere friends of the country. It seems evident to me

42. The administration was headed by Count Louis Mathieu Molé (1781–1855), prime minister from 1836 to 1839. Molé was an aristocrat, a peer of the realm, and a keen intellect; he had served both the empire and the Restoration well and did not hesitate to offer his services to King Louis Philippe. Molé was no friend to republican government and was wise enough to recognize that the July Monarchy would protect the landlords as well as the bourgeoisie.

43. Louis Adolphe Thiers (1797–1877) was an important political and intellectual figure, both gifted and arrogant, for over half of the nineteenth century. As a young man, he played an important role in the opposition to Charles X, but after the Revolution of 1830, he was instrumental in establishing, not a republic, but rather a constitutional monarchy headed by the duke of Orléans (soon to be King Louis Philippe). All his life he supported a constitutional monarchy, a conviction capsulized in his famous dictum: "The king reigns and does not govern."

Under the July Monarchy, Thiers was twice briefly called upon to form a cabinet and become prime minister, once in 1836 and again in 1840. Especially after 1840, Thiers headed one group in the Chamber of Deputies that formed a moderately left opposition to Guizot's ministry. Although Tocqueville strongly resisted assimilation into this opposition, he sometimes found himself in what he regarded as a most unsatisfactory alliance with Thiers. It was unsatisfactory precisely because Tocqueville regarded Thiers as unprincipled, opportunistic, and capable of swinging left or right as his own political interests demanded. Said Tocqueville: "I tell you that man is possessed by the devil."

Worse still, Tocqueville considered Thiers's so-called left opposition to be completely inadequate because it did not offer a clear and progressive political alternative to Guizot's conservatism. After all, Thiers was a man who had consistently proposed a small extension of the very restricted suffrage, but as prime minister in 1840, Thiers dodged an opportunity to push for electoral reform. In addition, he warned of the dangers inherent in extending education to all, he once labeled the working class a "vile multitude," and he was not a strong and consistent defender of civil liberties, something all too evident when he pushed through the repressive September Laws of 1835.

During the Second Republic, Thiers took a rather conservative position and supported the election of Louis Napoleon Bonaparte. After the coup of December 1851, however, he was briefly arrested and exiled, although he eventually returned and supported the rule of the Second Empire. After the fall of the Second Empire in 1870, Thiers was chosen temporary executive of the provisional republic, and in 1871 he directed the suppression of the Paris Commune. His most famous historical works were *Histoire de la révolution française* (1823–1827), and *Histoire du consulat et de l'empire* (1845–1862).

44. François Guizot (1787–1874) was an eminent historian whose lectures and whose *Histoire de la civilization en France* (1829–1832) greatly influenced

that it is necessary to reconstitute the ministry for the same reason that Louis Philippe was accepted, for want of anything better and for fear of something worse. This does not mean that it would be necessary to vote bad laws for them, when they ask for them. I cannot tell you, my dear friend, the disgust I feel in watching the public men of our day traffic, according to the smallest interests of the moment, in things as serious and sacred to my eyes as principles. These sudden conversions that we are seeing wound me inwardly more, perhaps, than what the opposition was doing. They frighten me sometimes and make me ask myself whether there are only interests in this world, and whether what one takes for sentiments and ideas are not in fact interests that are acting and speaking. What reconciles me a little to my century, however, is that I see something analogous to what we see now as far

---

Tocqueville's own thought. Although Guizot numbered among the opposition to Charles X, he cast himself in the role of defender of the bourgeoisie in the July Monarchy, for he regarded men of substantial property as the natural representatives of society's general interest. From 1840 to 1848, Guizot was prime minister, a favorite of Louis Philippe, and a defender of the status quo; as a result, he is usually remembered as a conservative, in contrast to the more liberal Thiers. Actually the differences between them are difficult to discern.

Guizot believed in widespread legal rights of property, free speech, and free trial but reserved political rights and political power only to a propertied elite. His famous advice, *"Enrichissez-vous,"* reflected his conviction that France offered ample equality of opportunity for men of merit to rise in the social hierarchy. Guizot appealed to Louis Philippe because Guizot provided order, policies facilitating the expansion of business, and resistance even to minimal change. The only far-reaching legislation that Guizot ever sponsored—and this was before he was prime minister—was his Education Law of 1833, which was certainly an important step forward in educational reform. Like Thiers, however, Guizot feared the social unrest that might arise from universal education and thus did not push these reforms too far. In sum, Guizot considered the July Monarchy an excellent system of government, the culmination of a centuries-old historical process that ended with the middle class finally taking its rightful position of political power. The system did not need reform, only proper administration. When the July Monarchy fell in 1848, Guizot of course fell with it and soon joined Louis Philippe in England. At this point, the politician once more became the historian, and Guizot wrote both a history of England and his memoirs. For more information, see Douglas Johnson, *Guizot: Aspects of French History, 1787–1874* (Toronto: University of Toronto Press, 1963).

back as the most beautiful times of antiquity, thanks to my
indiscreet and gossipy Plutarch. That raises my contemporaries a little, but lowers man in general. But this final idea I
retract: one must not despise man, if one wants to obtain
great efforts from others and from oneself. I was reflecting the
other day: going over in my mind the works of the human
spirit which have most seized the imagination of the human
race and which possess the most duration and brilliance, I
found that in a great majority of cases it was those books in
which the great principles of the beautiful and the good, as
well as the high and salutary theories of the existence of God
and the immortality of the soul have penetrated the most profoundly; these great works have best put in relief and exhibited those principles and those theories. There one finds, then,
the most durable and most efficient cause of the great literary
successes, which proves that after all it is in that direction
that the heart of mankind tends in the most energetic and
most continuous manner. Deprive Plato, for example, of this
aspiration toward immortality and the infinite which trans-
ports him, and leave him only with his useless forms, his incomplete and often ridiculous knowledge, his eloquence that
escapes us at such a great distance, and he falls into obscurity
and becomes unreadable. But Plato addressed himself to the
noblest and most persevering instinct of our nature, and he
will live as long as there are men; he will carry along even
those who only half-understand him, and he will always be an
enormous figure in the world of intellects.

I apologize for letting myself go on this way on the current
of my pen. What I am telling you does not interest you. Not
that you are not very capable of being interested in such ideas
at certain moments, but you cannot do two things at once.
Your mind is indivisible. You must not pity yourself too
much for this, because it is a sign of strength. You are always
ablaze, but you catch fire for only one thing at a time, and
you do not have any curiosity or interest in anything else. It is
for that reason that within the greatest intimacy, we have al-

ways had points at which we did not touch and never reached each other. I have an insatiable, ardent curiosity, which is always carrying me to the right and to the left of my way. Yours leads you just as impetuously, but always toward a single object. A thousand times I have been tempted to chat with you of the thousand strange ideas which cross my mind in the ordinary course of our studies, and I have always been stopped short by the thought that in this way of entering momentarily into a current other than yours, I could not hope to draw you with me. Which of us is right in the way he conducts his mind? In truth, I have no idea. I believe that the result will always be that you will know better than I, and I more than you. You would laugh if you were to see the confused and bizarre assemblage of books that are on my table and which I have devoured, almost all of them entirely, in four months. Rabelais, Plutarch, the Koran, Cervantes, Machiavelli, Fontenelle, Saint-Evremond, all of that has entered pell-mell for better or worse into my head. I would tell you at great length about all these readings, if you were not possessed of this type of madness that doctors call the fixed idea. I forgive you nevertheless, provided that you place me sometimes in your Ireland and that you think from time to time of the tender and lively friendship that I have pledged to you.

Please remember us to Madame de Beaumont. I embrace you.

33. *To Paul Clamorgan*

Tocqueville, January 1, 1839

You have done very well, my dear friend, to keep me informed of the rumors about which your letter speaks. Besides, they are completely groundless and, I may add, of rare absurdity. I have *never* received incense, either from up close or from afar, as you can well believe. I have *never* received holy water except from afar like the most unworthy of the faithful.

It is true my bench is in the choir. But there are more than two hundred people with me in this choir, and my place there is rented. More than three months ago, besides, I had to leave it to take a place in the nave. Not that it was more feudal there than elsewhere, but because it was colder. Therefore, they established a bench for me in another place.

After having given you these explanations, bear with me while I laugh from pity with you for being obliged to give them. What man, I will not say in France, but in Europe, has endeavored harder than I to prove that the aristocracy had lost its grand prerogatives forever? Do you believe that after that I am disposed to clutch onto its most childish and ridiculous privileges? Do you think that after having associated myself by my word with the great movement that is equalizing men, I would reclaim the exclusive right to strut between the beadle and the chorister and to sink myself there like a fox in his hole? Truthfully, my dear Paul, that makes me laugh. But we must not laugh, because everyone else is not laughing. Reestablish, therefore, the truth of the facts with all the seriousness and importance suitable to such a grave subject.

Moreover, add, if you want to, that I respect religion, but that I have never been nor will I ever be a man of the clergy. I honor the priest in church, but I will always put him outside of government, if I have any influence whatsoever in affairs. That is . . . a maxim that I preached quite loudly in my book, so that I may be permitted to be astonished that those who have read it are in doubt.

Farewell, my dear friend, I embrace you, first because I have a great deal of affection for you and in the second place because today it is January 1, the day for embracing good friends. Give a hug to Séry for me, who is not coming to see me despite the promises he had my brother give to me.

P.S. I forgot to pay you a compliment. I saw in the newspaper that you had won a work bag embroidered by Madame Adelaide. Fortune is just.

34. *To Gustave de Beaumont*

Valognes, March 7, 1839

I have just read in the newspaper, my good friend, of your defeat in Saint-Calais. It makes me indifferent to the victory I just won in Valognes.[45] That is not just a phrase or a manner of speaking. I am crushed, that is the word. It is as though people had named me to the Chamber after having previously torn away one of my principal faculties. I no longer know how or why I am going there or what I will do. In this state of profound sorrow, I need to clutch onto some hope again. If deputies of the opposition are named two times, why would you not stand again for their place? If this chance is open, I beg you, in the name of God, not to let it escape, but rather to make the most energetic efforts in this direction. I ask this of you for your own sake; I implore it for my own. If you do not join the Chamber, be certain that it would have been better for me not to join. Because I will wither away there rather than grow. I am writing Corcelle to this effect. I am informing him that, if he believes my presence to be useful, he inform me at once; two hours later I will be on the way. Write me from your end. No discouragement, this is the moment to act; we will mourn afterward, if there is occasion for doing so.

Farewell, I do not have the courage to speak to you of the details of my election; there remains to me only the desire to embrace you in my two arms and with all my heart.

45. In his second attempt, Tocqueville was elected to the Chamber of Deputies from the district of Valognes. He was elected on March 2, 1839, with 317 votes against 241 for his opponent. At the same time, Beaumont was defeated 175 to 155. Because of the death of a newly elected deputy, a special election was held on December 15, 1839, and Beaumont was elected to the Chamber of Deputies from the district of Mamers. Both remained in the Chamber throughout the July Monarchy.

Three

THE POLITICS OF THE JULY
MONARCHY (1839–1847)

Before Tocqueville entered the Chamber of Deputies, he had already expressed his distaste for what he regarded as the petty and unprincipled political quarrels of his day. When he joined the Chamber, he did not alter his opinion. To Royer-Collard he writes that in order to undertake even marginally effective political action, it appears he must ally himself either with Guizot or Thiers. Sadly, "both are fundamentally antipathetical to my way of feeling and thinking. I despise them." If he separates himself from both Guizot and Thiers, however, he can preserve a purity of political principle, but only at the price of being condemned to political inaction, isolation, and powerlessness. "That is an honorable role, but sterile" (Letter 42). As a consequence, the most obvious theme that threads its way through these letters from Tocqueville's parliamentary decade is his persistent attempt to revivify and reconstitute the left opposition. One can see this, for example, in his futile efforts to dissociate Barrot from Thiers so that the opposition, under the leadership of Barrot, might have "an attitude, a language, and a moral power that it has not yet had" (Letter 44).

The most dramatic example of Tocqueville's attempts to rejuvenate the opposition occurred in 1844–1845 when he helped reorganize an opposition newspaper called *Le Commerce*. Tocqueville here attacked the opposition for offering no clear alternative to Guizot's status quo; he sided with Guizot in defending the right of the church to establish secondary schools if it wished; he demanded that Thiers press more strongly for an extension of the franchise; and he discussed ways of alleviating the poverty of the working class. In the midst of these attacks, Tocqueville's friendship with Beaumont suffered from a serious misunderstanding, but the intensity of Tocqueville's letters to Beaumont makes it unmistakably evident that Tocqueville views this journalistic quarrel as a political "war" against Thiers and on behalf of the principles of "true liberty" (Letter 47).

In the end, Tocqueville of course failed to marshal an effective opposition, and during the twilight years of the July Monarchy, he resigned himself to joining with thirty or forty other disenchanted deputies who sought to form the nucleus of a future liberal opposition that had no ties with Thiers (Letter 51). As one reads through the letters of 1839–1848, one is not surprised that Tocqueville failed because in fact the sterility of the politics of the July Monarchy is everywhere apparent. Compared with the excitement in England at the same time—where Parliament debated the Poor Laws, the Factory Acts, the Irish Question, the Corn Laws, and Chartist agitation—France presents, to borrow from Lamartine, a picture of political boredom. Guizot thought that the July Monarchy was a model of political justice, that the opposition was not serious about reform, and thus that disputes centered on personality clashes and foreign policy issues such as the dispute between Turkey and Egypt, the Spanish marriages, etc. Virtually the only progressive social legislation under Guizot's eight-year ministry (1840–1848) was the Child Labor Law of 1841, a law that was both enacted and subsequently rendered ineffective with barely a political murmur.

All of this predictably frustrated Tocqueville because he still yearned both for grand political action and also for political power. "My nature is to be active and, I must admit, ambitious. I would like power if it could be honorably acquired and kept" (Letter 42). But Tocqueville wonders if ever again there will be a political world in which men of honor and principle might debate, dispute, and act. "Will people like me finally have their day?" (Letter 38). One might well ask, what principles is Tocqueville advocating? To Clamorgan he writes that he acts only "to keep our principles intact, which, finally, are only the principles of the Revolution of 1789" (Letter 51). But what does Tocqueville mean by describing his conception of liberalism in this fashion? Tocqueville believes the principles of 1789 can be summarized in this way: France must gradually, but steadfastly, extend both political power and also the material, educational, and moral benefits of society to all classes. To be more specific, as a member of the Chamber of Deputies, Tocqueville advocated free education for the poor, the abolition of slavery in the French colonies, the reform of prisons, a sequence of progressively larger extensions of the suffrage, free medical and legal advice for the poor, workers' banks and mutual aid societies, the encouragement of independently owned small farms to prevent the misery of rapid urbanization, a modest welfare program (even though he feared this would encourage the idleness of the poor), and rapid democratization of local government. (For more information, see Seymour Drescher, ed., *Tocqueville and Beaumont on Social Reform* [New York: Harper & Row, 1968], and also the issues of *Le Commerce: Journal politique et littéraire* that Tocqueville helped edit from approximately August 1844 to May 1845). Unfortunately, since the opposition never pressed for any such comprehensive program for reform, legislative quarrels pivoted on personality, political intrigue, and foreign affairs.

If Tocqueville's wish for significant political action found no outlet in the Chamber of Deputies, it did occasionally find an outlet in his remarks about foreign policy. In these letters, we discover what appears to be an active relic from his aristocratic heritage: a willingness to risk war and the perils of imperial expansion because he believed that such heroic events could be ennobling and could prevent internal political and moral decay. For example, it appeared in 1840 that France once more might engage a united Europe in a war caused by events between Turkey and Egypt. Even after admitting that France would probably lose such a war, Tocqueville still confides to Beaumont that he views "this crisis with a certain satisfaction. You know what a taste I have for great events and how tired I am of our little democratic and bourgeois pot of soup" (Letter 37). Again, in a startling letter to Mill, Tocqueville patiently explains his position; France, he says, must prepare herself for war because she must continue to believe in her grandeur, to perceive herself destined to accomplish great deeds, to be convinced that she should act from honorable principles. Those who preach peace at any price, he says, are in fact infecting France with the greatest possible disease—"the gradual softening of mores, the abasement of the mind," and a universal concern only for "material enjoyments and small pleasures." Says Tocqueville: "One cannot let this nation take up easily the habit of sacrificing what it believes to be its grandeur to its repose, great matters to petty ones; it is not healthy to allow such a nation . . . [to] console itself by making railroads" (Letter 40). Mill and most of Tocqueville's English friends regarded his bellicose attitude as irresponsible, even puerile, and Mill responded that France should not become so attached to these "low" intrigues of foreign affairs but instead should busy herself with "the love of liberty, of progress, even of material prosperity." After this exchange, the correspondence between Mill and Tocqueville cooled and diminished drastically.

In displaying an occasional fondness for what he considers heroic military adventure, Tocqueville was simply embracing the dominant events of nineteenth-century Europe, although not uncritically. Certainly he shows us his admiration for the grandeur of Napoleon, but he criticizes his authoritarian rule (Letter 43). He unflinchingly exhorted France to colonize Algeria and England to colonize India, but—rightly or wrongly—he joined many others in thinking Europe would be a progressive force in these nations. As a result of this conviction, he was an ardent critic of the destructive aspects of both British and French colonization. Once more, his letters on colonial conquest reveal his longing for grand events; to Reeve he writes of the pleasure he takes in watching England invade China:

So at last the mobility of Europe has come to grips with Chinese immobility! It is a great event. . . . Something more vast, more extraordinary than the establishment of the Roman Empire is growing out of our times, without anyone noticing it; it is the enslavement of four parts of the world by the fifth. Therefore, let us not slander our century and ourselves too much; the men are small, but the events are great. (Letter 36)

Still, even though Tocqueville may talk boldly of war, visit the battlefields of Algeria, and dream of civilizing China, none of that alters the central thread of the letters of this period, that is, the political torpor that distinguishes the July Monarchy. In some of the most intriguing letters of this section, Tocqueville tries to explain this phenomenon. First of all, he argues that political power is confined to the wealthiest segment of the bourgeoisie. Because this single class dominated political life, there was no substantial political conflict, and most political figures seemed to consent tacitly to allowing the state to manage middle-class interests. "The system of administration that has been practiced for seventeen years has so perverted the middle class, by making a constant appeal to the individual cupidities of its members, that this class is becoming little by little, for the rest of the nation, a little corrupt and vulgar aristocracy . . ." (Letter 52; see also Tocqueville, *Recollections*).

Second, without far-reaching political debate, the nation as a whole lost interest in political questions. One of the worst evils of the July Monarchy, Tocqueville confides to Beaumont, is the way it cultivates a "growing indifference" toward politics, an indifference caused in part by "the belief that is becoming more deeply rooted each day in the masses, that political life is no more than a game in which each person seeks only to win" (Letter 50). But Tocqueville outlines a third reason for political apathy. Because a middle-class ethic encourages one to withdraw from public concerns and worry only about material well-being, citizens sequester themselves in their private economic concerns, sacrificing passion and political principle to material security. Isolated and powerless, they have no practical experience in political participation. "I have never seen a country in which the first manifestation of public life, which is frequent contact of men among themselves, is less to be found. There is never a meeting of any kind" (Letter 38). Sometimes, Tocqueville writes Kergorlay, political freedom promotes prosperity and then a restless quest for material success; but this very obsession with material success can undermine all desire for political involvement, and the resulting indifference can destroy political liberty (Letter 53). In middle-class society, political freedom can sow the seeds of its own destruction. In sum, Tocqueville thought political questions had become subordinated to financial ones, a state of affairs that bred an omnipresent pettiness.

35. To Paul Clamorgan

Paris, March 7, 1840

You ask me, my dear friend, what has taken place concerning the bishop's project of establishing the Little Seminary at Montebourg. Here is what happened, simply and exactly: as soon as the bishop's project became known, three protests took place: (1) The first by the prefect who went so far as to *wish* there would be a salubrious reason for having the current site, such as it is, changed to Coutances. (2) The second came from the minister of public instruction, whom the rector of

Caen had avoided. The minister of public instruction strongly exhorted the minister concerned with religious practices not to authorize the transfer of the Little Seminary to Montebourg. The result of this measure, he said, would certainly be to ruin the only university establishment in the arrondissement of Valognes, and the most important of the whole peninsula, in order to replace it with an ecclesiastical school. The prefect's letter and that of the minister are in the dossier. (3) Finally, the town of Valognes protested with great vivacity by means of a petition by the Municipal Council that I was asked to deliver to the minister. I believe that M. Quénault[1] received the same mandate in the city of Cherbourg, which is interested, although to a lesser degree, in the question. I delivered the Municipal Council's petition to the minister, and, when he asked for my views, I did not hesitate to tell him that in my opinion the general interest of the arrondissement of Valognes was that the college of Valognes not be destroyed. That that establishment was very fine, very liable to acquire great importance. That it had already furnished men celebrated in science and in letters. That this college was the only lay establishment that existed in the arrondissement and received children from all the cantons; it was not solely a question of the interest of a locality, but of the general interest that I was charged to represent.

There you have, my dear friend, the language that I used and that I wrote down in a note delivered at the same time to the minister. I am certain that the region will approve of my conduct in this situation. In sending me to the Chamber, people undoubtedly wanted to put me in a position to defend not a part of the arrondissement, but the whole of the arrondissement. I would not have accepted the honorable mandate with which they entrusted me, if I had thought they intended otherwise. I was convinced that it was in the arrondissement's general interest that the Little Seminary not be established in

1. Hippolyte-Alphonse Quénault, secretary-general to the minister of justice.

such a way as to ruin our college; having this opinion and consulted on this point by the minister, I would have failed in all my duties if I had kept silent.

Farewell, believe in my sincere friendship.

36. To Henry Reeve

Paris, April 12, 1840

My dear friend, your letter of the 9th, which I have just received, proves to me that my last parcel was lost, I do not know how. Happily, just as I informed you yesterday, the publication is only going to take place on the 20th. Thus, between now and then, you have time to translate and to have what remains printed. I will forward this fragment to you by next Monday's courier. It is composed of a half-page of text and a page of notes. I suggest you translate the last chapter.

M. Guizot's remark, which you report, flatters me greatly. I know better than anyone else does how far I am from speaking well. But, it is quite a step just for me to believe I am in the process of getting there.

If I were English, I would not view the expedition that is being prepared against China without anxiety. In my capacity as a beneficent but disinterested spectator, I can only rejoice in the thought of an invasion of the Celestial Empire by a European army.[2] So at last the mobility of Europe has come to grips with Chinese immobility! It is a great event, especially if one thinks that it is only the continuation, the last in a multitude of events of the same nature all of which are pushing the European race out of its home and are successively submitting all the other races to its empire or its influence. Something more vast, more extraordinary than the establishment of the Roman Empire is growing out of our times, without anyone noticing it; it is the enslavement of four parts

2. In 1840, the British occupied Chusan and the Canton River forts as a prelude to the first Opium War in 1841.

of the world by the fifth. Therefore, let us not slander our century and ourselves too much; the men are small, but the events are great.

All my sincere affection.

37. *To Gustave de Beaumont*

Tocqueville, August 9, 1840

My dear friend, I do not know whether the most recent events make you desire, as I do, to see the horizon a little more clearly before launching into our enterprise.[3] If things become too confused, the Chambers will have to be convoked, and it would be annoying if we had to return from Africa almost as soon as we arrived. I believe that in a month we will know what to make of this possibility and can act accordingly. While waiting, I am studying the large blue books on Algeria that the government has had distributed to the Chambers in the last three years. I am abstaining from reading any polemic that would confuse my mind; for this reason I put the books of Desjobert[4] and company to one side. After having finished this study, I will try to glance at the consequences of the colonial acts since 1830.

I am not speaking to you of public affairs; there would be too much to say; besides, you are at the source of public life. I believe that the administration did, in this circumstance, what it had to do and that we have to support it (the Orient affair).[5] But I do not approve the language of the official

3. Tocqueville and Beaumont had planned to go to Algeria in September 1840.

4. Amédée Desjobert (1793–1853), a member of the Chamber of Deputies who strongly opposed the occupation and colonization of Algeria, especially in his 1837 book, *La Question d'Alger, politique, colonisation, commerce.*

5. For some time both England and Russia had supported the Turkish sultan in an attempt to prevent the collapse of the Ottoman Empire. Russia wanted Turkey as a satellite state, and England saw Turkey as an anti-Russian buffer. In 1839, urged on by England, Turkey renewed its quarrel with Pasha Mehemet Ali of Egypt, who was challenging the authority of the sultan by invading

press; these swashbucklers' pretensions do not mean anything.
Could not one be firm, strong, and prepared for everything
without boasting and without threatening? Surely it is necessary at such a juncture to make war, as is easy to foresee; but
such a war must not be desired or provoked, because we
would not be able to begin one with more odds against us.
In the current state of civilization, the European nation which
has all the others against it, whichever nation it may be, must
succumb in the long run; that is what one must never tell
the nation, but never forget. These wise reflections do not
prevent me, at the bottom of my heart, from seeing all this
crisis with a certain satisfaction. You know what a taste I have
for great events and how tired I am of our little democratic
and bourgeois pot of soup. I leave you with the above, not
without having embraced you with all my heart.

38. To Pierre-Paul Royer-Collard

Tocqueville, August 15, 1840

If I have not written you sooner, Monsieur, the blame must
be laid to the agitated life that I have been obliged to live since
my return to this country. I came here to rest, and I cannot
stay calm for two days. There are a multitude of local interests with which people wish me to busy myself and which I
have to go study on the spot. All of this is accompanied by
immense dinners, a dangerous pastime for a stomach as poor
as mine. I am a party to them, however, because, in this pro-

Syria. The Egyptians decisively defeated Turkey, which appeared to be a victory for French influence since the French had given substantial support to
Mehemet Ali. On July 15, 1840—in the Treaty of London—England and Russia united with Austria and Prussia to support the sultan of Turkey and to
demand that Mehemet Ali yield most of his military gains. Suddenly France
found herself insulted, mildly intoxicated with war fever, poorly led by Thiers,
and quite possibly confronted in war once again by a united Europe. Mehemet
Ali refused the demands, relying on the bluffing bellicosity of France; England
attacked Egyptian territory and, by the fall of 1840, Louis Philippe decided he
could not risk war and asked for Thiers's resignation.

vince, almost nowhere but at table does one have the opportunity to find several men gathered together and to form an idea of the reigning opinions. I have never seen a country in which the first manifestation of public life, which is frequent contact of men among themselves, is less to be found. There is never a meeting of any kind, not a place where a large number of men can freely exchange their feelings and their thoughts on any subject whatever. It is a distressing and alarming spectacle for those who, like me, dread, in the future, oppression more than anarchy. Besides, such mores lead as easily to the one as to the other. So, the dinners stay. It is between two of these large foodfests that I am writing you. Excuse me, therefore, if my ideas are not very clear.

What strikes me most as I have more opportunity to see this population is how little it is occupied with political affairs. It makes it all but impossible for me to speak of them myself. I have heard it said, and I believe it, that there are many voters who do not know that M. Thiers is prime minister. Do all of the arrondissements resemble this one, or would this one be the same in all circumstances? That I do not know. Still, the rumors of war have reached them, and I have noticed with pleasure that they supported this idea of war firmly and were not at all of the opinion that we should display weakness in order to avoid war. I do not know whether they would be as firm in the presence of dangers and above all in the discomfiture that war brings. But, at least, the first impression is good. I have always thought, besides, that the best thing our country has left is national pride, a pride which is often puerile and boastful, but which, with all its absurdities and weaknesses is still the greatest sentiment that we have and the strongest tie that holds this nation together. That alone gives it a great advantage over most of the peoples of Europe, among whom this sentiment is less developed. This idea we have of ourselves appears to me to be a very important resource and an outstanding trait which perhaps, let me say, you seem not to take sufficiently into account, when you pass judgment on this country.

This digression brings me back to present affairs. But, what could I say about them that you would not already know as well as or better than I? I confess that up to now I have not found fault with what the administration is doing, although the bluster of its newspapers seems to me ridiculous and dangerous. I believe that this dynasty could not bear the repercussion that the sight of Europe dividing up the Ottoman Empire with arms in hand and without us would produce in the country. I think that the best means that remain to us to prevent the European powers from going to this extremity is to persuade them calmly but firmly that such an event would bring on the general war that everyone dreads: I know that such an attitude can bring on this war. But I believe that on the whole it is even less dangerous than a submission from which sooner or later war would emerge and, finding us diminished in our own eyes, would be more dangerous still. The idea often comes to my mind that M. Thiers wants to launch us immediately on this immense affair, as much by the taste he has for movement as in order to make himself necessary. Nevertheless, upon reflection, I cannot believe it. This war, *without allies,* would present so many chances for catastrophe that I cannot imagine that, however much of a daredevil he is supposed to be, he would want to throw himself into it. Moreover, in the back of my mind, I have a misgiving about him that I must confide to you. M. Thiers is assuredly very unthinking, but is he also as coldly reckless as he is imagined to be? There are moments when I doubt this greatly. He has, I think, a less resistant nature than is imagined. And I do not think he is inclined to stiffen in the face of obstacles. I fear that a situation might arise in which one would see him soften in a manner surprising and very detrimental to the honor of the country. In short, he does not reassure me in any sense, and yet I recognize that there is nothing to put in his place and that he still towers by several arms' lengths over all this little world that surrounds him. He has adroitness without principles. The others have neither adroitness nor principles.

Do you believe, Monsieur, you who have seen so much and reflected so much, and probed so deeply into human nature, do you believe that the political world will long remain as destitute of true passions as it is at this moment and that it will be for a long time as far out of style, as it is now, to bring to it, as an element of success, a sincere taste for working for the general good? If this were so, I would not in truth have anything else to do but to get out of it. It is not that I want to proclaim myself before you a man of great principles. Experience has made me rather modest about the efficacy of principles. My integrity is not so lofty, but perhaps it is of a more solid kind. I am inclined to integrity by temperament. Should my will undertake to make me habitually act in a way contrary to the general interest, my instinct would resist, and, in the long run, I would be obliged to do good, if only out of weakness. There is therefore no resource for me in a world of rogues. Do you believe, Monsieur, that a time may come in which a love of the public good, as disinterested as our poor human nature permits, can render some service and finally put integrity in a place of honor? Will people like me finally have their day? I love good, but I also love the success that it brings. There is my weak side; I have never hidden it from your friendship. I have never known how to rest peacefully and steadily on myself, and this noise which rises from the crowd has always seemed to me the most beautiful music.

This leads me to speak to you about my book.[6] I very often receive testimonials which I value highly because of the nature of the people who address them to me. I am not deceived that, when it comes to the great public, I say great by number, the book is little read and badly known. This silence distresses me. It forces me to make an agonizing reappraisal of my position. I wonder if there is indeed something of worth

6. Tocqueville is referring to the second part of *Democracy in America*.

in this work. I am often brought to doubt it, and this doubt leads me to wonder if the ability that some were kind enough to see is to be found in me. Because, that a man who has some ability should spend four years of his life doing a book without merit, that is not to be supposed. I am baring my heart to you, sir, consenting to your seeing in it the small passions and rather miserable disturbances that are to be met there, provided that you perceive there at the same time the full confidence and affectionate respect I have for you.

In truth, Monsieur, I am taking advantage of your friendship in talking to you for such a long time about myself. I beseech you kindly to excuse a man who is as isolated in spirit in the middle of the crowd which surrounds him as the inhabitant of a desert island would be. Would you kindly present my respect to Madame Royer and believe in my respectful affection.

P.S. My wife wants especially to be remembered to you. You know she values your remembrance infinitely more than any other.

39. *To Edouard de Tocqueville*

Tocqueville, November 2, 1840

I cannot thank you enough, my good friend, for the long letter that I last received from you. It is truly admirable because of the elevated sentiments and ideas that it contains. Reading such letters is very wholesome therapy for the soul. Unfortunately, the illness you want to cure is hardly curable, because it results, in large part at least, from the very organization of the individual. It is this organization that must be modified, but which one cannot hope to destroy. It forms my strength in some cases, my weakness in a multitude of others. It is this anxiety of mind, this devouring impatience, this need for lively and recurring sensations that we have always seen in our father. This disposition gives me a great élan in certain moments. But most often it torments without cause, agitates fruitlessly and causes those who possess it to suffer greatly. This is very often my case, as I easily recognize. I am often unhappy without reason, and so I give too good a reason for being unhappy to those who surround me. Moreover, I am very conscious that this disposition could do me great harm in *action*. It keeps me for a while from having an exact perspective on things and makes external facts seem larger and smaller than life, depending on what my imagination brings me. I believe that my mind is naturally just and firm; but that is only on the condition that it is calm, which is not always the case, especially in the midst of small annoyances. The grandeur of affairs or of sensations in general makes me tranquil, but the daily jarring of practical life and habitual contact with men easily put me beside myself.

It is true, my dear friend, that I have a thousand reasons for being happy; because, aside from all the causes of happiness that you enumerate, this is one that must be added and that you do not name; that is having found the wife who suits me best. I lack some good things, the absence of which makes many people unhappy, and which I desire without ardor: a large fortune is one, and even, I will admit, children. I would passionately desire to have children as I imagine them, but I do not have a very keen desire to draw from the great lottery of paternity. Then what do I lack? You have thought it and have said it: peace of mind and moderation of desires. I have lived enough to know that there is not a single good thing in this world the enjoyment of which can hold me and satisfy me. I have attained a point for which I had no right to hope at the beginning of my career. It does not give me complete happiness. My imagination climbs easily to the summit of human grandeurs; and when it has carried me there, the bedazzlement that I experience does not prevent me from feeling with an irresistible force that, elevated to this point, I would experience the same painful sensations as today; just as those of today resemble the ones I formerly experienced so closely that they could easily be mistaken for them. What moves the soul is different, but the soul is the same—this anxious and insatiable soul that despises all the good things of the world and which, nonetheless, incessantly needs to be stirred in order to seize them, so as to escape the grievous numbness that it experiences as soon as it relies for a moment on itself. This is a sad story. It is a little bit the story of all men, but of some more than others, and of myself more than anyone I know.

40. To John Stuart Mill

March 18, 1841

I keep putting off writing you, my dear Mill, in order to be able to do so at greater length. I am beginning to think that if I wait this way until I have time, I will ultimately not write you, and that it would be better to write you briefly than not to do it at all.

I will say to you first that I still hear your article on my book mentioned frequently. M. Royer-Collard, who, as you know, is a great judge, undoubtedly the foremost in France today, told me again the other day that he has just read your article for the second time, and that he considered it not only a good review, but also an original work of great profundity and very considerable value. I wanted to let you know this judgment, because in these matters M. Royer-Collard delivers oracles. You recall the role the man played under the Restoration. He was for a moment master of the country, and he still exercises great power in the philosophical world.

The chance of war is becoming more and more remote. But the chance of a new and sincere alliance between France and England is not becoming any greater. Every day shows me more and more the irreparable harm of what has taken place. The governments can say all they want to that all is forgotten. The nation contradicts them in the bottom of its heart, and for this harm the protocols and diplomatic memoranda are no remedy at all. The violent irritation that the treaty of July 15 had produced has entirely abated, but there remains something worse than that, notably the tranquil and profound sentiment that there is neither security nor future in an alliance with England, that the rivalry of interests is a fact that can no longer be denied and cannot be ended, that such an alliance is only a makeshift, that in case of need it will always fail us and that as soon as a fulcrum outside of it can be found on our side, we must seize the opportunity. The nation is unhappy and humiliated. These feelings seem to become deeper as they become less keen, and, whatever the governments may do and say, the feelings turn more each day into bitterness against the English alliance. That is a great evil, to which I know only one remedy—few common concerns, some good conduct, and time.

Everything that has occurred in our foreign politics in the last six months, I confess my dear Mill, has caused me a great deal of confusion and difficulty. The situation has made two equally dangerous extremist parties on matters of foreign affairs appear in our parliament. One of them dreams of conquests and loves war either for its own sake or for the revolutions to which it can give birth. The other one has a love of peace that I would not fear to call dishonest, since it has as its sole principle not the public interest, but the taste for material well-being and softness of heart; this party would sacrifice everything for peace. The bulk of the nation is between these two extremes, but it has no prominent representatives in Parliament. Placed between these two extreme parties, the position of men like myself has been very difficult and very perplexing. I could not approve the revolutionary and propagandistic language of the greater part of the partisans of war, but to chime in with those who were loudly asking for peace, at any price, was even more dangerous. I do not have to tell you, my dear Mill, that the greatest malady that threatens a people organized as we are is the gradual softening of mores,

the abasement of the mind, the mediocrity of tastes; that is
where the great dangers of the future lie. One cannot let a
nation that is democratically constituted like ours and in
which the natural vices of the race unfortunately coincide with
the natural vices of the social state, one cannot let this nation
take up easily the habit of sacrificing what it believes to be its
grandeur to its repose, great matters to petty ones; it is not
healthy to allow such a nation to believe that its place in the
world is smaller, that it is fallen from the level on which its
ancestors had put it, but that it must console itself by making
railroads and by making prosper in the bosom of this peace,
under whatever condition this peace is obtained, the well-
being of each private individual. It is necessary that those who
march at the head of such a nation should always keep a
proud attitude, if they do not wish to allow the level of national mores to fall very low. The nation had believed itself
humiliated; it was humiliated in fact, if not by acts, at least
by the language of its ministers. Its government had told it so,
it had made threats in its name, and as soon as these foolish
and imprudent threats had brought on danger, this same government and this same prince, who had shown himself so
oversensitive and so proud, declared that it was necessary to
retreat. At this signal, a large part of the middle class gave an
example of the weakness and the egoism that is peculiar to it.
It asked loudly that they yield, that war be avoided at all cost.
The stampede was general, because the example had come
from the top. Do you believe that such circumstances could
be repeated without wearing out a people? Do you believe
that that is the therapy that suits us, and do not firm and
independent voices have to be raised in order to protest
against this weakness on behalf of the mass of the nation—
that men whom no party yet binds, who quite evidently have
neither Napoleonic tendencies nor revolutionary tastes, that
such men should come to adopt a language that raises again
and sustains the nation's heart and seeks to check it in this
enervating taste that drags it more each day toward material

enjoyments and small pleasures? If we were to cease to have pride in ourselves, my dear Mill, we would have suffered an irreparable loss.

I only wanted to write you a note, and here I am at the end of quite a confused letter, written in a great haste, from which perhaps nothing clear will reemerge for you, but where you will find, I hope, a new proof of the esteem and friendship that I profess and have for you.

P.S. Come, then, see us this summer at Tocqueville. From Southampton the steamboat takes you there in eight hours.

41. To Jean-Jacques Ampère

Tocqueville, August 10, 1841

My very dear friend, I just received your letter from Marseilles, and I am stopping everything to answer it, so as to be more certain that you will not pass to Ancône without hearing from me. I would rather write a few words that will get to you than to fling in your trail a long epistle that probably would not reach you.

I will respond to your kind questions, and I will tell you that, although I am not yet very well, I am all the same, I think, on the way to being so. My body and my spirit submit more and more to the good and peaceful influence of the life I lead here. You are familiar with it. I do not need to paint it for you. It only lacks the pleasure you used to add to it, and that pleasure was quite great, I assure you. We are longing for you to return to add this pleasure to the others and complete the picture. I am getting used to this life, and I take delight in it in a way that frightens me. Because I feel I have other duties to fulfill in this world, and I fear that they may ultimately seem painful to me and that I may no longer carry them out with passion, without which one can do nothing.

The further away I am from youth, the more regardful, I will say almost respectful, I am of passions. I like them when they are good, and I am not even very certain of detesting them when they are bad. That is strength, and strength, everywhere it is met, appears at its best in the midst of the universal weakness that surrounds us. I see only poltroons who tremble at the least agitation of the human heart and who speak to us only of the perils with which passions threaten us. They are, in my opinion, bad chatterboxes. What we meet least in our day are passions, true and solid passions that bind up and lead life. We no longer know how to want, or love, or hate. Doubt and philanthropy make us incapable of all things, of great evil as well as great good, and we flutter heavily around a multitude of small objects, none of which either attracts us, or strongly repels us, or holds us.

There I am falling again into my philosophical malaise. But you will pardon me because it is a malaise in friendship. One speaks to one's friends as one speaks to oneself. The thoughts that disturb me break through as if by themselves when I write you and, despite myself, fill my letter, which nonetheless has to be short. So I finish. So you have been thrown into that great Orient[7] where our thoughts will follow you; let us hear from you often and copiously. I ask this of you as much in my wife's name as in my own; and, if you do not have time to write long letters, at least write: "I am well." Be well indeed, and do not delay too much in recounting to us your new pilgrimages.

42. To Pierre-Paul Royer-Collard

Tocqueville, September 27, 1841

You indicated, Monsieur, that you wanted some news from me. I will be careful not to let this chance to write you escape, and, since you permit it, I will in fact start by telling you about myself. My health has recovered, without being completely restored. Mental work always tires me, although I

7. Ampère journeyed throughout the Mediterranean as far as Turkey.

hardly devote myself to it, and I fear that I will ultimately lose the habit of mental work and acquire the habit of idle musing, that is to say *touching* subjects without embracing them. It seems to me that I used to be capable of more penetrating and more sustained attention. I imagine that this energetic mental gait will return with my physical strength.

As for my soul, it is more tranquil than it has been for many years. The solitary life that I lead, peaceful and calm, holds charms for me that I did not think I was susceptible to tasting so keenly. I bitterly regret each day that ends. It is a friend who is fading away. When I am in this state of mind, the approach of the session appears to me a little like an enemy with whom one must fight bravely, but whom one would rather not meet on one's way. The future of this session, and even of those that should follow it, indeed has nothing in it that can satisfy me, I do not mean fully, for I think politics has never given such satisfaction, but even nearly. Here are the rather sad thoughts that this subject suggests to me: when I attentively consider our miserable political world and those who compose it, I do not see where I will find my place. To want to form a government or an opposition apart from both M. Thiers and M. Guizot seems to me an impossibility of the first order, for a thousand reasons that are either general or particular to those two men. Those who attempt it seem to me to give themselves over to a fruitless endeavor. There is today no power in parliament except in joining these two men or at least in using one of them. Now, I do not want to, nor can I, join with the one any more than with the other. Both are fundamentally antipathetical to my way of feeling and thinking. I despise them. Apart from them, however, there is nothing that can bring about anything noteworthy in our country's affairs; there is no action. And what is politics without action? To live in a public assembly and not to work effectively for public concerns, not to act and not to join with those who alone have the power to act, is that not manifestly absurd? Is that not to miss the principal character

of what one has undertaken to do and what one claims to be
doing? Does it not in the end amount to transferring one kind
of life into another, theoretical observation into the life of action, to the great detriment of both? That is, Monsieur, what
I say sorrowfully to myself when I am not in the Chamber
and with impatience and irritation when the session is open.
I go around hitting myself in turn against these two obstacles:
what is painful and almost untenable in isolation and inaction
in a political assembly induces me to try something, and before long the impossibility of my acting in common with
these men who alone can make action effective throws me
back into immobility and nails me to my seat. These tugs in
contrary directions fatigue and exhaust me, even more than
would energetic and continuous action. I compare myself to
a wheel that goes around very quickly, but which, having
missed its gear, does nothing and is useful for nothing. It
seems to me, however, that in other times and with other
men, I could have done better. But will the times improve?
And will the men we see, will they be replaced by better or at
least by *worse?* I would be disappointed about this last change
for the country, but not for myself. Because the true nightmare of our period is in not perceiving before oneself anything either to love or to hate, but only to despise. Permit me
to say, Monsieur, you cannot judge my sensations by your
own. You are isolated and inactive in the Chamber. But there
you are like a soldier who, after having fought actively and
gloriously all day, finally sits down on the edge of the arena
and considers what is being accomplished there. You have acquired in regard to others and yourself the right to judge
those who act and do not act. But myself, I do not have such
rights to assert. And yet what can I do? I feel an almost invincible repugnance to associating myself in a permanent manner
with any of the political men of our times and, among all the
parties that divide our country, I do not see a single one to
which I would want to be tied. I do not find in any of them, I
do not say *everything* that I would want to see in political asso-

ciates, but even the principal things for which I would
willingly give up the lesser (because I know that one can only
join at this price). Some seem to me to have an exaggerated,
pusillanimous and soft yearning for peace, and their love of
order is most often only fear. The others mix with their national pride and their taste for liberty (two things I value
highly in themselves) crass and anarchistic passions that repel
me. The *liberal but not revolutionary* party, which alone suits
me, does not exist, and certainly it is not given to me to create it. So I am almost alone and it only remains to me to
express my individual opinion as well as possible on the
events and on the laws as they are presented, without having
any hope of modifying them. That is an honorable role, but
sterile. Often I instinctively revolt against it, because my nature is to be active and, I must admit, ambitious. I would like
power if it could be honorably acquired and kept. Nevertheless, there is a thought which has always served powerfully
to hold me back: it is evident that all prolonged and intimate
contact with the political men or parties of our time cannot
fail soon to take away part of the esteem from anyone who
puts up with it, and what is given in return for this first of all
good things but an ineffective and transitory power? When
I see how little those who throw themselves pell-mell into the
arena manage to do, all things considered, then I console myself for my isolation and my powerlessness. I say to myself
that, on the whole, even putting to one side for a moment the
satisfaction of doing well, it is better still to preserve intact in
the eyes of the country, one's moral force, a power that has
become so rare, and to keep it for other times, than to let it
be diminished in order to acquire immediate advantages that
are always so inferior to it. There you have, Monsieur, what
I am thinking in my solitude and what has been the subject of
many long conversations between me and my companion,
whose upright and noble mind conceives and encourages so
well all that is courageous and honest. This is the way that
I have managed to be quite calm and to be as happy as it is

reasonable to hope for in this world. But I fear that this calmness may give way before the spectacle of the parliamentary fight, because the sight of a combat always excites me, however small the prize of victory is, and reason, which immobilizes me, is powerless to make me calm. Reason has always been for me like a cage that keeps me from acting, but not from gnashing my teeth behind the bars.

I will stop here. It is already now past the time I should have done so. Nonetheless, I could have, if I were not afraid of wearying you, spoken to you at length. Because it is a great delight for me to pour out my mind to you. I find it useful as well as pleasurable. But I fear that I may be abusing your indulgence. Please let me know if I am right to talk to you about myself this way and at such length. Please let me hear from you, Monsieur, so that I may have news of you and of all those you hold dear, and please accept this expression of the tender and respectful attachment that I have pledged to you.

P.S. My wife wishes to be expressly and particularly remembered to you. Since I have made one postscript for her, I want to add one for me. My inkwell has just fallen and made spots on my paper, for which I ask your pardon as well as for the numerous erasures that this letter contains.

43. To Paul Clamorgan

Paris, April 17, 1842

My dear friend, after the letter I wrote you three days ago and the one I am writing to Séry and which he will communicate to you, I have almost nothing more to tell you.

I do not see too clearly where the administration could find the candidate it wants to oppose me in Valognes. However, since that would be a good maneuver, we must expect that in the end they will have recourse to it.

What requires extreme circumspection on our part is the

affair in Cherbourg. I had declared to the Prefect himself that as long as M. Quénault would be presenting himself in Cherbourg, I would fight against him with all my might. It appears decided that the above said Q. is retiring and that Noël-A[gnès] is putting himself forward as an independent candidate. That requires at least a true neutrality on my part toward him. I very much wish that at least until I arrive my friends would strictly imitate this example. In a month I will be with you. We will come to a final decision on everything then. But until then it requires the most extreme circumspection.

My reception is definitely going to take place on Thursday.[8] It has been a long time since one has been so anticipated and so popular. There are already no more seats left to be given out, and I am forced into quarrels with ten people a day by refusing them tickets. This speech is a great affair for me. I am putting into relief more than ever the keen and tenacious love that I have for free institutions, a love that forms the essence of my politics. I will also be forced to speak of the Empire. I say things about it that will not satisfy you completely. I reproach it for the nonliberal side of its institutions, but at the same time I do full justice to the personal grandeur of Napoleon, the most extraordinary being, I say, who has appeared in the world for many centuries. I even enhance him at the expense of his work, since I say that the grandeur of the Empire is due to his person alone. I learned yesterday that the queen had asked that a seat in the gallery be kept for her.

Farewell, let us not seem anxious. I truly think that up to now there is nothing to be seriously anxious about.

I embrace you with all my heart.

---

8. Tocqueville was elected to the French Academy in 1841 and gave a speech at his formal reception on April 21, 1842. Tocqueville's speech is reprinted in his *Oeuvres complètes d'Alexis de Tocqueville*, IX, *Etudes économiques, politiques, et littéraires* (Paris: Michel Lévy Frères, 1866).

44. To Gustave de Beaumont

Carquebut, September 19, 1842

I am writing you, my dear friend, in the middle of an electoral tour that I found useful to undertake. The administration evidently is organizing a regular war against me in my district. That makes it more necessary for me to take action on my side. Positions are being given to my adversaries, and the administration is trying in this way to separate my friends from me. This method of attack has to be countered with more frequent personal contacts between me and the electors. I had, besides, promised that if I did not make any visits before the election, I would go see my principal friends afterward. That is what I am doing, to my great boredom, I confess. It is keeping me from getting back to Tocqueville, where I will return, nonetheless, in only a week. We live in a time and in a country in which, in order to have the right to speak and to act independently in the Chamber, you have to buy it by earning the individual good will of one's neighbors, so that they will support you out of friendship, in spite of your doing your duty.

Despite these excursions, I have not lost sight of what you told me in your letter. I wrote at great length to Barrot.[9] I have kept a copy of the letter, which I will show you, because

9. Odilon Barrot (1791–1873) took an active part in the 1830 Revolution, helping dissuade Lafayette from forming a republic. Although he originally hoped to be a minister of the government under the July Monarchy, he had to settle for being a key member of the left opposition (the so-called dynastic left) in the Chamber of Deputies. Of those in the left opposition, Barrot was one of those to whom Tocqueville felt closest, despite the fact that he thought Barrot mixed weakness with his virtues and despite the fact that he was unable to separate Barrot from Thiers as decisively as he wished. Barrot supported the constitutional monarchy but pushed sincerely for reforms, especially an extension of the franchise. In 1847–1848, frustrated by Guizot's intransigence and apparently thwarted by a law prohibiting public political meetings, Barrot took a leading part in the opposition's banquet campaign—"private" parties held enthusiastically all over France that demanded reform. After the 1848 Revolution, Barrot eventually supported the Second Republic and became prime minister twice, once in December 1848 and again in June 1849. In the latter instance, he chose Tocqueville for minister of foreign affairs.

this letter is important to us. I believe that it will make an impression on Barrot, and it will dispose him to put himself in the forefront of the endeavor to lead the left in better directions. I will let you know his response as soon as I receive it. I tell him, and I believe it, that he does not know his own strength and that, if he wanted, the moment would have arrived for him to found a powerful opposition and one with a great future. I believe that, in fact, and moreover I think the moment has arrived for us, if we ourselves do not lose heart, to exercise at last a great, and what will be worth more, a salutary influence. I believe that if we can isolate Barrot from Thiers and unite ourselves intimately with him, we will be in a situation to give the opposition an attitude, a language, and a moral power that it has not yet had. We have the integrity which M. Thiers and his friends lack, moderation and spirit of leadership that is not met on the left. If we can manage to govern it, the result will be very great. Our duty in any case is to try, and this idea sustains me in the midst of disgust with political life, which decidedly is not worth a damn. But we have started this, unfortunately; we have nothing more to do than to extract for our country and for ourselves the best advantage.

I did not forget that if it was useful to act on Barrot, it was no less so to act on Chambolle.[10] The one is the voice and the other the pen of the party (poor pen!). I therefore have written in the same vein to Chambolle, and as you had advised me, I offered him my cooperation. I am awaiting his response. If he accepts it and I see that he holds to it, on my return to Tocqueville, I will indeed put myself to work. Unfortunately, nature has not predisposed me to be a journalist. There is nothing

10. François-Adolphe Chambolle (1802–1883) was an important journalist, a member of the Chamber of Deputies from 1838 to 1848, and a friend to key members of the opposition, such as Barrot and Thiers. In 1837, Chambolle became the most important editor on the opposition journal Le Siècle, a position that brought him into conflict with Tocqueville in 1844 when Le Siècle and Tocqueville's Le Commerce quarreled.

more profoundly antipathetical than this trade to my moral and intellectual constitution. I mean the style as well as the mores. I will however do my best. But what subjects to treat? I confess that that perplexes me terribly and that if some ideas cross your mind on this point, you would be very charitable to transmit them to me, after having deducted in advance what suits you. What strikes me above all in the current situation is the danger and futility that there is in wanting to obtain great new institutions, while we have so much difficulty in defending those we possess. We are like an army embarking on the conquest of the world, while the enemy pillages and destroys its homes. We thus are frightening the country about our intentions and diverting its attention from what there really is to fear from our adversaries. Currently it is evidently a question not of making *progress,* but of stopping the retrograde steps and regaining lost ground, of conserving our liberties rather than of augmenting them. We will still be very adroit if we succeed. This role of defending them is the only one that temporarily suits us. Remember all the advantage the opposition in the Restoration drew from this, and all the strength this maxim gave it: the whole Charter and nothing but the Charter.[11] It is still on this basis that the sincere and energetic support of public opinion could be found. France is not much concerned with new liberties. But its attachment to those that it possesses can be awakened, and it can be put to shame for allowing them to be taken back. I wish, for now, that the opposition would restrict itself to showing that the

11. Tocqueville here refers to the Charter of 1814, granted by Louis XVIII with the Bourbon Restoration. The Charter, so staunchly defended under the Restoration by Tocqueville's friend Royer-Collard, established a government composed of a strong monarchy, a hereditary nobility that controlled an upper house composed of peers, and a Chamber of Deputies elected by a narrow franchise based on a high property qualification. The Chambers could only reject or accept proposals of the king and thus could not initiate their own laws. Ministers were not answerable to the legislature but to the king. Although the Charter was somewhat ambiguous on these points, it appeared to assure equality before the law, freedom of press and religion, trial by jury, and the right to private property.

government, which accuses us of wanting to innovate, is itself
innovating every day and that we are reduced to defending
what exists and not doing anything new. All that is very
badly explained, but you are in the habit of understanding me
on a hint. I believe my idea correct.

I leave you. Say the most affectionate things on our behalf
to Madame de Beaumont, whom we would have enjoyed so
much seeing with you at Tocqueville. Embrace Antonin[12] and
write me without delay. I imagine that I am at the end of the
earth, hearing and seeing nothing. Needing to learn everything. Farewell. I embrace you with all my heart.

45. *To Gustave de Beaumont*

Baugy par Compiègne (Oise),
December 15, 1842

My dear friend, you wanted me to let you read the letter
I wrote to Barrot last September. I am sending it to you after
having had it copied by my wife. Hold on to it so you can
deliver it to me in Paris, when we are there together. I am
very glad to acquaint you with this letter, so that you will
know how explicit I was with Barrot and how, while offering
him the most loyal and zealous cooperation, I made him understand clearly under what conditions and how, if I joined
forces with the left, it would not be to accept what I had
always condemned in it. The fact is that I would rather stay
all alone in a corner of the Chamber than let myself be *absorbed* in the midst of the left as it still appears to the eyes of
the country. I am joining forces with it only in order to try to
act upon it. And, if I do not succeed, I at least want to keep
the nuance that is my own. I believed it useful to have all that
heard by Barrot, who, I believe, has understood it all the better since his instincts on this point would be just like mine, if
he were free. We must surely keep ourselves from showing

12. Beaumont's son.

our intention of giving a new look to the opposition, but basically it is at this time the only great thing that we could contemplate doing. We must never forget it. The discomfiture of liberalism in France comes not only from the faults and vices of the nation, but above all from the vices and errors of the opposition, which, at present, represents nothing but the revolutionary spirit and would be perfectly incapable of transforming itself into a government, if need be. Your opinion has always been that with courage and perseverance, one could bring about a great transformation in the left. I know how much such an enterprise demands in the way of caution and presents in the way of difficulties, but it is a great one and it is not impossible to succeed at it. I ask for nothing better than to give myself to it body and soul, but with the resolve, however, not to let myself be carried away into the heat of battle up to the point of taking on colors that are not and never will be mine. I would prefer to stay in my corner.

I have studied my best since I have been here. I have not derived from it up to the present any great advantage, except in recalling, after all, details that I already knew. I fear, I shall confess to you, that the only great field of battle will be the treaties of '31 and '33.[13] I do not see any other question that generates any true interest across the country and on which the administration lays itself open. I confess to you, moreover, that the more I reflect on this subject, the more I am led to believe that the terrain is not bad for all those who did not

13. On November 30, 1831, France and England agreed to attempt to suppress the slave trade, and they agreed to the right of search on each other's ships, as long as this right was regulated and limited. A subsequent agreement on March 22, 1833, made these regulations more precise. A more comprehensive treaty concerning both the suppression of the slave trade and the right of search was signed on December 20, 1841, but the opponents of the right to search prevented ratification of this treaty. In 1843, Tocqueville and others spoke out against the right of search, and Guizot had to accept defeat on this issue. It is worth noting that Tocqueville was one of France's most ardent advocates of abolition, and one of his antislavery reports was translated and widely circulated in the United States. See Seymour Drescher, ed., *Tocqueville and Beaumont on Social Reform* (New York: Harper & Row, 1968).

take part in the negotiation. I am for my part very seriously and very profoundly convinced that after the experience we have had with the ineffectiveness of these treaties and with some of their pernicious effects in the state of mind of the two nations, which makes daily execution of these stipulations so thorny and so dangerous, finally since the American treaty, which shows that, whatever one does, the colors of one of the greatest maritime nations can always conceal the trade[14] and make particular arrangements illusory; all these facts, I say, convince me that it would be desirable to modify the treaties of '31 and '33. To call for this seems to me a good field for discussion, even for the declared enemies of the trade; it is the most direct road for bringing back to light the impossibility of ceding to M. Guizot the conclusion of this affair.

I have always believed, and I believe more than ever, that the Spanish question was not very good.[15] If it had been, the behavior of Espartero would have managed to spoil it. I know of nothing more odious in history than the bombardment of Barcelona.[16] Nothing could be both more sanguinary and more cowardly at the same time. It is very unfortunate that this event did not happen before the fortifications law. M. Thiers would no longer have been permitted to call those who supposed the bombardment of a capital to be possible dreamers and madmen. Not only has there been one, but, besides, a bombardment that was not even necessary to reduce the place.

14. The "trade" is of course the slave trade.

15. The hostility between England and France shifted to a matrimonial question in Spain, a question of who would eventually wed the young Queen Isabella II (1830–1904). In attempts to gain both diplomatic and commercial advantages, both the French and the British sought to arrange a suitable marriage for Isabella. The French sought to marry her to one of Louis Philippe's sons, and the British offered a reliable acquaintance of Queen Victoria's. The issue deadlocked, diplomatic threats followed, and the entente between England and France deteriorated.

16. In October 1840, the forces supporting Queen Isabella II, who was still a young girl and thus represented by her mother Maria Christina as regent, were defeated by those of General Espartero, and the queen was forced to leave the country. Espartero became a dictator who ruthlessly suppressed an uprising in Barcelona in December 1842. Espartero was defeated the following year.

As for the interior, I am occupying myself with seeing what guarantees have been removed from us by the conservative party for ten years. You have done an excellent piece of work in showing how much in positions, favors, and money the government could dispose of today in order to influence the elections. Could you not, in order to make the progress of the evil more perceptible, compare the budget of 1842 to that of 1830 or even of 1829 on this point? Familiar as you are with the budget, this study could be done very quickly. I believe that it is worth the trouble, and I urge you to try. If it gives you salient results, I would be much obliged if you would make them known to me.

Farewell. I lack daylight to write more. A thousand affectionate remembrances to Madame de Beaumont. I embrace you with all my heart.

I am sending you a splendid scrawl; pardon me, please.

46. *To Gustave de Beaumont*

Tocqueville, November 6, 1843

I am sorry, my dear friend, that you have not yet responded to my last letter, if only to tell me that you had received it in good condition. I distrust the Italian mail a little, and I am only moderately interested in making the king of Sardinia a third party in the intimacy of our correspondence.[17] I feel, however, that I need to write you and chat with you, because the session is advancing and I find that it is essential not to wait until the last moment to agree on what is to be done. Do not be mistaken about it, the situation is very critical, not only, as you say, because of our particular need to put ourselves more to the fore than we have previously; but also because of an ensemble of circumstances which undoubtedly is escaping you no more than it is me.

We had evidently waited too long for the unpopularity of M. Guizot and his imprudence. The nation, far from being

---

17. Beaumont is in Nice, a city that at this point in history was part of Sardinia and hence Piedmont. Not until the unification of Italy in 1861 did France gain final control over Nice.

more and more irritated with the administration that is leading it, is resigning itself more every day to tolerating it. The spirit of opposition instead of growing is subsiding. That seems evident to me, and the Chambers will come back softened rather than retempered by contact with voters. The cause of that is not only in the current tepidity of the country and its fatigue, but, it is very necessary to recognize this, in the adroitness of the administration which, as I wrote to I do not know whom the other day, performs many bad acts, but makes few mistakes. It is not easy to discover a flank on which it can be attacked with great success.

But your principal obstruction will originate in the opposition itself. You have, quite as I have, noticed the attitude M. de Lamartine[18] is taking. That he has acquired strength during six months in the country is incontestable. Our own journals have worked to this result, as much as they could. On his side too, he showed more spirit of leadership than I supposed him to have and that I supposed he in fact would have in a long series of acts: while going farther than we, he has not ostensibly thrown himself into the radical party, and he has taken care to envelop his old revolutionary rubbish

18. Alphonse de Lamartine (1790–1869) is perhaps best known as the Romantic poet whose *Méditations poétiques* aroused Paris in 1820. Under the July Monarchy, however, the royalist poet became a left-wing politician and served in the Chamber of Deputies from 1833 to 1848. Tocqueville generally showed considerable respect for and cautious fascination with Lamartine partly because Lamartine, like Tocqueville, found the quarrels between Guizot and Thiers to be insubstantial, hypocritical, and petty. When in 1839 Lamartine uttered his famous line, "France is a nation that is bored," Tocqueville was privately writing much the same thing. Nevertheless, Tocqueville avoided any open alliance with Lamartine because Lamartine too openly criticized the plutocracy that ruled France (Tocqueville used the word *plutocracy* only privately) and demanded reforms that, while not necessarily bad in themselves, could never be attained in the foreseeable future, according to Tocqueville, and hence would only encourage dangerous agitation. Lamartine's program for reform demanded an end to the well-known corruption of Guizot's government and a large extension of the suffrage; Tocqueville seemed to object, not to the content of these reforms, but to the ways in which these demands were issued.

By the 1840s, Lamartine claimed to be speaking on behalf of the French people, and in 1847 he once more excited the French reading public by publish-with a certain color which is modern, bright, and honest, and of such a nature as to carry along a lot of people. Besides, he has this incontestable merit of acting when others do nothing, of speaking when others hold their tongues, and of pointing out something considerable to do when others only present small reforms. The crowd is so constituted that it gathers more willingly around an idea that is false but great, than around several ideas that are true but small. It is incontestable that M. de L. is closer to being at the head of the opposition on the left today than he was at the end of the session. The times have marched forward for him.

The first question is whether we want to unite ourselves openly with him. I confess that I for my part have great repugnance for him. M. de L.'s aim is an aim not of government, but of revolution. M. de L.'s ambition goes farther than what is. What he is asking for will never be obtained in our day, or it will be obtained only at the price of a new overthrow of the government. The electoral reform he calls for, he has no more chance of having than O'Connell has a chance of

---

ing all eight volumes, one after the other, of his *Histoire des Girondins*. Here, with all the skill a great writer can bring to history, he (along with Jules Michelet and Louis Blanc) stirred up memories of the rights of man, the glory of the republic, the heroic nature of the Revolution (and especially the Girodins), and a thirst for liberty. All these ideals and passions formed, for much of the French public, a glittering contrast to the dull immobility of Guizot versus Thiers. Not surprisingly, Lamartine played an influential role in the banquet campaigns of 1847–1848 and at times hinted at reforms (such as an end to the monarchy) beyond anything that Barrot or Thiers dreamed of sanctioning. Lamartine warned that if the July Monarchy continued to stifle change and to foster corruption, then France would "have the revolution of the public conscience and the revolution of contempt."

In the February Revolution of 1848, Lamartine was chosen to head the provisional government, and in the elections for the Constituent Assembly held in April 1848, Lamartine polled an astounding million and a half votes in just ten districts. Then, Lamartine, as a member of the new Executive Council, tried to balance the radical republicans and socialists of Paris, the moderate republicans, and the monarchists, who comprised a third or more of the Constituent Assembly. He was unable to manage this balance, however, and after the tensions of 1848 exploded in the June Days, Lamartine fell rapidly into political obscurity.

having the union repealed. To call for it is to create agitation toward another end. That is a road on which neither our duty nor our interest advises us, as I see it, to enter. I feel I have to act with respect to M. de L. with a great deal of regard and circumspection, but at the same time I am inclined to believe that we would be wrong to intermingle ourselves with him. We need neither to wage war against him, nor to march with him farther than we want to go.

But where should we or can we situate ourselves? That is the great difficulty of our position, placed between M. de L., who wants to make great reforms which are impractical or dangerous, and M. Thiers, who wants to do nothing at all or who wants to do something only in a way that is not ours. How to distinguish our own stance?

47. To Gustave de Beaumont[19]

Monday morning [December 9, 1844]

I did not want to write you these last three days. I feared that the liveliness of my sentiments exceeded by far the reality

19. This letter requires some background information. From the summer of 1844 to the spring of 1845, Tocqueville joined with some friends in taking over and redirecting an opposition newspaper called *Le Commerce: Journal politique et littéraire.* He undertook this step and became the driving force behind this newspaper because he was convinced that the opposition press was sterile and devoid of any coherent program for reform. Unfortunately, Beaumont, who was always more strongly tied to Barrot's section of the opposition, had committed himself to writing some articles for *Le Siècle,* a newspaper loyal to Barrot and run by some friends of Beaumont's. Although Beaumont always intended to join Tocqueville at *Le Commerce,* he was unable to do so before journalistic warfare erupted.

One major issue concerned educational reform. Guizot's Education Law of 1833 had expanded the primary school system but had not eliminated the influence of the Catholic church, leaving some primary schools secular and some under control of the church. By the 1840s Catholicism had become increasingly tolerated and increasingly popular, and an organized Catholic movement turned to politics. Led by Charles de Montalembert, the Catholics focused on the school question and sought to end the state monopoly on secondary education. Here was an unusual development in the historically long of the facts. It is essential, however, that I do so today, because I fear that you might misunderstand the cause of my silence. You have, very involuntarily no doubt, distressed me and wronged me as, perhaps in all the world, you alone were capable of doing. I have only one vulnerable point. My birth and the opinions of my family can lead people to believe that I am attached to the legitimists and to the clergy, and, as I have not married, as you have, a granddaughter of General

---

dispute between French liberals and the church because the church was demanding political change based on liberal principles, i.e., the right to establish educational institutions that could compete with state-approved institutions and the right to do so without state interference. The left opposition faced at least two key questions: (1) can we trust this swing toward liberalism by such a historically conservative organization? and (2) can we really grant the church the authority to educate the future leaders of France?

As the issue emerged and enlarged, the opposition press—including *Le Siècle*—took an anticlerical stance. In 1844 Guizot's government proposed a law that would diminish the state monopoly on secondary education, but the suggested law did not go far enough to satisfy Montalembert, while it went too far to satisfy the left opposition. Tocqueville found himself in an awkward position: he did not consider the issue enormously important, he generally held the church in contempt whenever it entered the political arena, and yet he did not like state monopoly on education. Thus, he backed Guizot's moderate position, and, eventually, on November 29, 1844, *Le Commerce* attacked the major opposition journals. Soon after, Tocqueville perceived himself to be fighting desperately to preserve his political honor and his reputation as a progressive liberal.

In the very personal attacks that followed, Beaumont found himself caught between promises he had given to *Le Siècle* and loyalty to his oldest friend. On December 7, 1844, Beaumont publicly resigned from *Le Siècle* because of his devotion to Tocqueville. Even this did not satisfy Tocqueville, however, because he wanted Beaumont to adopt publicly Tocqueville's political position. At the urging of mutual friends, the two reconciled their differences, but in reading their subsequent letters, one gains the impression that their friendship cooled considerably, until they were together again in the hectic days of 1848. For example, during the banquet campaigns of 1847–1848, they were no longer coordinating their political efforts: Beaumont entered the campaigns enthusiastically, and Tocqueville warned of the danger of such agitation.

The educational question was not resolved until the Falloux Law in 1850, a law that gave the church the right to open secondary schools (*collèges*) in competition with state schools. By the last half of the nineteenth century, about half of all students involved in secondary education were attending Catholic schools.

Lafayette, this point of departure must naturally lead my enemies to attack unceasingly, not only my actions, but my intentions, not only my conduct, but my honor. At the first prick that their self-esteem receives, they do not fail to attack in this way, and the day after the one on which they waged this cowardly and disloyal war on me, you publicly separate yourself from me on the question that divides us. I am not reproaching you for that, I was expecting it. But you are leaving me alone without shielding me. Did you need the attacks of *Le Siècle* in order to know how my conduct would be interpreted by our common adversaries? Not only that, but you declare to them that they have your *complete sympathy*. Your friendship for me prevents you, it is true, from associating yourself with the war that is being waged on me. But cannot one be the friend of a legitimist or a Jesuit? What do you expect all these men of my region to believe when it is slipped every day into their crude hearing that I am play-acting and that a man in my social position is deceiving them? What do you expect them to think when, after *Le Siècle* for several days (because it began its attacks by naming me in every letter) depicted me to them as a miserable actor, they read a letter from you, from you for whom I have worked for four years to inspire in them full confidence, from you who do not protest, who, on the contrary, leave in doubt everything except your friendship for my person. And yet, who in the world knows better than you the dangers I am running on the terrain on which I am? Who better than you can say by what supreme effort of conscience I set about doing this despite all perils? Ah, Beaumont, my reason and my heart tell me that I would not have done the same in your place if you had been in mine. . . . In the eyes of the world you appear to be weighing equally in the balance on the one side me, and on the other a journalist about whom you have written me, and written a hundred times, that he was the agent or the dupe of M. Thiers, and probably both, and about whom you were telling me, less than six months ago, that he was excited

about you only to the extent that he feared to see you take
your talents to another journal. God is my witness that I do
not hold it against you, but you have caused me great sorrow.
I would have preferred it if you had abandoned me in the
virgin forest or in the camp at Eddis, instead of acting then
toward me as a brother.[20]

What drives me to despair is that now you are going to be
led despite yourself to search for and to find wrongs in me. I
do not believe, however, I have had any. . . .[21] At least all of
my friends and Lanjuinais[22] above all, affirm the contrary to
me. I was in the most critical position: *Le Commerce* became
my representation in the eyes of the political world. It was
representing only me. Now, this journal became a general object of derision. I was in a strait from which I could only
emerge with brilliance or with deadly ridicule. Not finding
anyone to assist me, deprived of your cooperation, I could not
hope once again to attract attention to the journal by the merit
sustained by the editorship. I knew besides that it was agreed
to extinguish me in the silence. Well then! I did not want it.
I suddenly gave the journal its true character; I placed it on its
true ground. I forced adversaries to see it and, if I believe all
the testimonies of sympathy I receive, the public to value it.
In the position which had developed I could not have acted
otherwise. And I believe I did so with moderation.

What will be the ultimate result of this letter? I do not
know. I am very troubled, but not weakened. I know well
what dangers I run in the isolated and perilous situation I occupy. I know that I can get myself out of this, only by dint of
courage, but if God permits my health to sustain me, I hope
to come out of it stronger than before I entered. The principal

20. Beaumont twice nursed Tocqueville through serious illnesses—once in
Tennessee in 1831 and once in Algeria in 1841.

21. Two words are missing.

22. Victor-Ambroise Lanjuinais (1802–1869) was a member of the Chamber
of Deputies from 1838 to 1848, elected to the Constituent Assembly under the
Second Republic, and, along with Tocqueville, a member of Barrot's second
cabinet in 1849.

subject of the quarrel is very unpopular. But I notice that M. Thiers is even more so. I feel more than ever that to combat his corruption and his power, there is only one resource, which is to appeal ceaselessly, without reservation, without timidity, to the principles of true liberty which still live in our country. It is a war that has never been waged against him openly and completely. We will see if I must succumb.

48. *Gustave de Beaumont to Tocqueville*[23]

La Grange, December 10 [1844]

I shall not speak to you of the profound sorrow I feel; it can only be great between friends who, after having overcome so many trials, come to the point at which we are in this moment. I do not doubt that you feel it as I do. And if I followed my natural disposition, I would keep silent, waiting to raise my voice and complain until the storm has calmed and passions are a little soothed. But I confess, on receiving your letter, which I was desiring so much and which I wish I had not received, and on seeing that all the wrongs were mine, when I was so much persuaded that they were not; on receiving from a friendship to which I had vowed a devotion I believed without equal, reproaches of weakness, not to say of treason, at the very moment when I expected to receive expression of other sentiments, it is impossible for me not to tell you with sincerity my thinking about your wrongs as well as my own. I will not forget, that is impossible, while setting them out to you, all the old attachment and current sadness that I have in my soul. The first of your wrongs was, in the midst of your efforts to place *Le Commerce* in its proper position, not to remember that I was still at *Le Siècle*. Do you believe that I did not have many worries about this journal? It was useful to us more than once, to you and to me. You had

23. This break with Beaumont was such an important and trying moment in Tocqueville's life that we have included this letter from Beaumont because it casts light on the sentiments of each man.

been of the opinion that I should enter into this publication; in a recent circumstance, you had thought, all our friends also had thought, that I should, instead of withdrawing from it, strengthen my ties to it, which I did. And then you believe that one can suitably and with dignity change opinions over-night! It is necessary that I go quickly and break the ties that the evening before I strengthened! This is necessary because at *Le Commerce* there is a difficult situation: but is it not also a difficult situation for me to leave a journal in which I spent three years establishing myself? At such a juncture, what do I do? I loosen little by little my ties with a man[24] whose behavior toward me has never been anything but good and delicate, but whose wrong is to be separating me from you. To reach that result, I refuse all cooperation with *Le Siècle* at a time when I could have been filling the journal with my articles and have been doing something that, perhaps would have been useful to our ideas, certainly would have been so for me. I had taken the commitment, a single commitment for a review of a historical work which had to appear signed by me; knowing the inconvenience of such a publication at the moment *Le Commerce* was making its efforts, I already had gotten this article to appear without my name. I had done more: I had established positively that my resignation would be presented by the supervising committee at the first meeting of its shareholders and that I would never again write a line in *Le Siècle*. This was the object of the most vigorous and most friendly protests from the editor-in-chief of *Le Siècle* to me. It was precisely at this moment that *Le Commerce* came to make a substantial charge against *Le Siècle,* to which as far as Chambolle was concerned I was no longer attached, but where as far as the public was concerned, I still belonged! That it was useful for *Le Commerce,* necessary perhaps for its success, for this keen aggression to be made against the various organs of the opposition, I will not discuss. That it was a courageous thing for its authors and that this thing will benefit the oppo-

24. Chambolle, at this point in time the most important editor at *Le Siècle*.

sition some day, I indeed want to admit. But admitting all the while what will be contested by others, I say that the effect of this aggression, in what concerns me, was to create for me at that very instant a situation that was not tenable. The side for me to take was never in doubt. To my mind you were absolutely wrong to have attacked *Le Siècle* as you did; in my view you would have attained your goal as well by attacking *Le Constitutionnel;* I did not understand how you came, without even shouting beware to me, to fall on *Le Siècle,* where you knew I was still located. But *Le Siècle* itself had a fault, which for me was above all others and effaced all those of *Le Commerce:* it *named* you, it made an allusion to a fact, which, six months ago, had been the subject of a calumny by *Le Constitutionnel.* Immediately and under the influence of its first articles and even before the malevolent insinuations that were found in other articles, I write to Chambolle, I give my resignation, and I forewarn you about it!

You were wrong to regard as an insignificant thing, and not even being worthy of an acknowledgment, the most serious act that I could do in the very situation which you had made for me. Was it necessary, because *Le Commerce* attacked *Le Siècle,* where I was located, that I at once desert the offices of *Le Siècle* to pass over to those of *Le Commerce?* Or rather while withdrawing to the side, without saying anything about the question of education, did I have to seem to be abandoning *Le Siècle* because of this question, that I encourage the accusation, founded on my having remained there for two years without protesting, that I was a man who was only awaiting the approach of the enemy camp in order to desert? No, no, do not speak to me of the compliments I pay to Chambolle while leaving him, which I owed to a long collaboration, to a relationship that was always affectionate, which I owed also to a man who had never done me a wrong and who could believe that I had done one to him; this journalist whose friendship I placed in the balance with yours, I declared publicly that I was leaving him because he committed the wrong of defending himself, being attacked, and be-

cause in defending himself he had pronounced your name! It is
true that a short time later, I regretted what I had done, because I would have wanted to have done more, seeing a polemic which came almost to the point of incriminating your
character by unkind insinuations, I asked myself if I could not
have found in it a cause or a pretext for going quickly to place
myself near you in order to receive there my part of the blows
to which it seemed to me I had the right; I expressed this to
you, and I almost regret it, because it seems to me that you
saw in my remarks an indication that I was reproaching myself for doing wrong. Besides, I could no longer do it without
falling into ridicule at taking two contradictory resolutions
one on top of the other. Be that as it may, there is no one
exempt from bias who, on reading my declaration in *Le
Siècle,* and having compared the fact of my resignation published by *Le Commerce,* did not take away with him this very
clear impression, that I separated myself from *Le Siècle* because of you and that this separation was the first step that
was drawing me closer to *Le Commerce.* About this impression
you were wrong, and to my mind this is the gravest and most
troublesome of all, you were wrong to fight in *Le Commerce*
by responding to a testimony of friendship with the deepest
disdain and with something more than disdain, with something that would be forever injurious, if in this sentiment
there had not been a visible anger. You were wrong not to
understand the act, the sole act that my affection could perform, you were wrong not to accept it in the spirit that had
inspired it; you were wrong to state publicly what you
thought of my act and so to deepen in another way the separation that kept me from *Le Commerce;* the tie which secured
me to *Le Siècle* once broken, only one circumstance was necessary, the least occasion, for me to rejoin you at *Le Commerce.* You were wrong to make the difficulty so great: if I
went there now or in a short while, after the way in which
you have treated me, I would be politically the poorest and
the least of men and would no longer be able to be any more
than your clerk. That is, I confess to you, what distresses me

most, because isolation is not to my taste and although the past appears very sad to me, I am very much more occupied with the future, and the future is no less saddening. Certainly it is not in my character to see an act of courage attempted by men of heart and to withdraw from them; I need rather to gather my strength in order not to place myself among them. But this strength will not be lacking any time care for my own dignity commands me to do a thing or to abstain. I do not deceive myself about how small I am, but, as small as that is, I insist on keeping my character honorable and consistent. It is not in response to your letter that I say this, because assuredly there is certainly nothing in your letter that induces me to the common efforts which have now become impossible; but I am answering my own thoughts, which, leaping to meet a hope, see with sadness the obstacle that exists and that might not have existed. Do not think me indifferent to the enterprise in which you are engaged; it would not suit me to tell you at this moment how excited we are about it: I do not stop being so when the crisis becomes strongest, and I understand all that is serious in it for men who bring to it all the talent, convictions, and devotion they have. But there is something more serious in politics than the perils attached to all common action; this is isolation. But I am persuaded that in the midst of all the natural agitation that you feel at this moment, and in the midst of the preoccupation that the chances for success or nonsuccess of the enterprise cause for your future, you will also think of the honor, of the character, and of the very existence of him who finds himself indefinitely thrown into isolation and inaction.

49. To Gustave de Beaumont

Friday [December 13 or 20, 1844]

The good friends who wanted to reunite us desired that there be no question between us of what had taken place these last two weeks. I think that they were right and that it would indeed be better not to recall unnecessarily these sad circumstances that have caused us both such sorrow. However, I need to tell you, my dear friend, how much I suffered at being next to you for an hour and a half without being able to express how I felt in any other way than by shaking your hand. When I went over in my mind the memory of the eighteen years that have just passed and when I thought of this part of our life, which is so large, that we have passed in a friendship so tender and so devoted, when I dream, my dear Beaumont, of all the proofs of affection that I received so often from you, instead of speaking politics I was tempted to fling my arms around you and to tell you that in spite of all that could happen, I will always love you with all my heart.

My wife will not only be content but happy to see your wife again. We would have been at your house tonight, if we could have gone out.

50. *To Gustave de Beaumont*

Bône, December 14, 1846

I am writing you, my dear friend, from Bône, where I arrived yesterday in spite of myself.[25] We had left Algiers for Stora on the 10th. A gale that made us run rather large risks on the coast ultimately brought us here. We will leave for Stora again as soon as good weather returns. I hope that it will be tonight. General Bedeau[26] wrote me that he has sent a

25. This is Tocqueville's second trip to Algeria. In May 1841, Tocqueville and Beaumont had toured Algeria, although their tour was interrupted after just over three weeks when Tocqueville was struck by a serious case of dysentery, an illness requiring continuous care by Beaumont while they carefully made their way back to France. On this second journey, Tocqueville and his wife visited Algeria during the months of November and December 1846.

26. Marie-Alphonse Bedeau (1804–1863) was an important part of the French military force in Africa from 1836 to 1848 and was appointed to the rank of general in 1841. Bedeau was one of the generals who attempted to

carriage to us in Philippeville which will be able to transport
Marie in one day to Constantine, where we will stay for
about ten days. We intend to be back in Philippeville in order
to take the liner on the 29th, which would bring us back to
France about the 1st of January. But it is possible that our
return will be delayed a week by a host of incidents impossible to foresee.

Up to now I have had a very beautiful trip, in which my
person behaved itself as it could have done ten years ago. It is
true that I have comported myself with a consummate prudence. I knew that, whereas the life of a traveler, even the
most fatiguing, is salutary for my health, nothing was more
perilous for me than the transition from sedentary life to
the former. I therefore followed the method the amateurs of
the jockey club practice with respect to their horses, which
they call *training*. I applied myself during a month in Algiers
to gradually changing my habits and to accustoming myself to
severe exercises, especially to riding a horse, doing something
more each day than the day before. When I thought myself
sufficiently seasoned, I accepted the invitation of the marshal,[27]
who left Oran by land. We have been on horses and sleeping
in tents in Médéa, Milianah, Orléansville. There I left him and
crossed the Dahra and made for Tenès, where I embarked to

---

control the February 1848 Revolution, and he was seriously wounded in the
June Days. As Tocqueville put it in his *Recollections,* Bedeau's "unlucky star
brought him back from Africa in time to bury the July Monarchy." Under the
Second Republic, Tocqueville and Bedeau became friends and allies in the
Constituent Assembly. After the 1851 coup, Bedeau was exiled.

27. Tocqueville here refers to Thomas Robert Bugeaud, Duke of Isly
(1784–1849), who was made marshal of the French forces in Algeria in 1841.
Bugeaud was an officer during Napoleon's Empire and took part in the Spanish
campaign. In general, Tocqueville had no strong quarrel with Bugeaud's military undertakings in Algeria, but he did disagree with Bugeaud on the government in Algeria. Unlike Bugeaud, Tocqueville wanted to educate the Algeri-
ans, to respect the indigenous Algerian culture, and to promote civilian instead
of merely military colonists. After Tocqueville presented his opinions in a
committee report to the Chamber of Deputies in 1847, Bugeaud resigned his
position.

go spend a day in Oran with Lamoricière. Having returned to
Algiers, I remounted immediately and, alone for ten days, I
visited most of the settlements of Sahel and all those on the
plain. I only returned to Algiers on the 8th; and on the 10th,
as I told you above, I embarked to come to Stora. It has been
years since I have fared as well as I have during this month of
physical fatigue. It remains to be seen if the end will go as
well as the beginning. Nevertheless, the hardest seems to me
to be over. I cannot tell you how admirable my wife was in
the courage and patience she has shown during this whole
trip. It often required, to tell the truth, some of both, and if I
had not counted greatly on both of them, I would never have
ventured to leave her all alone for nearly a month in Algiers at
an inn and without a servant.

I write you nothing of the result of my observations. Our
opinions on Africa seem to me to have been right on the
whole, although erroneous and above all incomplete on many
points. I will relate to you on my return everything without
exception that I will have learned and seen, and you will judge
yourself which of our ideas we must keep and which we must
abandon. My position vis-à-vis the marshal is perfectly simple
and clear. I told him on arriving and before accepting any
courtesy from him what I approved and what I disapproved in
his government. I announced on leaving him that I persevered
in the same views. What I told him I will be able to say before him in the Chamber. The relations we have had with
each other compel me only to great respect for his person, and
I had already resolved to have this respect before coming.

Now, I want to speak to you yet again about what has been
the principal subject of our last letters.

I see without a great deal of surprise, but with a great deal
of sadness that, although we are in agreement about the end
toward which our actions should tend, having in the last
analysis the same tastes and the same general opinions in politics, we are unhappily divided on the course of conduct to
take at this moment. That pains me extremely, and makes me

feel the need, even in the middle of the agitated life I lead, to take up the subject again with you and to explain to you thoroughly the motives that make me act in this situation, if not in a manner contrary to you, at least different from you. I would hope that this difference of opinion will not loosen in any way the tie of affection and esteem, so strong and so old, that unites us; that is, I believe, easy to prevent if we speak to each other with an open heart.

I have too much experience of the political world not to know that any ostensible separation from M. Thiers leads sooner or later to making war on M. Thiers. However, this conclusion can be more or less rapidly drawn. Neither my taste nor my interest nor my duty inclines me to combat M. Thiers immediately, and I believe that if some prudence is practiced on both sides, people can go along for a rather long time, making a *parallel* war on the cabinet without clashing with each other. Therefore, I am not disposed, for my part, to take a hostile and militant position concerning M. Thiers. But I consider it to be of immense importance to take vis-à-vis him one that in the eyes of the country is really and clearly independent, and I would have done so publicly long ago if I had not been alone. Here in very few words are my reasons:

As I am speaking to you with an open heart, I will acknowledge frankly that the first and strongest of my reasons is the need to satisfy myself. Of all the men in the world, M. Thiers is surely the one who most habitually shocks and offends all those sentiments that I generally consider the most elevated, the purest, and the most precious of all those I find both outside myself and within myself. I feel, without seeking to do so, differently from the way he does on almost everything in this world: what I love, he hate or ridicules; what he loves, I fear or despise and that, on both sides, by the sole instinctive movement of our two natures. To live in habitual contact and in a community of action with that man, to contribute to a certain extent to the accomplishment of his plans, to work in spite of myself to deliver power over to him, to

discover every day that I am, either voluntarily or without
any knowledge, the instrument of his plans and his politics—
this finally made mine such a miserable existence in my own
eyes that only the most absolute impossibility of having
another could bring me to lead it still. I wonder if I would not
prefer to leave political life.

Now that I have given as the first reason what, in speaking
to someone else, I would have given as the second, permit me
to be as explicit and as frank on this one:

Not only do I find alliance with M. Thiers painful and com-
promising but, from the point of view of the great interests of
our country and our homeland, I hold it to be very pernicious. I believe that those who, like Barrot and like yourself,
my dear friend, believe they can chain M. Thiers, alter him,
contain him, hold him, are deluding themselves. M. Thiers
has a personality too untamable in its suppleness, too dazzling,
too powerful for that to happen. You might well be able to
obtain from him some concession in return for something
else, make him yield on some point, even impose some sacrifice on him; you will change neither his nature, nor his tendencies, which are profoundly hostile to yours, and you will
not prevent him, once he has arrived in office, even by you
and with you, from giving to the government his spirit as
well as his name. One only dominates and contains M. Thiers
by strength, and one is only strong against him when one
relies on the portion of the country that has neither his sentiments nor his ideas. Now, it is this strength that you lose by
the alliance with him. We all consider the greatest evil and the
greatest danger of the present situation to be the profound indifference into which the country is falling, a growing indifference that manifests itself by the most formidable symptoms. There are many causes of this evil; but surely one of the
principal ones is the belief that is becoming more deeply
rooted each day in the masses, that political life is no more
than a game in which each person seeks only to win; that
politics has nothing serious in it but the personal ambitions

of which it is the means; that there is a sort of gullibility and almost stupidity and shame in growing impassioned for a game that lacks reality and for political chiefs who are only actors not even interested in the success of the play, but only in that of their particular roles. I may be mistaken, but I believe firmly that nothing was more suitable for causing and for increasing this belief than the alliance in which the parliamentary opposition lived with M. Thiers, because, whatever one might do, M. Thiers will always be for the country the most complete symbol, and the model, of selfishness, of *insincerity,* and of intrigue in political matters.

There you have, my dear friend, in very few words outlined in haste (because time is rushing me), the mixture of individual and patriotic sentiments that brought to me that deepest conviction that intimacy with M. Thiers, in whatever manner it would be established, whatever momentary advantage that it would have, was pernicious to ourselves and to our ideas, and which has determined me to place myself apart, if I can do so without falling into isolation.

Now, do not believe that I am hiding from myself the bad sides of this resolution. There are several which I have always envisioned. The first and the largest you point out yourself; it is that the ambitious of low condition who leave M. Thiers, after having been his flatterers and his friends, only because the ministerial chances of M. Thiers are not immediate, will find in persons who want to act as I do a commodious cloak behind which they will seek to make the transitional movement that has to lead them from M. Thiers to the current administration or to a very similar administration. I do not believe that cloak will be very useful to them for long. You seem to think that, in my opinion, those who would place themselves ostensibly outside the influence of M. Thiers would have to avoid political questions and shut themselves up in special affairs. I never meant anything like that. To conduct oneself thus would be to act in a way contrary to all our principles and at the same time to play too nicely into the hands of our adversaries. All that I wanted to say is this: the opposition, in being concerned only with political questions that cause administrations to come into being or to fall, has allowed people to believe that it lacks sincerity and serious-ness, because people finally have come to imagine that the op-position had only the fall of the administration in mind and not the questions themselves. Thus it has a particular need to apply itself now to dealing with questions that are not minis-terial in their nature when they interest the country, if only to deal at the same time with political questions properly so called with the moral strength that is lacking today. That is my thesis. It is, you see, very different from those ambitious people you speak to me about and will only serve to distin-guish us quickly from these, for anybody who wants to see clearly.

That will not prevent people from trying to confound us with them. I know that well. It is an evil of which I am very sensitive, but which seems to me preferable to the present evil. I could write you from here, if I had the time, the arti-cles that will appear in *Le Constitutionnel* and even, I greatly fear, in *Le Siècle,* once M. Thiers has given the theme. We will be a mixture of the ambitious and of the meddlers who only leave M. Thiers in order to come to power by a shorter route and who disturb the opposition and divide it for per-sonal purposes. The *principles* and the true flag of the Revolu-tion will be on the side of M. Thiers, we will only be de-serters. . . . These indignities will be extremely painful for me. I do not drape myself with you in a stoicism, from which I am very far. But in advance they cause me more irritation and sadness than fear. I do not believe that public opinion changes its view on men as easily as the newspapers fancy and that it suddenly transforms into political intriguers men whom for a long time it has been used to considering as honest and disinterested. I also count on the crude good sense of the pub-lic, on this intimate sense that is stronger than party spirit, which teaches to each that the broad political future of this

country is not away from M. Thiers, but near to him; that
sooner or later the vastest perspectives of personal ambition
will be opened on his side and that those who would separate
themselves from him, out of ambition, in the presence of a
74-year-old king, and in the present state of Europe, would be
ambitious men who are very badly advised, very mediocre
and very vulgar.

What I have told you, my dear friend, I have written you
on the run, without having the time to develop or to weigh
my words, but I was anxious to tell you this; because having
the great and forever regrettable misfortune of not being at
one with you at the moment concerning the proper course of
conduct to take, I would at least like for us always to stay
intimately tied by confidence and by the heart—which seems
to be easy.

51. *To Paul Clamorgan*

Paris, February 13, 1847

. . . I did not give you extensive details on the latest events
in the Chamber, because I supposed that, even from afar, you
would see the truth clearly; that is what has happened. With
your good sense, you have readily perceived the explanation
of my conduct and that of my friends, and I hope that the
country will be as clairvoyant as you have been. The events
that are emerging, M. Thiers's speech, the tone of the English
newspapers and of ours are already beginning to throw great
light on the scene and to clarify what until now was only seen
in the wings. It is evident that a great comedy is being played.
I did not want to be an actor in it. There in two words is the
key to all that has just happened.

You know what my opinions have been at all times concerning M. Thiers. They have never varied. I have always
thought that basically M. Thiers was the greatest enemy of

liberal ideas there was in France, and I have always believed that if he were to become master of the opposition, he would make it commit enormous mistakes for his private interest, that he would compromise it and would discredit it in the country and that he would ultimately make it lose the support of the liberal and generous sentiments that make up its strength. Without asking for war to be waged on M. Thiers, I have constantly worked within the opposition to see that it would hold itself apart from M. Thiers and that it would not let itself be dragged along by him into enterprises contrary to our principles, which the desire to retake power made him attempt. In this vein, I spoke and voted against the Regency law that was passed only thanks to him; in this vein, I spoke and voted against the fortifications of Paris of which he is the author. As long as M. Barrot, while ceding more than he should have to M. Thiers, kept some independence from him and did not let his personality be absorbed in Thiers's, I was patient and I avoided taking any side that could separate me from him. But, during the last two sessions, government of the entire opposition had fallen into M. Thiers's hands alone; I felt I needed to escape from responsibility for such conduct. I associated myself with thirty or forty members of the opposition who shared my sentiments. We have not broken with M. Barrot, we have not declared war on M. Thiers, but we have escaped the empire of this man. We have refused to allow ourselves to be blindly led any further by him. We had no desire to convey a public explanation, but necessity has forced us to it.

Do I need to tell you what just happened and what is happening with regard to the English question? Truthfully, I believe you have too much good sense not to have seen it for yourself. As long as the administration was relying on the English alliance, M. Thiers attacked this alliance with fury; he aroused, excited, influenced, a hundred times at the risk of leading to war, all the passions, all the prejudices, all the um-

brage that exist in the country against the English. He
dragged us all behind him along this road. An event happens
that embroils Guizot with England.[28] Immediately a change in
view takes place: the English alliance becomes the necessary
pivot of our politics; the Whigs are France's best friends; the
English nation has every right to complain about our government. And why this strange recantation, the greatest and most
subtle I have ever witnessed since I have been in Parliament?
Because M. Thiers understood that if affairs become more and
more entangled, as is probable, if the king after having been
plucky begins to tremble, if fear of war seizes the center, it
will surely be necessary to abandon Guizot as too compro-
mised, and then people will be compelled to throw themselves
into the arms of the only man of state who, agreeable to England, can restore good relations between her and us. In a
word, after having tried to overturn the cabinet by the hatred
to which the English alliance gives birth, a new campaign has
been started that has as its goal gaining power by means of
the English alliance and thanks to the fear the English inspire.

   And do you believe that I was a man who would take a role
in this shameful comedy? No, no, I did not want to, out of
respect for myself. I did not want to, out of respect for my

28. Guizot's quarrel with England in late 1846 and early 1847 again concerned the marriage of Queen Isabella II of Spain. In 1843, Guizot and Lord
Aberdeen had come to the following agreement: Queen Isabella II would marry
the duke of Cadiz (the nephew of her own father, Ferdinand VII), but King
Louis Philippe's plan to have one of his sons marry the Infanta, the sister of
Isabella, would be postponed until Isabella had married, had children, and
established a line of succession. In the summer of 1846, when Lord Palmerston
came back into power, he repudiated the agreement of Lord Aberdeen and
pushed strongly to have Isabella marry a German prince who was closely tied
to Queen Victoria. Guizot moved more quickly and more cleverly, and by
October 1846 Queen Isabella II married the duke of Cadiz, and the Infanta
married the duke of Montpensier, the son of Louis Philippe. France regarded
this move as revenge for the Treaty of London, England took it as a rebuff, and
Lord Palmerston could not disguise his anger. Thiers sought to exploit the
poor relationship with England to his own parliamentary advantage.

party. You tell me that the country is becoming indifferent to politics, that it is taking no further interest in opinions and men. And how do you expect it to be otherwise? What do you expect it to do when it is forced to witness developments of this kind? What interest do you expect it to take in this miserable game that is being played before its eyes? How would it grow impassioned for opinions that are only the instrument of the ambition of some men? How would it attach itself to leaders who only think of themselves and who treat it like a big child who is being made to act without being shown the hidden reason for things?

When I saw that a part of the opposition, either out of lack of intelligence, or out of weakness, or out of thirst for power, finally decided, after long agitation, to follow M. Thiers into the new terrain of foreign policy that he was taking, I protested publicly. I wanted to be on record that I was not an accomplice in the abandonment of ideas we have not stopped preaching in the country in the last six years. I did not mean in acting this way to break with the opposition, but on the contrary to stay faithful to its principles. I have confidence that time will justify me. The sequel to the discussion of the address, the admirable speech that M. Dufaure[29] gave has proven well, I think, that it was not personal motives that made us act, but the firm wish to keep our principles intact, which, finally, are only the principles of the Revolution of 1789.

I could speak to you about this longer. But I lack time.
Farewell, everything to you from the heart.

---

29. Jules Dufaure (1798–1881) was a lawyer and a member of the Chamber of Deputies from 1834 to 1848. Dufaure emerged as a friend and political ally in the Chamber, sharing both Tocqueville's political ideas and his desire to maintain some independence from Thiers within the left opposition. After 1848, Dufaure supported the Second Republic, was elected to the Constituent Assembly, and, along with Tocqueville, joined Barrot's second cabinet in 1849 under the presidency of Louis Napoleon.

52. To Nassau William Senior

Tocqueville, August 25, 1847

Thank you very much, my dear M. Senior, for having
given me your itinerary; not that I expect to meet you outside
of France, but what you tell me lets me arrange my affairs to
see you when you pass through Paris. I intend to be in that
city from the 1st to the 15th of October. Consequently, we
can find each other there. Kindly, then, let me know your
address before you arrive; I will promptly come look you up.
In Paris I live at no. 30 Rue de la Madeleine.

I will take immense pleasure in seeing you again after such a
long absence and in speaking with you about all that has
happened and is happening in the world. I will unfortunately
have little time to spend with you; to tell the truth, I am only
passing through Paris to visit my father, who lives near
Compiègne.

You will find France peaceful and prosperous enough, but
nonetheless uneasy. Minds here have for some time been experiencing a singular malaise, and, in the midst of a calm
greater than any we have experienced for a long time, the idea
that the current state of things is unstable is occurring to
many. As for me, although I view these symptoms with some
fear, I do not exaggerate the look of things; I think our society is solidly established, above all for the reason that no one
knows, whatever is desired, how to set it on another base.
However, this aspect of the state of minds must make one
reflect seriously. The system of administration that has been
practiced for seventeen years has so perverted the middle class,
by making a constant appeal to the individual cupidities of its
members, that this class is becoming little by little, for the rest
of the nation, a little corrupt and vulgar aristocracy, by which
it seems shameful to let oneself be led. If that sentiment has
grown among the masses, it could lead later to great misfortunes. But how to prevent the government from corrupting

when the elective regime naturally gives it so much occasion to do so, and centralization so many means? The fact is that we are attempting an experiment of which we have not yet seen the final result; we are trying to make two things proceed together that have never, to my knowledge, been united: an elective assembly and a very centralized executive power. That is the greatest problem of the time: it has been posed, but not resolved.

I long to know what you think of what you have just seen in Germany and what you are now seeing in Italy.

Adieu.

53. To Louis de Kergorlay

Clairoix, par Compiègne (Oise),
October 18, 1847

Your letter gave me great pleasure, my dear friend. You do what has to be done to reach an excellent conclusion, and you set about it with interest and with pleasure; great chances of success. I cannot believe that in studying the subject as you are doing, you will not produce a remarkable work.[30] I am fortified in this belief the more I see you working, and I am convinced that I am not mistaking my desire for reality. I urge you not to hurry your return too much, however strong may be your natural eagerness to see your wife again. What you are doing at this moment is capital, and if you are to succeed, you can be certain that it is where you are now that you will gather together the true elements of victory. I do understand the painful emptiness that the absence of Mathilde causes you. She is truly a very fascinating person. For my part, I am infinitely grateful to her, not only for her tenderness for you, but also for the true loftiness of soul with which

30. Kergorlay was in Germany, contemplating a work, which he never completed, on that country.

she knows how to love you, for the way in which she has
understood you, and the way in which she attached herself
with your plans from the day she perceived and continues to
see your destiny. These ways of thinking and feeling are unusual in any other society and in any time; but one no longer
encounters them these days in the society in the midst of
which Mathilde was raised, and she must have found in her
soul a very real nobility in order to have raised herself this
way above all the petty images others in her position ordinarily form of life. You undoubtedly contributed greatly to this
élan, but you would not have succeeded if you had not found
in her an aspiration that was natural and perhaps unknown to
herself toward something higher than she had before her. I
received from her, a week and a half ago, a letter full of all
the sentiments in your regard that I most desire to see in her.
I hope that you have captured that soul by its most vigorous
side and that you will always keep a very great hold on her.

I am delighted to hear you say that in general the political
men you see agree with you on the affairs of Germany. Two
years ago, in Paris, I saw an Englishman of great merit, M.
Senior, who was returning from Germany. I talked with him,
and I found with satisfaction that he appeared to be as impressed as you were with the affairs of Prussia; at least that is
what I believed him to think. That is for me a substantial
guarantee that you are right, and that is what makes me hope
so much that some day you will decide to write about the
country you perceive so well. If you ever do it, here is what
I would recommend. The difficulty would be in creating a
picture accessible to the French reader of a state of society and
of mind so different, not only from what we picture to ourselves, but above all from what our sentiment about ourselves
inclines us to imagine. The real difficulty with the subject is
not our ignorance, but that natural prejudice that is born of
the contemplation of our country and of the recollections of
our history. Unfortunately, on this point I cannot give you
any advice, except to take stock of yourself constantly, to ask

yourself what you were inclined naturally to think about Germany before studying, and to investigate by what pathways you passed from your instinctive opinions to your reasoned opinions, and to attempt to make your readers follow the same routes. I am sure that that must be your goal, but by what process is it to be attained? Only the author can be the judge of that question. Is it necessary to explain the differences and the resemblances between the two countries, or to speak only with a view to making people understand? I don't know. In my work on America, I almost always followed the second method. Although I very rarely spoke of France in my book, I did not write one page of it without thinking about her and without having her, so to speak, before my eyes. And what above all I have sought to put in relief in relation to the United States and to have well understood, was less the complete picture of that foreign society than its contrasts and resemblances to our own. It is always either from opposition or from analogy with one that I set out to give a just and interesting idea of the other. I am telling you that not as an example to follow but as a good item to know. In my opinion, that continual reflection that I was making without saying so on France was one of the prime causes for the book's success.

You pose to me, concerning religious passions, a question that I think is insoluble, that is to say, one that is not capable of being resolved by a general and absolute truth. I think it incontestable that political liberty has sometimes deadened, sometimes animated religious passions. That has depended on many circumstances: on the nature of the religions, on the age at which they occurred, either the religious passion or the political passion; because, for passions as for everything in this world, there is growth, manhood, and decay. When religious passion was in its decline and political passion in its first flight, the latter made people forget the former. These circumstances, and many others that I am not pointing out, explain the prodigious differences that different times and places have presented in this respect. If, however, it were necessary to seek, through all these particular cases, what can be considered the most regular and most general truth in this matter, I would side with the opinion of your Germans rather than with yours. I believe that as a general rule political liberty animates more than it extinguishes religious passions. There exist more family ties than are supposed between political passions and religious passions. On both sides general goods, immaterial to a certain degree, are in sight; on both sides an ideal of society is pursued, a certain perfecting of the human species, the picture of which raises souls above contemplation of private interests and carries them away. For my part, I more easily understand a man animated at the same time both by religious passion and political passion than by political passion and the passion for well-being, for example. The first two can hold together and be embraced in the same soul, but not the second two. There is another reason that is less general and less grand, but perhaps actually more conclusive, which explains to me why the two passions go together and stimulate each other: that is the service that they are often called upon to render to each other. Free institutions are often the natural and sometimes indispensable instruments of religious passions. Nearly all the efforts that the moderns have made toward liberty they have made because of the need for manifesting or defending their religious opinions. It is religious passion that pushed the Puritans to America and led them to want to govern themselves there. The two English revolutions were made to win liberty of conscience. It is the same need that made the Huguenot nobility tend toward republican opinions in the 16th century in France. Religious passions in all these cases aroused political passions, and the political passions served the free development of others. If religious passions had never been impeded in their movements, this effect would perhaps never have been produced. But they almost always are. When they have obtained all the satisfaction they desired, this effect can as easily cease to be reproduced. Your theory may be applicable in a society that is religious without being agitated by controversies or religious passions. It is possible that public affairs then little by little and almost exclusively absorb the attention of citizens; and yet I am not sure of that, unless political circumstances are very stirring. Most often, the agitation which created and which fosters political liberty in the depths of souls will agitate all the religious ferment that may remain in the country and arouse it. That is, in my opinion, what is happening in America, about which you have been telling me. In my opinion, the march of time, the developments in well-being, . . . have, in America, taken away from the religious element three-quarters of its original power. However, all that remains of it is greatly agitated. Religious men in the United States meet, speak, act in common more than anywhere else. I believe that the habits of political liberty and the movement it has given to all things count for much in the particular movement that is perceived within the religious element that still exists in the country. I believe that, without being able to restore to it the omnipotence it used to have, these circumstances are maintaining it and producing in it all the strength that it can still give. One must take care not to confuse political liberty with certain effects it sometimes produces. Once it is well established, and exercised in a peaceable milieu, it impels men to the practice and the taste of well-being, to the care and passion for making fortunes; and, as a repercussion, its tastes, its needs, its cares extinguish religious passions. But these are the distant and secondary results of political liberty, which scarcely harm political passion itself less than religious passion.

That is what I had to say on this particular point, which I am far, moreover, from having examined with all the care that its importance requires. The only absolute truth that I see in this matter is that there is no absolute truth. Thus it is wise, as I see it, to apply oneself to the examination of particular circumstances.

You tell me, in finishing your letter, that our correspondence no longer has the frequency and expansiveness that it used to have. I notice that as much as you do. But, even though I am sorry that it is so, I am not distressed beyond measure, because I believe that I see clearly that that does not result from a change in our mutual dispositions. When I consider attentively the kind of feeling that I have for you, I see no diminution in everything that formerly made up the basis and the bond of our friendship. If it lacks something of the élan that youth brings to everything, one encounters in our friendship a certain stability and real knowledge of life and of men that cannot be found in youthful élan. As I have grown more experienced and as I have seen the political world more closely, I have understood better how you are a friend on whom I can absolutely count and in whose soul those little passions that in the long run untie the tightest knots of ordinary friendships could never interject themselves. Our intimacy is also like this for me and I could say much more precious than it has ever been, and I think that you feel something similar. Now why do we feel the need to pour it out to one another less often? That results from two causes: from all the positive occupations that fill our lives, and that leave less time and less interest for these long conversations, which almost always had for a subject the debate of several general *questions;* and especially from the difference of our occupations. The first reason, as I was saying, takes away the time and sometimes the taste for general conversations; the second, the possibility of conversing about private and everyday facts. These reasons do not seem to me to be sufficient to justify what you complain about, but they explain it and in some degree, they excuse it. All the same, I am of your opinion that we have to make an effort to combat such tendencies.

Farewell, I embrace you with all my heart.

Write me soon.

Four

FROM THE FEBRUARY REVOLUTION TO THE ELECTION OF LOUIS NAPOLEON (1848)

Tocqueville's *Recollections* will always remain one of the indispensable descriptions and analyses of the 1848 Revolution in France. Still, Tocqueville wrote his *Recollections* about two years after the fact, when he had time to reflect, synthesize, research, converse with others, and interpret. Certainly his letters of this period will never replace his *Recollections,* but they do offer a fascinating and complementary account of the time. For example, it is one thing to reconstruct a marvelous description of the ferocity of the June Days two years later, but Tocqueville reveals his feelings more directly and forcefully in a letter written "in the noise of cannon and fusillade," warning a friend that the struggle is "the most terrible of all civil wars, the war of class against class" and indeed a war against "property, family, and civilization" (Letter 58). To take one more example, we can see for ourselves that Tocqueville, even in times of accelerated and disordered change, does not lose his uncanny ability to analyze and predict. So many in France were astonished at the conservative character of the Constituent Assembly elected in April 1848, but Tocqueville predicted this nearly seven weeks before the election (Letter 54).

As the events of 1848 unfold, one is not surprised to discover that, despite some misgivings, Tocqueville is pleased that France has rid itself of Guizot and Thiers and established a republic. "I breathe more easily feeling myself outside the atmosphere of these small and miserable parties among which we have lived for ten years. . . . The Thiers, Molé, and Guizot dynasty is overthrown, thank God, with the royal dynasty" (Letter 56). Still, although Tocqueville seeks to help steer France to a "republic strongly and regularly constituted like that of the United States" (Letter 54), he rapidly finds himself isolated and frustrated in this effort. After the June Days, the Constituent Assembly polarized, in his view, between the extremes of left and right. "We are situated between a small minority, which wants the socialist or red republic, and an immense majority, which does not want to hear of any republic whatever" (Letter 60). Once more Tocqueville can find no significant and satisfactory parliamentary alliance, and once more he feels a stranger to the political aspirations of his time. So desperate does he become that on one rare occasion he wonders if France might need a dose of force to save it from the extremes of left and right. "What can I tell you? It would be necessary to go to *reaction*. This would be the only way to save the Republic" (Letter 60).

These letters of 1848 also help disclose Tocqueville's views on historical causality and on social classes. In responding to Senior, who had suggested that the economic misery of the working classes had caused the revolution, Tocqueville emphatically denies it. Yes, admittedly there was some misery, often intense if not widespread, but, argues Tocqueville: "The revolution was not brought about by the misery of the working classes. . . . Not needs, but ideas brought about this great upheaval" (Letter 55). Thus, at first glance Tocqueville appears to be suggesting that ideas can propel history, not class needs or technological change. But what kind of ideas is Tocqueville speaking about? Tocqueville is here referring to a collection of utopian socialist ideas whose message to the working class, according to Tocqueville, is that the rich are responsible for the misery of the poor and that in a reorganized, state-controlled economy, every person can attain "ease and well-being" (Letter 55). Actually, in his other writings, Tocqueville acknowledges that the *intended* message of utopian socialists is not one laden with such hedonism and greed, but he argues that this is in fact the *communicated* message. All this might depict Tocqueville as just another defender of the middle classes, but he made it amply clear in his previous letters and in his January 1848 speech warning of an imminent revolution that the self-interest, hedonism, and greed that was infecting all of French society *originated* with the bourgeoisie.

Still Tocqueville regards these lower-class ideas about reorganizing the economy and equalizing wealth as chimerical, misguided, and dangerous. Such ideas are chimerical because France in 1848 was a nation of scarcity, clearly unable—even if willing—to eliminate poverty. These ideas are misguided because every time the socialist faction threatens a redistribution of property, business actually brings on additional working-class misery by, in a sense, going on strike—"making capital disappear, . . . suspending transactions, . . . stopping work, . . . leading immediately to the ruin of almost all private industries" (Letter 54). And, last, these ideas are dangerous because they do not capture the imagination just of the greediest "good-for-nothings" of the lower classes. They are dangerous precisely because these ideas are powerful enough to persuade so many honest and hard-working people.

Many of these men, who were marching toward the overthrow of the most sacred rights, were led by a sort of erroneous notion of right. They sincerely believed that society was founded on injustice, and they wanted to give it another basis. It is this kind of revolutionary religion that our bayonets and our cannons will not destroy. (Letter 59)

This leads to two observations. First, Tocqueville does not in fact argue that ideas *alone* propel history; indeed, in his earliest writings, he borrowed from Guizot to argue that French history was propelled by the material needs, the political aspirations, *and* the ideological struggles of the middle classes. For example, the driving idea of his century, the idea of equality, was once brandished as a weapon by the bourgeoisie in a battle with aristocratic privilege. Now, however, this idea of equality, clothed in more proletarian garb, is a weapon serving the material and political interests of the working classes. Thus, Tocqueville actually argues that ideas *and* class needs propel history, a belief we can see in a letter to Lord Radnor. "The upper classes of England would be very wrong to slumber in absolute security. We are in the midst of a general revolution. . . . There is only one way to avert and attenuate this revolution, which is to do everything that is possible to ameliorate the lot of the people before being forced to do so" (Letter 57).

The second observation serves to qualify the first. Despite the fact that Tocqueville never ceases to talk of history, politics, and revolution in class terms, he always contends that it is *possible*—if very improbable—to avoid class conflict, to establish a harmony among classes. We again see a residue of his aristocratic heritage, a belief in the desirability of cooperation and mutual obligation (however paternalistic) among classes. How else to explain the fact that at least twice in 1848 he openly puts his faith in the good sense, instinct for justice, and patriotism of the "people." Without question, his respect for the peasantry and the non-Parisian working class contrasts sharply with his contempt for the middle classes. In fact, Tocqueville attributes the immediate cause of the 1848 Revolution to the nation's leadership, a narrow plutocracy of the bourgeoisie, who (1) corrupted France with a miserable example of greed and hedonism, (2) sought neither to educate nor to improve the lot of the lower classes, and (3) used their power to extend their own self-interest, to increase poverty, and thus to nurture class conflict (Letters 55 and 57).

In the end, Tocqueville confides to Stoffels that he sees no end to France's revolutionary voyage. "Are we not on a stormy sea without a shore?" France seems fated, he says, to alternate between the self-interested rule of the middle classes and the understandable but woefully misguided revolutionary outbreaks of the working classes. "But do we not see today . . . that the cause of the illness is deeper; that the illness, in an intermittent form, will be more durable than had been imagined; that . . . any durable government whatsoever [seems impossible], and that we are destined to oscillate for a long time between despotism and liberty, without being able permanently to support either?" (Letter 59).

54. To Paul Clamorgan

Paris, March 7, 1848

My dear friend, yesterday I received your letter of March 5. First let us speak of you for a moment. I had been thinking a lot from the outset about the collector's office at Valognes. This is evidently what you have to do. It is in your interest, it is in ours, since otherwise you are leaving us just when we need both energetic and moderate people. How to place you at Valognes? That is easy, I believe, if Havin[1] actively becomes a party to it. Today's newspaper will inform you that Garnier-Pagès[2] is minister of finance. You know on what friendly terms I am with him. He spent two days at Tocqueville last year. Although I have made it a rule to ask nothing of the new government, I have decided to violate it one time in your favor and to go find Garnier-Pagès. If Havin asks on your behalf from the political point of view and I as a proof of friendship, I do not doubt that a place will be found for the current officeholder and that you will be installed at Valognes.

1. Léonor-Joseph Havin (1799-1868), a member of the Chamber of Deputies from a district very near Tocqueville's.
2. Louis-Antoine Garnier-Pagès (1803-1878), member of the Chamber of Deputies under the July Monarchy, participant in the banquet campaigns, and minister of finance under Lamartine's provisional government.

Why couldn't M. Gouget be sent to Cherbourg? I am in general an enemy of dismissals. But when it is a question of a man like M. Lemaître who has won his place only through fifteen years of electoral roguery, in truth I do not see any inconvenience in what justice might be done. Be that as it may, if M. Gouget can be accommodated, we should find a way to put him elsewhere. He must take an active part in it himself for the reason you tell me. Inform me quickly of what you have done and what must be done.

I was just now speaking of Havin, but I do not know what he can do himself at this time. I was informed a week ago that his nomination had been the occasion for an altercation at the city hall. The *violents* had reproached Ledru-Rollin[3] for the nomination of Havin.[4] Ledru-Rollin excused himself by saying

3. Alexandre-Auguste Ledru-Rollin (1807-1874) was an important radical figure in the 1848 Revolution. Under the July Monarchy, Ledru-Rollin had been a radical republican in the Chamber of Deputies and an editor of the newspaper *La Réforme*. In the February 1848 Revolution, Ledru-Rollin joined the cabinet of Lamartine's provisional government as minister of interior. In April 1848, he was easily elected to the Constituent Assembly, but the moderate Constituent Assembly sought unsuccessfully to block his appointment to the new Executive Council. Lamartine, probably sensing that he needed to make concessions to the more radical Paris population, insisted that he would not head the Executive Council if Ledru-Rollin was not chosen.

In the Constituent Assembly, the left—a distinct minority—divided itself into old-style revolutionaries who dreamed of 1789 (and called themselves Montagnards) and the new socialists. Ledru-Rollin, as a radical republican, was among the Montagnards and, as part of the government, hoped to gain progressive reform in a parliamentary fashion. Thus, radicals such as Lamartine and Ledru-Rollin offered no support to the insurrection of the working people that came to be known as the June Days. One year later, however, after Ledru-Rollin had been elected in May 1849 to the new Legislative Assembly, certain radical leaders attempted a second June insurrection that was unsupported by a skeptical populace and easily crushed. Ledru-Rollin fled to England.

In *Recollections,* Tocqueville describes Ledru-Rollin this way: In 1848, "the nation saw Ledru-Rollin as the bloody image of the Terror. . . . Ledru was nothing but a great sensual sanguine boy, with no principles and hardly any ideas; he had no true courage of mind or heart, but he was also free of malice, for by nature he wished all the world well" (p. 138).

4. Havin was appointed, along with Vieillard, commissioner of the republic in the *département* of La Manche.

that this nomination had been a surprise to him and by promising that he was going to remove Havin and name Vieillard.[5]
I had been informed too that Vieillard had refused to attain
the position in this manner. Then I saw his name in *Le Moniteur*. I imagine there was an arrangement and that Vieillard
was not substituted for but joined with Havin. I would keenly
hope that it was so, because all the little party rivalries or
rancors have ominously disappeared in the midst of this awful
torment, and if Havin had been dismissed today, moderation
would be defeated in his person. Besides, what you tell me
about his dispositions makes mentioning him still more necessary in my eyes. The nominations that he made in Valognes
are excellent. These are the people I would have named
myself.

Now let us speak of general affairs: the situation is beginning to take shape. We are seeing more clearly than we could
a week ago where the reasons for hoping and for fearing are
to be found. The news that is arriving from abroad proves
that if war is still possible, it is no longer probable. The news
that has been collected from all parts of France reveals that the
most profound tranquility reigns everywhere, that nowhere is
there serious disorder, that an immense aspiration by all
classes toward order is making itself apparent, that finally
never have fewer traces of quarrels been seen, of passions between citizens. The same truth is appearing with equal clarity
to everyone: after what has just occurred, it can no longer be
a question of royalty. The whole question is whether we will
have a good or bad republic. So it is with me; my conviction
is quite sincere. Great errors and great misfortunes could lead
France back to a dictatorship, an armed despotism. But as for
a limited monarchy, it is dead. Nothing but a republic is pos-

5. Narcisse Vieillard (1791-1857), an officer in Napoleon's army, a member
of the Chamber of Deputies under the July Monarchy, a representative to the
Constituent Assembly and Legislative Assembly under the Second Republic,
and, finally, to Tocqueville's displeasure, a senator under the Empire of Napoleon III.

sible now. Thus the fears of civil war and foreign wars are either disappearing or receding. But there are other perils. What threatens the government and society itself with more terrible disasters are not political difficulties, but economic and financial difficulties. Those are immense and formidable. For ten years, in books and today in the street, doctrines have been preached whose application is irreconcilable with the general laws that today regulate production and property. The heads of people in the working and proletarian classes have been filled with expectations that, I greatly fear, are absolutely chimerical. Each attempt that is made or that threatens to be made to realize them has the effect of making capital disappear, of suspending transactions, of stopping work, of leading immediately to the ruin of almost all private industries. I said to you in my first letter that I was expecting a great industrial crisis. I fear that it will surpass the limits I assigned to it myself in my thoughts. There is reason to fear that *all* the bankers of Paris will be led in a few days to suspend their payments. Already yesterday, the Central Bank of Gomie went bankrupt. At this news the Stock Exchange, which was going to reopen, closed, and the panic has been inexpressible. With work, comfort will disappear; with comfort, a part of the indirect revenues. Never have more calls been made on the treasury and never has the treasury found itself closer to being empty. And where is the remedy?[6] If there were still the goods of the clergy or the émigrés on which a mortgage could be taken out in order to create some paper money. It is impossible today to touch the property of someone without unsettling that of everyone else. Neither this resource nor any

6. The financial crisis that Tocqueville describes diminished greatly within a few weeks, but only after (1) all banks, including the Bank of France, sharply limited cash withdrawals, forcing people to take treasury notes instead that were redeemable only in four to six months, (2) the government increased its revenue by adding a 45 percent increase on all direct taxation (a measure angering both large and small property holders), and (3) the crisis atmosphere became less intense, allowing both stocks and bonds to recover much of their value.

other presents itself. Also, M. Goudchaux,[7] who was a very able man, just handed in his resignation. There is the cloud that floats on our horizon, the cloud from which will emerge first misery and then perhaps the popular tempest. The whole nation is now calling loudly for the National Assembly. This is indeed the only safe plank. I believe firmly that the majority of this Assembly will be very moderate. I believe this because the country as a whole is less impassioned than it has been at any time. I believe this because the people will be impelled toward men of moderation and order by *all* those who have an influence on them. Of all the men of property the most evidently exposed today are those who have those kinds of ideal properties that rest on a privilege, the bailiffs, the solicitors, the notaries, the lawyers, the doctors. Those are the men who are most threatened by the ultrademocratic doctrines of the free commune, of offices open to all without conditions, of the capacity of everyone to do everything. They are too intelligent not to sense it, and their interest, coming to the aid of their reason, will impel them energetically toward men who want to contain the movement and not to accelerate it. I therefore have the firm expectation that, if there is no oppression or treachery in the elections, the majority of the Assembly will be moderate, that it will want the republic because a reasonable man cannot imagine the possibility of anything else today, but that it will want a republic strongly and regularly constituted like that of the United States. But will it be free in Paris? Faced with this abused and hungry working population, whose ambitious members are determined to turn needs into passions, will it be able to deliberate with independence and achieve the good intentions with which it will be full? That is doubtful. In my opinion, it will have to confer all the political

7. Michel Goudchaux (1797-1862) was, as Tocqueville put it, both a banker and a radical, an unusual combination. Under Lamartine's provisional government, he was very briefly minister of finance until he resigned and was succeeded by Garnier-Pagès. After the June Days, when Cavaignac formed a new government, Goudchaux was again chosen minister of finance.

liberties possible, in order to have the right to hold firm on
the questions of property and order. But even in doing that,
will it avoid being blown away by a gust of popular wind like
the assembly that just ended, if not blown away, at least com-
pressed? I unfortunately have great doubts in this regard. And
these are doubts that make me persevere in the feelings I expressed to you the first day. My desire is not to present myself, but if my country names me, I will certainly accept, and
I expect to risk just as readily as anyone else my peace and
quiet and if need be my life in the great cause of order and
civilization in France. I will do nothing either directly or indirectly to prevent the country from choosing me. I would
think myself acting with cowardice in doing so. But if it does
not name me, I confess I will not complain of it. But if it is a
question of me or another, the people of quality must not
slumber at the approach of the election that is on the way.
The mode chosen by the decree that was in *Le Moniteur*
yesterday had this grave inconvenience, that it leaves the
population of each canton uncertain of the result of the vote
and that it delivers the election over to those who will draw
up the lists of candidates for the departments, which will
make them the most readily accepted. No kind of election
lends itself more to surprises and to disputes, and I fear the
men who got Lamartine to adopt it, despite my advice and
that of several others, had in effect the expectation of carrying
away the election with the aid of clubs and newspapers. However that may be, the instrument exists; it is only a question
now of making the best possible use of it. For that, here is my
advice: it is necessary to hasten to form electoral committees
in each arrondissement, committees composed of everyone
who has any influence on the people. It is necessary that the
committees settle on their choice and begin to communicate
with the committees of other arrondissements in order to try
to reach agreement, with the help of mutual concessions. That
is easy, since there are fifteen choices to make. And once they
are agreed, to settle on the list and have it circulate through-

out the department in the ranks of the people. If all the men interested in order do what I say, they will remain masters of the elections, and if it happens that the moderate majority is immense in the Assembly, it is possible that it will impress by its mass the popular violence and that it will save the Republic and order. Preach, my dear friend, this kind of peaceful agitation. If as a consequence of this action and of those negotiations between all the moderate men of the department, I am put forward, I have already told you, for my part, I will obey this call. If other names than mine are chosen, I will energetically lend my cooperation to this new arrangement, and I will use all the influence that remains to me to make it succeed. And so, may our friends, even the most intimate, act *with every kind of freedom of mind* and may they be convinced in advance that I will join them with all my heart in making a man other than me, one who would provide guarantees to property and good order, triumph. Everything that this letter contains, except what relates to private affairs, is not at all secret. Thus, you may make such use of it as you judge suitable.

I am stopping. My hand is tired. In several days, after I have terminated some matters that are keeping me here, I will return to Valognes and to Tocqueville. I am very impatient to chat with you and with all my friends. Until then, please continue to write me often.

I embrace you with all my heart.

P.S. Shake hands for me with Léon and Sébire. I wrote specifically to the latter yesterday morning in order to get some news.

55. *To Nassau William Senior*

Paris, April 10, 1848

My dear Monsieur Senior, I was absent when your letter arrived; I found it on my return, which took place only three

days ago. I at once proceeded to M. Austin's[8] house to find
out what had prevented you from coming to Paris. I learned
with sorrow that your health had forced you to give up your
plans. I doubly regret your absence, since it is due to this
cause; I would have been all the more satisfied to see you
since I would have drawn from your conversation especially
useful enlightenment concerning the circumstances in which
we find ourselves.

It has not escaped you that our greatest ill comes not from
violent political passions, but from the prodigious ignorance
in which the mass of the nation has been plunged concerning
the true conditions of production and social prosperity. Our
illness comes much less from false notions on politics properly
so called than from false notions on political economy.

I do not believe that the poor law about which you speak to
me is the remedy that suits the ill, for the present at least. The
revolution was not brought about by the misery of the working classes. This misery surely existed in certain respects, but
in general one could say that in no country, in no time, had
the working classes been in a better condition than in France.
That was especially true of the agricultural working class.
There, it was not the worker who lacked work, it was everywhere work that lacked workers. As a consequence of the division of landed property, the number of hands for hire was
barely sufficient. The crisis that tormented the workers of the
great factories was transitory and, although intense enough,
did not surpass known bounds. Not needs, but ideas brought
about this great upheaval: chimerical ideas on the relative condition of worker and capital, exaggerated theories on the role
that social power could fill in the relations of worker and
master, ultracentralizing doctrines that had ultimately persuaded multitudes of men that it depended only on the state
not only to save them from misery, but to give them ease and

8. John Austin (1790-1859), an eminent English lawyer, a professor of law,
and the author of *Province of Jurisprudence* (1832). Austin was an opponent of
parliamentary reforms that would extend the vote.

well-being. You understand that for this malady of minds a poor law would not be a very efficacious remedy; I am far from saying that it might not be necessary to have recourse to it. I even believe that this legitimate satisfaction should have been given to the people long ago; but it is not with the aid of this law that we can extricate ourselves from today's affair, because, I repeat, we have before us ideas even more than needs.

Three weeks before the revolution I gave a speech[9] that, reproduced by the stenographers, was inserted in *Le Moniteur.* I just had it reprinted word for word as it appears in *Le Moniteur.* I am sending you a copy; please read it; you will see that, although the form and moment of a revolution were unknown to me, I appreciated with great clarity that a revolution was going to take place. This speech, which made the Chamber clamor violently, has since been recalled to me many times by people who recognize that it is they who were wrong and I who was right. I believe that in making this speech I was on the road that would lead to uncovering the prime and profound causes of the revolution. [All my recent experience has had the effect of confirming me in the same opinions.

The great and real cause of the revolution was the detestable spirit which animated the government during its long reign; a spirit of trickery, of baseness, and of bribery, which has enervated and degraded the middle classes, destroyed their public spirit, and filled them with a selfishness so blind as to induce them to separate their interests entirely from those of the lower classes from whence they sprang, who consequently

9. Tocqueville here refers to his famous speech, delivered to the Chamber of Deputies on January 27, 1848, less than one month before the February Revolution. In this speech Tocqueville warned that the egoism, the material self-interest, the political apathy, and the corruption that originated with the middle-class leadership of the country was penetrating to the working classes. As a result, the country was in danger, perhaps immediate danger, of a new and dreadful revolution propelled by the powerful but unrealistic dreams of workers who were learning to strive solely for material self-interest.

have been abandoned to the counsels of men who, under pretence of serving the lower orders, have filled their heads with false ideas.

This is the root of the matter;] all the rest were accidents, very singular and very pressing accidents, I confess, but in the end accidents that alone would have produced nothing. Imagine on the one hand the causes I have indicated, on the other our centralization that makes France subject to one bold stroke undertaken in Paris, and you will have the whole explanation for the Revolution of 1848, as history will assuredly give it one day and as I will develop it myself, if God lends me life. Will you be so good as to offer a copy of my speech to Lord Lansdowne and remember me especially to him? I have spoken to you only of the past in this letter; to deal with the *future* would require more than one letter.

We are in the most extraordinary situation into which a great nation has ever been suddenly thrown. We are witness to great misfortunes and surrounded by great perils. My principal hope comes from the spectacle presented to me by the people properly so called. They lack enlightenment, but they have instincts that I find worthy of admiration; one encounters in them, to a degree that astonishes me and which would by its nature surprise foreigners, the sentiment of order, true love of country, and very great sense in things about which they can judge by themselves and in matters about which ambitious dreamers, to whom they had been abandoned, have not fooled them.

Farewell, my dear Senior, etc.

56. *To Gustave de Beaumont*

Tocqueville, April 22, 1848

You must have been surprised, my dear friend, that I did not answer the entirely friendly letter you wrote me the

fourth of this month and that I did not allude to it in our
interview in Paris. That is explained by the very simple reason
that I had not received it, at least not when I should have
received it. It came to Valognes while I was going to Paris.
I only found it on my return to this region.

I am writing you from Tocqueville, where I came to take
refuge from all the little electoral wrangling that is naturally
growing as the election approaches.[10] For two weeks the new
candidates have been swarming in an extraordinary manner,
and the candidates are rushing like real devils in order to make
up for lost time. The only talk is of clubs, of open-air meetings; lists cross by the thousands. The consequence of all this
movement is that outside of seven or eight names, the result
of the battle is completely in doubt and it is possible that the
Chamber will finally contain three or four members who not
only are not sympathetic to the majority of the population,
but who represent ideas that are the most antipathetical to it.
This is, one must admit, a glorious method of election! What
also disturbs me a little is the dreadful weather that there is
today and that there could very well be tomorrow. At this
moment, questions of rain or good weather are questions of
politics.

On my return here, at your direction I pushed des Essarts[11]
warmly. You will answer for it before God, if he is named
and he turns out badly. I fear that you will find it more
trouble to contain him than you think. He is terribly involved
with the violent party. The night before last, in a club in
Cherbourg, he strongly praised M. Ledru-Rollin's circular and
declared himself for a single assembly. Worse still, the evening
before in another club in which minds were of another bent
he kept to a much more moderate language, which makes one
think that he changed doctrine in changing audience. Be that

10. Both Tocqueville and Beaumont were elected to the new Constituent
Assembly on April 23, 1848.

11. Eugène des Essarts (1802-1869), local political figure in Caen, member
of the Constituent Assembly in 1848.

as it may, I had him admitted to our lists. However, I regard his election as doubtful.

As you do, my dear friend, I see clearly all the reasons that should make us hardly desire to enter the future Assembly. Like you, I believe that we will be in a very difficult position there, surrounded by difficulties, if not by perils, and perhaps called upon to pay for mistakes we will not have committed. I am no more sure than you that we will even have frequent opportunities to do anything useful for our country. I see and I believe all that, and still I would not see the doors of this Assembly closed in front of me without regret. I have several reasons for thinking so. Politics has become our career. We perhaps were wrong to take it up, but in the end we did take it up. It would grieve me to quit it at the moment that such great events are to be encountered, to become a stranger to the affairs of my country when my country is subject to such tests. I would have preferred never to have been mixed up in these affairs than to abandon them voluntarily today. It is probable that we can do nothing about it. That I concede. But it is not certain. This is such a moment of crisis that our experience, our sentiments, our ideas and, I hope, if need be, our courage can suddenly be of much greater help to our country than they would be if we simply became private persons again. Up to now we have seen only the difficulties and the annoyances of public life. Perhaps a moment will come in which the action we will undertake can be glorious. At least that is what I tell myself when I feel myself becoming discouraged at the spectacle that is presented to us by the inexperience, the profound ignorance, the madness[12] (the word often is not too strong) of those who have governed us for two months. I am not cheerful, assuredly; I expect little in the future. I hardly see anything there but disastrous events for us and for France. But I try to make myself calm and serene by thinking of what I said above. Besides, what could I tell you? I breathe more easily feeling myself outside the atmosphere of

12. Fr. = "la folie."

these small and miserable parties among which we have lived for ten years; I breathe more easily feeling myself no longer enchained by the ties of this kind of ministerial trinity that has been the divinity of these last eighteen years. We will assuredly see worse, but at least we will not see this again and that itself is something. The Thiers, Molé, and Guizot dynasty is overthrown, thank God, with the royal dynasty. Still, there is some gain in that. It seems to me that we are going to begin a new political life again, a stormy and short life perhaps, but different from the one that preceded, which hardly pleased me. What will give us our bearings in this, I hope, is our friendship, a friendship that has become more enlightened and more tolerant with experience without having become less sincere and less deep than before. Therefore, I do not want to let myself go too much to the sad thoughts that besiege me as often as they do you, and which I am trying to face up to as I am sure you do yourself.

I am not asking you for news of Antonin whom I left recovered. Give my most affectionate regards to Madame de Beaumont. Remember me to your father and believe, my dear friend, in all my feelings of lively and tender friendship.

57. *To Lord Radnor*

Paris, May 26, 1848

My lord, I do not want our friend M. Senior to leave without charging him with bringing you a letter. Yours caused me a great deal of joy and gratitude. You know what feelings of respect and affection I profess for you, and you can understand that it is never with indifference that I receive a sign of your remembrance and testimony of your friendship.

M. Senior will tell you more than I could myself at this moment on the present state of France, pressed as I am by the necessities and labors of public life. Our situation is certainly very serious; however, the integrity and good sense of the mass of the people reassures me. The conduct of this part of the nation has as yet been above all praise, and if chiefs of state capable of utilizing its good dispositions and of leading it were found, we would soon emerge from all dangerous and impracticable theories to establish the republic on the only durable bases, those of liberty and of right. Our greatest peril comes from the absence of chiefs. The old parliamentary men who appeared under the monarchy cannot take hold of affairs at this time. They would be suspect: and those being out of the way, a great scarcity makes itself felt; one does not know on whom to confer the high political offices.

England seems to me the only country in Europe in which the ground at this moment is not shaking. I nonetheless believe, if I may be permitted to express an opinion on a foreign country, that the upper classes of England would be very wrong to slumber in absolute security. We are in the midst of a general revolution of the civilized peoples, and I believe that none of them will escape it in the long run. There is only one way to avert and attenuate this revolution, which is to do everything that is possible to ameliorate the lot of the people before being forced to do so.

Mme. de Tocqueville thanks you, my lord, for remembering her. She asks you, as I do, not to fail to remember her to Lady Jane Ellice. Also please give my affection to M. Edouard, and believe in all my feelings of respectful affection.

58. To Paul Clamorgan

Paris, June 24, 1848

I am writing you, my dear friend, in the noise of cannon and of fusillade after the most terrible day and the most cruel night that one can imagine.[13] It is not a riot, it is the most terrible of all civil wars, the war of class against class, of those

13. The fighting of the June Days began on June 23, 1848, and ended on June 26.

who have nothing against those who have. I hope that we will be the stronger; the national guards from the surrounding areas are arriving en masse, the line regiments also. Nonetheless, God alone knows what will be the outcome of this great battle. If we are vanquished, something I do not believe, the reddest Republic is mistress of Paris. If this is so, the resolution of the Assembly would be to leave Paris en masse and call France to arms. I hope that France would hear it, because it is not a political form that is at issue here; it is property, family, and civilization, everything in a word that attaches us to life.

If we are vanquished, obey no order emanating from Paris; on the contrary, organize resistance in the most energetic way and trust that we will not fail you. I embrace you.

Paris, 8 o'clock in the morning

All the troops are doing their duty admirably.

3 o'clock. Fighting is continuing fiercely. But I believe we will triumph. Our forces are growing minute by minute and those of the insurgents do not seem to be increasing. But what a war, my friend, what a dreadful war! At 10 o'clock the danger became so impending that the National Assembly decided to put Paris under a state of siege, and to confer all power on General Cavaignac.[14] Immediately afterward, the Assembly decided that 60 of its members would go circulate throughout Paris with their sashes and stir up the national guard. I was chosen to be one of these 60 and for four hours I wandered about the districts that were indicated to us. I found everywhere the most energetic *resolution* to be victorious and

14. General Louis Eugène Cavaignac (1802-1857), a veteran of Algerian fighting and now given the responsibility of suppressing the June insurrection. After the June Days, the Assembly gave him extraordinary powers and named him president of the new Executive Council. Between June and the December presidential elections, Cavaignac enjoyed the strong support of both the bourgeoisie and the wealthy landlords, and virtually all of the social reforms (e.g., shortening the work day to ten hours) of the early Second Republic were abolished.

I believe that we will indeed be victorious. But what a war! Never in 60 years has such a day been seen. The bloodiest days of the French Revolution compared to this are child's play. The whole province is flocking in. 1,500 men just came to us from Amiens. Farewell. Our destiny is still in the hands of God. But I am full of good hope and above all of good courage.

59. *To Eugène Stoffels*

Paris, July 21, 1848

I do not need to tell you, my dear friend, that I wanted to write you earlier, but the events that have taken place since I received your letter speak loudly enough and furnish me easily with an excuse.

You ask me to talk politics. I would do so quite willingly if I had more time; but I lack time, and I am obliged to limit myself to very general and very summary observations.

I have never doubted for an instant since February that we would have to have a great battle in Paris. I said, repeated, and wrote it a hundred times. So the days of June surprised me only by the colossal proportions the combat took. The victory kept for us a part of the ground that the social order had lost. For the first time in four months, a regular government is possible; and although I am sure that the men who are directing affairs at this moment, and the Assembly itself, will be outdone by the necessities of the situation, and will not do all there is to do in order to achieve this goal promptly and firmly, I believe that in spite of them and by virtue of the irresistible force that events have given to ideas of order, the goal will be achieved; but great dangers are nonetheless to be feared in the very short run, others in the more distant future. The most immediate arise from the condition of financial affairs. If we continue to vote expenditures and if receipts continue to decline, we can hardly escape a financial crisis the consequence of which no one can calculate. . . . Those are the immediate perils. They are very great, very frightening. I am inclined to believe, however, that we will not succumb to them. I would not be surprised if, after these trials, the republican government takes a distinct position and works with regularity for a while. But I do not have faith in the future. I feel a profound sadness that arises much less from immediate apprehensions (although they are great) than from the absence of hope. I do not know if I still should hope to see established in our country a government that is at the same time regular, strong, and liberal. This ideal was the dream of my entire youth, as you know, and also of the portion of my adulthood that has already passed. Is it permissible to still believe in its realization? I have thought for a long time (this belief was thoroughly shaken long before February) that we had traveled and were still traveling on a stormy sea at the other side of which the port was to be found. Wasn't this a mistake? Are we not on a stormy sea without a shore? Or, at least, isn't the shore so far away, so unknown that our life and perhaps that of those who will come after us will pass before the shore is encountered and people are settled on it? It is not that I believe in an uninterrupted succession of revolutions. I believe, on the contrary, in rather long intervals of order, of tranquility, of prosperity; but in the firm and definitive establishment of a good social and political state, how can one still believe in that? One would have thought in 1789, in 1815, even in 1830, that French society was stricken by one of those violent maladies after which the health of the body social becomes more vigorous and more durable. But do we not see today that it is a matter of a chronic complaint; that the cause of the illness is deeper; that the illness, in an intermittent form, will be more durable than had been imagined; that it is not only such a government that seems impossible, but any durable government whatsoever, and that we are destined to oscillate for a long time between despotism and liberty, without being able permanently to support either? I am frightened, moreover, at the state minds appear to be in. It is far from proclaiming a revolution that is ending. It has been said many times, it is still being repeated every day, that the June insurgents were the scum of humanity, that only good-for-nothings of all kinds were to be seen among them, and that they were acting only out of the crude passion for pillage. There were many such people among them, surely; but it is not true that is all there was. Would be to God that it had been so! Men of such nature are never anything but small minorities; they never prevail. The prison and the scaffold rid you of them; all is settled. In the insurrection of June there was something other than bad propensities: there were false ideas. Many of these men, who were marching toward the overthrow of the most sacred rights, were led by a sort of erroneous notion of right. They sincerely believed that society was founded on injustice, and they wanted to give it another basis. It is this kind of revolutionary religion that our bayonets and our cannons will not destroy. It will create difficulties and perils for us that are nowhere near to being finished.

In short, I am led to ask myself if it will be possible to build anything solid and durable for a long time on the moving soil of our society, even absolute power, which so many people, weary of storms, would make do as a port for lack of anything better. We did not see this great revolution of the human species begin; we will not see it end. If I had children, I would repeat that to them unceasingly, and I would tell them every day, that we are in a time and in a society in which a person must make himself versatile and be prepared for everything, because nothing is certain about its destiny. I would add this, above all, that in this country one would be wise not to rely upon what could be taken from you, but to think solely of acquiring what can be lost only by ceasing to live: energy, courage, knowledge, active spirit. Farewell, my dear friend; in what I am saying to you that is somber about the future make allowances for the melancholy disposition into which I have been flung by the moment at which I am writing to you, and always believe in my tender affection. . . .

60. To Gustave de Beaumont

Paris, September 24, 1848

My dear friend, my last letters must have given you a fore-boding that I was uneasy about the situation, and that I found that, rather than improving, it was deteriorating. Since then, it has very much worsened or rather what I perceived at the bottom of things has appeared at the surface. You saw what happened a week ago Saturday in the Assembly and how the cabinet nearly fell on the question of sending commissioners to the départements. The idea had all sorts of external inconveniences; it had, besides, the very serious inconvenience of being as new to the greater part of the ministers as to the Assembly itself. So that the ministers were in the same mood and as suspicious toward each other as the Assembly was to-ward them. You have since seen the result of the elections. What is most serious is the nomination of Louis Napoleon[15]

15. Louis Napoleon Bonaparte (1808–1873) was the nephew of Napoleon and now heir to France's growing fascination with Bonapartism, a fascination that ignored Napoleon's authoritarian tendencies and instead pictured him as an everyday corporal who rose to greatness, an ardent patriot, a defender of the common man, a French martyr sacrificed to British intrigue. With the 1832 death of Napoleon's only legitimate son, Louis Napoleon proclaimed himself the representative of the Napoleonic tradition.

Louis Napoleon was a complicated man. He had grown up in exile, never learned to speak perfect French, fought for Italian freedom with the Carbonaros in 1830, and yet was certain he was the rightful leader of France. In 1836, at the age of twenty-eight, he appeared dramatically at a barracks at Strasbourg, persuaded some soldiers to follow him in restoring the glories of empire, and was arrested ignominiously. But after exile in the United States and England, he once more tried to storm France, this time crossing the channel with fifty followers; again he was humiliated, arrested, and sentenced to life imprisonment. After six years of prison, he escaped in the disguise of a stonemason.

By 1848 Louis Napoleon appeared to stand for almost everything; he spoke of the strong government of the empire but praised republican freedom; he wrote a mildly anticapitalistic book called *Extinction of Poverty* (1844) but had been in England working with Wellington against Chartist agitation. Above all, he seemed farcical and incompetent; too many politicians ignored him, and others like Thiers foolishly felt he was weak enough to be manipulated. It was only as the December 10, 1848, presidential election approached that the coun-try began to realize what magnetism the name Napoleon still carried. The in Paris. It is known now that he is not making his way by means of the socialists, but by means of the national guard, which misery is pushing to this kind of despair as it pushes the workers to the barricades. This symptom and many others that are appearing in the provinces and that indicate the kind

---

poems of Hugo, the songs of Pierre Jean de Béranger, the histories of people such as Thiers, and the pictures of Napoleon in homes all over the country—all had kept alive Napoleon's mystique. The election was an avalanche; Louis Napoleon received 5.4 million votes to Cavaignac's 1.5 million, and the three moderately radical candidates (Ledru-Rollin, François Raspail, and Lamartine) could not even total a half-million votes among them.

In his presidential years, Louis Napoleon relied upon the moderate-to-conservative majority in the new Legislative Assembly; he rescinded universal suffrage, sent troops to defend the pope against Mazzini's successful republican revolt in Rome, and signed the Falloux Law in 1850, which gave the church much more influence in secondary education. From the Assembly, however, he sought two things: (1) a constitutional reform allowing him to run for a second term, and (2) more money to pay his enormous, and widely suspect, personal debts. When the Assembly refused, he planned for a coup d'état. On December 2, 1851 (the anniversary of Austerlitz), he dissolved the Assembly, arrested its members (including Tocqueville), and suppressed resistance by killing several hundred and arresting at least 25,000 people across France. At the same time, he reinstated universal suffrage, declared a ten-year term for a president, and severely curtailed the Assembly's powers. He asked the voters to approve the new arrangement, and on December 20, 1851, the voters ratified the changes overwhelmingly. In 1852, he announced the Second Empire and declared himself Napoleon III.

The Second Empire was, of course, oppressive, and its institutions were but the shadow of real parliamentary government. The emperor's support came partly from the church hierarchy, which applauded his support of the church, the pope, and social order. Yet Napoleon III, drawing on ideas from his Saint-Simonian youth, also proved adept at using the state to engineer economic growth and prosperity. Thus, as railways, mines, and factories prospered, he also enjoyed the backing of the Second Empire's bourgeoisie, a class famous under the Second Empire for wild speculation, vulgar taste, and corruption. Finally, Napoleon III even made some attempts at social legislation to help the working classes: a land bank to lend money to peasants, hospitals and free medicine, improved public education, and the legalization of unions and strikes in 1864.

In the late 1860s, Louis Napoleon began hesitant steps toward liberalization and quasi-parliamentary government, steps that may or may not have been successful. But in July 1870, France and Prussia went to war. Sensing defeat, Napoleon III sought a hero's death in the battle of Sedan but instead was captured on September 1, 1870, and his empire ended.

of horror with which the Republic is viewed, and the eagerness with which any alternative would be adopted, no matter what, has thrown a profound alarm into every mind, those of governors as well as those of the governed. Some great ruckus is expected from Louis Napoleon at any moment. I am convinced this is exaggerated and that most of these fears are chimerical. But this situation is very serious all the same. What is more serious in it in my eyes is the rapid diminution of Cavaignac's popularity within the Assembly and without. You tell me that Cavaignac's fall would be a great misfortune. By God! I know it only too well. It is because of this that I am so frightened. You add that, for fear of unsettling him, his cabinet must not be unsettled. I know this well, that is surely my own opinion and I am voting accordingly. This is why I feel this mixture of fear and irritation when I see the inability, the blundering and, let us say it, between ourselves, the profound mediocrity with which these indispensable and irreplaceable men today are conducting affairs; when I perceive them being diminished gradually without anything growing up beside them; when I discover at last that the *improvement* bought so dearly in June is disappearing and that we find ourselves again facing a country that is so uncertain, so divided, so uneasy and that is more miserable than before, I confess to you that for my part I believe less today in the future of the Republic than I did on June 22. Then we had, it is true, the perspective of battle, but also the hope of victory, and after victory, of a definite, energetic reaction in favor of order. And today, this unique opportunity is almost lost. I know well that the government is being asked to do an impossible thing, to reestablish order suddenly and to provide for the recovery of business, and that it is making itself less popular not only by its mistakes and its incapacity, but also by events that merit and good behavior would not prevent. They surely could never have done all that was expected of them. But how much better they could have done than they are doing! They themselves feel that the ground is beginning to give way beneath

them and that is what induced them yesterday to request a
vote of confidence in the Assembly. I knew that the previous
evening Cavaignac himself had had an interview, which he
demanded (this very much between us), with Rémusat[16] and
Barrot, and that he asked them for their support in case he
needed it. In such a way that I was expecting that before requesting the vote of confidence, he would give an account of
his politics likely to establish a new line between these men of
tomorrow and himself and to sever himself definitively from
the Mountain.[17] But not at all. They had chosen an unknown
dolt whose name is, I believe, Sautayra, to bring the question,
and he carried out his task very ridiculously. After which, Cavaignac came to make an appeal for conciliation in good
terms, but in basically a most insignificant manner. After
which, the man who had been chosen to propose the order of
the day and who belongs to the active party read its formula.
And the Assembly voted almost unanimously. All that as you
might believe did not strengthen anyone and it is not such
remedies that will cure the formidable sickness to which one
has to administer. It is a case of saying, like Sieyès:[18] "We are

16. Charles de Rémusat (1797-1875), a member of the Chamber of Deputies
throughout the July Monarchy and, in the 1840s, part of Thiers's opposition.
Rémusat was also elected to both assemblies under the Second Republic.
Rémusat, however, was more than a politician; he was a journalist, a historian,
a member of the French Academy, a writer for Le Globe (along with Sainte-
Beuve, Vigny, and Balzac), and eventually the author of Mémoires de ma vie (5
vols., not published until 1958-1967), covering nearly eight decades of French
history.
17. During the French Revolution, the National Convention, which first
met in 1792, divided into the more moderate Girondists and the radicals. The
radicals gathered in the highest seats of the chamber, and they were therefore
referred to as the Mountain. Members of the Mountain were called Mountain-
eers or Montagnards. The most famous Montagnard was, of course, Robespierre. In the Constituent Assembly of 1848, the radicals once again climbed to
the highest seats of the chamber and called their group the Mountain. Tocqueville regarded these Montagnards as poor imitators of the past.
18. This is the 1789 revolutionary, Abbé Sieyès (1748-1836), whose famous
pamphlet What Is the Third Estate? (1789) attacked the nobility and declared that
the Third Estate represented the nation. Sieyès was also a member of the

today what we were yesterday, we are deliberating"; in my opinion, there is only one remedy; it would be heroic and perhaps it is too late to use it. It would involve the government, breaking openly and violently not only with the Mountain, but with all the *hills* that adjoin it, throwing itself boldly to the head of all those who want to reestablish order to whatever nuance they belong; circumstances are too serious for one to stop even before men for whom one feels the most legitimate repugnance. It would even be necessary to call upon some of M. Thiers's friends. In the provinces, it would be necessary energetically to put power solely back into the hands of those who would exercise it in this way. What can I tell you? It would be necessary to go to *reaction*. This would be the only way to save the Republic, to bind hearts and hopes to it a little and to make Cavaignac's candidacy succeed. Do not judge affairs, I pray you, by your memories of a month ago. They are misleading. The position, without being absolutely different from what it was when you left it,[19] is nonetheless prodigiously changed. The honest and moderate part of the Republic has almost disappeared outside of the Assembly. We are situated between a small minority, which wants the socialist or red republic, and an immense majority, which does not want to hear of any republic whatever. That is the true situation. The Assembly today is suspended between these two extremes without anything to support it. Its majority no longer, as it were, represents anything in the country. You understand that in such an illness, it is not suitable to apply palliatives and that to believe that it is enough to prolong the legislative powers in order to keep them for a long time, in the face of a country so disposed, is a chimera. You will understand the sadness I feel in seeing the government, which, facing this formidable situation, vacillates, gropes,

Convention in 1792, then of the Directory, and finally a key figure in Napoleon's coup d'état in 1799.

19. Beaumont was named ambassador to England on August 7, 1848, and was now living in London.

maneuvers, strikes at the right after having struck at the left, wants to conciliate things and men that are irreconcilable and in this way is losing the hours of grace that fortune is leaving to it. Do I need to tell you that confidence is not being reestablished, that business is not recovering, that the future is short for everyone, that everyone is anticipating something unknown of which people have a foreboding without being able to define it and that in the end misery is taking colossal proportions?

Pardon me for blackening your imagination this way. Perhaps I am exaggerating. I hope so without believing it. In any case, I needed to unburden myself of this weight with you. Although you are hardly in a better state to find a remedy for this evil than I, it is a sort of pleasure for me to complain to you, all the more as I am confiding all that I have just told you to you alone.

Everything you tell me about foreign politics is very curious and very wise.[20] Do not believe that I am of the opinion that one should appear *easily satisfied* in advance. That is neither my thought nor my ostensible language. But I thought it useful to let you know what I believe to be the truth, as seen not only by me, but by informed political opinion itself. War at this moment, I will confess, would appear to me to be the end of the world. I will give you, in the greatest secrecy, a piece of news that has given me great pleasure and that will do the same for you, undoubtedly. I believe it to be certain that Vivien[21] is being sent to conclude the arrangement of the Ital-

20. The question concerns how France should react to Italian attempts—especially by Piedmont, Venice, and Milan—to remove Austria from Italy. At this point in time, France was reluctant to become involved, fearing war with Austria and perhaps England.

21. Alexandre-François-Auguste Vivien (1799-1854), a member of the Chamber of Deputies under the July Monarchy. Tocqueville is referring to the following development. Austria agreed to accept mediation by France and England in the Italian struggles for independence, and Vivien was selected to represent France in negotiations with Austria at Brussels. On October 13, 1848, Cavaignac appointed Vivien minister of public works, and the negotiations

ian affair, I imagine to Vienna. Although his mind lacks a little in breadth, this is nevertheless an excellent choice. Vivien's intention is to stay in close contact with you. Perhaps he has already written you. In any case, if I am the first to let you know of this, keep it *entirely to yourself* and do not appear to know about it.

I end where I should have begun, which is to thank you for all the very kind things that you said to me concerning my address. These testimonials of your old friendship went straight to my heart. That is all I can say to you. I will seize the first opportunity to have some copies of this address passed along to you. They will bear the names of the people to whom I ask you to have them forwarded.

The life I lead has, besides, so fatigued me that last Saturday I finally fell ill, or at least became so indisposed that I had to ask for a few days vacation. I returned to the Assembly yesterday. I am no longer ill. But I am not in good health and this circumstance together with several other factors will no doubt prevent me from taking my turn at speaking on the question of the two Chambers,[22] as I was hoping to do.

Farewell, a thousand affectionate remembrances to Madame de Beaumont and to you a very tender and very sincere friendship.

61. *To Paul Clamorgan*

Paris, December 22, 1848

My dear friend, I have amends to make to you and I hasten to offer them. The most recent events had made me, I con-

---

were about to fall to Tocqueville himself. Soon, governmental changes in Austria and Louis Napoleon's election in France put an end to this enterprise before it began.

22. Tocqueville was chosen by the Constituent Assembly to be on the committee responsible for drafting a new constitution. He and Barrot argued for the necessity of two legislative chambers, but the committee voted overwhelmingly in favor of only one.

fess, doubt in your friendship; various lying rumors that were directed to my attention had made this distressing impression so serious, that I thought I had to write some of my friends and yours to clear up the painful doubt I was experiencing. Well, I have just received their responses, including that of Ste. Colombe, who furnished me the proofs that I had been mistaken. I therefore ask you to pardon me for my absurd doubts, and I extend you my hand in friendship. This much said and understood, let us return again to chatting as freely as before.

I will not speak to you of politics in general. You know as much on that point as I can know myself. I therefore will limit myself to informing you about what concerns me personally. The new administration very much wanted to offer me, and even to press me into keeping, the diplomatic mission that the preceding had charged me with.[23] I refused, even though the position is magnificent. I did so for reasons of delicacy that you better than anyone are in a position to understand. To accept from one's friends in power a great office and to keep it when they yield the place to others, to pass without any transition from the *confidence* of one cabinet to the *confidence* of another, that would be to conduct oneself with vulgar ambition and like an upstart. I have too much pride for that. Besides, at all times, but especially in times of revolution, power is worth very little, whereas moral power doubles in price. Moreover, by the medium of Vieillard, I explained at length to the new ministers themselves and to the President that I was not intending to make of this action an act of opposition. That on the contrary my intention was to support the new government with all my strength, if it intended to stay within the terms of the constitution. I would even be able to do so much more freely when it was clearly to be seen that I

23. Tocqueville here refers to the negotiations with England and Austria scheduled to take place in Brussels. Soon after the election of Louis Napoleon on December 10, Beaumont resigned as ambassador to England, and Tocqueville declined this diplomatic mission.

was not acting out of any interested motive. If, on the contrary, I kept my mission, my consent could appear interested, and consequently I would not give it in a lax manner, out of fear of public opinion. Today, I am free to show what I think, namely that it is the duty of all friends of the country to sustain the new government and the distinguished men it has called to itself. I also feel great relief in thinking that this action retrospectively negates all the calumnies that could have been spread on account of the support I gave, and that I do not repent having given, to General Cavaignac's candidacy. How many people, on reading in *Le Moniteur* of my nomination, said to their neighbor or said to themselves: we finally have the secret and interested motive that made M. de Tocq. act. M. de Tocq. is no more than anyone else above the motives of ambition that have directed so many others? Hand on your heart, did you not yourself feel these detestable thoughts cross your mind? All right! There you are *done in,* convicted of injustice, of calumny, of the crime of outrage against friendship! That is the only revenge I want to extract from you.

Farewell, I embrace you with all my heart.

Five

LOUIS NAPOLEON AND THE EMERGENCE OF THE SECOND EMPIRE (1849–1851)

In the middle of the Second Republic, Tocqueville describes to Gobineau the "more and more profound obscurity" that surrounds the future. "Picture to yourself a man who is traveling on a December night that is moonless and accentuated by mists. . . . This man is the whole of France" (Letter 65). An opaque future frustrates Tocqueville because, as much as any political thinker in history (including Marx), Tocqueville focuses one eye on the approaching horizon, always evaluating the tendencies and conflicts of the present in order to infer probable developments in the future. He now begins to wonder, in a letter to Harriet Grote, if the future might be incomprehensible to the men and women of his time. Yes, he says, we do cherish the principles of liberty, individual self-reliance, and private property, but perhaps the old world built on such virtues is "quite used up" and "breaking down a little every day."

History teaches me that none of the men who have been present at the destruction of religious or social organizations that the world has already seen, could foretell or even imagine what was to follow. (Letter 67)

Despite his confession of modesty, Tocqueville characteristically is able to offer a rather accurate assessment of the second half of the nineteenth century, a half-century more characterized by armed force—in securing domestic order, national unification, and colonial expansion—than the previous half-century. In the first letter of this section, Tocqueville emphatically declares that the peaceful attempt of the Frankfurt National Assembly to unify Germany will fail, and he correctly predicts that Prussia will unify the principalities by force because it has "the only organized force that exists in Germany, the army" (Letter 62). In a similar vein, Tocqueville offers us one of the most enduring portraits of the contradictory personality of the soon-to-be-Emperor Napoleon III: "audacious" yet "lymphatic," a man who dreams of absolute power, yet apparently remains content to work within republican institutions for as long as possible, a man unwilling to "abandon the imperial idea at his last breath," yet hesitant to violate the law (Letter 63; also see Letter 64). Nevertheless, Tocqueville sees an inevitable clash between Louis Napoleon's desire for power and a hostile Assembly, and he eventually acknowledges that the solution will involve force. Again, however, the pettiness of the spectacle bothers Tocqueville as much as the inevitable clash. "The President . . . is the poorest usurper who will ever present himself before a great nation. . . . After having passed through the hands of the greatest men of modern times, here we are ready to throw ourselves into the arms of I do not know what weak and mediocre conquerer, who would be classified only somewhere between Espartero and Iturbide" (Letter 64).

Still, Tocqueville deems the fight to preserve republican liberty the most important fight of his time, and he does his best, though frustrated by his renewed parliamentary isolation: "There is only one determination that I am sure of always following: to make our liberties triumph through this crisis, or to succumb with them. All the rest is secondary, but this is a question of life or death" (Letter 69). When Louis Napoleon's coup finally descended, Tocqueville, along with about 230 other representatives, resisted as well as a powerless Assembly could, but parliamentary words were far too late to defeat rifles, prisons, and deportation. At some danger to himself, Tocqueville made one final plea on behalf of the republic, a plea to English public opinion. In a strongly worded letter to the *London Times,* he condemned the coup and attempted to kindle English moral outrage against Louis Napoleon.

Such, Sir, is the condition in which we stand. Force overturning law, trampling on the liberty of the press and of the person, deriding the popular will, in whose name the Government pretends to act. . . . If the judgement of the people of England can approve these military saturnalia, . . . I shall mourn for you and for ourselves, and for the sacred cause of legal liberty throughout the world. (Letter 70)

After a brief flurry of concern, England became content that order had been restored in France.

Tocqueville's participation in a defiant but dissolved Legislative Assembly was his final political act, and one is tempted to be grateful that he had to turn away from what even he regarded as the sterile, insubstantial debates of everyday politics and return to more far-reaching political speculation. Actually, in his 1850 winter vacation to Sorrento, more than a year before the end of his political career, Tocqueville was able to distance himself from day-to-day politics, and he began to reflect on broader political issues. He continued to make progress on his *Recollections,* but now he projected his lifelong yearning for accomplishing something grand onto a new intellectual task, eventually of course *The Old Regime and the French Revolution.*

It seems to me that my true worth is above all in works of the mind; that I am worth more in thought than in action; and that, if there remains anything of me in this world, it will be much more the trace of what I have written than the recollection of what I will have done. The last ten years, which have been rather sterile for me in many respects, have nonetheless given me the truest insights into human affairs and a more practical sense of the details. (Letter 68)

He confides that he is seeking a "great subject of political literature," one that would allow "an ensemble of reflections and insights on the current time, a free judgment on our modern societies and a forecast of their probable future" (Letter 68).

In this letter, Tocqueville reveals several key ideas underlying his method of understanding and writing about politics. First, like his contemporary Michelet and his later admirer Wilhelm Dilthey, Tocqueville contends that the historian must not only recount factual information but must also resurrect and re-create for the reader the feelings, aspirations, and meanings of a particular epoch. Thus, the discipline of history is a hybrid; it must embrace both the factual demands of a social science and the communicative skills of literature or art. Tocqueville in fact uses artistic metaphors in describing his methodology; for example, a historical event "serves me as an occasion to paint the men and the affairs of our century, and permits me to make one picture out of all these detached paintings." Second, the historian or political analyst must not merely reconstruct and depict historical facts and events. The historian cannot avoid, and should not pretend to avoid, interpretation—judgments about what is significant, what is causally important, what is beneficial or pernicious. "What I have best succeeded in up to now is in judging facts rather than recounting them." Finally, Tocqueville openly acknowledges that he weaves history and political analysis together with philosophy. "The difficulties are immense. The one that most troubles my mind comes from the mixture of history properly so called with historical philosophy. I still do not see how to mix these two things (and yet, they must be mixed, for one could say that the first is the canvas and the second the color . . .) ." When Tocqueville says flatly that it is essential to choose the facts well in order to "support the ideas," it is hardly surprising to any reader of *Democracy in America* or *The Old Regime and the French Revolution,* but it does have an odd ring to the modern social scientist (Letter 68; see also Letter 74). After 1851, in his forced isolation from politics, Tocqueville became free to pursue his political ideas with all his available energy.

62. To Gustave de Beaumont

Frankfurt, May 18, 1849

My dear friend, although I wrote you a week ago from Bonn,[1] I have not received any news from you. As a result I am absolutely without letters from France, because I had only asked for correspondence from you and from my father (who must not be in Paris). My father's silence is explained by his remoteness. But yours disturbs me. However, I do not want to speak to you of all the more or less painful impressions I am receiving from France. I hardly know what has happened since my departure and, besides, what I would say to you now would perhaps no longer have any connection with the state of things when you receive my letter. I would rather say something to you about this country, the affairs of which are becoming more and more serious. The newspapers must have informed you that Germany has been in a state of crisis. Nothing could be more true. The moderate party, which wanted unity without the destruction of the old order of things, having failed in its attempt to find a point of leverage on the princes and particularly on the king of Prussia, lost its balance and has fallen into the arms of the purely revolutionary party, to which it delivered itself, but with hesitations and anxieties that are paralyzing its strength. The revolutionary party has thus acquired the majority in the Diet[2] and has put

1. Tocqueville visited Germany in May 1849, partly in order to witness the political events sparked by France's 1848 Revolution. While he was gone, elections for the new Legislative Assembly were held on May 13, and despite the fact that he did not campaign, that he was not in the country, and that he had supported Cavaignac, he was still reelected handily. Beaumont was also elected without difficulty.

2. What Tocqueville mistakenly calls a "Diet" is actually the German National Assembly. During the March Days of 1848, when France's Revolution sparked revolutionary activity in Austria, Prussia, and other German principalities, a self-constituted committee, calling itself a preliminary parliament, organized parliamentary elections based on universal manhood suffrage for all of Germany. As a result, the German National Assembly—theoretically represent-

legality on its side; thus it cries "Long live the Constitution!" as "Long live the Charter!" on July 27 and "Long live reform!" on February 24 were cried. Almost all the small governments of Germany, which happen to be in the most revolutionary part of the country, are being more or less dragged along after this party. On their side, the great states, at the head of which is Prussia, are finally being cast down the road of resistance, and lean resolutely on their armies. There are therefore two laws, two governments, two German forces facing each other, between which all dealings have become impossible. You must perceive that from afar as well as I, but of what you can have no idea, is the inexpressible confusion that exists at this moment in this country, the universal agitation, the revolutionary centers that are swarming from all sides in the midst of this excessive decentralization and, most of all, the profound ignorance which everyone confesses to having about the nearest future. Moreover, yesterday in Frankfurt, the fight began officially between the Assembly and the vicar of the Empire, and at any time it may descend into the street; so, I have my bag packed and am ready at any instant to reach the railroad train and the Rhine.

---

ing all the people of Germany but unfortunately without power to enforce any legislation—met in Frankfurt on May 18, 1848.

The aspirations of most members of the National Assembly were moderate enough. The members sought a united or federated Germany, a parliamentary government that was democratic without becoming too egalitarian, and a constitutional government that secured private rights. In short, most delegates sought to bring about a united and liberal Germany through peaceful means. In April 1849, they completed a new constitution for a new empire or Reich. After Austria refused to join, the National Assembly proposed a new federation of states (minus Austria) headed by Frederick William IV, king of Prussia. The king, however, refused to accept; he feared trouble with Austria, he knew this National Assembly had no authority to bind the smaller German principalities, and he did not like elected assemblies. In the end, he said he would accept only if all his fellow princes freely offered him this authority.

Thus, peaceful unification of Germany failed, and most delegates went home, although some radicals remained to urge more forceful political action. The Prussian army easily managed to suppress them. As Tocqueville predicted, Germany would be unified only by force of Prussian arms.

What will be the result of this immense conflict? No one can say. However, I believe the princes will be victorious. They possess the only organized force that exists in Germany, the army. When I say *they,* I mean to say only the king of Prussia, because Austria is too occupied at home to busy itself with Germany, and the secondary states are not sure of their soldiers. But everything indicates that the Prussian army remains sound. The army in Prussia is the homeland, and an esprit de corps reigns there which will apparently hold it together for some time yet. There were symptoms and even acts of rebellion in the Landwehr, but these events do not appear to be spreading. The army of Baden, however, just gave a very dangerous example to all the German armies. It expelled or killed its officers and put noncommissioned officers or soldiers in their place. Be that as it may, what I have heard gives me reason to believe that the Prussian army will remain loyal, and, if so, I believe the princes will be victorious. As an additional reason, they are up against the revolutionary party, which seems to me to be similar in every respect to our own, that is to say violent, thoughtless, and always obedient to its passions and not to its reason. But the victory of the Prussians will end nothing, I believe. This country appears to me deeply agitated and discouraged by the spirit of revolution, by disgust at existing institutions, by the vague passion for change. Moreover, because there is nowhere either a head or a center to be found, if it is difficult to make the revolution triumph with a single blow, it is impossible too to suppress it with just one. Moreover, it must be assumed that, even in the middle of this formidable crisis, Prussia is not abandoning the tradition of ambitious politics that has been its distinctive characteristic for a century. I believe that the king of Prussia has refused the supremacy the Assembly offered him in the name of the revolution only with the intention of obtaining it by repressing this revolution, and that all his acts are going to bear the imprints of an *interested* passion, which will very much increase the perils, already so great, of the position this king has taken. He plays a part in which his throne and his life are at stake, and it is very foolish of him to dream of increasing his power when he will already have so much trouble saving his old power.

The entire part of Germany that is adjacent to us is going to become an immense, very active, revolutionary center. I believe that, faced with this state of affairs, we would do well to reinforce our garrison in the east. But above all not the army for reconnaissance that has been announced. Its presence alone behind the Rhine would turn against us the revolutionary passions of Germany and would serve the restoration of the old order of things more than anything else. Speak of this and repeat it, I beg you, to those who are conducting affairs.

Although my wife's and my health have caused me many annoyances since my departure, nonetheless, the spectacle that I have before me excites my interest to the highest degree and every day presents me with a thousand new ideas, even on things I thought I knew. Frankfurt was marvelously chosen for the purpose of obtaining an idea of the revolutionary party of which it is the head. But the trip would be very incomplete if I could not go spend a week in Berlin, where the head and the center of the resistance is. I would therefore desire very strongly to be able to prolong my absence for about a week; that would put my return in the first week of June instead of the end of May. I find that, since I have come so far to make so useful a study, it is painful, for want of a week, to leave it almost barren. That will depend, however, on the news I receive from France. Write me, please, at general delivery in Cologne. I believe there is nothing to put in the newspapers about my trip. That would uselessly attract sufficient attention to my absence for some of our colleagues to be able to reprimand me.

I will tell you no more right now. My letter can only leave tomorrow morning. I will wait until then to close it.

Thursday night. The mail from France just arrived and still does not bring me anything from you. This absence of all

communication makes me despair, all the more so as reading
the newspapers gives me greater desire to know in more detail
what is happening. I hope that you are not ill. I saw your
name and those of our friends in the last ballots. How does it
happen that I am not receiving anything?

63. *To Gustave de Beaumont*[3]

Paris, November 4, 1849

I am taking advantage of the courier who leaves tomorrow,
my dear friend, in order to complete the news that the letter
I wrote you by mail contained.

There are accidental and superficial causes that could
have precipitated the crisis[4] that has just taken place. But the
profound and permanent cause is, on the one hand, the conviction the President had formed that not only would we not
aid him in the final coup d'état, but that we would not let him
prepare himself for it and place himself in a situation to do
without us on that day; on the other hand, the desire to govern and above all to appear to govern by himself. He believed
that little by little he was being allowed to fall into obscurity
and that the country would ultimately lose sight of him. He
wanted to appear completely independent of us and the National Assembly. It is for that reason that he chose the moment when we were most assured of having the majority,
and, instead of taking the leaders of this majority as ministers,
he sought the men he wanted to use in the lowly parts of the
parties. Those, indeed, will neither cover him nor hide him
from scrutiny. There you have the true causes of the event.

It is more difficult to say what the consequences will be.

3. Tocqueville was named minister of foreign affairs in Barrot's second
cabinet on June 2, 1849. On September 17, 1849, Tocqueville selected Beaumont to be ambassador to Vienna.

4. On October 31, 1849, President Louis Napoleon formed a new cabinet,
and Tocqueville's brief appointment as minister of foreign affairs was over. As
soon as Beaumont heard the news in Vienna, he resigned his post.

Probably, someone will write you that an imperialistic attempt is imminent; that this is only the very near precursor of something greater and more decisive; this is the most widespread belief and I must say that the leaders of the parties themselves are fairly disposed to think this way and they feel a great anxiety. I think they are wrong. I have studied the President enough to have insights on him that are peculiar to myself. The President is a monomaniac who will only abandon the imperial idea at his last breath; he is audacious to the point of imprudence and folly; but at the same time he is lymphatic and apathetic; he does not do two things in succession. He has just given himself great satisfaction for his self-esteem; he believes himself to have humiliated the Assembly and all the party leaders and to have become considerably enlarged in the eyes of France. That suffices him for the moment. He is going to live on that for some time until a new thorn prick wakes him up and makes him leap over the ditch. I know that what is true of him is not true of the members of his entourage. There, they only breathe adventure. If I am well informed, they are summoning all the *ruffians* of the party around him; they are forming a new association of the *tenth of December;* in a word, they are preparing themselves for war. But they will not carry the master along immediately. Such, at least, is my forecast. We will see whether the future proves me wrong.

What is going to happen now between the President and the Assembly? A great and difficult question that embraces our entire future.

By this time, the President has the *entire* majority of the Assembly against him.[5] He has injured it deeply, and prudence alone is containing it. But will he not want or will he not be able to win it back?

I believe he is on bad terms with Thiers.[6] The latter sensed

5. The legislative majority under Louis Napoleon's presidency was conservative and, to a large extent, monarchist.

6. Thiers had supported Louis Napoleon's presidential efforts, thinking Louis Napoleon would be easily controlled. Thiers had even chosen many of

that he had no role to play with this man who is as *ungovernable as he is incapable of governing.* Several incidents that would take too long to recount to you have, moreover, put incurable wounds of self-esteem between them. I repeat that, however mobile Thiers may be, I believe him alienated forever. I think I can say the same of the legitimists. You see that they have no representative in the cabinet. The message was particularly insulting to them. Moreover, I think the President's idea is that he must make himself popular at their expense. Therefore they are and will remain, I believe, enemies.

Molé is always for sale. He is the dirtiest intriguer of the whole pack. He reminds me of those old libertines who still do their filthy acts with women when they no longer can do anything else, so irresistible a habit has vice become to them.

Thus, there are several principal parties in the majority that appear to be alienated for all time and determined not to concur in the resurrection of the Empire. I would not dare say as much of the total mass of it, and I am even inclined to believe that the President would win it back easily and make it serve his plans if he had the will and the talent for it. The mass that does not like the Empire likes the Republic even less and above all shudders at giving access to the reds. To avoid them, the mass would throw itself into the arms of the devil. It is, moreover, composed in part of men who have *local* satisfaction to pursue and who could be taken one by one by means of that. The new administration is going to apply itself to that bluntly; it is going to place itself on its knees before all the members of the majority and cry mercy to them. Composed for the most part of people who have been paid for, but who are mediocre and timid, it is going to try to make peace between the majority and the President, so that the coup d'état toward which they feel themselves being dragged along will

---

the president's first ministers, but the president soon began to quarrel with them.

have the least amount of violence and the least possible danger.

But that is not the master's point of view. He has among a number of fixed notions this, *of the existence of which you can be certain:* he does not want at any price to be or above all to appear to be the instrument or agent or creation or protégé of a parliamentary majority. Far from fearing war with the Assembly, he wishes for it; he seeks opportunities to humiliate the Assembly, to appear in the eyes of France larger and stronger than he is. Charles X was never more infatuated with his name and with his prerogative than this man is. Count on the above. I believe, therefore, that, however much good will the majority may have to give, it will find it difficult to succeed, and that, in injuring its self-esteem, it will be given the impetus of anger. But this is only a forecast and the external forces that are pushing the majority and the President to be on good terms are so great that perhaps union will ultimately be reestablished between them. I do not need to tell you that that would be the almost immediate ruin of the Republic.

As for us, our path is so clearly marked that there is no merit to be had in following it. We must, for a time, hold ourselves very much aside. This attitude is consistent with our dignity, with our interests. The best way to bring about a repatriation between the majority and the President would be to intervene. It is necessary to leave these two powers face to face. They very likely will collide. They would draw closer if we intervened. We must therefore hold ourselves in observation, ready to take advantage of all the opportunities that will permit us to aid the majority in its fight with power, if this fight must take place. This role is all the easier now than if we were in the Assembly, as in the country we enjoy a universal good will. Never has a fallen administration had fewer enemies. The intriguers who attacked us thinking to succeed us are kicking themselves about it, and the bulk of their friends, seeing that they had been made to undertake a bad campaign, are trying to demonstrate their regrets at not having been more sympathetic to us and, were it not for fear of the reds, they would wage a violent war tomorrow against the President on our behalf. The most useful and most worthy role to play, faced with this situation, is to watch and wait. That is the one we are going to take until there is a new order.

The whole diplomatic corps demonstrated very keen regrets that seemed sincere to me. Hübner,[7] whom I met yesterday evening, cordially repeated these impressions. He assured me again in the same conversation that you had caught on admirably in Vienna, that M. de Schwarzenberg[8] set the highest value on you. He added: *"He is certainly the most distinguished agent you have today in your diplomatic service."* Thus you see, my dear friend, that I did not make too bad a choice.

I am sending you two private letters from Lamoricière, one of which arrived the day after the departure of our last courier and the other of which arrived yesterday. Things went as well in St. Petersburg as in Vienna. People were hesitating, and yet they were not growing cool with us. The twofold goal was attained. In short, you will have rendered, you and Lamoricière, an immense service to the country in this affair.

Farewell, I will add a postscript to my letter if some new incident occurs before the courier's departure. I embrace you with all my heart. Remember us very affectionately to Madame de Beaumont.

I was just named president of my bureau, even though the President's friends did join together with the reds in order to get me out of the way.

---

7. Joseph-Alexandre Hübner (1811-1892), ambassador from Austria to France.

8. Prince Félix Schwarzenberg (1800-1852), chief minister to Emperor Francis Joseph I, who ascended the throne in December 1848. With a finesse that perhaps exceeded even Metternich, Schwarzenberg opposed self-government, constitutional rights, and nationalistic aspirations within the Austrian Empire. At the same time, he sought to use the centralized state to promote commercial and industrial interests.

64. To Gustave de Beaumont

Paris, November 28, 1849

My dear friend, after having received the letters in which you urged me not to let M. Marchand leave for Vienna, I had indeed placed obstacles in the way of his departure, although I thought that the complaints that M. de Quer brought down on me from all sides were at least exaggerated, considering that he was crying he was *removed from office,* whereas his situation was not *materially* changed, although in importance it might be lessened. A letter has been brought to my attention, moreover, in which M. de Quer himself recognized that people were not wrong about M. Marchand: however, as I told you, because of you I had stopped M. Marchand just as he was leaving and I was seeking another destination for him when I myself left the Ministry. My successor carried out M. Marchand's nomination, who, independently of his merit, of which people speak highly, and of his numerous and warm friends, furthermore belongs to the de Lesseps[9] tribe, a tribe powerful in the Ministry of Foreign Affairs. M. Marchand therefore leaves tonight to take his post directly and I am taking advantage of it to write you with an open heart, which I could not do three or four days ago, by mail.

By a rather singular coincidence, Lamoricière's resignation arrived almost at the same time as yours. General La Hitte,[10] who reported this situation to me yesterday, told me that

9. Members of the de Lesseps family had been associated with the diplomatic service since the seventeenth century. During the Second Republic, Ferdinand de Lesseps (1805-1894)—most famous for later building the Suez Canal (1859-1869)—was sent to negotiate between Mazzini's newly proclaimed Roman republic and the French forces sent to suppress the revolt and restore the conservative papacy. De Lesseps signed a treaty, allowing French troops to enter the city only if France respected the republic. De Lesseps resigned after being swiftly recalled and denounced. The French forces were reinforced, and despite further resistance from Garibaldi, France took Rome and restored the papacy to power.

10. General Ducos de La Hitte (1789-1878) had replaced Tocqueville as minister of foreign affairs.

yours was stated in the most suitable terms that could be imagined, which I knew before he did, whereas Lamoricière's was drawn up in a very rough and brief form, which seemed to have very much flabbergasted L'Elysée. Lamoricière finished, however, by saying that he was awaiting his successor and would not leave before having received orders. In short, these two resignations have given the government a very disagreeable impression, a vivid reflection of which appeared in *Le Constitutionnel*. Both of you, but principally you, were found to be very useful to the conduct of the difficult affairs that are under way; above all, they were disagreeably affected to see eminent men do, from afar, what all the leaders of the parliamentary parties are doing here, that is to say, stand aside. This result of your action was inevitable. This does not make me any the less persistent in saying that you acted very well. I would never have pushed you to it, and if you had stayed, I would have defended you to and against everyone (that is the role I had already taken), but this resolution would have lessened you and, hand on my heart, I have no doubt that you grasped the situation well. You either had to withdraw, as you have done, or remain with the firm intention of following the President wherever he wishes to go. Every half-resolution had only drawbacks, would have estranged or cooled you with everyone, and, finally, would have made you play the part of a dupe. If, therefore, as I think, you do not want to follow the lot of Louis Napoleon, you have done the only thing there was to do. I think so, as I say it, with all the sincerity I have, and I do not believe that there is a political man who would not be of this opinion.

Before leaving what concerns you in order to tell you something of the general situation, I must report that yesterday I received the letter you wrote me on the 21st, a letter which contains rectifications of the facts of the Duke de Nemours's voyage to Vienna.[11] These facts had produced no impression

11. The Duke de Nemours (1814-1896) was a son of deposed King Louis Philippe, and he had been in exile in England since 1848. In 1849 he made a

here. No one had believed them, no one had paid any attention to them, and above all everyone has forgotten them today. I therefore did not believe, after having taken the advice of Dufaure, who was of my opinion, that there was reason to send your letter to *Le National*. That would have been to give this affair an importance that you supposed it to have from afar, but that it has never had from up close. I therefore restricted myself to giving the rectification you had transmitted to me to Chambolle; I will try to have it reproduced today in *Le Pays*. These are the only newspapers on which we have a direct influence.

If you remember the letter I wrote you by the courier of the 5th, you will recognize that I never believed either in an immediate coup d'état or in a series of violent moves on the part of the President. I therefore did not share in the surprise that was generally caused by the indecisive and soft attitude the President has resumed since the effort of his message. It was in his nature. Not only does he not have *continuous* energy and passion, but his mind is muddled, divided between different points of view; wanting contrary things all at once, resolved to come to sovereign power and not being absolutely decided to violate the laws, dreaming I do not know what chimerical compromise among all these mutually exclusive courses of action. In truth, that is the man. But he is swept along by a movement and by a combination of circumstances that he has neither the capacity nor the will to combat effectively. We are marching every day, not rapidly, but invincibly, toward a crisis. The time and the forms alone remain to be known. What will be the upshot of it? The actor is very insufficient for the role and he still has only very mediocre players around him, but all the same the play has great chances of success. Since

---

private visit to relatives in Austria. Beaumont was concerned because *Le National* had reprinted a paragraph from an Austrian paper that claimed that Beaumont, representative of the French Republic, was seeing the deposed king's son on a regular basis. Beaumont needlessly assured Tocqueville that there was not a word of truth to the rumor.

the defection of *Le Constitutionnel,* which has become the monitor of the Elysée Palace, the reconciliation of *La Presse,* the semibenevolent attitude taken by the vile scamps of *Le Siècle,* the President has none of the great newspapers against him. The Assembly is deeply hostile to him. But, with submissiveness, M. Molé assisting, it is hoped to mollify, if not to win over, the majority or at least to reduce and discredit it so that it can soon be had cheaply. This majority, besides, resolute enough and adequate for resistance, is too divided to be very fit for action. The Chamber presents a strange spectacle and one which has not been seen for thirty-four years. On one side, almost all the eminent men of the country, closer together and more in accord among themselves than they have ever been. Behind them, a very large numerical majority. In front, a feeble and mediocre government that no one dares either to avow or to support and which everyone bears in silence without either esteeming or fearing it. There is the situation. It results from the crude and unintelligent aspiration of the popular masses for a constitution of any power whatsoever and from the discouragement of the enlightened classes, who hardly know any longer what to wish for. As for the masses, one would be wrong to believe that they were very infatuated with Louis Napoleon; I do not believe he has gained in the provinces, and, in the working classes in Paris, he has certainly lost; but what has gained is the taste for a strong and stable power, whatever it may be. Louis Napoleon is a makeshift, but people are ready to make the best of him, for want of anything better. As for the enlightened classes, and, among them, the political men, only they, with contempt and an inexpressible disgust, see the bastard revolution emerging that is being prepared; but they lack two very useful things for fighting spiritedly and effectively against it—the feeling that they are supported by the nation and, most of all, a well-settled goal. They agree that they should resist either actively or passively; but beyond that, they do not know what they want. All the chiefs, however, have arrived at this doc-

trine, that for now, it is not possible to do anything but maintain the Republic, and that is what must be done. But they
lack faith in it and this doubt enervates their intelligence and
their will. What will make the President fail, if he fails, is less
the obstacles that he will find before him than the weaknesses
that he encounters in himself and around him. His faults will
perhaps be stronger than the hazard of fortune. The tide is
coming in and it is powerful, the wind is good, the harbor
will open; but the boat is small and badly manned. Although
the President has in his heart and even in his mind certain
uncommon qualities, as a whole he is the poorest usurper who
will ever present himself before a great nation, and nothing
demonstrates better than the possibility of his success the
skepticism, the enervation, the softness of spirit and of heart
into which these sixty years of revolution have thrown us.
After having passed through the hands of the greatest men of
modern times, here we are ready to throw ourselves into the
arms of I do not know what weak and mediocre conqueror,
who would be classified only somewhere between Espartero
and Iturbide.[12]

Besides, if it is possible for his enterprise to succeed, it is
not possible for his government to endure. The one is an accident that can happen in the poor intellectual and moral state to
which we are reduced at this moment. The other would be
contrary to the very laws of humanity and will not occur. If
he succeeds, which is still very doubtful, what will we see
afterward? The future has often been more frightening, never
more obscure.

While we wait, our particular situation here is very difficult,
despite all the testimonies of consideration and sympathy we

12. In an earlier letter, Tocqueville expressed his strong dislike for General
Espartero, dictator of Spain from 1840 to 1843, who ruthlessly bombarded the
city of Barcelona. Augustín de Iturbide (1783–1824), a military adventurer who
in 1821 proclaimed the independence of Mexico (an effort supported mainly by
the upper classes and the clergy), was crowned Augustín I in 1822, was deposed by Antonio López de Santa Anna in 1823, and was executed in 1824.

receive. If we took an offensive initiative against the President, and that could be done in a thousand ways every day, we would be playing his game; we would give pretexts for people to draw closer to him and we might recompose a sort of majority in the Assembly for him; we would lay ourselves open to attacks in the newspapers. On another side, this universal silence, this tacit adherence of a great power to a government that it is known to hold in contempt, ultimately enervates the public spirit. I know well that because this government has not been fettered, responsibility is ascribed to it for all the faults and all the weaknesses into which it falls daily. But public opinion, which is not very excited, does not pay great attention either to the one or to the other. People are waiting for a good opportunity to resist, which will perhaps not come or will perhaps come too late. Nevertheless, as I have told you above, a crisis is inevitable, and on that day it will be necessary to be at one's post. I urge you to remain absent for only the time you need to place your family in its winter quarters.

I did not want, my dear friend, to speak to you of a situation that for two days has been tormenting me, because I believed it useless to torment you with it, if, as I think, nothing serious will come of it. But, on thinking it over, I think it is useful to inform you. A decree of last June 15, which only put into effect the imperious prescriptions of the budget commission, contains an absurd principle, which is very worthy of being the result of M. Sauvaire-Barthélémy's initiative: it is that, when a diplomatic officer leaves his duties before three years and is replaced during this period, he is not again given moving expenses. That would have made a difference of about 15,000 francs in the sum you thought you had at your disposal, according to Brenier. He, who should have known about this when you left, but discovered it himself only a few days ago, came to warn me of it. We are agreed that he would speak of it to the new minister who, of his own accord, declared that it would not be right to make you pay for your return, an expense on which you could not have been able to base your expenses; and he stated that they would take into account the 15,000 francs on the secret funds. Yesterday I spoke to him myself very forcefully along the same lines. I do not need to tell you that I am making this affair a matter of principal concern to me, and, to speak truthfully, I do not doubt that things are happening as M. de La Hitte has indicated and as Brenier requested. The latter does not seem to doubt it, either. Nonetheless, I believed I must make you aware of the difficulty, so that you could act or write me, at least, accordingly. At first, I was very upset and desperate about this discovery, and, despite the positive assurances that are being made, I would like to see the difficulty resolved. I am, besides, on the best of terms with M. [de] La Hitte, who came to look for me at my home and at my bench in order to ask me for information.

Farewell, I embrace you with all my heart. Our affectionate regards to Madame de Beaumont.

65. *To Arthur de Gobineau*

Paris, January 7, 1850

For a long time, my dear friend, I have been wanting to answer your letters; it has not been that time has been lacking for doing it, but rather that I have lacked that kind of spirit that puts a pen into one's hand or makes one want to talk. Since I have little to do, I am doing nothing at all. You are too good a philosopher, although you may not have developed your philosophy, not to understand that. But what you will have difficulty understanding is the degree of apathy into which I have fallen. I am scarcely even in the position of a spectator, for, at least, the spectator *watches* and I do not even take this much trouble. That results above all from this more and more profound obscurity that is spreading over the always so obscure picture that is called the future. Picture to yourself a man who is traveling on a December night that is moonless and accentuated by mists, and tell me what amusement he would take in looking through the carriage door at the impression of the countryside. This man is the whole of France. It is a night like this that surrounds us. Men who have glasses do not see any farther into it than those who have only their eyes to use, and all the blind men make their way together hitting each other in the gloom while expecting to arrive all together at the gulf that may be found on the other side. What a somber night! I would prefer day, even if it were to show us the inevitable precipice.

M. de Serre told me that you had finally established yourself very comfortably, if it is possible to be very comfortable in Berne during the winter. But, come summer, and your stay in that city will, I believe, be very agreeable. I have only seen Berne in the summer, and, at that time of year, it charmed me.

Mme. de Gobineau was, I am told, quite ill during the trip. I hope that her health is firmly reestablished. Please remember me especially to her and believe in all my feelings of sincere friendship.

66. To Gustave de Beaumont

Tocqueville, June 14, 1850

My dear friend, I received your letter of the 9th. It gave me great pleasure, as much because of the interesting news it contains as the testimonies of confidence and friendship that it included and which, coming from you, will always be, as you know, very touching to me.

Our journey went very happily, and we arrived here in good health, although nearly worn out.[13] The first week that followed, I was marvelous. In the last few days, I have be-

13. Due to illness, Tocqueville took a six-month leave of absence from the Legislative Assembly and went home to his château early in June.

come listless again. I am not ailing at all; but I grow weary without taking exercise, and my strength is not returning. The illness I just had seems not to have left any particular traces in the organ it attacked, but one might say it produced a uniform weakening in all organs, from which I cannot manage to recover. The length of this convalescence, because I am still a true convalescent, persuades me that this time youth has gone for good and that what you have driveled to me for twenty years about the first effects of decline is really beginning to be true. I do not know if you also will see a premonitory sign of this old age in the cooling off of my impressions. The truth is that I am less impatient, calmer, and infinitely more even tempered than I ever was before. I am growing rich, as you see, in negative qualities. I am becoming sterile and easy-going; still, despite my philosophy of recent date, I cannot free myself from being strongly preoccupied in my solitude with what is happening in the great theater you continue to inhabit. Revolutionary times have this benefit, that they do not permit indifference and egoism in politics. Although, seen from afar, the diverse incidents of our current history appear to me to have less importance than when they are considered from up close, nevertheless, I, like you, find that there is gravity and great difficulty in the affair of the three million.[14] One point appears to me, as it does to you, perfectly clear, and happily it is that which concerns our particular conduct. Our role is to stay completely in reserve, whether at the speaker's platform or in informal talks. The only advantage that can result from the President's demand is to put him in a difficult position for him with his new friends and protectors on the right; we would be very foolish to come to the aid of the latter and to be used by them as a trumpet.

14. On June 4, 1850, President Louis Napoleon's minister of finance proposed that the Assembly grant the president 3 million francs for expenses of state. The Assembly hesitated but eventually paid the debts (which did not total 3 million francs) of Louis Napoleon, requesting that he be more frugal in the future.

I noticed the position that *L'Ordre* took and, like you, it made me shrug my shoulders. What a dull-witted fool that poor Ch[ambolle] is, if he is sincere. How could he not see that new circumstances necessitate new conduct; and that, if it were opportune and wise to put ourselves forward against the President when the leaders of the majority wanted to defend the Republic against him with us, it would be foolish and dangerous to act the same way when what is to be feared is that the Republic may be overthrown by the union of the President and these same men? It is not necessary to vote for the project, but it is necessary to speak like the least ardent of its adversaries; that is my opinion. Up to that point, it is easy to have one. That becomes far more difficult when it is a matter of deciding the other question your letter poses: is it more to be desired than to be feared that the demand will be rejected by the Assembly? On this point, I cannot say that I have a very settled opinion, but nonetheless I have a clear enough impression. On the whole, I am more inclined to desire the rejection than the adoption of the law. Both results pose dangers, but the one seems to me less to be feared than the other. I know that rejection of the law diminishes the President, which is not desirable for the moment, and may throw him, through misery and despair, into some adventure. That may be. Nevertheless, it seems to me very unlikely, at the point things have reached, that the President could, outside and in opposition to the Assembly, by the mere military forces that he has at his disposal, overthrow the Constitution and the Republic. If he attempts it, I believe he will fail. In any case, we will have the majority with us then to fight against him, and, if the Chamber is the stronger, we will be able to influence the consequences of the victory. If, on the contrary, the law passes, the bond between the President and the leaders of the majority will be drawn tighter. The current tepidity of the latter may irritate him, but in the end, if he has his millions, he will owe it to the step they made him take and to the care they have taken to break in and discipline the majority. Now, I have always believed and I believe still that the most certain danger that the Constitution and the Republic could run would come from the union, even momentary and hypocritical, of the leaders of the majority and the President, and that, moreover, of all the ways in which the Republic could perish, that would be the most disastrous for us in particular, something that would be likely to leave us in the middle of the country in the most false and most isolated position after the event occurred. That is the impression I have in my solitude.

But, whatever may be the importance of the question with which I have just dealt, and its importance is great, I confess to you, my dear friend, that as I withdraw from the field of battle, the incidents of the fight disappear and my mind searches for more general outlooks on the situation of the country, and I ask myself where we are going, what we are doing, what ought we to do? There often cross my mind, I confess, doubts that I express to you, as if I were all alone. I ask myself if the Constitution is tolerable, as it is, and regularly modifiable, if the Republic itself is possible in the present state of minds; if, of all the forms the government could have taken, it is not the most dangerous to the liberty we love. This leads me to ask myself if we are right to persist in maintaining this Constitution and in defending this Republic, and if we would be making better use of our moderation and our recognized integrity to seek ways to get out of the Constitution in the least irregular fashion and the fashion that is most respectful for the national will, and to try to see whether, not being able to save the Republic, one could not prevent liberty from perishing with it. In a word, if it would not be more useful to the country for us to try to exert an influence on the character of the revolution which is preparing itself rather than resisting it limitlessly and to make allowance for this in our ideas instead of acting so that they are completely excluded. There you have some of the thoughts that are floating through my mind in the midst of my desert. Only take them for what they are worth: a vague chat. When I myself examine their detailed and practical application, I find so many obstacles both outside of us and within ourselves, in present events and past events, that, were they correct, I am still inclined to think that we would have great difficulty in following them through and that it would be better to walk along the road we are on, which is still the easiest and most certain.

Farewell. I embrace you with all my heart. Do not forget me in my *wilderness*[15] and write me soon. Remember us with great affection to Madame de Beaumont.

P.S. Examine thoroughly the condition of the seal that closes my letter and inform me of it.

67. *To Harriet Grote*

Tocqueville, July 24, 1850

I could, Madame, if I had not been instructed properly, complain that, although you know me to be one of the most proclaimed admirers of your intellect, you yourself have not thought to send me your pamphlet on pauperism,[16] and have left me to ask you for it by the intercession of our friend M. Senior. But I would much rather, instead of making a quarrel with you, thank you for the pleasure that this little piece of writing has brought me. I received it on leaving Paris, and I read it on arriving here: I could not have better employed the leisure time that illness has forced on me. I encounter in your work the good sense of the English economists, only sharpened and colored by the intelligence and imagination of a woman, of which it is often in very great need. You defend the constituting principles on which our old European society rests, liberty and the individual responsibility that is its conse-

15. Tocqueville here uses the English word.
16. *The Case of the Poor Against the Rich, Fairly Stated by a Mutual Friend*, published in 1850. Here Grote argues that poverty cannot be alleviated by interfering with the sanctity of property rights.

quence, above all property. You are quite correct, you could
not conceive of men living outside these primordial laws, nor
could I. However, I confess to you, I often find that this old
world, beyond which neither of us sees anything, seems quite
used up; that this great and respectable machine is breaking
down a little every day, and, without understanding what
might come to be, my confidence in the duration of what is,
is shaken. History teaches me that none of the men who have
been present at the destruction of religious or social organizations that the world has already seen, could foretell or even
imagine what was to follow: this has not prevented Christianity from succeeding idolatry, domestic service from succeeding slavery, the barbarians from succeeding Roman civilization, and feudal hierarchy from succeeding barbarism. Each of
these changes took place without having been foreseen, least
of all by any of the writers (you know, Madame, that the
French have had the impertinence of not making *auteur* femi-
nine) who have lived in the time that immediately preceded,
and before the fundamental revolution. Who thus can affirm
that one form of society is necessary and that another cannot
exist? But the duty of honest people is not any the less to
defend the only one they understand, and even to be killed for
it, while waiting to be shown a better.

M. Grote has continued to have his excellent and very interesting history of Greece[17] sent to me; I would regret not already having thanked him for the last volumes I received, if I
did not have the opportunity to make you the interpreter of
my gratitude. I just read his eighth volume (the last I possess);
I find in it, as in the preceding ones, a mass of unknown facts
or of insights that are new to me, which give to me an idea
of the Greeks different and often contradictory than I had before. Notably, until now I had never known Socrates and the
sophists of antiquity. I am startled by the erudition and astonished by the liberty of mind that such a work supposes—two

17. *The History of Greece,* the first volume of which was published in 1846.

qualities that are so rarely joined. Please, Madame, speak to
him with great affection in my name, and accept for yourself
the homage of my respectful devotion. Mme. de Tocqueville
wishes to be remembered to you fondly; neither of us is
yet in good health, although we are no longer precisely ill,
etc., etc.

68. To Louis de Kergorlay

Sorrento, December 15, 1850

I do not know, my dear friend, if you heard from my parents and our friends the news of our journey.[18] In that case,
you should know that we suffered great fatigue and still more
vexation. Marie was so tired by the sea that, on arrival in
Naples, she felt an extreme repugnance to reembarking to go
to Sicily. I believed it necessary to give up that part of the
journey, but not the way of life I was counting on adopting in
Sicily. In this respect we have not changed our plans at all.
We are doing, near Naples, in a charming place called Sorrento, what we wanted to do in Palermo; that is to say, we
have leased a furnished apartment, in which we have settled
with our servants and in which we are living a very retiring
life. The place, as I told you, is charming; the home in which
we live is very well situated, very well furnished, and, in
short, infinitely agreeable; the country that surrounds us is admirable, the walks are without number, and, up to now, the
climate has been delightful. Among all these fine things, however, it would not be long before I grew bored if I could not
create a vigorous occupation for my mind. I brought some
books here. I intend to continue what I had already begun at
Tocqueville this summer, with great spirit and pleasure,
which was an account of what I had seen in the Revolution of

18. Tocqueville and his wife left France in November 1850 in order to spend
the winter in Italy's milder climate. From December 1850 to April 1851, they
rented a home in Sorrento.

1848 and since, things and men.[19] I have not yet been able to get back into the current of ideas and recollections which can give me the taste for this work; and, while waiting for the inspiration to come back, I have contented myself with musing about what could be the subject of a new book for me; because I need not tell you that the recollections of 1848 cannot appear before the public. The free judgments that I hold on it, both on my contemporaries and on myself, would make this publication impractical, even if it would be to my taste to produce myself on some literary theater or other, which assuredly it is not. For a long time, I have already been occupied, I could say troubled, by the idea of attempting a great work once again. It seems to me that my true worth is above all in works of the mind; that I am worth more in thought than in action; and that, if there remains anything of me in this world, it will be much more the trace of what I have written than the recollection of what I will have done. The last ten years, which have been rather sterile for me in many respects, have nonetheless given me the truest insights into human affairs and a more practical sense of the details, without making me lose the habit that my intelligence had taken of regarding the affairs of men by wholes. Thus, I believe myself in better condition than I was when I wrote *Democracy* to deal well with a great subject of political literature. But what subject am I to take up? The possibility for success lies mostly in the subject, not only because it is necessary to find a subject that interests the public, but especially because it is necessary to discover one that animates me and draws out of me all that I can give. I am the man least fit in the world for going up with any advantage against the current of my mind and my taste, and I fall well below the mediocre when I do not take an impassioned pleasure in what I am doing. I have therefore

19. Tocqueville is working on *Recollections,* a private set of reflections on the 1848 Revolution and subsequent events. It was not intended for publication and was not published until 1893. Even this version was incomplete, and the complete text did not appear until 1942.

often sought for several years (every time, at least, that a little
tranquility permitted me to look around and see something
else and farther than the little tangle in which I was involved),
I sought, I say, some subject that I could take up; and I have
never seen anything that pleased me completely or rather that
seized me. However, now that we see that youth is gone by,
and time marches or, to say it better, runs down the slope of
mature years, the limits of life are discovered more clearly and
more closely, the field of action shrinks. All these reflections,
I could say all these mental agitations, have naturally brought
me, in the solitude in which I live, to search more seriously
and more deeply for the mother-idea of a book, and I have
felt the inclination to communicate with you what has struck
my imagination and to ask your advice. I can consider only a
contemporary subject. Basically, only affairs of our time interest the public and interest me. The greatness and singularity of
the spectacle that the world of our time presents absorbs too
much attention for anyone to be able to attach much value to
those historical curiosities that suffice idle and erudite societies. But which contemporary subject to choose? One that
would have the most originality and that would best suit the
nature and habits of my intelligence would be an ensemble of
reflections and insights on the current time, a free judgment
on our modern societies and a forecast of their probable future. But when I try to find the crux of such a subject, the
point where all the ideas that it generates meet and tie themselves together, I do not find it. I see parts of such a work,
I do not perceive the whole; I have the threads well in hand,
but lack the woof to make the cloth. I must find somewhere,
for my ideas, the solid and continuous basis of facts. I can
encounter that only while writing history, while applying
myself to a period whose account serves me as an occasion to
paint the men and the affairs of our century and permits me to
make one picture out of all these detached paintings. Only the
long drama of the French Revolution can furnish this pe-

riod.[20] For a long time I have had the thought, which I have expressed to you, I believe, of choosing in this great expanse of time that goes from 1789 to our day, and which I continue to call the French Revolution, the ten years of the Empire, the birth, the development, the decline and the fall of that prodigious enterprise. The more I reflect on it, the more I believe that the period would be well chosen for painting. In itself, it is not only grand, but peculiar, even unique; and nonetheless, up to the present, at least in my opinion, it has been reproduced in false or vulgar colors. It throws, moreover, a vivid light on the period that preceded it and on that which follows it. It is certainly one of the acts of the French Revolution that enables one to judge the whole play best, and permits one to say the most on the ensemble, all that one can have to say on it. My doubt bears much less on the choice of subject than on the way of dealing with it. My first thought had been to redo M. Thiers's book[21] in my own manner: to write the plot of the Empire, avoiding only expatiating on the military part, which M. Thiers has reproduced with so much self-satisfaction and a very ridiculous pretension that he understood the profession of warfare well. But, in reflecting on it, I developed great hesitation about dealing with the subject in this manner. Thus envisioned, the work would be a very long and exacting enterprise. Moreover, the principal merit of the historian is to know how to handle the fabric of the facts, and I do not know if this art is within my reach. What I have best succeeded in up to now is in judging facts rather than recounting them, and, in a history properly so called, that faculty which I know all about would be exercised only every now and then and in a secondary manner, unless I left the genre

20. Already Tocqueville is thinking of writing his history of the French Revolution, of which he completed only one volume, i.e., *The Old Regime and the French Revolution* (1856).

21. *Histoire du consulat et de l'empire,* 20 vols. (1845–1862). Tocqueville may also be thinking of Thiers's earlier work, *Histoire de la révolution française,* 10 vols. (1823–1827).

and burdened the narrative. Finally, there is a certain affectation in taking up again the road that M. Thiers has just followed. The public is rarely grateful to you for these attempts,
and when two writers take the same subject, it is naturally
inclined to believe that the second has nothing more to teach
it. There you have my doubts; I disclose them to you in order
to obtain your opinion.

 To this first manner of envisioning the subject another has
succeeded in my mind which goes as follows: it would no
longer be a matter of a lengthy work, but of a rather short
book, one volume perhaps. I would no longer do, to speak
properly, the history of the Empire, but an ensemble of reflections and judgments on that history. I would point out the
facts, no doubt, and I would follow the thread, but my principal concern would not be to recount them. Above all, in
order to clarify the principal facts, I would need to illuminate
the diverse causes which emerge from them: how the Empire
came about; how it was able to establish itself in the midst of
the society created by the Revolution; what were the means
used; what was the *true* nature of the man who founded it;
what caused his success, what caused his reverses; the passing
influence and the durable influence which he exercised on the
destinies of the world and in particular on those of France. It
seems to me there is in that the material for a very great
book. But the difficulties are immense. The one that most
troubles my mind comes from the mixture of history properly
so called with historical philosophy. I still do not see how to
mix these two things (and yet, they must be mixed, for one
could say that the first is the canvas and the second the color,
and that it is necessary to have both at the same time in order
to do the picture). I fear that the one is harmful to the other,
and that I lack the infinite art that would be necessary in order
to choose properly the facts that must, so to speak, support
the ideas; to recount them enough for the reader to be led
naturally from one reflection to another by interest in the narrative, and not to tell too much of them, so that the character

of the work remains visible. The inimitable model of this genre is in Montesquieu's book on the grandeur and the decline of the Romans.[22] One passes there, so to speak, across Roman history without pausing, and nonetheless one perceives enough of that history to desire the author's explanations and to understand them. But independently of the fact that such great models are always much superior to every copy, Montesquieu found in his book opportunities he would not have in the one of which I am speaking. Occupying himself with a very vast and very remote epoch, he could choose only every now and then the greatest facts, and, with respect to those facts, say only very general things. If he had had to restrict himself to a space of ten years and seek his road across a multitude of detailed and precise facts, the difficulty of the work would assuredly have been much greater.

I have tried in all the above to enable you to grasp my state of mind completely. All the ideas I have just expressed to you have put my mind very much to work; but it still bustles about in the darkness, or at least it perceives only half-lights which only permit it to perceive the grandeur of the subject, without putting it in a position to recognize what is to be found in that vast space. I very much wish that you could help me to see it more clearly. I am proud enough to believe that I am better suited than anyone else to bring to such a subject great freedom of mind, and to speak without passion and without reticence concerning men and things. For, as regards to men, although they have lived in our time, I am sure I do not hold toward them either love or hate; and as regards to the forms of what are called constitutions, laws, dynasties, classes, they have, so to speak, I will not say no value, but no existence in my eyes, independently of the effects they produce. I have no traditions, I have no party, I have no *cause,* if it is not that of liberty and human dignity; of that, I am sure;

22. *Considérations sur les causes de la grandeur des Romains et de leur décadence* (1734).

and for a work of this sort, a disposition and a nature of this kind are as useful as they are often harmful when it is no longer a matter of speaking about human affairs, but of being entangled in them.

Farewell; I am looking for a long letter from you soon. Write me in the following manner: put the sealed letter that bears my name in an envelope and on this envelope write: *to M. Desage, foreign affairs agent in Marseilles.* Prepay it to there.

I am ashamed to say that I received, a very long time ago, a very friendly letter from Mathilde. I wanted to attach a letter to her to this one, but I am so tired from talking to you of history and philosophy that I would be a very boring correspondent today. My wife intends to write yours one of these days and I will add my letter to hers. In the meantime, give our warm regards to your wife. We embrace you.

69. *To Gustave de Beaumont*

Versailles, September 14, 1851,
Grille du Grand Montreuil

I would have answered the very kind letter you left for me in Paris if I had not been detained longer than I expected in the département of La Manche. My council[23] lasted two full weeks and only finished the night of the 7th or 8th. On returning from Saint-Lô, I spent 24 hours at Corcelle's home, which caused me to arrive here only last Wednesday. I leave you to judge whether I took pleasure in returning to my home after this pestered life that I have been leading and after

23. Since 1842, Tocqueville had been a member of the General Council in the *département* of La Manche and had occasionally served as president of the council, an office to which he had just been reelected in August 1851. Despite the tone of this letter, Tocqueville found enormous satisfaction in participating in local government precisely because he valued decentralization so highly. Because he refused the oath to the new Empire, he felt compelled to resign from the General Council in 1852.

the real solitude in which I had been living without ever being alone. Otherwise, things went as well as I could want. The revision of the laws was passed just as the Assembly's commission proposed it after a speech I made.[24] Previously, I had had a vote passed in favor of the revision of the law of May 31.[25] Those very colleagues of ours who belong to the council and who voted for this law did not dare oppose me, and the resolution passed without discussion. That was a little abuse of my influence, but the occasion seemed to me worth the trouble.

It is rather difficult, after all, to tell what public opinion is in my département, so great is the reserve with which everyone expresses his ideas, half out of prudence, half out of not knowing what to think. That fact is that silence is the almost universal fact here and that there has never been a population that had its mind more preoccupied with public affairs and its mouth more shut. Nonetheless, I believe that I have finally discerned this: no passion at all, scarcely any taste for the President of the Republic; great tolerance for those who do not like him, but almost a general attraction for reappointing him, *because he is there.* Anyone else in his place would have almost the same chance, so strong is the repugnance to stirring things up, and the horror of the *unknown.* I believe, how-

24. In June 1851, Tocqueville had been elected a member of an Assembly committee designated to explore the question of whether or not to revise the Constitution to permit the president to run for a second term of office. In July 1851, Tocqueville and the committee declared themselves for such a revision if the revision were undertaken by a Constituent Assembly elected expressly for revising the Constitution. The recommendation passed the Assembly, but not with the necessary three-fourths majority. Louis Napoleon now felt he had no alternative but a coup d'état.

25. The law of May 31, 1850, effectively disenfranchised about 3 million voters out of about 9.5 million registered. It did this by requiring each voter to live in the same district for the past three years, a measure that affected migratory workers and especially industrial workers who moved frequently (and tended to be radical). In a conversation with Louis Napoleon on May 15, 1851, Tocqueville said he regarded this law "almost as a crime."

ever, that the Prince de Joinville[26] will receive a rather large
number of votes, because there is no repugnance to his name,
and on the contrary a certain favor is attached to it, because
beef was sold better under his family's government than at
any other time. But that is good will that will remain, for all
appearances, productive of little, if not altogether unfruitful.
This candidacy would have only, in my judgment, one chance
of success and even that is very doubtful (except for accidents
of the moment that always play such a large role in the conduct of voting by universal suffrage), if, after the candidacy
had been suitably presented and become widely known, the
National Assembly took an energetic attitude toward the
President and the administration, intimidated the civil servants
and even the electors who would want to violate the law, and
especially showed itself to be determined not to allow the
illegal election to take effect without resistance. One could
turn the fear of disturbances against the President, a fear
which is today his best support, and induce many people to
vote against him for precisely the same reasons that today induce them to vote for him. But the National Assembly will
not take this attitude, that is certain; and the President's luck
decrees that the only man who can compete with him is at the
same time the one who, in emerging, renders any union of

26. François Ferdinand Philippe Louis Marie d'Orléans, Prince de Joinville
(1818-1900), the most popular of the sons of Louis Philippe, now a candidate
representing the House of Orléans and former leaders of the July Monarchy
(Guizot, Thiers, etc.). But the Orleanists and their supporters were understand-
ably opposed by another branch of monarchists, the Legitimists, who sought a
full restoration of the House of Bourbon and consequently put forth as a
pretender to the throne the grandson of Charles X—Henri Charles, Count de
Chambord (1820-1883)—calling him Henri V. Despite much talk and energy
expended in trying to "fuse" these two monarchist factions, these attempts
failed—partly because neither the Legitimists nor the Orleanists could agree on
which monarchy to restore, partly because the Legitimists dreamed of the
Restoration dominated by the landed aristocracy whereas the Orleanists
dreamed of the July Monarchy controlled largely by the industrial bourgeoisie,
and partly because the Prince de Joinville detested the Legitimists and all attempts at "fusion."

the natural enemies of the current power, or even the creation of a firm majority in Parliament in any sense, most impossible.

I therefore hold to the opinion I have always had, as you know, that the reelection of the President is an inevitability and that the only question is how large the majority will be; a question still very important, it is true.[27]

The kind of light that seems to me to clarify this particular point in our future does not make the rest of the picture any the more visible to me. What will happen as a consequence of this popular coup d'état? I do not know. It seems to me it will be very difficult to escape from some sort of crisis and from passing through a very painful and perhaps very cruel moment. I confess to you that I expect it much less to come from the red party properly so called, as is the common apprehension, than from the generals of the Assembly. These are resolute men, accustomed to perils, and so committed as to be unable to retreat. That they will attempt an unsuccessful attack seems to me almost certain, and, whatever they say, that they will fail is very probable. That is the darkest cloud on the horizon and one of the most terrible tests that await us. I think, as do you, that it is desirable, between now and then, that we be able to hold ourselves, not in neutrality, but in reverse, and especially, as you say, without any obligation in civil war, in the hope of being able, in that last moment, to invervene and, if the President triumphs, to hold firm on the ground of constitutional liberty. But how little one feels master of oneself in advance, in such times! There is only one determination that I am sure of always following: to make our liberties triumph through this crisis, or to succumb with them. All the rest is secondary, but this is a question of life or death.

27. Under the 1848 Constitution, the president could not run for reelection, but he might still win office in the following manner: if no candidate received a majority of votes cast, the Assembly would choose a president.

I have still only seen Dufaure and Rivet.[28] The first returned from his council. Both are very excited about the new candidacy. I saw that great efforts were being made to push Dufaure to the fore and to make him the official promoter and guarantor of the new candidate. I fought this tendency strongly. I said that I understood that people who, like us, want and profess to want to continue a fair trial of the republican system, looked with pleasure upon a serious candidacy arising against the unconstitutional candidacy of the President; that the Prince de Joinville—if, in presenting himself, he only had the effect of diminishing his competitor's majority and of diminishing likewise the moral strength that the latter will be able to make use of after reelection—that this would still bring about a great benefit, and that, accordingly, we should do nothing against his candidacy, but, on the contrary, should favor his development to some extent. But to propose his candidacy to the nation, to make ourselves, in some way, its guarantors, would be dishonest or ridiculous: dishonest if, seeing that it is a question only of playing out the current comedy under another name and with another purpose, we do not say so; ridiculous, if we do not see it at all. This reasoning seemed to me to make a profound impression, and it was agreed to remain in a *kindly reserve* and to wait for events and especially for what the prince himself was going to do; because that would be a big point. I know *with certainty* that, although he is determined to act, he is hesitating over the manner and the moment. He is waiting for the Duke d'Aumale,[29] who is going to come spend several days with him in order to settle the plan that is to be followed. Thiers, who was invited to go confer with them, was still hesitating yesterday, either as a consequence of that fear which seizes him readily, as you know, in decisive moments, or for the very reasonable motive

28. Jean-Charles Rivet (1800-1872), a member of the Chamber of Deputies under the July Monarchy, a representative to the Constituent Assembly, and later, under the Second Empire, involved in the expansion of railroad lines.

29. Another son of Louis Philippe, also former governor-general of Al-

he gives that the prince's candidacy can only lose by contact with his unpopularity. The fact is that, as a consequence as much perhaps of what good he has done as of what harm he has done, the little man is at this moment one of the most unpopular men in France. I have reason to think that one of the ideas that the President's friends are entertaining is this: to profit on the one hand from the irritation Joinville's candidacy causes Legitimists, and on the other from the near unanimity of the general councils in favor of the revision in order to get the Assembly to dissolve itself while calling, under the old election law, for the electors to name a Constituent Assembly. If this plan exists, indeed, it seems to me to be very chimerical, and in general the illusions that are developing on both sides of the Assembly seem very great. The Orleanists believed that from the moment that their candidate leaps the moat, the friends of his family who today belong to the majority under the name of fusionists or conservatives will pass over from their side; in that, they are mistaken, in my opinion. All those men no doubt cherish the house of Orléans, but only in their hearts; and they will expose themselves neither to the anger of their electors nor to the chances of new disturbances in order to do its business. The majority, besides, is attached to that house as pigs are attached to the memory of their sty, and so long as they are offered another lair, they will not budge. One will perhaps be able to draw part of them into the Créton proposition,[30] but not beyond.

As for the President, if he believes he can carry along these same men or even the Legitimists with him into getting out of the Constitution, I think he is equally mistaken; he will perhaps be able to lead everybody to the point of having the elections three months before the natural time, which would already be a great deal; but further, I think not. In general the illusions that seem to me to be developing at the moment are

30. A proposition to repeal the law forcing exile on members of the Bourbon family.

strange. When I chat with certain people, it seems to me I am walking through an insane asylum. It is true that I do not possess the mother of illusions, which is passion. I have no passion and how could I have any? Of all the solutions that present themselves, there is not a single one that is to my liking and I have only sorry choices from which to choose. People are living on illusions about the true state of the country, on illusions about the army; as for the latter, a general whose name I do not want to reveal thus described his mind yesterday rather well when he said: "The army is a well-raised young girl who does not ask for more than to give herself, but who will not allow one to violate her and will only consent to surrender herself with the permission of her grandparents." He understood by that, the President and the Assembly. The remark is nice, and I wanted to amuse you with it.

Let us come now to your decline, with which you have entertained me this time with a certain melancholy that made me laugh. If you are speaking about it in order to joke, I very much want to be a party to the joke. But if you are saying that seriously, it is not among the helpless you should be classed, but assuredly among the insane. Because you are quite in the prime of life for what you have to do. I admit that for doing the things that would have pleased us more 25 years ago, we may well be a little in decline; but as for the rest, I deny it, and I will tell you that in no period of my life have I felt myself more fit to judge and, consequently, in our trade, to act, to think, and to write. The same must be true of you, since you are my contemporary and in better health. The truth is that you have been tested for two years in an extraordinary manner and one which is very liable to leave a certain momentary fatigue of the spirit.[31] But, as I was telling you a

31. Beaumont's father-in-law died in November 1849; Beaumont's daughter died in June 1850, a death that crushed Beaumont's spirit and left Beaumont's wife very ill and upset even a year later; finally, in May 1851, Beaumont's father died.

little while ago, I am convinced that you are now at the end
of this streak of bitter luck, because there are streaks of luck
in everything as in games, or rather life is only one great
game in which one is sometimes losing and sometimes winning according to the combination of luck and skill, until
death reverses the dice suddenly and ends the game. I am convinced that you will now enjoy a happier time than you have
known for many years. You have finally found the little her-
mitage without which there is neither complete tranquility nor
complete happiness, you have an already grown son and one
that every father would desire, and here comes a second for
the pleasure of your old days and who undoubtedly will follow in the footsteps of the first. I do not doubt that, under the
impression of all these good things, the soul of your excellent
and charming wife will do nothing but recover and rediscover
the serenity she had lost. Courage, then, and set yourself to
work! I do not know what advice to give you about how to
employ the six weeks that remain to you, but you are never
perplexed in finding an object of work when you are in the
mood, and I will wager that my letter will find you already
at work and giving yourself over to it with extreme ardor
despite your decline.

For my part, I am going to try once again to take up the
work I had started at Sorrento and would like to finish. It
concerns politics, as you know, without being connected with
affairs of the moment; that is as it must be, because, for us,
it is difficult now to think ardently and fruitfully about anything else but politics and difficult to think with pleasure
about what is being done today. I cannot tell you, but I do
not have to tell you because you may judge for yourself, what
delight I find at this moment in the calm between two storms
and with what sadness I will see November 4 arrive. Write
me often, at length and with as much friendship for me as I
have for you. I do not need to ask you to remember us to
Madame de Beaumont or to tell you that she is very often

present in our thoughts and often, just as you are, the subject of our conversations.

70. To the editor of the London Times[32]

[Published December 11, 1851]

Sir, — The opinion expressed by certain organs of the English press on the events which have just occurred in France has caused a painful surprise to men who, like myself, preserve a steadfast attachment to the principles of regulated lib-

32. This letter appeared anonymously in the December 11, 1851, issue of the *London Times* under the title "The State of France—A Narrative by a Member of the National Assembly." Since no French original has survived, the version given here is a reproduction of the letter as it appeared in English in the *Times,* except for the list of signatures to the December 2 decree, which is not given in full. The letter was smuggled out of France by Tocqueville's friend Harriet Grote and published because of Reeve's influence at the *Times.* The editors of the *Times* added the following introduction:

"The following narrative of the events which accompanied the dissolution of the National Assembly of France is from the pen of a member of that body, whose name, in the present state of that country, it is of course impossible to disclose. But we submit this important document to the judgement of the world with entire reliance on the strict accuracy of every detail which it contains. These particulars are now published by us in an authentic form, as no means any longer exist in France of bringing the truth to the knowledge of the public. The opinions are those of the writer; the facts belong to the history of these times."

Since Tocqueville himself had been briefly imprisoned after the December 2 coup, along with 230 other representatives of the Assembly, and since so many were deported or exiled, he took a considerable risk in publishing his letter. Ultimately, Lord Palmerston recognized the new government with rather embarrassing swiftness, and Tocqueville was unable to generate any substantial condemnation by England or the English press of the new empire. See Mayer, *Alexis de Tocqueville: A Biographical Study in Political Science,* pp. 61-64.

Since the text as it was published in the *Times* includes some French phrases, the following translations are provided: the *Conseils Généraux* means General Councils; *Conseil d'Etat,* Council of State; *Chasseurs,* light infantry soldiers; Mairie, town or district hall; *Commissaires de Police,* police commissioners; *"Vive l'Assemblée Nationale,"* "Long live the National Assembly"; *forçat,* convict; *bagne,* prison; *lettres de cachet,* arbitrary warrants of arrest notorious under the Old Regime; *sous-prefets,* subprefects; the Court of Cassation, the highest French court of appeals; Greffier, court clerk; and *procès-verbal,* official report.

erty and a fixed respect for legality. We are grieved to remark the purpose to which these observations of a portion of the English press are turned by the new Government, and that any English writers should seem to applaud what all honest Frenchmen condemn. It is for this reason that, as a witness of these events, I wish to make them known to you in all sincerity, convinced as I am that when Englishmen approve violence and oppression, it is only because the truth is not yet before them.

Permit me to offer some general reflections before entering into details.

Louis Napoleon, in order to endeavor to palliate in France and abroad the audacious violation of the laws which he has just committed, has caused a report to be circulated that he only anticipated the hostile measures of the Assembly, which was conspiring against himself, and that if he had not struck that body it would have struck him. This sort of defence is no novelty to us in France. All our revolutionaries have used it these 60 years. The members of the Convention, who sent each other to the scaffold, invariably treated their adversaries as conspirators. But in the present instance this accusation, as far as the majority of the Assembly is concerned, is without a pretext, and can only pass current among strangers ignorant of the true course of events.

No doubt history will have weighty charges to bring against the Legislative Assembly, which has just been illegally and violently dissolved. The parties of which that Assembly was composed failed to come to an understanding; this gave to the whole body an uncertain and sometimes contradictory policy, and finally discredited the Assembly, and rendered it incapable of defending either liberty or its own existence. History will record thus much; but history will reject with contempt the accusation which Louis Napoleon has preferred against us. If you do not believe my assurances, judge at least by the facts—not the secret facts which I could disclose to you, but the public facts printed in *Le Moniteur*.

In the month of August last, the Assembly voted the revision of the Constitution by an immense majority. Why was the revision of the Constitution desired? Simply to legalize the reelection of Louis Napoleon. Was that an act of conspiracy against him?

The Assembly prorogued itself soon after this vote; the *Conseils Généraux,* convoked immediately afterwards, and principally consisting of representatives, also expressed an almost unanimous desire for the revision of the Constitution. Was that an act of conspiracy against Louis Napoleon?

The Assembly met again on the 4th of November. There was an Electoral Law—that of the 31st of May—which the great majority of the Assembly had voted. This law was unpopular, and to catch the favour of the people, Louis Napoleon, who had been the first to propose and sanction the law of the 31st of May the year before, demands its abrogation, and proposes another law in a message insulting to the Assembly. The new Electoral Law proposed by him was, indeed, rejected, but by a majority of only two votes; and immediately afterwards the Chamber proceeded, in order to comply with the President's policy, to adopt in another form most of the changes which he had proposed. Was that an act of conspiracy against Louis Napoleon?

Shortly afterwards a proposition was made by the Questors to enable us to place the Parliament in a state of defence, if attacked, and to call troops directly to our assistance. This proposition was, as nobody can deny, in strict conformity with the Constitution, and all that the proposed resolution did was to define the means of exercising a power which the Assembly incontestably possessed. Nevertheless, from fear of a collision with the Executive Power, the Legislature dared not assert this incontestable right. The proposition of the Questors was rejected by a large majority. Was that an act of conspiracy against Louis Napoleon? What! the Assembly was conspiring, and it renounced the command of the troops which might have defended it, and made them over to the man who was compassing its ruin! And when did these things happen? A fortnight ago.

Lastly, a bill on the responsibility of the President and the different officers of state was sent up to the Assembly by the *Conseil d'Etat*. Observe, that this proposition did not emanate from the Assembly, that the Assembly had no right, by law, to refuse to entertain it. The bill was, therefore, brought up, but the committee to which it was referred showed at once that its disposition was conciliatory. The provisions of the bill were rendered more mild, and the discussion was to be deferred, in order to avoid the displeasure of the Executive Power. Were these the actions of enemies and conspirators? And what was happening in the meanwhile? All the journals notoriously paid by the President insulted the Assembly day by day in the coarsest manner, threatened it, and tried by every means to cover it with unpopularity.

This is history—the truth of history. The acts of which I speak are the last of the National Assembly of France, and I defy our adversaries to find any other facts to oppose to them. That an Assembly of 760 members may have included in that number certain conspirators, it would be absurd to deny. But the manifest truth, proved by its acts, is that the majority of this Assembly, instead of conspiring against Louis Napoleon, sought for nothing so much as to avoid a quarrel with him; that it carried its moderation towards him to the verge of weakness, and its desire of conciliation to a degree of pusillanimity. That is the truth. You may believe my assertions, for I participated in the passions of none of its parties, and I have no reason either to flatter or to hate them.

Let us now proceed to examine what the Assembly did on the 2d of December; and here I cease to express any opinion, I merely relate, as an actual witness, the things I saw with my eyes and heard with my ears.

When the representatives of the people learned, on waking that morning, that several of their colleagues were arrested, they ran to the Assembly. The doors were guarded by the

Chasseurs de Vincennes, a corps of troops recently returned from Africa, and long accustomed to the violences of Algerian dominion, and, moreover, stimulated by a donation of 5*f.* distributed to every soldier who was in Paris that day. The representatives, nevertheless, presented themselves to go in, having at their head one of their Vice-Presidents, M. Daru.[33] This gentleman was violently struck by the soldiers, and the representatives who accompanied him were driven back at the point of the bayonet. Three of them, MM. de Talhouet, Etienne, and Duparc, were slightly wounded. Several others had their clothes pierced. Such was the commencement.

Driven from the doors of the Assembly, the deputies retired to the Mairie of the 10th arrondissement. They were already assembled to the number of about 300, when the troops arrived, blocked up the approaches, and prevented a greater number of representatives from entering the apartment, though no one was at that time prevented from leaving it. Who, then, were those representatives assembled at the Mairie of the 10th arrondissement, and what did they do there? Every shade of opinion was represented in this extemporaneous Assembly. But eight-tenths of its members belonged to the different Conservative parties which had constituted the majority. This Assembly was presided over by two of its Vice-Presidents, M. Vitet[34] and M. Benoit d'Azy.[35] M. Daru was arrested in his own house; the fourth Vice-President, the illustrious General Bedeau, had been seized that morning in his bed and handcuffed like a robber. As for the President, M.

33. Napoleon, Count Daru (1807-1890), once a peer of France, elected a representative to the Legislative Assembly from La Manche, and much later, in Emile Ollivier's cabinet during the more "liberal" empire of the 1860s, minister of foreign affairs.

34. Louis-Ludovic Vitet (1802-1873), son of a man who participated in the Revolution of 1789, a member of the Chamber of Deputies in the July Monarchy, a representative in the Legislative Assembly since 1849, and now co-presiding officer during this parliamentary protest.

35. Denis Benoît d'Azy (1796-1880), a representative in legislatures under the Restoration, the July Monarchy, and the Second Republic. After 1851, he concentrated on industrial and financial interests.

Dupin,[36] he was absent, which surprised no one, as his cowardice was known. Besides its Vice-Presidents, the Assembly was
accompanied by its secretaries, its ushers, and even its shorthand writer, who will preserve for posterity the records of
this last and memorable sitting. The Assembly, thus constituted, began by voting a decree in the following terms: —

"In pursuance of Article 68 of the Constitution—viz.: the
President of the Republic, the Ministers, the agents, and de-
positaries of public authority are responsible, each in what
concerns themselves respectively, for all the acts of the Government and the Administration—any measure by which the
President of the Republic dissolves the National Assembly,
prorogues it, or places obstacles in the exercise of its powers,
is a crime of high treason.

"By this act merely the President is deprived of all authority, the citizens are bound to withhold their obedience, the
Executive power passes in full right to the National Assembly. The Judges of the High Court of Justice will meet immediately under pain of forfeiture; they will convoke the juries in
the place which they will select to proceed to the judgement
of the President and his accomplices; they will nominate the
magistrates charged to fulfil the duties of public Ministers.

"And seeing that the National Assembly is prevented by
violence from exercising its powers, it decrees as follows,
viz.: —

"*Louis Napoleon Bonaparte is deprived of all authority as President of the Republic.* The citizens are enjoined to withhold their
obedience. The Executive power has passed in full right to
the National Assembly. The Judges of the High Court of Justice are enjoined to meet immediately, under pain of forfei-

36. André Marie Jean Jacques Dupin (1783-1865), famous lawyer, an unpopular member of the Chamber of Deputies under the July Monarchy, elected
to the Constituent Assembly in 1848, chosen president of the Legislative Assembly, and an Orleanist. Tocqueville called him selfish and cowardly (despite
recognizing Dupin's bursts of integrity) in *Recollections,* and in fact Dupin suffered some ridicule for his excessively frightened behavior of December 2. He
later became a senator under the Second Empire.

ture, to proceed to the judgement of the President and his accomplices; consequently all the officers and functionaries of power and of public authority are bound to obey all requisitions made in the name of the National Assembly, under pain of forfeiture and of high treason.

"Done and decreed unanimously in public sitting, this 2d of December, 1851."

[A list of 230 signatures follows; among the signatures are those of Barrot, Beaumont, Berryer, de Broglie, Chambolle, Corcelle, Dufaure, Duvergier de Hauranne, de Falloux, Lanjuinais, Rémusat, Sainte-Beuve, Tocqueville, and Eugène Sue.]

All the members whose names I have here given were arrested. Several others, having left the room after having signed, could not be taken. Among these, the best known are M. de Tracy, M. de Malleville, Ferdinand de Lasteyrie, and General Rulhière.

After having voted this first decree, another was unanimously passed, naming General Oudinot commander of the public forces, and M. Tamisier was joined with him as chief of staff. The choice of these two officers from distinct shades of political opinion showed that the Assembly was animated by one common spirit.

These decrees had scarcely been signed by all the members present, and deposited in a place of safety, when a band of soldiers, headed by their officers, sword in hand, appeared at the door, without, however, daring to enter the apartment. The Assembly awaited them in perfect silence. The President alone raised his voice, read the decrees which had just been passed to the soldiers, and ordered them to retire. The poor fellows, ashamed of the part they were compelled to play, hesitated. The officers, pale and undecided, declared that they should go for further orders. They retired, contenting themselves with blockading the passages leading to the apartment. The Assembly, not being able to go out, ordered the windows to be opened, and caused the decrees to be read to the people and the troops in the street below, especially that decree which, in pursuance of the 68th article of the constitution, pronounced the deposition and impeachment of Louis Napoleon.

Soon, however, the soldiers reappeared at the door, preceded this time by two *Commissaires de Police*. These men entered the room, and, amid the unbroken silence and total immobility of the Assembly, summoned the representatives to disperse. The President ordered them to retire themselves. One of the commissaires was agitated, and faltered; the other broke out in invectives. The President said to him, "Sir, we are here the lawful authority, and sole representatives of law and of right. We know that we cannot oppose to you material force, but we will leave this chamber only under constraint. We will not disperse. Seize us, and convey us to prison." "All, all!" exclaimed the members of the Assembly. After much hesitation, the Commissaires de Police decided to act. They caused the two Presidents to be seized by the collar. The whole body then rose, and, arm-in-arm, two-and-two, they followed the Presidents, who were led off. In this order we reached the street, and were marched across the city, without knowing whither we were going.

Care had been taken to circulate a report among the crowd and the troops that a meeting of Socialist and Red Republican deputies had been arrested. But when the people beheld among those who were thus dragged through the mud of Paris on foot, like a gang of malefactors, men the most illustrious by their talents and their virtues, ex-Ministers, ex-Ambassadors, Generals, Admirals, great orators, great writers, surrounded by the bayonets of the line, a shout was raised, *"Vive l'Assemblée Nationale."* The representatives were attended by these shouts until they reached the barracks of the Quai d'Orsay, where they were shut up. Night was coming on, and it was wet and cold. Yet the Assembly was left two hours in the open air, as if the Government did not deign to remember its existence. The representatives here made their last roll call in presence of their shorthand writer, who had followed them. The number present was 218, to whom were added about twenty more in the course of the evening, consisting of members who had voluntarily caused themselves to be arrested. Almost all the men known to France and to Europe, who formed the majority of the Legislative Assembly, were gathered together in this place. Few were wanting, except those who, like M. Molé, had not been suffered to reach their colleagues. There were present, among others, the Duke de Broglie, who had come, though ill; the father of the house, the venerable Keratry, whose physical strength was inferior to his moral courage, and whom it was necessary to seat in a straw chair in the barrack yard; Odilon Barrot, Dufaure, Berryer, Rémusat, Duvergier de Hauranne, Gustave de Beaumont, de Tocqueville, de Falloux, Lanjuinais, Admiral Lainé and Admiral Cécille, Generals Oudinot and Lauriston, the Duke de Luynes, the Duke de Montebello; twelve ex-Ministers, nine of whom had served under Louis Napoleon himself; eight members of the Institute; all men who had struggled for three years to defend society and to resist the demagogic faction.

When two hours had elapsed, this assemblage was driven into barrack-rooms upstairs, where most of them spent the night, without fire, and almost without food, stretched upon the boards. It only remained to carry off to prison these honourable men, guilty of no crime but the defence of the laws of their country. For this purpose the most distressing and ignominious means were selected. The cellular vans, in which *forçats* are conveyed to the *bagne,* were brought up. In these vehicles were shut up the men who had served and honoured their country, and they were conveyed like three bands of criminals, some to the fortress of Mont Valerien, some to the Prison Mazas in Paris, and the remainder to Vincennes. The indignation of the public compelled the Government two days afterwards to release the greater number of them; some are still in confinement, unable to obtain either their liberty or their trial.

The treatment inflicted on the Generals arrested in the morning of the 2d December was still more disgraceful. Cavaignac, Lamoricière, Bedeau, Changarnier—the conquerors of Africa, were shut up in these infamous cellular vans, which are always inconvenient, and became almost intolerable on a lengthened journey. In this manner they were conveyed to Ham—that is, they were made to perform upwards of a day's journey. Cavaignac, who had saved Paris and France in the days of June—Cavaignac, the competitor of Louis Napoleon at the last elections, shut up for a day and a night in the cell of a felon! I leave it to every honest man and every generous heart to comment on such facts. Can it be that indignities which surpass the actions of the King of Naples find a defender in England? No; England knows but a small portion of what is taking place. I appeal to her better judgement when these facts are known to the world.

Such are the indignities offered to persons. Let me now review the series of general crimes. The liberty of the press is destroyed to an extent unheard of even in the time of the Empire. Most of the journals are suppressed; those which appear cannot say a word on politics or even publish any news. But this is by no means all. The Government has stuck up a list of persons who are formed into a "Consultative Commission." Its object is to induce France to believe that the Executive is not abandoned by every man of respectability and consideration among us. More than half of the persons on this list have refused to belong to the commission; most of them regard the insertion of their names as dishonour. I may quote among others M. Léon Faucher, M. Portalis, First President of the Court of Cassation, and the Duke d'Albuféra, as those best known. Not only does the Government decline to publish the letters in which these gentlemen refuse their consent, but even their names are not withdrawn from a list which dishonours them. The names are still retained, in spite of their repeated remonstrances. A day or two ago, one of them, M. Joseph Périer, driven to desperation by this excess of tyranny, rushed into the street to strike out his own name with his own hands from the public placards, taking the passers-by to witness that it had been placed there by a lie.

Such is the state of the public journals. Let us now see the condition of personal liberty. I say, again, that personal liberty is more trampled on than ever it was in the time of the Empire. A decree of the new Power gives the prefects the right to arrest, in their respective departments, whomsoever they please; and the prefects, in their turn, send blank warrants of arrest, which are literally *lettres de cachet,* to the *sous-prefets* under their orders. The Provisional Government of the Republic never went so far. Human life is as little respected as human liberty. I know that war has its dreadful necessities, but the disturbances which have recently occurred in Paris have been put down with a barbarity unprecedented in our civil contests; and when we remember that this torrent of blood has been shed to consummate the violation of all laws, we cannot but think that sooner or later it will fall back upon the heads of those who shed it. As for the appeal to the people, to which Louis Napoleon affects to submit his claims, never was a more odious mockery offered to a nation. The people is called upon to express its opinion, yet not only is public discussion suppressed, but even the knowledge of facts. The people is asked its opinion, but the first measure taken to obtain it is to establish military terrorism throughout the country, and to threaten with deprivation every public agent who does not approve in writing what has been done.

Such, Sir, is the condition in which we stand. Force overturning law, trampling on the liberty of the press and of the person, deriding the popular will, in whose name the Government pretends to act—France torn from the alliance of free nations to be yoked to the despotic Monarchies of the Continent—such is the result of the *coup d'état*. If the judgement of the people of England can approve these military saturnalia, and if the facts I have related, and which I pledge myself are accurately true, did not rouse its censures, I shall mourn for you and for ourselves, and for the sacred cause of legal liberty throughout the world; for the public opinion of England is the grand jury of mankind in the cause of freedom, and if its verdict were to acquit the oppressor, the oppressed would have no other resource but in God.

One word more, to record a fact which does honor to the magistracy of France, and which will be remembered in its annals. The army refused to submit to the decree of the captive Assembly impeaching the President of the Republic; but the High Court of Justice obeyed it. These five judges, sitting in the midst of Paris enslaved, and in the face of martial law, dared to assemble at the Palace of Justice, and to issue process commencing criminal proceedings against Louis Napoleon, charged with high treason by the law, though already triumphant in the streets. I subjoin the text of this memorable edict: —

"THE HIGH COURT OF JUSTICE,

"Considering the 68th article of the constitution, considering that printed placards commencing with the words 'the President of the Republic,' and bearing at the end the signatures of Louis Napoleon Bonaparte and De Morny, Minister of the Interior, which placards announce, among other things, the dissolution of the National Assembly, have this day been affixed to the walls of Paris; that this fact of the dissolution of the Assembly by the President of the Republic would fall under the case provided for by the 68th article of the constitution, and render the convocation of the High Court of Justice imperative, by the terms of that article declares, that the High Court is constituted, and names M. Renouard, counsellor of the Court of Cassation, to fill the duties of public accuser, and to fill those of Greffier M. Bernard, Greffier in Chief of the Court of Cassation; and, to proceed further in pursuance of the terms of the said 68th article of the constitution, adjourns until tomorrow, the 3d of December at the hour of noon.

"Done and deliberated in the Council Chamber. Present,

M. Hardouin, president, M. Pataille, M. Moreau, M. de la Palme, and M. Cauchy, judges, this 2d day of December, 1851."

After this textual extract from the Minutes of the High Court of Justice, there is the following entry:

"1. A *procès-verbal* stating the arrival of a *Commissaire de Police,* who called upon the High Court to separate.

"2. A *procès-verbal* of a second sitting held on the morrow, the 3d day of December (when the Assembly was in prison), at which M. Renouard accepts the functions of public prosecutor, charged to proceed against Louis Napoleon, after which the High Court, being no longer able to sit, adjourned to a day to be fixed hereafter."

With these extracts from the judicial records I terminate this communication.

Six

FROM THE BEGINNING OF THE SECOND EMPIRE TO THE PUBLICATION OF *The Old Regime* (1852–1856)

The first letter in this section begins with a bitter description of the crimes and injustices of the new Empire, but Tocqueville saves his most intense bitterness for the French people, who apparently have accepted the new regime. "But what is heartbreaking is to see the bulk of the nation applaud and feel that it is not suppressed, but supreme." He attributes this deplorable spectacle to three causes: first, the "immoral" government of Louis Philippe, which encouraged a "softening" or lack of courage and bold ambition; second, the willingness of the middle classes to trade public liberty for private prosperity; and third, the irrational terror of the "phantom of socialism," a fear that drives men to assist in their own oppression provided the government guarantees them from the so-called socialist menace (Letter 71). In France, Tocqueville writes, the socialist has taken the place that "the devil occupied in the imagination of the Middle Ages" (Letter 79).

One might expect that a new emperor, bearing the name Napoleon, would establish a government that at least pretended to boldness, to grandeur, and to military expansion. In fact, writes Tocqueville, the new government adopted all the fundamental and detestable features of the July Monarchy. Napoleon III's boldness "is little by little being extinguished and enervated in the more material and more bourgeois enjoyments that the hazards of fortune . . . have put within his reach. He seems to me, more and more, to be reduced to the basic principle of Louis Philippe; powerlessness and modesty outside, industrial politics inside." Thus, underneath a façade of occasional imperial rhetoric, lies a government very similar to the July Monarchy, a government that draws its support from the industrial bourgeoisie. Napoleon III has merely made a bad arrangement worse, by muzzling the press and making a mockery out of what was once an ineffective, though partially representative, Chamber of Deputies (Letter 72).

Tocqueville argues at great length in *Democracy in America* that the beliefs, habits, and mores of a nation are as important, indeed probably more important, than institutions in securing political freedom. Any nation might write excellent laws or compose a remarkable constitution, but democratic freedom will not flourish unless the habits of participation, self-reliance, cooperation, and morality penetrate into the daily thoughts and activities of citizens. Tocqueville repeats these ideas in a letter to Corcelle, saying that institutions have only a secondary influence on the shape of society. If one could merely legislate a republic, then Tocqueville could at least hope that "by chance we might, someday, stumble onto the precious piece of paper that would contain the recipe for all wrongs." Instead, "political societies are not what their laws make them, but what sentiments, beliefs, ideas, habits of the heart," and the history of the culture have shaped them to be (Letter 74).

It is this conviction that habits and mores are the foundation on which a nation establishes political freedom that so disheartens Tocqueville because he contends that first the July Monarchy and now the Second Empire have engendered a corruption of French mores. First, France, once so self-confident and proud that she believed she could reorganize the world, now seems mired in feelings of powerlessness, timidity, lack of confidence, a sort of fatalism. This concern emerges most clearly in Tocqueville's dispute with Gobineau. After attacking Gobineau's racial theories, Tocqueville adds that the practical effects of such a doctrine are more pernicious than its theoretical flaws. The suggestion that events are determined because of race only reinforces the fatalism, sense of powerlessness, and resignation that is "the great malady of the time" (Letter 78). Second, Tocqueville feels that France has lost all of her aspiration for noble ideals, moral principles, and great deeds. Instead, citizens have become subjects who dream only of petty, private affairs and material comforts. "People believe strongly in nothing, they love nothing, they hate nothing, and they hope for nothing except to profit at the stock exchange" (Letter 103; see also Letter 87). Tocqueville, by the way, reveals his own aristocratic attitude toward wealth when he confides to Beaumont his contempt and horror at the prospect of consecrating his days to commerce or industry (Letter 73). Third, freedom requires a certain rugged independence, a willingness to throw oneself into public disputes, an occasional challenge to authority; but Tocqueville sees around him only growing centralization, bureaucratization, and docility. This concern lies behind his warning to Theodore Sedgwick that the German immigrants to the United States, bringing with them only habits of deference to authority, were a threat to the mores of democratic America (Letter 81).

Confronted by what he regards as the continuing deterioration of France, Tocqueville withdraws into his writing. In fact, only his intellectual pursuits can divert his gaze from France and avert a bitter melancholy. "I confess that I am often struck by terrible attacks of discouragement; I sometimes have hours or days of great bitterness and of infinite sadness. How could it possibly be otherwise when one compares what we imagined, desired, hoped for our country during all those years with what we see? . . . For my own part, I would be surely dead of low spirits if I had not found work" (Letter 85). Saddest of all, perhaps, Tocqueville believes that the best men of his time are learning to accommodate themselves to the empire, even learning to acquire a "taste for servitude." Thus, more than at any point in his life, Tocqueville feels a stranger to his times. To Madame Swetchine, he writes: "You could not imagine, Madame, the pain and often the cruelty I experience in living in this moral isolation, to feel myself outside the intellectual community of my time and my country. Solitude in a desert would seem to me less harsh than this sort of solitude among men" (Letter 87).

As early as *Democracy in America*, Tocqueville had painted, with broad strokes, the most fundamental force for change in the nineteenth century: the relentless unfolding of equality and democracy. The word *democracy* has a host of connotations for Tocqueville, but to a great extent he equated it with the demise of the landed aristocracy and the rise of the middle classes. He restates this thesis bluntly in a letter to Beaumont when he talks of the "great revolution that is operating slowly but as irresistibly [in England] as elsewhere: the prevalence of the bourgeois classes and the industrial element over the aristocratic classes and landed property. Is this a good or an evil? Your grandchildren will discuss this question" (Letter 72). Tocqueville had always hoped that, despite certain deplorable characteristics of the middle class—an obsession with private affairs, lack of any vision for the future, a tendency to selfishness, etc.—wise statesmanship could steer this middle-class democracy toward freedom, morality, and even grandeur. Now Tocqueville has become profoundly pessimistic about whether middle-class government, in any nation, can produce anything lasting, free, or great. France, it seems, has tried but failed.

Is it really true that there were political assemblies in France? That the nation was enthusiastic over what was said in them? . . . Those passions, those experiences, those fears, those friendships, those hatreds, . . . do they refer to a time we really saw or are they memories of what we learned reading the history of times past? I would truly be tempted to believe the latter; because what has really existed leaves some trace, and I see none of what we imagined we perceived or felt. (Letter 85)

71. *To Henry Reeve*

Paris, January 9, 1852

As I told you, my dear friend, I was counting on writing you a long letter, but I lacked the courage to accomplish this task. What should I tell you that you do not know about what is happening in France? When I finally want to speak of our affairs, even to my best friends (and you are among them), a sadness so bitter and so profound seizes me that I have trouble continuing such distressing conversations or correspondence. This affliction, besides, does not date from the most recent events. It preceded them. You were able to perceive in the letter that I wrote you at the end of November that I saw that all was lost and expected all sorts of disgrace and misfortune. However gloomy my presentiments were then, the event has surpassed them. What has happened can be defined: the most odious conduct of revolutionaries has been employed to serve the grudges and above all to calm the fears of the conservative party. Indeed, one has to go back to the Committee of Public Safety and the Terror to find anything analogous in our history to what we are seeing now. And even the Terror kept in the crime a certain hypocrisy of forms and of fairness that is lacking here. Then they at least pretended to judge those who were being sent to death. Now, they send thousands of unfortunates to die in the wilds of Guiana[1] (already so dismally renowned in our annals) who have not even been the object of a judicial investigation or inquest. And that is nothing: because what else is one to expect from the wretches who are the counselors or principal agents of this government? But what is heartbreaking is to see the bulk of the nation applaud and

1. In the end, about three thousand people were imprisoned in France, ten thousand sent to Algeria, and several hundred to Guiana.

feel that it is not suppressed, but supreme. Nothing shows two things more clearly: the first, the softening of souls, which the immoral government of Louis Philippe brought about; the second, the dreadful terror into which this violent, but above all mad, Revolution of February has thrown these souls, softened and ready to bear anything with joy and even to assist in anything provided that the phantom of socialism that disturbed their enjoyment by threatening their future would disappear.

Although this government has been established by one of the greatest crimes known in history, nevertheless it will last a long enough time, unless it hastens itself to ruin. Its excesses, its wars, its corruption must make the country forget its fear of the socialists, which necessarily requires time. God be willing, in the meantime it will not find its end in a fashion nearly as prejudicial to us as to itself, in some mad foreign adventure. We know this only too well in France; governments never escape the law of their origins. This one, which arrives by means of the army, which can only endure by means of the army, which finds its popularity and even its reason for existing only in the memories of military glory, this government will be dragged fatally into wanting territorial expansion, spheres of influence, in other words, into war. That is, at least, what I fear, and what all sensible people dread with me. In war, it will surely find death, but perhaps then its death will cost us very dearly.

As for me, my dear friend, I have been exerting great effort for a month to recapture my peace of mind, which alone can let me give my attention to some useful occupation. I am beginning to succeed in this, but from time to time the sight of the violence of some, of the cowardice of others, stirs me up and there I am carried away anew into a violent but sterile indignation; because for the moment there is nothing to do but to try to create in one's own mind the silence that the government is causing to reign in the country. Little by little, however, I am applying myself to work again and I am awaiting impatiently the moment when the season will permit me to go and give myself over entirely to Tocqueville, in such a way as to forget what is happening and disinterest myself, if possible, from my time and from my country.

You have the deepest expression of affection from my heart.

72. *To Gustave de Beaumont*

Paris, March 23, 1853

I will only write you a few words today, my dear friend, because my wife must have given yours news of us and especially because your letter gives me reason to believe that I will see you in a week or ten days. In all times, but principally in ours, correspondence is only a makeshift to which one must be reduced when conversation is forbidden. One makes oneself so badly understood by letter, even when one dares to write everything!

I admire what an exact concord exists in our ways of feeling. I feel, as you do, that the present state of things, instead of growing lighter by habit, becomes heavier the longer it lasts and seems more painful to bear today than at its beginning. This is true for the reason you give and also because of the fact that, after all, its chances of lasting are increasing. It seems evident to me that the times and the use of sovereign power are producing certain effects in the mind of the master, which while diminishing the worth of the man, increase the chances of his government. It seems to me that what he had of life, of boldness, and to a certain extent of grandeur, although always badly proportioned in his imagination and in the image he made from his accession, is little by little being extinguished and enervated in the more material and more bourgeois enjoyments that the hazards of fortune and the folly of the authors of the February Revolution have put within his reach. He seems to me, more and more, to be reduced to the basic principle of Louis Philippe; powerlessness and modesty outside, industrial politics inside; the whole disguised or colored by a press to which no one can respond. In the current state of the country, no striking virtues serve him as well as the mediocrity of such vices.

You ask me for news of our friends: several of them will dine with me next Tuesday the 29th. I hope that Reeve will also be with us. For the first time we are daring to have another housewarming. So try to be in Paris for this day and come take your place with such good company!

It is certain that the agreement between railroad companies is being consummated. That business is accomplished. I do not know the details on Rivet's position. But, he does not seem to be discontented. He seems to believe that a small council will be formed on which the current heads of the lines will serve as the main authority over their line.[2]

The Orient affair will yet be a soap bubble that will burst without making a sound.[3] At least everything portends that

2. In 1853–1854, the emperor reorganized and helped finance a much needed extension and coordination of the railway system. In 1853, the railways were controlled by about twenty companies, each with its separate tariff, each afraid to risk investment to establish much needed commercial lines, and all of which needed intelligent planning to provide a comprehensive, national rail system. In the 1850s, the government of the Second Empire addressed the problem; it formed larger companies that could coordinate several smaller ones, it practically eliminated the risk of investment, and by the end of the decade the number of miles of railway track in France was four times what it had been in 1848.

3. In January 1853, Czar Nicholas I proposed to England that Turkey was a "sick man" and thus England and Russia should control Turkey's fate and share the spoils of a shattered empire. When Prime Minister Aberdeen gave an ambiguous response to this offer, the czar sent Prince Menshikov in March 1853 to seize Constantinople under the pretext of protecting Greek Orthodox churches in Turkey. At first this move appeared to be another in long negotiations over Christian rights in Holy Places throughout the Turkish Empire, but soon Russia's belligerence became apparent. In effect, Russia was asking the impossible: the right of protection over the 10 million Greek citizens in Turkey.

Turkey rejected the demands in May, Menshikov sailed and occupied another Turkish province (Moldavia), France protested vigorously, and English public opinion, led now by Palmerston, turned against Russia. Vienna tried to negotiate a peace in July 1853, but the effort failed, and Turkey declared war on Russia in October. Palmerston welcomed French and English cooperation, but people only aspire to emerge from it battered and content. Nevertheless, what is happening is *news* and probably one of the last phases in the life of the Turkish Empire. For the first time, it is clear that England herself is renouncing the hope of keeping it alive, and, although its hour has not sounded, it will hardly be long in coming. Volumes could have been written above; but the necessary policy, which this affair and many others put in relief, is: first, the impossibility, recognized by the English government, of conducting any business of long duration with our government, which inspired an *incurable* defiance everywhere; second, the gradual, but continuous change in the English temperament, which each day is becoming more pacific, less irritable, less proud than it has shown itself in any period of modern history. This, seen clearly, is only the addendum to the great revolution that is operating slowly but as irresistibly there as elsewhere: the prevalence of the bourgeois classes and the industrial element over the aristocratic classes and landed property. Is this a good or an evil? Your grandchildren will discuss this question. A society calmer and duller, more tranquil and less heroic, such will without a doubt be the spectacle that those who will follow us will have before their eyes, without perhaps being capable of noticing what is new; because it is necessary to be at the point of division, as we are, to perceive the two routes distinctly.

My health seems to be recovering gradually. I am beginning to work again very actively. But still without producing anything. I am lost in an ocean of research, in the midst of which fatigue and discouragement sometimes overcome me. It is not only discouragement with myself but with men, at the sight,

---

as late as January 1854—after Russia had destroyed the Turkish fleet and after the British-French fleet had entered the Black Sea—Napoleon III was still trying to avert war. Finally, in March 1854, almost one year exactly after Tocqueville wrote this letter, France and England declared war on Russia, allied themselves with Turkey, and entered the Crimean War (1854–1856). Tocqueville was wrong; when this soap bubble burst, it created quite a roar.

which is clearer every day, of the small number of things that we know, of their uncertainty, of their unceasing repetition in new words, for three thousand years; finally with the insignificance of our kind, of our world, and with our destiny, with what we call our *great* revolutions and our *great* affairs. It is necessary, nonetheless, to work, because this is the sole resource that remains to us for forgetting what is sad about surviving in the empire with its ideas and about feeling more estranged in one's own country than one would be among foreigners.

I long to be able to chat with you about what occupies and will occupy you, I hope, to your great honor. Remember us fondly to your family. I embrace you. Until later.

73. *To Gustave de Beaumont*

Friday, April 8, 1853

My dear friend, yesterday I was paid for you the sum of 415 francs 94 centimes at the Academy, which I am holding for Jacques's disposition. The attendants asked me if you were not counting this year, as in preceding years, on making them a New Year's Day present. I said that I would follow your instructions in this regard. Give them to me when you write me.

Your last letter saddened me greatly without surprising me. Several days before, Laubespin had come to speak to my wife in terms that had prepared me for what you told me. (It is vital for you to know that the said Laubespin, if he speaks to others as he has to us, makes the secret you rightfully desire to keep, at least in regards the most regrettable truth, impossible; because he expatiates on the subject at great length and even exaggerates, I believe, what is regrettable in this situation. It is right to add at the same time that he does not run dry of praise for people with regard to their affairs and, in particular, yours, in which, however, he only does do you

justice.) To come back to the real question, with true sorrow
I see that you are constricted and in such tight straits that the
least extraordinary expense must be avoided. This state of fortune, which goes so far as to remove from you all freedom of
action, and which will soon be an obstacle even to the education of your children, fills me with diverse thoughts of which
several, assuredly, must have occurred to you and which you
no doubt had good reasons for rejecting. I asked myself,
among other things, if the situation did not make it necessary
for you to find a way to augment your revenue in industry,
which would be very easy for you. I know you refused to do
it eighteen months ago, when it was yet easier. But things
were not then in the state they seem to be in today. I know
your objections. They appeared all-powerful to me then and
I still find much strength in them. I want to say to you only
that I no longer have, on this point, an opinion as clear and as
decided as I had at that time. Surely, I would not want, even
from the point of view of your well-intended interest in your
children, to see you devote your life to increasing your fortune, as poor Louis[4] seems bent on doing, but the question is
whether several years devoted in this way would not at least
procure for you the ease that brings independence of movement, the single goal that I desire to see you attain. I am so
ignorant in these matters that I do not know if what I say here
is possible, or, at least, if in order to attain this goal, it would
be necessary not only to enter into business, but to do business, which is different. I therefore am saying nothing on this
subject that you do not know better than I, a subject on
which your mind must have fixed. What is certain is that I am
very painfully occupied with your situation and the effects
that it cannot help producing on the mind of your wife, whatever efforts you have made in order to hide your own preoc-
cupations from her. I am indignant against destiny, when I see
people who are so worthy of being happy, in such distress,

4. Louis de Kergorlay.

without it being their fault, and if something could increase the tender attachment we both feel for you two, it would be to see you subjected to this test and to see you bearing it so nobly.

I am not any better informed than you are about public affairs, although I am closer than you to the place where they are being decided. It appears evident to me that for the moment the government has entered fully into Louis Philippe's system: immoderate development of material interests and administration by knaves internally; extreme modesty externally, masked as well as possible by certain shows of force or proud speeches. I persist in believing that nothing will come of the Orient affair, that it has been decided to yield on all the *substantial* questions and to ask only for some satisfaction of self-esteem concerning the Holy Places.[5] Still, if nothing is obtained in this regard, people will peacefully swallow the shame of an enterprise begun so thoughtlessly and finished in so cowardly a way. But what do the French people know of it and even more what does it matter to them? This absence of publicity and supervision permits the people of Paris to consecrate themselves to making by their labor and by assistance, sums of which people had no idea in preceding regimes. The suburbs are particularly *cared for* and, I have heard it said, not without success. The poor denounce each other as socialists in order to have part of the pie. Do not speak to me of the people or of those who are of the people by temperament; persons who only have instincts and no principles; sometimes pushing, by a sudden flight, up to heroism, but generally floundering in the gutter.

You ask me what are our plans. The difficulty of finding anything at this moment to buy and even to rent in the vicinity of Paris, the desire to economize for a year and, above all, the need I see in my wife to have a long and uninterrupted

5. Since 1851, France's chief dispute with Turkey concerned the right of access to the Holy Places in Palestine for Catholics.

rest, have made us think about spending next summer and winter in some very tranquil, small corner of a province. We would go with delight to T[ocqueville] if we could spend summer and winter there. But my health does not permit us to hazard such an undertaking at this moment. We therefore have been thinking of the Loire Valley, Blois or Tours; Blois rather on account of the nearness of Paris and on account of Mme. B[elam],[6] who is growing old. The climate is mild, and the country agreeable. The more I live, the less I feel the need of external distractions; this is the sole gain I have found up to now in aging. As yet we have confided these ideas to no one. Therefore do not circulate them. But, tell us, since you know this entire region, if you believe that we could find in one of the two places I have named, or just outside, an unfurnished dwelling that could suit our plan. I will be grateful if you would not delay long in answering these questions, if you can answer them.

You confuse me greatly when you speak to me of my new chapters. I have not *written one line* since we parted. I have however worked a great deal for about six weeks, but as I already told you, the subject is almost limitless, as research. I want to try to understand what, in truth, the France of the Old Regime was at the moment the Revolution surprised it, the state of the people, the habits of public administration, because there was scarcely anything but habits. . . . That is already more difficult to rediscover than the rules of the curia in Rome and the constitution of the three orders of which Roman society was composed, two thousand years ago. I do not know if I will extract something interesting and new from this study, which is making progress; I am finding in it, at least, the advantage of forgetting, in surrendering myself to it, the things and the men of our time and of isolating myself, without boredom, from human beings, which appears to me, more and more, the great goal to attain. Because I never leave

6. The aunt of Tocqueville's wife, Marie.

contact with them, whatever they say, without being of-
fended. If they are not of my opinion, they irritate me; if they
are, they sadden me in forcing me to stir up the blackest of
my thoughts.

Farewell, my very dear friend, write me often and freely;
because, like you, I am in the habit of never giving anyone
else a full letter to read, but rather communicating only passages. I embrace you. Extend our warmest feelings of friendship to your household.

Your Macaulay[7] should be brought back to me this very
day from the bookbinder's. I was not able to make him bind
it earlier for fear of making it illegible. If that man, who is
making me wait two weeks, keeps his word to me this time,
I will give the two volumes in question to Jacques. If not, as
soon as they are brought to me.

Always examine the seal well to see if it has not been lifted
and pasted back on again. I chose one as complicated as possible in order to make that operation difficult. The opening of
letters is not only an established fact, but now is officially admitted, since the basis of the case against M. de Rovigo and
others are letters by them which were opened in the mail,
before the presentation of presumptive evidence, and which
someone had the effrontery to attach to the dossier. Dufaure
pleads Tuesday in this affair.

74. To Claude-François de Corcelle

Saint-Cyr, près Tours, September 17, 1853

I have very often been thinking and speaking of you, my
dear friend, in the last fortnight. I therefore can explain my
silence only by the rather lulling effect produced by a life that

---

7. Tocqueville is probably referring to the 1853 translation, by Jules de Pey-
ronnet, of Thomas Macaulay's famous history of England: *Histoire d'Angleterre
depuis l'avènement de Jacques II*. Beaumont had recommended this book to Tocqueville in a letter of January 12, 1853, as a good model to follow in writing history.

is so regulated that in the end I can imagine nothing but what I did the days before. It is a sort of voluntary *treadmill*[8] on which one dreams only of lifting one foot after the other until the wheel stops.

I will tell you right away, to answer your friendly question, that since your departure, I have been happier with my health, and that my doctors continue to assure me that I will recover completely. On this last point, I am radically incredulous, and I do not believe that I will see my complete recovery any more than that of France. These illnesses, in both cases, are too old to admit hope of a complete cure, and I limit myself to desiring a tolerable state for both of them. You see that I am becoming moderate in my desires as I grow old.

I have just reread your letter, and it seems to me that you were mistaken about the meaning of what I said when we were talking about my new book; that is not astonishing, since it is very difficult to make someone else perceive clearly the plan of a work as vast as the one I have in my head.

I told you that my intention was not to investigate what remained to be done in order to heal France as the Old Regime, the republic, and the empire have formed it. That is true. My firm resolution is to stop at the entrance to this terrain, to consider it only from afar, and not to aim at doing a book just for the present occasion. But it does not follow at all that a clear meaning is not to be extracted from the historical study I have undertaken; that it must leave the opinions and sentiments of the author indefinite and the mind of the reader uncertain as to the judgments he should adopt on the facts and on men, on the events, their causes, and the lesson that emerges from them. It would be very odd if—bringing to this study tastes so decided and often so impassioned, ideas so set, a goal to reach for that is so visible to me and so fixed—I left the reader without any impetus whatsoever, wandering at random in the midst of my thoughts and of his.

8. Tocqueville uses the English word.

I believe that the books that have made men reflect the most and have had the most influence on their opinions and their actions are not those in which the author has sought to tell them dogmatically what it is suitable to think, but those in which he has set their minds on the road leading to truths and has made them find these truths for themselves. If God leaves me the time and strength necessary to finish my task, no one will have any doubt, be certain of that, about the goal I had in view.

You say that institutions are only half of my subject. I go farther than you, and I say that they are not even half. You know my ideas well enough to know that I accord institutions only a secondary influence on the destiny of men. Would to God I believed more in the omnipotence of institutions! I would have more hope for our future, because by chance we might, someday, stumble onto the precious piece of paper that would contain the recipe for all wrongs, or on the man who knew the recipe. But, alas, there is no such thing, and I am quite convinced that political societies are not what their laws make them, but what sentiments, beliefs, ideas, habits of the heart, and the spirit of the men who form them, prepare them in advance to be, as well as what nature and education have made them. If this truth does not emerge, at every turn, from my book, if it does not induce the readers to reflect, in this way, unceasingly on themselves, if it does not indicate at every instant, without ever having the pretense of instructing them, what are the sentiments, the ideas, the mores that alone can lead to public prosperity and liberty, what are the vices and errors that, on the other hand, divert them irresistibly from this, I will not have attained the principal and, as it were, unique goal that I have in view.

Passing to another subject, you are perhaps right in saying that I attach too much importance, in matters of faith, to the irregularities in the conduct of the clergy. You must pardon me a little because of the sadness, I could almost say the despair in view of what is happening, that is felt by a man who is as convinced as I am that man's true grandeur lies only in the harmony of the liberal sentiment and religious sentiment, both working simultaneously to animate and to restrain souls, and by one whose sole political passion for thirty years has been to bring about this harmony.

I am far from saying that among the greatest number of our compatriots consideration for religion is not growing now, but that is unfortunately not the same thing as the growth of faith.

At the beginning of next month my father is supposed to come spend several days with us. After which we will renounce the living and live only in the company of the illustrious dead, whose books will be our sole society. I do not give up hope, however, of seeing before spring a good friend like you tear himself away from Paris for a while to give us the favor of a little visit. Would I be mistaken? The world is contracting more and more for me, to the point that it no longer contains more than five or six people whose company pleases me, soothes me, and comforts me. You head the list of these last of humans. You will judge if I make the best of going so many months without chatting with you except by letter.

75. To Pierre Freslon

Saint-Cyr, September 23, 1853

I regretted, my dear friend, that you did not receive my last letter before you left for Belgium. . . .

I am still continuing the labors in which you were interested, but very slowly. . . .

When one studies, as I am doing in Tours in the archives of an old generality,[9] the details of administrative affairs before

---

9. A financial and administrative division of France, before 1789, that was headed by an Intendant. Tocqueville lived near Tours from June 1853 to June 1854, doing research in these archives in order to prepare to write *The Old Regime and the French Revolution*.

the Revolution of 1789, one finds a thousand new reasons for
hating the Old Regime, but few new reasons for loving the
Revolution; because one sees that the Old Regime collapsed of
itself and rapidly under the weight of the years and by the
imperceptible change of ideas and mores; and that, with a
little patience and virtue, one could have transformed it
without destroying at the same time both the detestable and
the good that it contained. It is curious to see how different
the government of 1780 already is from that of 1750. There
are the same laws, there are in appearance the same rules,
there are in abstract the same principles, there is the same look
on the surface. Fundamentally, there are already different
methods, different habits, a whole different spirit. Those who
are governed and those who govern are already changed beyond recognition. People did not fall from the excess of evil
into revolution, but from the excess of progress into revolution. Having come to the middle of the staircase, they threw
themselves out the window in order to arrive at the bottom
sooner. Thus, moreover, does the world almost always go. It
is almost never when a state of things is the most detestable
that it is smashed, but when, beginning to improve, it permits
men to breathe, to reflect, to communicate their thoughts
with each other, and to gauge by what they already have the
extent of their rights and their grievances. The weight, although less heavy, seems then all the more unbearable.

Around October 15, I am figuring on taking my winter
quarters. It is then that I flatter myself I will be able to work
seriously. I will put books to one side, I will cease digging
through old papers. I will finally undertake to write and really
begin my work; because as yet I have only been preparing
myself, and I am at one and the same time beginning to become excited and irritated in this long novitiate. I will throw
onto paper the first chapter of the work somehow or other,
and, judging by the result of this effort, I will see if I really
have a great book in my head or only its fleeting image. I
need to succeed in this first effort in order to have the courage

to go on. The sight of what is occurring is not good for anything, not even for getting a book done in solitude. You want me not to be downcast; that is a lion's advice, but how to follow it! . . .

76. To Arthur de Gobineau

Saint-Cyr, près Tours, November 17, 1853

I have all kinds of apologies to make to you, my dear friend, first for not having written about your work,[10] and next for having left your last letter without a response for ten or twelve days, very much in spite of myself. As for the first misdeed, it was induced by a sort of perplexity that reading your work caused in my mind and by the confusion I was in amidst the criticism and the praises I had to address to you. As for my silence, for two weeks, it was necessitated by the obligation of rapidly reading books that were borrowed from libraries in Paris and that were being reclaimed. Now, let us come to the matter at hand: I will behave differently from most people, I will begin with the criticisms. They bear on the mother-idea itself. I will admit to you frankly that you have not convinced me. All my objections still stand. You are, however, quite right to defend yourself as not being a materialist. Your doctrine is indeed rather a kind of fatalism, or predestination if you wish; different however from that of Saint Augustine, the Jansenists, and the Calvinists (it is these you resemble most by the absoluteness of the doctrine) in that there is with you a very tight bond between the fact of predestination and matter. Thus, you speak unceasingly of races that are regenerating or deteriorating, which take up or lay aside social capacities by an *infusion of different blood* (I believe that these are your own terms). Such a predestination seems to me, I will confess, a cousin of pure materialism and be sure

10. *Essai sur l'inégalité des races humaines,* the first volume of which was published in 1853.

that if the crowd, which always takes the great beaten tracks
in matters of reasoning, were to accept your doctrine, that
would lead it straight from the race to the individual and from
social capacities to all kinds of capacities. Besides, whether fa-
tality is placed directly in a certain organization of matter or in
the will of God, who wished to make several human species
in the human genus and to impose on certain men the obligation, by virtue of the race to which they belong, of not having certain sentiments, certain thoughts, certain behavior,
certain qualities that they know about without being able to
acquire them; that would be of little importance from the
point of view in which I place myself, which is the practical
consequences of different philosophical doctrines. The two
theories result in a very great contraction, if not a complete
abolition, of human liberty. Well, I confess to you that after
having read you, as well as before, I remain situated at the
opposite extreme of those doctrines. I believe them to be very
probably wrong and very certainly pernicious.

It is to be believed that within each of the different families
that compose the human race there are certain tendencies, certain characteristic aptitudes born of a thousand different
causes. But whether these tendencies, whether these aptitudes
are invincible, not only has that never been proven, but it is,
of itself, unprovable, because it would require having at one's
disposal not only the past but the future as well. I am sure
that Julius Caesar, if he had had the time, would have readily
done a book to prove that the savages he had encountered on
the island of Great Britain were not at all of the same human
race as the Romans and that, whereas the latter were destined
by nature to dominate the world, the former were destined
to vegetate in a corner. *Tu regere imperio populos, Romane,
memento,*[11] says our old acquaintance Virgil. When it is only a
matter of human families that, differing among themselves in
a profound and permanent manner by *external appearance,* can

11. "Roman, you are ruled by an empire, having remembered the people."

make themselves known by distinctive traits in the whole course of time and be related back to a kind of different creation, the doctrine, without being in my opinion more certain, becomes less improbable and easier to establish. But when one places oneself in the interior of one of these great families, such as that of the white race for example, the thread of reasoning disappears and escapes at each step. Is there anything in the world more uncertain, no matter what one does, than the question of knowing by history or tradition when, how, and in what proportions men who do not preserve any visible trace of their origin are mixed? These events all took place in remote barbarous times, which have left only vague traditions or incomplete written documents. Do you believe that in taking this route to explain the destiny of different peoples you have greatly illuminated history and that the science of man has gained in certitude for having left the road traveled, since the beginning of the world, by so many great minds who sought the causes of the events of this world in the influence of certain men, of certain sentiments, of certain ideas, of certain beliefs? Again, if only your doctrine, without being better established than theirs, were more useful to humanity! But it is evidently the contrary. What interest can there be in persuading the base people who live in barbarism, in indolence, or in servitude, that since they exist in such a state by virtue of the nature of their race, there is nothing to do to ameliorate their condition, change their mores, or modify their government? Do you not see that your doctrine brings out naturally all the evils that permanent inequality creates— pride, violence, the contempt of fellow men, tyranny, and abjectness under all its forms? What are you saying to me, my dear friend, about making distinctions between *the qualities that make moral truths be practiced* and what you call *social aptitude?* Are these things different? When a person has seen for quite a while and from up quite close the manner in which public affairs are conducted, do you believe that he is not perfectly convinced that they succeed precisely on account of the very

means that make one succeed in private life; that courage, energy, integrity, foresight, good sense are the true reasons for
the prosperity of empires as well as for that of families and
that, in a word, the destiny of man, either as an individual or
as a nation, is what he wants to make of it? I stop here; allow
us, please, to let the discussion rest there. We are separated by
too great a space for discussion to be fruitful. There is an intellectual world between your doctrine and mine. I would
much prefer to get from that to what I can praise without
restriction. Unfortunately, although I was not less keenly affected in this way than the other, I am obliged to be more
brief, because I cannot dwell in detail on what I approved;
but, on the whole, I will tell you that this book is, by far, the
most remarkable of all your writings, that there is very great
erudition, as far as I can judge, in the assembling of so many
facts and great talent, rare perspicacity in the profit you draw
from it. Those who approve your mother-idea or who desire
it to be true (and in our day, after the fatigue of these sixty
years of revolution, there are many people in France who aspire to just such a belief), must read you with true captiva-
tion, because your book is well constructed, proceeds very
well toward the goal and leads up to it with great delight for
the intelligence. I proved my sincerity to you in criticism; believe equally in my sincerity in praise. There is real and very
great merit in your work and assuredly it puts you at the head
and above all those who have maintained analogous doctrines.

Having written all this very rapidly and with a sort of *furia
francese* (I am reentering here into your system), my hand is
tired, and I ask you to let me stop here. Besides, it is not a
subject that can be treated by letter. It is too complicated and
too vast, but we will chat about it *abundantly,* when we see
each other. Tell me only if the press is already occupying itself
with you? I am receiving an English newspaper and a German
newspaper (because I am applying myself bravely to learning
German), but I save money on French newspapers, which,
as I have told you, I believe, seem to me to have resolved a
problem that was until now believed to be insoluble, which

is to be more vacuous than censored newspapers. I thus know only what they contain by way of hearsay. It seems to me that the *Débats* should have readily given an account of such a considerable book.

We will be here until the month of May. I would very much like at that time to have the opportunity of finding you in Paris. You are being left buried for a very long time in your Alpine snows. I am aggrieved with it, without being able to do anything about it. I am very well. I am working a lot, and the days seem to fly. Farewell. Be assured of my very sincere friendship.

P.S. Do not fail, I entreat you, to remember us to Mme. de Gobineau.

77. *To Adolphe de Circourt*

Saint-Cyr, December 7, 1853

I learned with great sorrow, my dear Monsieur de Circourt, of the sad event that forced you to go to Franche-Comté almost as soon as you returned from your long trip in the south of France. . . .

I brought with me from Paris and I have almost completely read, I say almost, because such reading is rough going, a book that I believe you had pointed out to me, the one by Haxthausen on the agricultural classes in Russia.[12] One could not come across anything more tiring, in my opinion, than the study of this work, but nothing in the world is more instructive. The author, who seems to possess a very mediocre mind, is a very honest witness and had the good sense to consider the only thing that is interesting and at times great in Russia, and the only thing that no one else goes to see: the people. I found in this book a great mass of facts of which I had no idea and which seemed to me to throw great light on this little known part of our Europe, if indeed it is still Eu-

12. August von Haxthausen, *Etudes sur la situation intérieure de la vie nationale et les institutions rurales de la Russie,* 2 vols. (1847).

rope. I would not want to say too much that is bad to you about Russia, because you have an excellent reason at least for thinking well of it; consequently I will limit myself to remarking that I have never had less taste for going to live in the empire of the czars than after having read Haxthausen. What above all would make that society uninhabitable for me would be the boredom; one breathes boredom merely in hearing it described. Uniformity in liberty has always seemed boring to me, but what can be said of complete uniformity in servitude, of these villages that are so perfectly alike, populated by people who are so perfectly similar, doing the same things, in the midst of the deepest slumber of intelligence? I confess to you in a whisper that I would prefer disordered barbarism.

Just as I had finished writing to Mme. de Circourt the other day, I received a letter from her, the kindest and friendliest letter in the world. I would have written again at once to thank her, had I not feared making her tired of me by sending two letters like that in rapid succession.

Farewell, dear Monsieur de Circourt; please think of me occasionally, and give me news of everything, because everything interests me and especially what concerns you; a thousand affections.

78. To Arthur de Gobineau

Saint-Cyr, près Tours, December 20, 1853

I have your second letter, my dear friend, which makes me regret not having responded earlier to the first. I did not wish to treat the subject with you except in conversation. If discussion only manages, shall we say, more often than not, to root people in their opinions, what about discussion by writing? It is time lost or at least badly employed. Perhaps you are right, but you have taken precisely the thesis that has always appeared to me the most dangerous that could be maintained in our time. That, independently of the fact that I persist in believing your principle to be false in the extreme extension that you give it, is sufficient not to allow you to convert me, especially from afar. The last century had an exaggerated and a rather puerile confidence in the power that man exercises over himself and in that of peoples over their own destiny. That was the error of the time; a noble error, after all, which, if it brought about the commission of many follies, led to the accomplishment of some very great things, beside which posterity will find us very small. The fatigue of revolutions, the tedium of emotions, the failure of so many generous ideas and so many vast hopes, all this has now precipitated us in the opposite excess. After having believed ourselves capable of transforming ourselves, we believe ourselves incapable of reforming ourselves; after having had an excessive pride, we have fallen into a humility that is no less excessive; we believed ourselves capable of everything, today we believe ourselves capable of nothing, and we like to believe that from now on struggle and effort will be useless and that our blood, our muscles, and our nerves will always be stronger than our will and our virtue. This simply is the great malady of the time, a malady completely opposed to that of our fathers. Your book, however you arrange things, favors it instead of combatting it; in spite of yourself, it inclines the already too soft soul of your contemporaries toward softness. That does not prevent me from seeing that there is something very remarkable in your work and even from being keenly interested in it as one is toward those brats who have your best friends for fathers and who besides, which often occurs with brats, know how to please. But I did not become sufficiently German in studying the German language for the novelty or philosophical merit of an idea to make me forget the moral or political effect that it can produce. I will therefore need to have your *spoken* eloquence to convince me absolutely.

As for the Academy of Moral and Political Sciences, I do not have to tell you, my dear friend, that I agree with Rémusat's idea with all my heart. In what section does he

believe your candidacy belongs? I imagine that it can only be
philosophical and general history? There, Rémusat has a considerable influence, since Thiers, Mignet,[13] Guizot, three principal members whom he can at present predispose very well,
belong to that section. If I were in Paris, I would join with
him very readily, but I will not return to that city, as I have
told you, before the month of May. From afar, one can do
nothing in this matter, especially since there is no *proxy voting*.
Do you know if there is a vacancy in this section? Because the
number of corresponding members is fixed. As for the time at
which you will have to run openly and push your candidacy
keenly, that will depend absolutely on the noise that your
book will make or that it is making, because no noise whatever is penetrating here to my hearing. The preliminary step
will consist of offering your book to the Academy, if you
have not already offered it, and of arranging things so that
this offer is made in your name by a member who will attract
the attention of the body to the writing. Rémusat would perform this service readily. In everything that can depend on
me, depend, I need hardly tell you, on my very sincere friendship. If I do not like the work very much, I like the author,
and that is worth more, although perhaps that does not satisfy
you completely. Depend likewise on Beaumont, I think I can
tell you that in advance.

What interests me as much as your academic advancement,
is your advancement in diplomacy, about which you do not
tell me anything. I imagine however that, during your stay
in Paris, you are looking for a way to keep from returning to
Berne.[14] You surely should have let me know if you have
some chance of succeeding. We are continuing to lead a life
here that is very useful to us and, what is more difficult to

13. François-Auguste Mignet (1796–1884), an eminent historian and secretary to the Academy of Moral and Political Sciences since 1837.
14. Gobineau, who was both a writer and a career diplomat, had been a
member of France's diplomatic delegation to Switzerland. In about a month's
time, he was happy to report that he was being transferred to Frankfurt.

believe and no less true, which seems more and more agreeable to us despite the winter and the solitude. Farewell. Remember us very especially to Mme. de Gobineau and believe in my unalterable attachment.

79. *To Gustave de Beaumont*

July 16, 1854

I want to add several words, my dear friend, to the long letter my wife has just written yours in order to express my regret at not having written earlier. For more than two weeks now I have been wanting to do so every morning and I have been prevented by some pressing work and still more by the difficulty of finding something to tell you about this country. I am ashamed at being in Germany for more than three weeks without having any idea to express about it; I am speaking of the living Germany because as for the dead Germany,[15] I could already speak of it for an hour. But, for the Germany which thinks and acts in our day, I am living, up to now, in ridiculous ignorance of it. What are the general dispositions of this country with relation to politics, what are its sentiments in the particular circumstances in which Europe finds itself? I do not know at all. But I could tell you rather well how things occurred in 1754. Thus I have not yet been able to unravel the state of thinking here on the matter of free institutions. The only fact that I confide to you is this: on seeing the proceedings of the Chambers of Prussia reduced, last winter in the *Gazette de Cologne,* to the proportions of a meager written summary and placed right next to the announcements, we figured that Prussia enjoyed the same institutions as we do in matters of the press. Not at all, nothing prevents them from

15. Tocqueville undertook this journey to Germany, in part, to help him reconstruct the spirit or mores of the old European aristocracy. Although he felt the old Germany was dead, still he discovered that aristocratic beliefs and institutions lingered in parts of Germany and were accessible to investigation.

reproducing the speeches of parliamentary orators and commentary on the text; the newspaper does not do it, because the public does not take any real interest in the debates. Now, where did this indifference of the public originate? Is it only, as I am assured, that the Chamber is composed in such a manner and is in such a position that hardly any more independence is expected from it than could be expected from ours in France? This is in general the response people make to me. And I believe there is a lot to that. But I believe, also, that the fact of which I speak is still due to a very predominant tepidity in political matters. Nonetheless, I must say that I do not perceive here the signs of moral stiffness, which are so sad to see in France. Fear is by no means the dominant sentiment. The socialist has not taken here, as among us, the place the devil occupied in the imagination of the Middle Ages. People are preoccupied very little with the socialist. They seem still to believe firmly in the usefulness of constitutional forms, and they demonstrate a firm confidence in their future. But it is evident that they are not pressed, that the institutions of absolute government cause no great discomfort and no great impatience, and that mores, habits tend strongly in this direction, although new ideas and new needs push from the other.

I am not speaking to you of my way of life in Bonn, because I imagine that my wife must have spoken of it very abundantly to yours. We now spend our time marvelously, usefully and agreeably. But the first days were painful. As I told you above, since my arrival here I have lived only the Germany of the last century, and I see with a certain satisfaction that the ideas of it that I had developed for myself without knowing the country and only by abstract reasoning, in researching why the Revolution took place among us rather than among them, those ideas appear to me fully confirmed by the detail of the facts. The political condition and especially the social condition of this country seem to be exactly what I had supposed.

Farewell, my dear friend, I embrace you with all my heart. Do not delay in writing me. Tell me what you are going to do for Antonin,[16] who occupies our thoughts often—he, his mother, and even his brother—because we tenderly love everyone there.

80. To Gustave de Beaumont

Bonn, August 6, 1854

We are preoccupied with Antonin, my dear friend, and we hope that you will let us know the results of the examination as soon as you know them yourself, whatever they may be. I hope very much that your young man will qualify and, above all, I desire it very ardently; because it is good to start life with a success. That sets things going and facilitates everything else. But, still, if Antonin were to fail, he is so young, that it would be very foolish for him and for you to be discouraged.

We are still in Bonn, where I would still be getting along marvelously if a week ago Marie had not suffered a very acute rheumatic pain in the joint of her wrist and in that of the thumb of her right hand. She could not make any use of that hand without crying out. So it was wrapped up and put in a sling. She has to do everything with only one hand and, what is even worse, with the left hand. You can judge the unbearable discomfort that results from that. Also, this indisposition has deeply depressed my traveling companion and is beginning to depress me greatly myself. We truly seem destined for the hospital. Aside from that, as I told you above, we are spending our time well. I am working a lot, and I hope, if I

16. Antonin, Beaumont's eldest son, successfully completed an examination for a Bachelor of Letters degree in 1854, yet still the choice of a future occupation remained, and the choice was circumscribed by Beaumont's constricted financial position. After continuing his studies for a couple of years more, Antonin entered Saint-Cyr (the famous military school) and eventually became an officer in Algeria.

do not succeed in knowing Germany, at least I will have an idea of what is most important for me to know about it. No one could show more regard for me than the people are doing here, to the point of having made an exception in my favor to the absolute rule which requires that at this time of year all the books lent by the university library be brought back and no new ones be lent. We have also found several families here among whom we are familiarly received and whose mores please us greatly. Private life in Germany evidently has very engaging aspects. But what poor citizens! When I see the long use they have made of absolute power, the gentleness of that power, the tradition of liberty so effaced in the mores, the centralization, the universal passion for places and the universal dependency everywhere, I ask myself if they will ever be much different from what they are. Still, one can recognize that the feeling of *instability* in all things seems general.

The other day I had a conversation that seemed rather interesting with a Prussian who had returned from the United States, where he had been ambassador for ten years. His largest job was to supervise matters of emigration. He astounded me by telling me that last year German emigration to the United States rose to the incredible figure of 140,000 individuals, and it is continuing at this pace. Formerly, only the poor arrived but, today, many well-off and even wealthy families are arriving. I asked him from which countries in general these men were arriving and what motives made them emigrate. Comparatively few Prussians are counted among the 140,000 Germans. But those were nearly all people well brought up and well-off. The others came particularly from the small states in the center of Germany and also in large numbers from Baden, from Württemberg, and from Bavaria. All these Germans bring their ideas to the United States and to a certain extent, according to the person of whom I told you, keep them there. They preserve their language, they do not mix much with the inhabitants, they generally stay together, and, although in the end, by imitation, they take on something of American political practices, especially in the second generation, they nonetheless remain a distinct and foreign element. In short, what he told me confirms what I had always thought, that the rapid introduction into the United States of men foreign to the English race was the greatest peril that America would have to run, and what makes the final success of democratic institutions still an unresolved problem. I forgot to tell you that my interlocutor attributed the departure of the greater part of the families who leave Germany in order to go to America to the urgent invitations that their already emigrated parents or friends send them. But what *German* cause induced those to emigrate? That is what I could not get him to say clearly, and what would be especially important to know.

The other day, here, I saw Reeve, who is taking the waters at Aix. I even returned to Aix with him in order to say farewell to Lamoricière. Yesterday, your friend and correspondent Lewis and his wife Lady Theresa Clarendon[17] arrived here; they came to see us at once, and we will see each other again today. I have not yet brought up politics with him and will bring it up as little as I can: this is now a very delicate and rather painful subject to discuss with an Englishman.

My wife has received a letter from yours, whom she is in a hurry to thank for it. But her infirmity, of course, makes all writing impossible for her. Please relate that to Madame de Beaumont, while offering her as always the expression of our tender friendship.

Farewell, dear friend. I embrace you.

17. Sir George Cornewall Lewis (1806–1863), the famous Whig statesman and lawyer; author of books on Ireland, Malta, political philosophy, and philology; editor of the *Edinburgh Review;* and at various times a Poor Law commissioner, Chancellor of the Exchequer, and under Palmerston in 1861 head of the War Office. His wife, Lady Maria Theresa Lewis (1803–1865), was the sister of Lord Clarendon and a correspondent of Tocqueville's.

81. To Theodore Sedgwick

Bonn, August 14, 1854

I received, dear Monsieur Sedgwick, your letter of last July
20 three days ago. It brought me great relief. I was very wor-
ried about the state of commercial affairs in America, and, in
particular, about the panic that seemed to reign in railroad
transactions. Thanks to you, I now see clearly what are the
causes and what is the extent of the problem. From what you
tell me, I do not think that I have anything to fear, because I
have no need of my capital, and I can wait until the crisis
passes and prices go up again. I cannot tell you how grateful
we are for the persistent care that you take in giving us warn-
ings you think can be useful or agreeable to us. This is the
action of a true friend, and one cannot refrain from responding to such a way of acting with true affection. So, that is
what I am doing, I assure you, and very heartily. I hope that
you will count on me if I, for my part, can ever do something
in France that would be agreeable for you.

I wrote you from Bonn the 17th of last month. It is again
from Bonn that I am writing you today. But just when I am
leaving this small city, where I have spent two very profitable, and even very pleasant months, I have the good sense to
find great pleasure in seeing the new mores and conforming
myself comfortably to them. Introduced here into a society of
German professors and admitted into the midst of their families, I have not been slow to feel myself one of them. I found
among them great instruction, often great intellect, and almost
always a true simplicity of habits and geniality of disposition.
What I have seen here of the private mores of Germany
seemed to me very interesting and even engaging. But as for
public mores, one must not speak of them. They are what
two centuries of absolute government, sixty years of centralization, and a very long practice of administrative dependence,
as bureaucrats or as the administered, have been able to make

of them: that is to say that they lend themselves only to servitude or to revolution. What can you do with those people when they come to you in America? Meanwhile, they come to you in an ever-growing throng, already 140,000 a year, according to what I am told. Whatever your power of assimilation may be, it would be very difficult for you to *digest* quickly enough so many foreign bodies in order to be able to incorporate them into your substance and make them sufficiently *yourselves,* so that they do not disturb the economy and the health of your body social. I would wish you were growing less quickly. But you are carried away by an inevitable destiny toward grandeur and perils.

Farewell, dear Monsieur Sedgwick, thank you a thousand times again. No longer write me at St.-Cyr, près Tours, which I have left, but at my father's home, M. le Comte de Tocqueville, *at Clairoix, par Compiègne (Oise).* That is where I will be. Many, many regards.

82. *To Gustave de Beaumont*

Compiègne, February 21, 1855

I received a letter from you, my dear friend, the day after I had written you, and my wife likewise has received one from yours which gave her great pleasure.

I am writing some lines to you right away again, because I do not want to leave you with the impression of the bad news that I gave you the other day. God be thanked, Marie's indisposition seems not to have had a sequel and seems only to have been caused by an external accident and not to have any internal cause. All the symptoms of the illness have nearly disappeared, and I hope that within two days there will no longer be any question of it. These illnesses are often only the symptoms of a deeper illness. That is what disturbed me, and my imagination was already carried back to

the long malady Madame Roederer had two or three years
ago. In a word, I hope I will not have to speak of it any
more.

Continuation of the bohemian life we lead more each day:
we have been sleeping and working in the same room; now
we are eating there. We could not do anything, were it to get
any colder. I am nonetheless getting used to this style of life,
and, when I feel myself in good spirits, I begin to find that
our miserable room is a comfortable enough place to stay.
This renewal of winter has done me no harm, up to the present. And not once in the last week have I missed taking a
walk for more than an hour in the forest. These great trees,
seen in the snow, remind me of the woods of Tennessee that
we traveled through, it will be 25 years ago before long, in
weather still harsher. What was most different in that picture
was myself. Because twenty-five years in the life of a man,
that is an entire revolution. I had this melancholy thought all
the while tracing my way across the snow. But after going
over this large number of years in my memory, I consoled
myself by thinking that if I had to start this quarter of a century over again, I would not want, all things considered, to
do things very differently from what I have done. I would try
to suppress many of the errors of detail and several distinctive
and foolish actions, but as for the bulk of my ideas, of my
sentiments, and even of my acts, I would change nothing. I
also noticed how little I had changed my point of view on
men in general during this long interval of time. One speaks a
great deal of the illusions of youth and of the disillusionment
of maturity. I have not noticed that at all in my personal experience. The vices and weaknesses of men leaped to my eyes,
from the first, and, as for the good qualities that I found in
them then, I cannot say that I have not encountered them
nearly the same since. This little retrospective review put me
back in better humor and in order to complete cheering myself up again, I considered that I had kept to this day the same
friend with whom I hunted parrots in Memphis, and that time

had only managed to strengthen the ties of confidence and friendship that existed between us then. This point of view seemed to me even more heartening to consider than all the others.

No new *Allgemeine*. This is a true suppression. That shows better than anything it could say that what is coming from the Crimea is not fit to make known, since even the news friends give is suppressed. I know that people are very disturbed in Paris about the fate of the army. I do not think, however, that there will be a sudden *disaster* to dread, but it is certain that this army is dissolving from illness and misery, and that this situation can at any time impel some dangerous attempt. Everything seems to portend that an act of strength is being prepared. I do not know what. But what has most preoccupied Paris these days has been the scheme that the Emperor disclosed of making his way to the Orient himself. This announcement, giving patriotism the stimulant of fear, seemed to me to have greatly troubled people's minds. My brother Edouard, who arrived from Paris two days ago, was still breathless from this news. To be several months without the actual presence of a master! How to escape from the peril of such a situation? I tried to reassure him by telling him that since this scheme is one of those that is good to make known, but very imprudent to execute, there were good odds that such a great danger would not be run. Duvergier de Hauranne, who wrote me today, maintains that England, having been warned of the Emperor's design, made known to him that if he executed it, it would consider the Vienna Conference[18] as broken off and would not have Lord J. Russell leave, and that, on this threat, it had been adjourned.

18. Tocqueville here refers to the conditions of peace agreed to by France and England on August 8, 1854; the conditions included free passage at the mouth of the Danube, a new treaty on the Bosporus Straits and the Dardanelles that favored France and England, and an end to Russia's claim to a protectorate over Christians in Turkey.

Despite these warlike impulses, I believe peace to be not more probable, but less improbable than it has been up to the present. Basically, England, which is the principal interested party in the question, seems to me to desire it, something which had not been the case before; war gives birth in that country to a terrible clamor against the aristocracy. I am often sent the *Times,* and in it I read articles, the democratic violence of which appears to me of such a nature as to make the governing class take pause. If it were led by a Chatham,[19] it would confront the storm and would understand that the only way to escape the peril that the poor success of the war makes it run is not to conclude peace, but to wage successful war. But England has become as barren as we of great men. And I believe that its aristocracy is hastening to escape from current difficulties by peace, in which I am inclined to believe it is making a mistaken calculation and that, if it dwells on the uneffaced recollection of the army's loss, it will have a great deal of difficulty regaining its place in public opinion. From this seed will emerge great misfortunes for it. Besides, and in order to return to the subject of peace, whatever may be the chances for it, these chances will be increased or destroyed by what is probably going to happen in the Crimea; and, until it is known if something, indeed, has happened there, and what has happened there, all that one can say on the end or continuation of the war has little value. I am informed from Paris that it appears certain that a treaty, what sort is not known, is going to occur between Prussia and France.

Farewell, dear friend. I do not need to tell you all the affection we bear toward your household.

P.S. Since yesterday when I wrote this letter, a foot of snow has fallen. That is necessarily going to interrupt my American walks.

19. William Pitt, first earl of Chatham (1708–1778), probably the statesman most responsible for England's defeating France in the Seven Years' War (1755–1763); later prime minister (1766–1768).

83. To Gustave de Beaumont

Compiègne, March 8, 1855

I must reply at once to your last letter, my dear friend, and tell you how much that letter interested me and touched me.[20] It has been years since I received one from you that produced such an effect on me. I could not thank you too much for all the testimonies of good friendship it contains. What is most precious to me is perhaps the one of which you are least conscious; I mean to speak of the openness of mind and of heart with which you spoke about yourself. The only reproach I used to make to you sometimes was that you did not like to speak enough about yourself, to paint what was happening at the very depth of your mind. That results in part from one of your great qualities, courage. You have less need than other people to lean on your neighbor, confiding in him what may either agitate or trouble or simply occupy your mind; you ordinarily prefer to withdraw rather than to pour yourself out. The general rule is good. But the exceptions are too, and I lay claim to one.

Besides, you were very unjust in your judgments about yourself, the flu interfering with them. Human life must be judged by its broad strokes. This is a duty with respect to others; it is a right with respect to oneself. Despite having a nature more impressionable and consequently more easily moved than that of many others, have you not always followed the same pathway through the kind of labyrinth within which we have lived? Did you not embrace, at the start, what

20. On March 6, 1855, Beaumont wrote Tocqueville a rather sad letter describing a severe illness that temporarily struck his young son Paul, his wife's exhaustion and depression, and Beaumont's own bout with the flu and with melancholy thoughts. In short, whereas Tocqueville had glanced back on his life with a certain satisfaction, Beaumont felt only disappointment. "I perceived in my entire life only plans badly conceived and still more badly pursued." His fondest thoughts were those of his friendship with Tocqueville, but even these thoughts were partially spoiled by the memory of a regrettable moment (1844) that came between them. Beaumont tried to dismiss these thoughts as merely the companions of illness, but his sadness was evident.

I still call the good cause, even though it may be the vanquished cause: did you not adhere to it to the end, so as to fall
only with it and so as to be likely to rise with it, if it should
ever rise again. Are there many of your contemporaries who
could say as much? Have you not borne adversity better than any
among them? You have done so, so that your friends have
joined respect to the affection and esteem they already held for
you. Consult the good judges in these matters: hear what
Corcelle and Lanjuinais say about you. Assuredly it would
please you to hear their remarks, and it is a pleasure in which
your wife would share. We live, it is true, in a time and in a
country in which every fifteen years a revolution comes to
pass, as the laborer passes each year in his field with the plow,
returning below what was above, and above what was below.
But that is the common destiny. There are many of our contemporaries whom this operation has buried; I hope that it has
done nothing but cover us over and that, with time and courage, we will finally break through to the surface again.

What you say about England is well conceived and well
expressed.[21] It could neither be better conceived nor better expressed. The evil is perhaps even greater than you imagine it
from afar. I just went to Paris to vote at the Academy. There,
I received, from several sides, many confidences; I read of the
prodigious indiscretions written by an Englishman you know.
All of that proved to me that the English political world is in
abominable disarray and that the institutions of England will
come out of this very much affected. As a result, the nation is
bending to fortune and yearning for any peace whatsoever. As
a result, in the end (each one of these things would require a
long conversation to develop), this war, which seemed the

21. On March 2, 1855, Czar Nicholas I died, and his successor, Alexander
II, was inclined toward peace. Beaumont wrote that England, due to a growing
"softness," would now seek a peace that would preserve English "self-esteem,"
although effectively leaving the field of battle to Russia. Beaumont seemed to
want England to fight on, despite enormous losses, and to "show the world
what resiliency and resources there are in the genius, passions, and the institutions of a free country."

guarantee of the English alliance, will very probably bring
about the end, the Emperor perceiving that absolute government permits him other, more profitable alliances and seeing
that the liberty of the English does not give rise to the mira-
cles that people said it would, but on the contrary disturbs
and upsets the enterprises in which it mixes. I knew, of certain knowledge, two facts very probative of what I am saying
there: the first is the irritation that our government has been
caused by the inquiry of the House of Commons[22] and the
unavailing efforts that our government has made to stifle it.
Second, the excitement evidenced to Senior, not a week ago,
by Van de Weyer.[23] The latter, returning to London after an
absence, is speaking with his colleagues in the diplomatic
corps and in particular with our representative. And then he
exclaims that he is beginning to tremble again for Belgium,
that England's prestige in the eyes of the nations on the Continent, and especially in the eyes of France, which was his
homeland's salvation, this prestige is being destroyed and replaced by a contrary sentiment that was indicated by con-
temptuous remarks, even on the part of the principal ally of
the English.

If it were only a question of them, how I would be tempted
to rejoice in their disgrace! But, as you say, it concerns ourselves. I regard what is happening as more deadly to liberty
than the 2d of December. That ruined it, but this discredits it.
I feel, for my part, so struck by it, that disgust often seizes me
in my work and I am sometimes more discouraged and sadder
than I was three years ago. *E pure si torna!*[24] Truth lives, what-

22. Under the leadership of John Roebuck, the House of Commons began
to carry out an inquiry on March 5 into the allied siege of Sebastopol, a siege
now unsuccessful and nearly six months old. It was during this siege, in the
winter of 1854–1855, that the allies suffered horribly from casualties, lack of
supplies, and disease.

23. Jean-Sylvain Van de Weyer (1802–1874), ambassador from Belgium to
London.

24. "Nevertheless, it turns"; Galileo's famous remark after he was condemned by the Roman Inquisition.

ever one does, and liberty remains the greatest thing in this world. But who, before long, will be worthy of it? One thing that would be pleasant, if it did not have another side that is so sad, would be to hear the English bourgeoisie say to the nobles: "We did not ask for more than to let you govern, but you only commit blunders," and the nobles to respond to the bourgeoisie: "In order to humor you, we have half-disorganized the aristocracy, and now that we need you in order to govern, you can generate no man of genius to emerge from your ranks, not even an eminent man we could employ." And both are right. The truth is that England has at its service neither the wisdom nor the vigor of its former masters, nor the coarse, but powerful mettle that democracy gives to its children in America. It now has only a mediocre and soft government to serve it, a government that would not suffice for the needs of war and that may have some trouble now even sufficing for those of peace. Fortunately, the people are tranquil. Its first agitations will be very dangerous.

Marie is not doing badly. The erysipelas has disappeared, and the remainder continues. I have been well up to now. If I emerge entirely from this winter without having suffered any more from it, that will be a good sign.

The nature of your dear little Paul's bronchitis should greatly reassure his mother and you for the future. Everyone has been stricken more or less this year, and since this child has resisted so keen an attack so well, you can conclude that his chest and its surroundings are vigorously constructed. We did not know of his illness. We would have been terribly anxious about the condition of a child whose health has such an influence on his mother's health.

The last time I wrote you I was so carried away by our memories of America that I finished my letter without responding to the question that you had posed to me about my father. He was already better, as Corcelle informed you, and the improvement has not ceased. Nonetheless, his health has not returned; his cough has not entirely ceased; his strength is still very much diminished and, in short, his condition, without still alarming me, preoccupies me. This time I see a serious blow from age, and although I do not fear that he will succumb to it, it will leave, I fear, lasting traces. I imagine that even strangers are interested in him. You cannot imagine what a tender and likable old man he is. Never has he shown more affection toward his children than in the last several years nor a more charming evenness of humor toward everyone. He was very unwell the day you dined with him. You would find him better now, although far from the man you have seen.

We definitely are going to see him again the 20th of this month. This will happen, I think, at long last. This stay pleased Marie so much that I did not want to make her leave, before she herself desired it.

The *Allgemeine* came again two days ago. It had disappeared completely. These long interruptions take away all the taste one might have for reading it.

It is very likely that the death of Emperor Nicholas will lead to peace. But nothing is indicating so yet. That depends absolutely on the secret thought that makes L. N. work, a thought which no one knows, not even, I think, those who live with him, which is all the more reason for those who, like us, inhabit his antipodes not to know it. If he really wants peace, that will make him ultrapacific and in the contrary case ultrawarlike. Because this event can lead as readily to an easy peace as to a war to the bitter end. One has only to be set on the condition of the abandonment of Sebastapol and the limitation of Russian vessels in the North Sea; the young Emperor[25] is obliged not to lay down arms, as was his father and perhaps more so than his father. However, if I had to bet, I would still bet on peace.

Speaking of games of chance, the most diverting ventures were being recounted during my stay about the master's con-

25. Alexander II.

fidants, who, knowing that the decision to leave for the Crimea had been made, had speculated on the slump and had been ruined by their patron's good fortune. I am finishing, not for want of matter, but of paper. A thousand feelings of affection from the bottom of my heart. Marie absolutely wants to answer your wife's letter, which gave her so much pleasure. I wanted to keep her from doing so, because, of all exercises, this is the one that is still the most difficult and the most painful for her, but I could not.

84. To Claude-François de Corcelle

Tocqueville, October 16, 1855

Like you, my dear friend, I have never had much taste for metaphysics, perhaps because I never seriously devoted myself to it, and because it has always seemed to me that good sense led to the goal it contemplates as well as metaphysics. But, nonetheless, I cannot avoid recognizing that it has had a singular attraction for several of the greatest and even the most religious geniuses who have appeared in the world, notwithstanding what Voltaire says about metaphysics being a romance about the soul.

The centuries in which metaphysics has been most cultivated have been, in general, those in which men were most drawn outside and above themselves. After all, however little of the metaphysician there is in me, I have always been struck by the influence that metaphysical opinions have had on things that seemed the most distant from them and even on the condition of society. There is, I think, not a man of state who could see with indifference that the dominant metaphysics, in the scholarly world, takes its point of departure in sensation or outside of that. Condillac has, assuredly, contributed greatly to driving to materialism[26] many people who have

---

26. Etienne Bonnot de Condillac (1715–1780) was one of the great French *philosophes* of the eighteenth century. His most famous work was *Traité des sensations* (1754). Borrowing from Locke, Condillac argued that knowledge

never read him, because the abstract ideas that do relate to man always infiltrate in the end, I do not know how, into the mores of the crowd.

You would like for the truth to be reached with no great fuss and:

That Aronce with ease should marry Clélie.

Your outburst certainly made me laugh, but it does not change my opinion on the essence of things.

I embrace you with all my heart.

85. To Gustave de Beaumont

Tocqueville, November 22, 1855

The minor indisposition of which we spoke, my dear friend, has not had any sequel, and I have returned to the condition I was in before. It is very disagreeable to be subjected several times a year to these stomach attacks, which hardly affect the mind less than the body. During all the time that these lasted, although they were not very intense, I was unable to devote myself to any work whatsoever, and I lived in a languishing and useless manner. But it is superfluous to describe to you a condition you have witnessed so many times. The idea of leaving this country, which you suggest to me out of friendship, occurs to me rather naturally. However, I still do not perceive any definite sign that the influence of the climate is harmful to me. I felt marvelous for four months; the stomach attack I just had, where have I not had it the same and with the same intensity? In Paris, in Saint-Cyr, in Compiègne, I experienced attacks, at the same time of year, that were completely the same. As for my chest, I have not

---

derives from sense experience; and against George Berkeley, Condillac held that there is a material world that causes our sense experience. If Tocqueville means by "materialism" the philosophical position that the real world consists only of matter, then he is wrong in attributing this position to Condillac, who believed in the existence of matter and mind.

yet perceived any sign whatsoever that it was bad because of the stay in Tocqueville. I did not have a cold there. Thanks to the work that took us a lot of time and money and caused us a great deal of annoyance, but that is completed, the interior of the house is transformed; and we are also sheltered there from the drafts and from the humidity to which we were exposed in the past. You could not imagine how *comfortable* our establishment has become in this respect, as well as in all others. The life we lead in our retreat seems more and more sweet to me and conforms to my tastes; I am in the process of concluding a work here that I would have a lot of trouble finishing in Paris. I am not speaking of the question of money, which, in this matter, must be secondary. All these reasons combined are inducing me to want to prolong my stay by at least a month, unless I perceive that the climate really does influence my health in an appreciable way.

I will send Icilius the note that he requests; I will make it, as did you, very succinct. Returning of necessity to my parliamentary life, I will think I am dreaming. Is it really true that there were political assemblies in France? That the nation was enthusiastic over what was said in them? Were those men, those constitutions, those forms, not shadows without reality? Those passions, those experiences, those fears, those friendships, those hatreds that stirred around us and that aroused us, do they refer to a time we really saw or are they memories of what we learned reading the history of times past? I would truly be tempted to believe the latter; because what has really existed leaves some trace, and I see none of what we imagined we perceived or felt.

If the past is a dream, at least let us try not to let the present escape and to make it bring forth something more effective. However well my life may be arranged, I feel that I will not be altogether content if I do not see you employing yours as one has a right to expect from a man as active and as intelligent as you are. I am afraid of tiring you. It is sufficient for you to know that I think about it often and always with sorrow. An occupation for the mind that is keenly interesting is an indispensable condition for happiness after the existence we have led and are leading today. Nothing could take its place, and however things may seem, I dare to affirm that you will never have a tranquil and contented heart unless you can find that occupation. Myself, I am playing the preacher here; I confess that I am often struck by terrible attacks of discouragement; I sometimes have hours or days of great bitterness and of infinite sadness. How could it possibly be otherwise when one compares what we imagined, desired, hoped for our country during all those years with what we see? But it is precisely the fortunate use I have made, and that I am making of work (I mean work animated by a certain ardor), to extricate myself from this state, which makes me desire so much to see you furnished with such a remedy. You have, it is true, less need of it than I. Your mind is by nature less anxious. But no one in our position can do without work. For my own part, I would be surely dead of low spirits if I had not found work.

We narrowly escaped burning down the other night. A piece of wood that was placed in a wall along a stove caught fire and spread the fire to the neighboring woodwork. We were going to bed. The incident happened in the dining room, where no one goes any more at that hour. The servant passes there by chance, sees the fire, gives the alarm. The burning part was knocked out of the woodwork by blows from an axe and the fire was very easily extinguished. A quarter of an hour later, everything was over. But without the good fortune of which I have told you, the château would have been in flames in no time, and we would have been awakened only in order to clear out of there as fast as possible. Advice to people who like large fires.

Farewell, dear friend. Remember this household with great affection to Madame de Beaumont. She has written two letters in succession to my wife which have, as usual, charmed and touched her.

86. To Gustave de Beaumont

January 1, 1856

My dear friend, I want to add a word in order to tell you once again an old story, which you know well, namely, that I have a tender affection for you and that I wish you all the good things of which you and Madame de Beaumont are so worthy. We never separate her from you in our thoughts and in our wishes. Because what greater good is there in this world than a wife so worthy of being loved? May God preserve her to you! We can ask nothing better of Him for you. It is not the end of December that suggests these thoughts to us. We always have them, just as I always feel for you this keen affection, which, although it is not always expressed, is nonetheless a continual and habitual fact that you know without one speaking of it to you.

I was very sick to my stomach for a week. Ailing in body, ailing still more in mind, because I was fearful of the return of a *crisis*. It did not come. The illness has left, but a certain malaise and a great languor remain. This incident has greatly disturbed and very much saddened me. I feel that I have today greater capacity and means for being happy than I have ever had in my life. But the means for being happy while ailing? In my youth, I used to have a disordered mind in a fairly healthy body. Now, my mind is nearly healed, but its envelope does not lend itself any more to what is asked of it. I did not know how to be happy then; I cannot be so now. There you have the whole story of man.

I hastened to take a six-month subscription to *Allgemeine,* the reading of which interests me greatly. But however much haste I put into it, I fear the paper will not be sent to me precisely on the 1st of January. Do not accuse me of delaying.

Farewell. I will write you more at length soon. I embrace you from the depth of my heart. I do as much to your children, especially to my friend Antonin. Please present the very sincere and keen expression of my good wishes to Madame de Beaumont.

87. *To Sophie Swetchine*

Tocqueville, January 7, 1856

It is a very long time, Madame, since I have availed myself of the permission that you gave me of writing you. I thought I would return to Paris and see you earlier, which would have been better still. But the way affairs have piled up has detained me here and will very likely detain me for three more weeks. I do not want to wait until then to thank you for your last letter, which interested me and touched me. You are to be found in it entirely. You evidence in it a kindness toward me that I would like to deserve, because the affection of a person like you is binding. It obliges one not only to be grateful but also to do what can be done to justify it. Toward this end, I would very much wish absolutely to cure this disposition toward discouragement that you combat by writing me. The malady, unfortunately, is nearly as old as I am, and it is not easy to recover from it completely. I have nevertheless made great efforts against it for several years, and surely I have greatly diminished the violence of it. Your letter has helped me to pursue this task and has been of real benefit, for which I thank you. Furthermore, Madame, do not think that the particular attack of which I told you was due uniquely to this sort of sickly sadness by which I have been tormented from time to time throughout my life. It arose above all from reflections that had their origin in facts that are only too real. The further I go in the work in which you see fit to take an interest, the more I perceive that I am being carried away in a current of sentiments and ideas that goes precisely contrary to the one that is carrying away many of my contemporaries. I continue to love passionately things about which they are no longer concerned.

I regard liberty as the prime good, as I always have; I have always seen in it one of the most fertile sources of manly virtures and of great actions. Neither tranquility nor well-being can take its place. By contrast, I see most of the men of my time, I mean to say the most respectable because the sentiment of the others would matter little to me, dreaming only of accommodating themselves as well as possible under a new regime, and, what ultimately casts turmoil and a sort of terror into my mind, seeming to make the taste for servitude a sort of ingredient for virtue. I would like to think and to feel as they do, but I cannot: my nature resists it even more than my will does. An indomitable instinct forces me to be on this point as I have always been. You could not imagine, Madame, the pain and often the cruelty I experience in living in this moral isolation, to feel myself outside the intellectual community of my time and my country. Solitude in a desert would seem to me less harsh than this sort of solitude among men. Because, I confess my weakness to you, isolation has always frightened me, and to be happy and even calm, I have always needed, more than is wise, to find a certain concourse around myself and to count on the sympathy of a certain number of my fellows. This profound saying could be applied especially to me: it is not good to be alone. This state of mind, Madame, which I have the confidence to show you, will explain the profound discouragement with which I am sometimes seized when I write, because when a person works for the public it is especially sad to perceive that it differs from him. I would very much like to have the virtue of being indifferent to success, but I do not possess it. Long experience has taught me that the success of a book lies much more in the thoughts the reader already has than in those the writer expresses.

Besides, Madame, do not think that the object of my book is either nearly or distantly related to the events or the men of the time. But you know as well as I that the work which is most foreign to the particular circumstances of a period is stamped in all its parts with a spirit sympathetic or contrary to that of its contemporaries. That is the soul of the book. By that it attracts or repels the reader. I have been speaking about myself for a very long time, Madame, but it is you who drew me into this fault, and I assure you that I am not accustomed to it. I would much rather speak to you of yourself, Madame. . . .

88. To Gustave de Beaumont

Paris, February 22, 1856

I still have not sent you anything, my dear friend, and will not have anything to send you for some time, because we only begin printing Monday at the earliest. Didot[27] found the manuscript so indecipherable that I had to go through it again in order to facilitate the work of the head of the print shop. This review, which will cut short the ulterior operations, is starting out by taking me a great deal of time.

Give me some peace from your jeremiads on the effects that age and solitude are producing on you. You are the same man you were twenty years ago, except that you are worth more. I therefore wish to submit my proofs to you and to obtain your advice; if she permits it, I also would like to have Madame de Beaumont's impressions, since she has fine literary discretion and such naturally high thoughts. The comings and goings of these proofs will take place without difficulty. What is more difficult is to keep my mind in the state in which it must be in order to do useful work. You know that it is subject to a malady that I dare confess only to my best friends. Reviewing what it produced, when the first excitement of composition has subsided, is painful and enervating to an unbelievable degree. I have never been able to take it on

27. Tocqueville is now in the final stages of publishing *The Old Regime and the French Revolution* with the publishing house of Michel Lévy Frères. Didot is the printer.

myself to reread *Democracy* since it appeared, although that would have been essential for introducing to it the improvements that the successive editions permitted me to make. And today, this unhappy manuscript burns my fingers and suggests to me, as I go over it, the most disagreeable sensations (the word is well chosen, because it is a matter of a kind of physical horror). To that anxiety there is joined the anxiety that the future of a book always causes even those who see themselves in a good light. But that is enough on that subject.

I will tell you that the other day my publisher, who is supposed to have a good *flair,* asked me if you have been writing anything. To which I replied that I did not know, but that I hoped that you were occupied with some work. He then entreated me to tell you that he would very much like to have your business. He asked me that on his own accord and with a liveliness that appeared to me to augur well, if ever the avowed weakening of your capacity permits you to do a book again. I confess to having expressed the indignation your torpor was causing me perhaps a little strongly to your son, but that young man expressed to me the desire to see you at work so strongly, with such tenderness for you, with an ardor so juvenile, that he carried me away perhaps a little too far into his point of view. He is truly a charming young fellow. I do not discount anything of what I said of him.

I expect my wife tomorrow night. She will be well received, and my condition as a bachelor begins to weigh on me terribly. I am so used to telling her everything that occupies me and everything that concerns me that to be separated from her at the present time was almost unbearable. Thank God, we are going to be reunited.

My father has been very unwell these last days. Although he is better now, I do not fail to retain some anxieties, if not for the moment, at least for the future.

I see that that little rascal Paul has done harm to his mother. I hope that when you receive this letter she will be as well recovered as he. Offer her the most affectionate remembrances on my part. I embrace you with all my heart.

89. *To Gustave de Beaumont*

Paris, April 24, 1856

As I happen to have a free moment this morning, my dear friend, I want to take advantage of it in order to chat with you a little more at length than I could when I sent the proofs. I cannot thank you too much for the care you took, as did Madame de Beaumont, in reviewing my old papers again. You have only one fault, which is not being bold enough in your opinion. I would appreciate it if, when an idea or an impression comes to you, even if you abandon it after more mature reflection, I would appreciate it, I say, if in that case, you let the trace of what you are not maintaining subsist. Thus, in the chapter on *men of letters,* your first impression was that it had to stop on the next-to-last-page. You recorded it on the paper; then you erased your remarks on that subject with so much skill that I wore my eyes out uselessly in order to read the stricken lines. The expression of your ideas here would have been all the more precious to me as I myself entertained some doubt on the end of that chapter. The entire chapter, and that on religion which follows and which you are without doubt going to send back to me, are, of all the parts of my book, the ones that cost me the most in reflection, work, and worry. I felt strongly that in those chapters I was walking on burning ground, because what remains perhaps most alive in the original spirit of the Revolution is in the literature, and because the only Frenchmen who today can be connected by a kind of esprit de corps to their fathers are the men of letters. Nevertheless, I did not believe I had to stop; but Madame de Beaumont's first impression disturbed me, because I attach an infinite value to her judgment and I feared that my thought did not *stand out* very clearly for her; in that chapter I did not want to criticize the ideas of the 18th century or, at least, the correct, reasonable, applicable portion of those ideas, which, after all, are my own. I wanted only to show the singular effects that had to be produced by a politics, which, although it contained those ideas, was professed solely by people who had no notion of how to apply them. My whole book has as its purpose making the innumerable abuses that condemned the Old Regime to perish stand out; I therefore do not mean to blame those who wanted to destroy them, but rather the manner in which they went about it and the spirit which their style of life and their inexperience suggested to them in this necessary destruction. Men of letters may perhaps have something to complain about in what I am saying, but I believe that the adversaries of the Old Regime are not harmed in the least.

I have acquiesced without hesitation in all the observations about details. At the point where you remark correctly that the writers in every country are often strangers to the world of affairs, I added a sentence which observes that in France not only did they not involve themselves practically in government, but they did not even have any idea of things that were done within the government, because of the absence of all political liberty. In free countries, the men of letters themselves breathe in the *practical* in some way without taking a hand in affairs.

I could still not change *efficacious*,[28] because I could not find another word that suited me. It is excellent French, but very old and almost out of use. I believed equally, in the chapter on liberty under the Old Regime, that I have to leave my quotation: *Skillful at refining and squandering precious metals*[29] . . . because I did not know what to put in its place and because I had to have something in order to finish. I only accompanied it with several words to make it pass.

28. Fr. = "efficace."
29. Fr. = "Habile à fondre et à dissiper les métaux."

My wife is leaving the day after tomorrow to spend two weeks at her aunt's. During that time, I am going to take the room I had as a schoolboy at my father's. That is where you will have to write me.

You will have another chapter at once. But as the entire text will hardly exceed 300 pages and as you are already at 250 at least, you will not have to give your attention for very long to the work I am giving you. I am myself approaching the end with great relief; you cannot have any idea of the disgust I feel for myself seeing myself again passing ceaselessly before my eyes this way. I compare this to being imprisoned with a single companion who would finally wear one out by virtue of the single obligation of seeing him endlessly and nothing but him. I experience hours of abominable discouragement in which I tell myself that I believe I am doing something considerable because I am doing it laboriously; whereas in this matter, as Molière says, the time, and I add the difficulty, puts nothing into the value of the thing. This is a common illusion of those who do not work easily, just as the illusion of others is often in believing that they have done something great, when they have done a host of little things. In short, I answer you that, for this quarter of an hour, I am not *proud.* There is the summary of my mental state.

A word slipped into one of your letters the other day that astonished and saddened me. After having spoken of what you call a little complacently my position in the world, you added a word of discouragement about your own. I believed firmly, on the contrary, that you had brought back from Paris a completely different impression, and we were congratulating each other, my wife and I, on the good effect that this trip could not fail to produce on you, in which it seemed to us that you had come within an inch of feeling for yourself how little your absence had harmed you and how, on the contrary, the esteem people had for you had still increased. We are surely all in *the gloomy kingdom,* but in this region your position is not only as good, but better than I have ever seen it.

How is it that it must be I who has to teach you that? Have you not seen it in all sorts of signs yourself? Decidedly, I no longer recognize you. If there is change, it is in yourself and not elsewhere. I have passed on to you my principal fault, which is a sickly despondency. Or rather circumstances have accomplished in you what in me was the work of nature. But will you never become yourself again? The end of my paper puts an end to my sermon.

Farewell, I embrace you with all my heart. Remember us with great affection to your wife.

[Tocqueville's *The Old Regime and the French Revolution* appeared in June 1856.]

Seven

THE FINAL YEARS (1856–1859)

The letters in this final section reveal Tocqueville's ambivalent attitude toward France and toward his age, an ambivalence that reflects a blend of his hopes and fears, loves and hates, memories and present realities. Consider first his ambivalent attitude toward France. On the one hand, Tocqueville unquestionably has been and continues to be an ardent critic of France. The nation, he says, is "fatally boring," and France can boast only of an oppressive regime "in which the greatest event can be brought about in the shadows with a view to a stock market coup" (Letters 91 and 92). On the other hand, Tocqueville exhibits a certain ambivalence because his love for France will not allow him to despair entirely. When Gobineau argues that the French have fallen irretrievably into a childlike decadence, and hence need rule by a master, Tocqueville rushes to defend his country. France has corrupted her citizens in countless ways, he admits, but "I believe that a better upbringing could redress the evil that a bad upbringing has accomplished."

No, I will not believe that this human species, which is at the head of visible creation, should become the debased flock that you tell us it is and that there is nothing more to do than to deliver it without future and without recourse to a small number of shepherds who, after all, are not better animals than we are and often are worse. (Letter 92)

Later, when Gobineau proclaims the mediocrity of French culture, Tocqueville offers a qualified defense, but shows both his love for and faith in France: "I know of no foreigner, unless perhaps some cad of a German professor, who holds the opinion about France that you, a Frenchman, hold of it" (Letter 103).

Tocqueville's ambivalence emerges in other areas. After his 1857 journey to England, he writes Corcelle that England presents a marvelous spectacle of class cooperation, such a wonderful contrast to "those class hatreds and jealousies that, after having been the source of all our miseries, have destroyed our liberty" (Letter 96). But less than a week later, he writes Kergorlay that while England's class cooperation is remarkable, Tocqueville still dislikes upper-class and especially aristocratic domination of political power (Letter 97). Similarly, Tocqueville has mixed feelings about colonialism. He describes the suppression of India's Sepoy Mutiny as a triumph for "Christianity and . . . civilization," but he insists that England pursue fair and mutually beneficial colonial policies, that England's task is "not only to dominate India, but to civilize it" (Letter 98).

And, finally, Tocqueville has an ambivalent regard for religion. Once again, he is critical of religion for promoting the habits of passivity, withdrawal into private affairs, resignation, and political or public inaction. There are, says Tocqueville, two parts to morality, and religion teaches us only one. Religion does instruct us in private obligations and duties, but not in our duties toward public life, "the duties that every citizen has toward his country." Tocqueville reaches back into his memory of aristocratic times for an example: "I have often heard it said that my grandmother, who was a very saintly woman, after having recommended to her young son the exercise of all the duties of private life, did not fail to add: 'And then, my child, never forget that a man above all owes himself to his homeland' " (Letter 90). On the other hand, critical as he is of religion, Tocqueville shows no inclination to abandon his religious convictions and his religious-based morality. To both Corcelle and Kergorlay, he praises the harmony England achieved between political freedom and religion (Letters 96 and 97). And Tocqueville uses religious arguments against Gobineau. "Christianity," says Tocqueville, "certainly tended to make all men brothers and equals," but Gobineau's racial theories violate this most central of Christian beliefs (Letter 92). And in the face of Gobineau's fatalism, Tocqueville argues— much like Bossuet—that surely the plan of providence has not been to lead us through all these centuries just in order to arrive in a state of perpetual childhood. "You will permit me to have less confidence in you than in the bounty and justice of God" (Letter 92).

Despite his ambivalence on so many subjects, one theme runs consistently throughout these letters: his attempt to escape from his decade. Often, Tocqueville escapes into books. He describes his library of books, mostly ones from past centuries, and the reading habits adopted by his wife and himself: "We take down, to read, sometimes one book, sometimes another: it is as though we were forcing the man of intellect who had written it to come converse with us" (Letter 91). At other times, Tocqueville escapes into his dreams or hopes for a somewhat distant future. To Beaumont he reiterates his established view that liberty "alone can give to human societies in general, to the individuals who compose them in particular, all the prosperity and all the grandeur of which our species is capable." But alas, he says, France will not be free for a long time because France does "not seriously want to be free." Then, strangely enough, Tocqueville indulges in revolutionary hopes. After France has rid herself of the fear of anarchy and socialism, after France has settled into the routine of despotism, then perhaps a new revolution, guided by members of the "enlightened classes" but propelled by the energy of the people, can restore freedom (Letter 100).

And finally, Tocqueville escapes into a certain nostalgia for the past. He agrees with Gobineau that it was easier to establish liberty in an aristocratic society (Letter 92), and he writes his nephew of the "sweet and paternal relations that [three hundred years ago] still existed between the upper and lower classes" (Letter 94). Most of all, we see his nostalgia when he encountered a man from the Revolution of 1789, an encounter that provoked in Tocqueville great pride in his country but great shame for his own time. This ninety-six-year-old revolutionary spoke very highly of the eighteenth century and of the Revolution, and, in Tocqueville's view, this man confirmed that France had declined since the Revolution in morality, in ambition, in principled political action, and in confidence. Has France changed much, asks Tocqueville, and, as his illness worsened along with his conviction that France's malady would last at least for his lifetime, no passage could summarize Tocqueville's own feelings better than this old revolutionary's reply: " 'Ah! Monsieur, . . . then people had a cause; now they have only interests. There were ties between men then; there are none any more. It is very sad, Monsieur, to outlive one's country!' " (Letter 101).

90. To Sophie Swetchine

Tocqueville, September 10, 1856

Nearly three weeks ago you wrote me, Madame, the kindest and most interesting of letters, and I have still not answered you. I hope you will find in your heart, which contains so much indulgence, some reason to excuse me. For myself, I find none; and I have nothing to say, except that I have always been the worst correspondent in the world, the most irregular, the most intermittent, and that my best friends, who have always complained of this fault, have al-

ways pardoned me by considering that it is neither forgetful-
ness nor indifference that will ever prevent me from writing,
but a sort of sluggishness of mind of which I am not the
master. I would readily do what a compatriot I met in America did, who, when he had something urgent to say to his
friends, went a hundred leagues rather than write a letter.
Very different in this from a neighbor of mine who, by contrast, was so little the master of his speech and so habituated
to his pen that, if in conversation you put forth to him an
argument that was a little lively, he left you at once, mounted
a small horse that he had left at the door on coming, and went
back at a gallop to his manor house to write what he should
have answered. I am at antipodes to the former, but I would
gladly draw closer to the latter.

Your opinion on my book delighted me. No one could
penetrate further into my thought and better understand the
meaning of the work. Your letter will be set apart from all
others that express opinions on my work. In general, you
must know, Madame, that everything that concerns you is set
apart in my mind. The place you occupy there is all your own
and resembles that of no one else. I have a mixture of respect
and affection for you that makes the feeling I hold for you
very special, and that a very rare combination of diverse qualities can alone explain.

How I love to hear you speak so nobly against everything
that resembles slavery! I am very much of your opinion that a
more equal distribution of goods and rights in this world is
the greatest aim that those who conduct human affairs can
have in view. I would only wish that equality in politics con-
sisted of everyone being equally free and not, as one hears so
often in our days, of everyone being subjugated to the same
master.

I very much suspected, I admit, that what I say on the
clergy of the Old Regime and on the advantage there was in
binding it to the homeland by terrestrial interests, would not
have your complete assent. I do not want any more than you
do to broach this great question by letter. But I keenly desire

one of those precious and very rare hours to present itself in
which I may chat freely with you, so that I can set out to you
all my thought on this point and search for the truth in contact with a mind as sincere as mine and more enlightened than
mine in such a matter. I will only tell you today, if you permit it, the sentiment that underlies the impression of which I
wrote.

There are, it seems to me, two distinct parts to morality,
each of which is as important as the other in the eyes of God,
but which, in our days, His ministers teach us with a very
unequal ardor. The one relates to private life: these are the
relative duties of people as fathers, as sons, as wives or hus-
bands. . . . The other concerns public life: these are the duties
that every citizen has toward his country and the human society to which he belongs. Am I mistaken in believing that the
clergy of our time is very occupied with the first portion of
morality and very little occupied with the second? That seems
to me especially apparent in the way in which women feel and
think. I see a great number of them who have a thousand
private virtues in which the direct and beneficial action of religion is to be perceived; who, thanks to it, are very faithful
wives, excellent mothers; who show themselves to be indul-
gent toward their servants, charitable toward the poor. . . .
But as to that part of duties that is related to public life, they
do not seem to have the least idea. Not only do they not
practice them for themselves, which is natural enough, but
they do not seem even to have any thought of inculcating
them in those on whom they have influence. That is an aspect
of education that is as if it were invisible to them. It was not
like this under the Old Regime, which, amidst many vices,
included proud and manly virtues. I have often heard it said
that my grandmother, who was a very saintly woman, after
having recommended to her young son the exercise of all the
duties of private life, did not fail to add: "And then, my child,
never forget that a man above all owes himself to his homeland; that there is no sacrifice that he must not make for it;
that he cannot rest indifferent to its fate, and that God de-

mands of him that he always be ready to consecrate, if need be, his time, his fortune, and even his life to the service of the state and of the king."

But I see, Madame, that I am penetrating imperceptibly further than I would like into the subject about which I would like to chat with you and on which there would be too much to write.

Nevertheless, I do not want to finish without thanking you for the quotation from Bossuet that you sent me.[1] Nothing is more beautiful, not even comparing Bossuet with himself. I find in this single passage all that uplifts man and all that at the same time retains him in his place. It presents both the sentiment of our grandeur and of that of God. It is proud and it is humble. Where did you extract that, Madame? I was not acquainted with this admirable morsel.

Farewell, Madame; give me news of yourself. My wife always asks me to remember her particularly to you, and I, on my own behalf, ask you to believe in my tender and respectful attachment.

91. To Jeanne-Rachel de Cordoüie, Countess de Mandat-Grancey

Tocqueville, December 28, 1856

Your letter is so kind, dear cousin,[2] and your temper so benevolent that I want to thank you right away. I will confess

1. Madame Swetchine had sent Tocqueville the following excerpt from Bishop Bossuet: "I do not know, my Lord, if you are happy with me, and I even recognize that you have many reasons for not being so. But, for me, I must confess to your glory that I am happy with you and that I am perfectly so. It matters little to you whether I am or not. But, after all, this is the most glorious witness I can make to you, because to say that I am happy with you is to say that you are my God, since there is only one God who can make me happy."

2. Like Tocqueville, the countess was a great-grandchild of the famous eighteenth-century statesman and lawyer Lamoignon de Malesherbes. As cousins, they had known each other since childhood.

first that I am an awful scribbler. The blame for that is due a
little to that good and spiritual old man who raised me; you
knew him, Abbé Lesueur,[3] a saint, and a kind saint,
which is not always to be encountered. He had the singular
idea of making me learn to write before teaching me spelling.
As I did not know very well how to write my words, I muddled them as best I could, in this way drowning my errors in
my scrawl. As a result, I have never learned spelling
thoroughly and have continued indefinitely to scrawl. Please
rest assured that my dear abbé succeeded better in other parts
of my education. To come back to the word you declare illegible, undoubtedly with reason, I imagine that it must be
distance or something like that. I hardly, as a matter
of fact, see anything but time and distance that could
separate us. Everything else brings us together, and above all
so many common remembrances that could never be effaced
entirely from our memory. How can one avoid recalling the
friends of one's youth with pleasure? One loves them for
themselves and for the charming remembrance of youth itself
they bring back to mind. Nor could I ever forget your
mother, not only her kindness, but her mind: that mind,
strong and brilliant, peculiar to a generation that had
learned to think and to feel for itself, instead of breathing in I
know not what dull and insipid commonplaces, like today's
generation.

I am not surprised the world bores you; I have too good an
opinion of you to doubt it. It is, indeed, fatally boring, especially what is called the great world, undoubtedly because
people above all come together in large houses and in large
apartments.[4] Paris is nonetheless still the city where most of
the people of a kind and spiritual fellowship meet; but one
must fish for them in an ocean of fools and once one catches
them, it is difficult to bring them together. I imagine however

3. His childhood tutor.
4. Fr. = "grand monde . . . grandes maisons . . . grands appartements."

that it would not be impossible for one to create a very agreeable society in Paris, in the midst of which one could spend several pleasant months every year. But for that, one would require much time, effort, care, and I must add, alas, many good dinners. For, in general, nothing has a better appetite than fine wits.

Pardon me for chatting this way with you. That will prove to you, at least, that I am writing you with pleasure. Why aren't you our neighbor, as you say? I assure you we would spend some good evenings together. I live, whatever the weather, almost all my days outside; but when night comes, I go back in, no longer to the drawing room, but into a very peaceful study, where a large clear fire burns in an old-fashioned and enormous fireplace. We stay there, until going to bed, my wife and I and in addition, as at this moment, one or two special friends. We are surrounded by the best books that have been published in the principal languages of Europe. I have admitted nothing into this library but what is excellent: it is enough to tell you that it is not very voluminous, and above all that the nineteenth century does not occupy a very great place. We take down, to read, sometimes one book, sometimes another: it is as though we were forcing the man of intellect who had written it to come converse with us. Time flies in the midst of these peaceful occupations: we always find that it goes by too quickly; and, indeed, life moves on. It is a pity that one does not truly know how to take advantage of it, except when one becomes old.

I am stopping here so as not to bore you. Farewell, very dear cousin, or rather, see you soon; because, at the end of February, we will be returning to Paris, and I imagine you will be there. Do not completely forget us until then. Be well and above all believe in my old and very sincere friendship. Do not forget to remember me either to your husband or to your children, especially to the sailor in whom we are indeed heartily interested.

92. *To Arthur de Gobineau*

Tocqueville, January 24, 1857

Your letter of November 29, which I received about a month ago, my dear friend, has filled us with genuine emotion. What a horrible journey.[5] All mine are only child's play beside that one. If at the same time I received your letter I had not received one from d'Avril, which announced the happy arrival of Mme. de Gobineau and your daughter, I avow that your letter would still not have reassured me on the latter's fate. I confess to you that I have all the trouble in the world understanding how, after considering the nature of what you are telling me about, you could decide to precipitate your wife and your daughter into the perils of such a route, so well known for its dangers and in the middle of which you had to abandon your own family. I admire Mme. de Gobineau's temerity, and I am full of joy and almost of surprise that this temerity succeeded. Now, I hold Mlle. Diane to be immortal. Your friends can tell you how anxious I was when I saw her leave. I swear to you that, knowing the effects the Orient ordinarily produces on travelers of her age, I had little hope of seeing this charming child again and that the image of Lamartine's daughter[6] sorrowfully besieged my imagination in making my farewells to you. There she is safe from that horrible danger. God be praised!

You have taken very seriously I know not what silly joke I have apparently made to you on your religion. That proves that one must not jest with friends whom two or three deserts and just as many seas separate from us so that one word taken awry can only be redressed at the end of a year. No, my dear friend, calm yourself, I have never taken you for a base hypocrite, I know you too well, as you say, ever to hold this opinion of you. God keep me from it! I believed you to be one of

5. Gobineau had recently completed a long, rather dangerous overland journey to be France's ambassador to Teheran.

6. Lamartine's daughter had died of illness on a journey to the Orient.

those people, as there are and always will be so many of
them, even in centuries of faith, who are full of veneration
and a sort of filial tenderness for the Christian religion, without unfortunately being for all that absolutely convinced
Christians. In that state of the soul, a person does not believe
himself to be performing an act of hypocrisy in evidencing all
sorts of respect for a religion that is so beneficial and holy
(taking this word at least in the sense of one of the great instruments of morality and civilization with which God has
ever been served). Several of the noblest geniuses of modern
times have assuredly been hypocrites of this sort; those especially who have professed doctrines that, all the while appearing true to them, had in their eyes even the inconvenience of
appearing contrary to Christian dogma and consequently of
being capable of shaking the faith in the souls of those in
whom it was still to be encountered, if some effort were not
made to attenuate that deadly result. I had placed you among
those knaves, pardon me for that. I admit that it seemed to
me impossible to believe that you had not perceived the difficulty of reconciling your scientific theories with the letter and
even the spirit of Christianity. As for the letter, what is more
clear in Genesis than the unity of humankind and the emergence of all men from the same man? And as for the spirit of
Christianity, is not its distinctive trait having wanted to abol-
ish all distinctions of race that the Jewish religion had continued to allow to subsist and making only one human species,
all of whose members were equally capable of perfecting
themselves and of becoming alike? How can this spirit, naturally and for the great good sense of the crowd, be reconciled
with a historical doctrine that makes for distinct, unequal
races, more or less made to understand, judge, act and that as
a consequence of a certain original disposition which cannot
change and which irresistibly limits the perfecting of some?
Christianity certainly tended to make all men brothers and
equals. Your doctrine makes all of them cousins at most, the
common father of whom is only in heaven; here below there

are only conquerors and conquered, masters and slaves by
right of birth, and this is so true that your doctrines are approved, cited, commented on by whom? By the owners of
slaves and on behalf of the eternal servitude that is founded
on radical differences in race. I know that, just now, there are,
in the southern United States, Christian priests and perhaps
good priests (owners of slaves nonetheless) who are preaching
in the pulpit doctrines that no doubt are analogous to yours.
But rest assured that the mass of Christians composed of those
whose interest does not incline their thinking your way; rest
assured, I say, that the bulk of Christians in the world cannot
feel the least sympathy for your doctrines. I am not speaking
of materialist opinions, which you say are not contained in it.
All right, but out of which it is impossible that many minds
will not extract them. I admit therefore that reading your
book had left me doubts on the solidity of your faith and that
I had placed you disrespectfully among those men whom
doubts do not prevent from treating Christianity with a real
and profound respect, and who do not believe they are performing an act of hypocrisy in working to make their ideas as
compatible as possible with it. You tell me that I am wrong in
this and that you have become an absolutely convinced Christian. May heaven hear you! You will be the happiest of men
in this world, to say nothing of the other; I am deeply convinced of this, and rest assured that no one will rejoice more
than I to see you persist in this course. Alas! It is not open to
all minds, and many who seek it sincerely have not so far had
the good fortune of encountering it. If I perhaps spoke hu-
morously (I no longer recall) of the devout, it is because my
heart rebels daily at seeing the little gentlemen who pass their
time in clubs and wicked places, or great knaves who are capable of any base action as well as of any act of violence,
speak devoutly of *their holy religion*. I am always tempted to
cry out to them: "Be pagans with pure conduct, proud souls,
and clean hands rather than Christians in this fashion."

I descend from these heights toward a very small subject,

which is the Institute.[7] I am finding the chances for your making your way into it very good. Until just recently, the enterprise seemed to me to present almost insurmountable difficulties. In the Academy of Moral and Political Sciences, a person is only admitted through presentation by a section. The two sections to which you most naturally belong, philosophy and history, seemed to me, for a host of reasons that would take too long to explain, to be scarcely accessible. But now there is a new state of affairs that is going to give us great opportunities: a year ago we had a small coup d'état, imperceptibly directed against the Institute and in particular against the Academy of Moral and Political Sciences. Ten colleagues have been added to us under the name of the political section. Villemain[8] has named them *the garrison,* because indeed they have entered the place in force to hold it in subjection. As these scarcely academic academicians for the most part were not *elected,* according to organic and always followed law, but named by the government contrary to that law, we do not altogether consider them to be colleagues and we do not express much respect toward them. But the same feeling does not adhere to those members of that section who, at each vacancy, will be elected. Now, in the said section as in all the others, there has just been created a body of corresponding members, ten I think, whom the government has refrained from naming and whom it strongly wants to leave to election. For you it is a matter of becoming one of those. If the section presents you, you will probably be elected, because we will form a majority for you in the Academy. Now, the qualifications required to

7. Technically, the French Academy, the Academy of Moral and Political Sciences, and three other academies were all part of the Institut National, organized along these lines in 1801.

8. Abel-François Villemain (1790–1870), a famous essayist, literary critic, historian, and once professor at the Sorbonne. Under the Restoration, he defended freedom of the press, and under the July Monarchy he became minister of public instruction for five years. Since 1832 he had been secretary of the French Academy.

become a member of the political section are so diverse that I
do not see what kind of study could be prevented from aspir-
ing to it. It would thus be a matter of being presented by
the section. The natural intermediary to it seems to us, to
Rémusat and me, necessarily to be M. Lefebvre. D'Avril must
have informed you that, on our advice, he had seen M. Lefebvre and had been content with him. Rémusat is in excellent spirits. I am returning to Paris in two weeks, and you can
rest assured that I will advance your case vigorously and will
do my best to make it succeed.

I ask you, my dear friend, for permission not to discuss
your political theories. Not being able to have the same liberty as existed five hundred years ago, you prefer to have
none: all right. Out of fear of undergoing the despotism of
parties under which a person could at least defend his dignity
and independence through word and press, you find it good
to be oppressed in a single way and by a single individual at
the same time, but so well that no one, you no more than
anyone else, can breathe a word. All right again. There is no
disputing taste. Rather than witness the intrigues that prevail
in the assemblies, you would prefer a regime in which the
greatest event can be brought about in the shadows with a
view to a stock market coup or to a success in an industrial
enterprise. Better and better. I have to confess that I am disappointed with you. I have found you, since I have known you,
to be of an essentially troublemaking temperament (you see
how I hold you incapable of hypocrisy). It has to be just now
that I see you finally satisfied with things and men! Seriously,
what could political discussions between us result in? We belong to two diametrically opposed schools. We thus cannot
have any hope of convincing each other. Now, it is not necessary to discuss matters of serious questions and new ideas
with one's friends, when one has no hope of persuading them.
We are both perfectly logical in our way of thinking. You
consider the men of our days to be big children, very degen-
erate and very poorly raised. And, consequently, you find it

good that they be led by spectacles, noise, a lot of tinsel, by pretty embroidery and superb uniforms which, very often, are only so much livery. Like you, I believe that our contemporaries are rather poorly raised, which is the first cause of their miseries and their weakness; but I believe that a better upbringing could redress the evil that a bad upbringing has accomplished; I believe that it is not permissible to renounce such an enterprise. I believe that they can be turned, as all men can, to some account, by an appeal to their natural integrity and to their good sense. I want to treat them as men, in effect. I may be wrong. But I follow the consequences of my principles and, moreover, I find a profound and noble pleasure in following them. You profoundly despise the human species, at least ours; you believe it not only fallen but also incapable of ever raising itself up. Its very constitution condemns it to servitude. It is very natural that in order at least to maintain a little order in this rabble the government of the saber and even of the baton seems to you to have some very good aspects. I nonetheless do not believe that, in what concerns you, you are tempted to offer your back in order to render a personal homage to your principles. For myself, feeling that I have neither the right nor the taste to entertain such opinions on my race and on my country, I think that it is not necessary to despair of them. In my eyes, human societies like individuals become something only through the practice of liberty. That liberty is more difficult to establish and to maintain in democratic societies like ours than in certain aristocratic societies that preceded us, I have always said. But that it is impossible I will never be so rash as to think. That it might be necessary to despair of succeeding in it, I pray that God will never inspire me with such an idea. No, I will not believe that this human species, which is at the head of visible creation, should become the debased flock that you tell us it is and that there is nothing more to do than to deliver it without future and without recourse to a small number of shepherds who, after all, are not better animals than we are and often are worse. You will permit me to have less confidence in you than in the bounty and justice of God.

Although your solitude in Teheran seems to agree with you, I confess to you that it is with sadness and not without some anxiety that I see you being left all alone in a country so removed and so lost. My sole consolation is that you are going, I hope, to gain the right to leave soon. It seems that Persia has in recent times taken on an importance that must, naturally, strongly enhance the position of the person who conducts France's affairs there and make him prominent in the master's eyes. Distinguish yourself there, but do not stay there too long. While waiting, give me your news. I would never dare to send you so long and so indecipherable a scrawl if you were not so expert in the art of divining what I intended to write. Take good care of yourself. Be assured of our very sincere affection. Have faith that I will not forget your academic interests.

93. To Sophie Swetchine

Tocqueville, February 11, 1857

. . . I have applied myself rather seriously to work since I last wrote you, but that does not suffice to give my mind the desirable balance. It is still a little *unhinged,*[9] as they say in English. This disorder is so natural to it that one must not be astonished. Vague restlessness and an incoherent agitation of desires have always been a chronic malady with me. I am only astonished that it can affect me so much in circumstances in which everything should generate internal peace. Certainly I cannot complain of the part providence has made for me in this world. I have no more right than I have any desire to say that I am unhappy; and nonetheless I lack the greatest of all conditions of happiness: the tranquil enjoyment of present good. I live, however, beside a person whose contact should

9. Tocqueville uses the English word.

long ago have sufficed to cure me of this great and ridiculous misery; and indeed, this contact has been very salutary for me for twenty years, enough to fortify my mind in my condition, not enough to produce regular and complete equilibrium. My wife, whom the world knows so little, feels and thinks in an impassioned and vehement manner; she is very capable of experiencing fierce sorrow and of feeling with extreme emotion any evil that happens; but she knows how to enjoy fully the good that arises. She does not become disturbed over nothing; she knows how to let tranquil days and happy circumstances flow in a perfect repose and calm. Thus a serenity is established in our home that overtakes me now and then, but which soon escapes me and abandons me to this turmoil that is without cause or effect, which often makes my soul turn like a wheel that has fallen out of gear.

94. *To Hubert de Tocqueville*

Tocqueville, February 23, 1857

If I have not answered your letter sooner, my dear friend, you must not conclude that it has not interested me. Your letters, in general, give me very great pleasure: but I do not always write you in my turn as often as I would like. My mornings are consecrated to study, and my days are spent in the fields supervising the workers. At this time, we have great tasks to do that we are pushing faster than we can go, in order to make our outdoors nearly what it should be. Once that is done, we will no longer undertake anything but small tasks; for we are not idlers who can endure the country only on the condition of having a multitude of workers there, and no sooner have succeeded in becoming well settled there than they are bored. I believe that you will find Tocqueville very much changed for the better when you come back here: I would like that to be this year. For the first time in the twenty years that I have lived in this country, I have under-

taken to put a little order into all the old papers that are
heaped up here in what is called the charter room. A complete
examination would have taken me more time than I had at
my disposal. But the little I have seen of these family documents interested me greatly. I have encountered the line of
our fathers through nearly four hundred years, always finding
them again in Tocqueville, and their history mingled with that
of the whole population that surrounds me. There is a certain
delight in thus treading on the ground that our ancestors inhabited, and in living in the midst of people whose origins are
mingled with our own. I await you in order to complete these
studies, which have an interest only for us, but which for us
have a very great interest. I also was curious to cast a glance
at the old baptismal and marriage records in the parish; they
exist in part to the sixteenth century. I noticed, in doing this
reading, that three hundred years ago, we served as godfathers
for a very large number of the inhabitants of the village: new
proof of the sweet and paternal relations that, in that time,
still existed between the upper and lower classes; relations that
were replaced in so many places by sentiments of jealousy,
suspicion, and often hatred.

I am delighted with what you tell me about your studies.
You do well to master German history, especially the period
since the Reformation. What you tell me about Schiller[10] has
often been said to me by Germans of taste. As a historian,
Schiller is a great colorist, but not a faithful copyist of nature.
His book, I believe, would be a very bad guide if one read it
to know the exact detail of facts and even the particular mo-

10. Johann Christoph Friedrich von Schiller (1759–1805), the famous German poet, dramatist, and philosopher. Schiller's historical play, *Don Carlos*
(1785), kindled an interest in history, and he wrote a book on the history of
Spain. With this success, Goethe obtained a professorship at Jena for Schiller
where Schiller delivered a famous address on the study of universal history and
published a second historical work on the Thirty Years' War. Schiller then
returned to the study of philosophy and literature. Tocqueville is probably
referring to Schiller's *Geschichte des Dreissigjährigen Krieges* (1791–1793).

tives that made certain figures act and produce certain incidents in that great play. But I believe that he points out well
the general causes of the occurrence and the movement of the
ideas and passions that produced it or sprang from it. After
all, only that is absolutely *sure* in history; all that is particular
is always more or less doubtful. What is more, Schiller above
all deserves to occupy the first rank among men of genius
because of his poems. His great plays for the theater and his
little detached pieces are, in my opinion, among the most
beautiful poems that can be encountered in any literature. If I
knew German well enough to judge in such a matter, I would
say that Schiller appears at least equal to Goethe as a poet, and
he is infinitely superior to him as a man. The god Goethe,
immobile in his Olympus, describing human passions without
ever feeling them or sharing them, has always appeared to me
hardly an attractive being, a defender of the devil by his insen-
sitivity, his egoism, and his pride, and of man only by his
small passions.

There is a general history of Europe in the eighteenth century, done by a German, Schlosser:[11] it is a solid work and
very good to read in the parts that deal with Germany in that
century. I recommend it to you when you come to the period
he describes.

Your father writes me that if I could find you a good
woman, I should point her out; and that you would be disposed to marry her, if the opportunity presented itself and the
person pleased you. Therefore, let me know something about
what you are thinking along this line. I am interested in your
domestic happiness as much as in your career, and anything
that could contribute to making you happy as you understand

11. Friedrich Christoph Schlosser (1776–1861), a popular German historian
who openly passed judgment on men and events of the eighteenth century and
simultaneously expressed the German nationalist aspirations of the nineteenth
century. Tocqueville is probably referring to his *Geschichte des 18ten Jahrhun-
derts,* 2 vols. (1823).

happiness would cause me great joy, and I would work with all my might, if this were possible, to help you. There is nothing solid and truly sweet in this world but domestic happiness and intimacy with a wife who knows how to understand you, to help you, and if need be to support you in the difficulties of life. I have felt that too much from my own experience not to be convinced of it. At bottom, it is only in a father or in a wife that true and continual sympathy can be found. All other friendships are only incomplete and ineffective sentiments compared to that. I would like you to find this happiness, since you can understand it and aspire to it. But with the way in which people marry in France, it is very difficult to succeed in this; the greatest concern in life is concluded, in general, more lightly than the purchase of a pair of gloves.

Here I am at the end of my paper and my time; I embrace you with all my heart.

95. To Gustave de Beaumont

[End of February 1857?]

. . . Marmont's memoirs.[12] That is necessary reading. The author is one of these heroic adventurers (very well brought up besides) whom the French Revolution brought to the fore, who is without any very lofty morality, without moral grandeur, who is animated by a great hatred of liberty and in general of everything that hinders the preponderance of material force, but, what is more, who is very intelligent, moderate, and has a clear and easy narrative that enables one to become

12. Maréchal de Marmont, *Mémoires,* 9 vols. (1857). Auguste de Marmont, Duke de Raguse, was one of Napoleon's generals.

well acquainted with the men of his time and especially with the most extraordinary of all. But I am always astonished that someone can have taken part in such great things, been close to such great affairs, and lived with such great company, and have only that to say! What little he has to say, however, is well worth reading, especially if one restricts oneself to the narrative and skips three-fourths of the supporting material. Another book that I draw your attention to is the sequel of Macaulay's work, the 3d and 4th volumes.[13] We have just read it in English. But a translation must already have appeared. It is almost as superficial, but more amusing than a novel. But even when I say *superficial,* I speak of a profundity of mind that makes one perceive over the particular passions of time and country the general character of an epoch and the development of the human spirit. The work is not superficial as to the particular facts about which the author speaks and which he has thoroughly studied. It is necessary to read it to see how the base of integrity, of good sense, of moderation and of virtue which is to be found in a nation, and the good institutions that these qualities have established or allowed to subsist, can struggle against the vices of those who direct them. I do not believe that there have been men of state in any country more dishonest than those of whom Macaulay speaks in this part of his work, as there is no society greater than that which ultimately came from their hands. There are among peoples as among individuals, certain temperaments that struggle not only against maladies, but also against physicians.

This immense piece of gossip only leaves me time to tell you without explanation that we shall remain here the greater part of the month of March. After that things follow as usual. My wife wished to include in my letter a letter for. . . .

13. Thomas Macaulay, *The History of England.* Tocqueville must be referring to vols. 4 and 5, published in 1855.

96. To Claude-François de Corcelle

Tocqueville, July 29, 1857

I have so much to say on England,[14] which I have seen
again after twenty years and with a much greater experience
of men, that I would need several letters to give an account of
the sensations I have received and the ideas that have passed
through my mind in the presence of the spectacle I had before
my eyes.

It is the greatest spectacle there is in the world, although
everything in it is not great. One above all encounters things
entirely unknown in the rest of Europe and the sight of which
has comforted me.

I do not doubt that among the lower classes a certain
amount of hostility toward the other classes exists; but one
does not perceive it, and what one sees everywhere is the union
and understanding that exist among all the men who belong
to the enlightened classes, from the beginning of the bourgeoisie to the highest of the aristocracy, for defending the society and freely leading it in common. I do not envy England
its riches and its power, but I envy it that; and I took a deep
breath on finding myself for the first time in so many years,
beyond those class hatreds and jealousies that, after having
been the source of all our miseries, have destroyed our liberty.

England made me feel a second joy of which I have been
deprived for a very long time: it made me see a perfect accord
between the religious world and the political world, private
virtues and public virtues, Christianity and liberty. I heard
Christians of all denominations there commend free institutions not only as necessary for the good, but also for the morality of societies, and I did not once have before my eyes that
sort of moral monstrosity that today is to be seen on nearly

14. Tocqueville made a last visit to England in June and July of 1857, and
largely because *The Old Regime and the French Revolution* was so well received,
he was something of a celebrity. To the astonishment of many, the English
navy provided a ship to transport Tocqueville home to Cherbourg.

the entire continent, where there are religious men who commend despotism, leaving to those who are not religious the honor of speaking in favor of liberty.

97. *To Louis de Kergorlay*

Tocqueville, August 4, 1857

I do not want to go a long time, my dear friend, without giving you news of us and asking for news of you. I came back here two weeks ago today after having made a trip to England that was rather useful and the pleasure of which exceeded my expectations. I was so admirably received in that country, I was so overwhelmed with the testimonies of esteem, that I came back at once confused and charmed. Nevertheless, I am very happy to have returned home, and the tumult of the life I have just led seems only to have added to the value of the peaceful life I am leading now. My health is quite good, as is Marie's. I am now going to try to set myself seriously to work again. I certainly am encouraged about this in every respect. But, my mind can only be set in motion on its own, and it is not easy for my will to push it. As soon as I have finished with some visits we are having just now, I will make a great effort.

You know well that I did not spend my time in England without casting some curious glances around me. I found England more aristocratic in appearance, at least than I left it twenty years ago. The democratic ferment that then had risen to the surface has disappeared, and all the superior classes seem to have reached a better understanding, compared to the past era to which I was referring, about how they can jointly manage public affairs. What a great spectacle, but for a Frenchman who takes stock of himself, what a sad spectacle! Besides, there is not a single one of my theoretical ideas on the practice of political liberty and on what allows it to function among men that does not seem to me fully justified once

again by everything I have been seeing before me. The more
I have delved into the detail of the way in which public affairs
are conducted, the more these truths seem to me to be demonstrated; for it is the manner in which the smallest of affairs
are managed that leads to a comprehension of what is happening in the great ones. If one were to limit oneself to studying
the English political world from above, one would never understand anything about it. But to return to this great problem of today: not only does the aristocracy seem to be more
solidly in place than ever, but the nation is, without mutter-
ing, apparently leaving the government in the hands of a
very small number of families. Nonetheless, and despite all
appearances, I believe that the movement that is imperiously
pushing all other nations in an anti-aristocratic direction, is
softly and little by little dragging England itself. It would take
more time than I have to explain to you what makes me think
this. I will limit myself to giving you my general impression,
which is that aristocracy, and especially that which is combined with birth, is continuing to govern, like before, less by
a preponderant force that belongs to it, than by a sort of tacit
and voluntary consent of the other classes, which voluntarily
leave it at the head of public affairs, as long as these affairs are
well managed. I believe that great reverses and especially mistakes will readily enough make the other classes appear in the
government. It seems to me that this is the sentiment of able
people even within the governing class, and this sentiment
will undoubtedly preserve them a long time yet from a
downfall. Yet they are now put to a rugged test, and the current affairs in India constitute a crisis that can be compared
only to the one the war in America caused eighty years ago.

I was struck this time in England, as I had previously been,
to see how a religious sentiment conserved its power, without
becoming something that absorbs and destroys all other motives of human action. Nothing could be further from what
one sees in so many Catholic countries in which the great

bulk of people do not think about religion at all, and a small number of people think of nothing but religion. I have always thought that there was danger even in the best of passions when they become ardent and exclusive. I do not make an exception of the passion for religion; I would even put it in front, because, pushed to a certain point, it, more than anything else, makes everything disappear that is not religion, and creates the most useless or the most dangerous citizens in the name of morality and duty. I confess that I have always (*in petto*)[15] considered a book like *The Imitation of Jesus Christ*,[16] for example, when considered other than as instruction intended for the cloistral life, as supremely immoral. It is not *healthy* to detach oneself from the earth, from its interests, from its concerns, even from its pleasures, when they are honest, to the extent the author teaches; and those who live according to what they read in such a book cannot fail to lose everything that constitutes public virtues in acquiring certain private virtues. A certain preoccupation with religious truths which does not go to the point of absorbing thought in the other world, has therefore always seemed to me the state that conforms best to human morality in all its forms. One remains in this milieu most often, it seems to me, among the English, than among any other people I know.

This said, I leave you, asking you to write me soon and embracing you with all my heart. All our best to Mathilde.

P.S. I have a little money coming from Paris. Perhaps, for your part, you have some coming from Normandy. Could we not exchange debtors? Do not delay too long in responding to this.

15. "In my heart."
16. A book written by Thomas à Kempis in 1427 and revived and translated in the nineteenth century by Félicité de Lamennais. The book stresses the importance of an ascetic or even monastic life, a contempt of all worldly concerns, and the need for self-mortification in preparation for the grace of God.

98. To Lord Hatherton

Tocqueville, November 27, 1857

Not long ago, my lord, I received a letter from our friend Sumner,[17] dated from Teddesley. He claims that you have spoken to him about me with affection. I very much appreciated this kind thought on your part, and I wanted to write you to thank you for it. Indeed, I gladly seized this occasion to ask for news of you. This is not a gesture of politeness; I am sincerely interested in what is happening to you. I remember with gratitude your simple and cordial hospitality, and as I have already told you, I believe, I consider my little expedition to Teddesley with you to be one of the most agreeable episodes of my trip to England. Writing to you makes the time I spent so usefully and rapidly with you and at your home vivid in my memory once again.

Many thanks for all the trouble you took in writing me in regard to my little bit of agriculture. This always occupies me greatly, although I can do it only on a very small scale. All my land is rented, except for some meadows that are near to my house and on which I feed animals and harvest hay. That is enough both to make me very curious about all that concerns agriculture in general and to spread a great charm over my solitude. My daily life is divided into two almost equal parts: before noon I am a writer, and after noon a peasant. My books never make me forget my fields, whereas the latter often distract me when I am among my books. The evening brings my wife and me back together in front of a great ancient fireplace, before which a great number of my predecessors have sat and in which a bright flame burns. Together we reread the books that please us most, and time flies. You know that our habits in the country are a little different from

17. Charles Sumner (1811–1874), a Republican senator from Massachusetts, famous as an abolitionist and during the Reconstruction period following the American Civil War as a leading Radical Republican.

yours: in summer we receive our friends; winter is consecrated to retreat.

We have not, however, become such strangers to the world that we do not follow what is happening with attention and curiosity. Your dramas in India[18] have caused genuine emotion within the Tocqueville walls. I have, besides, never for an instant doubted your triumph, which is that of Christianity and of civilization. I even believe that this very painful jolt will ultimately be salutary and that, after this shock, your power in India will be established on a more solid foundation than that on which it has rested until now, but that will necessitate the development of larger military forces than you have had until now. That is the greatest harm that will result from this revolt. Whatever you do, you seem to me to be dragged little by little into establishing a considerable standing army. I sincerely regret seeing you enter onto this road, but everything seems to be pushing you onto it with an irresistible force.

I once wanted to do a work on the establishment of the English in India, and, to this end, I gathered together and read many documents on that country.[19] I long ago renounced this enterprise. I would have had to go there in order to understand well what I wanted to talk about; I admit to you that the thought still stays with me from this study that the English had not in a century done anything for the Indian populations that might have been expected from their enlightenment and their institutions. It seemed to me that they had

18. The Sepoy Mutiny of 1857–1858. The Sepoys, native Indians who served in the British army, constituted one of the few organized forces that could resist or protest against British colonialism. Thus the Sepoy rebellion became a focus for a more general resentment against the British—resentment by those who had lost land, by rulers long deposed (including the Great Mogul), and by those who feared the British would try to end the caste system and forcibly convert the people of India to Christianity.

19. Tocqueville's unfinished but very enlightening work on India was written from 1841 to 1843. See *L'Inde,* in *Oeuvres* (M), III, *Ecrits et discours politiques* (Paris: Gallimard, 1962).

limited themselves, generally, to assuming the place of the indigenous governments, and to making use, with more equity, mildness, and intelligence, of the same methods. I think that more could have been expected of them. I hope that the event we are witnessing will attract and fix the attention of the entire nation on the affairs of India, and will cause some light to penetrate into them. It is this part of your government that had remained until now the most obscure, not only for foreigners, but, if I am not mistaken, for yourselves. For this reason especially, I would like to see the East India Company abolished and the administration of this vast country fall, like all the rest, under the scrutiny of Parliament and the public.[20] Only then will you attain the level of your task, which is not only to dominate India, but to civilize it. These two things, indeed, are closely connected.

My wife particularly wants to be remembered to Lady Hatherton, to whom I ask you very kindly to offer the homage of my respect. Please accept for yourself, my lord, the expression of all my sentiments of high esteem and friendship.

99. To Henry Reeve

Tocqueville, January 30, 1858

I should have thanked you earlier, my dear friend, for the issues of the *Review*.[21] But I have suffered the common fate: I had a cold, and that illness kept me from writing for a while. On the other hand, the enforced rest to which it condemned me (and still condemns me a little, since it is not completely cured) permitted me to read at my ease the entire issue in question. I have read it completely with the sole exception of the last article, which I have not yet begun, and I have been

20. In fact, after the Sepoy Mutiny, England abolished the British East India Company and ruled India directly, though relying heavily upon and supporting Indian landlords and other members of the upper classes.

21. The *Edinburgh Review*.

very satisfied with it. Almost all of the articles interested me and taught me something. The historical fragment on M. Addington's administration[22] and the last years of M. Pitt's career pleased me greatly. There one finds our friend Lewis[23] completely. Little that imagination and coloring could add in life and brilliancy to a picture; but the clarity, the precision, the truth in detail that one would look for in the product of an excellent engraver working from nature. This manner of writing, applied to representing the appearance of a man as considerable as Pitt and a moment as important in history as that with which it is concerned, has great merit, and I hope that L. will keep the promise that he gives to finish in a subsequent article the work he has begun. Tell L., if you please, not the detail of my judgment, but the conclusion, which is that I have read the article with infinite pleasure. Give him, in addition, all my best regards, and present to him all the compliments one should make to a Chancellor of the Exchequer who, having to manage England's finances during the war in China and the war in India, still finds the time and the freedom of mind to write excellent chapters of history. Do not fail to remember me to Lady Theresa either, when you have a chance to meet her.

From that I come to your work,[24] which, sincerely, seems to me by far the principal work of the issue. I read you with extreme interest. It is what has struck me most in what has been written on the subject. This immense subject refuses to be contained in a single article. One does not find in yours all that one would wish to encounter. There are a lot of questions which it leaves to the side and that are nonetheless quite considerable. The matter that is treated, perhaps also the position of the *Review,* which is not a collection of historical philosophy but rather one of the great organs of the political parties

22. Henry Addington, prime minister of England, 1801–1804.

23. George Cornewall Lewis.

24. Tocqueville refers to Reeve's article on India that appeared in the January 1858 edition of the *Edinburgh Review*.

that conduct affairs, made it a rule for you to circumscribe yourself and commanded you, by example, neither to examine too closely the manner in which India had been governed before the war, nor the system that was adopted to govern it after the war. You have wanted only to make an exposition of the general situation in which the government habitually finds itself in this immense annex to your empire, and on this subject you have taught me much and have made me reflect a great deal. Perhaps you will not find that a great compliment to pay you. Although I may have studied the affairs of India more than is ordinarily done in France, I am still quite ignorant of it, compared with those Englishmen who are really occupied with the matter. But I believe that their number is rather small, and I imagine that the bulk of your public must have received from your article the same impression I did. You have made me see clearly, among other things, a capital truth of which I had only a very confused idea: the difficulty of raising revenues from India and the singular character of that territorial duty that is more the product of a joint ownership by the state than of a subsidy that is paid to it. I knew there was hardly in India anything but direct taxes or monopolies. But I did not know the difficulty that is encountered in deducting in advance any duty under other forms: a capital fact that makes India more onerous to England than I thought and makes its possession more precarious. The large number of men in arms who are in India, outside the army of the government, is equally a very important fact that I did not know well. I had never calculated it closely. It would require not a letter, but a volume, or a very long conversation, to tell you all the thoughts that reading your article suggested to me. I riddled it with strokes from my pencil. One point on which you are very affirmative and on which I permit myself to have the greatest doubts is the usefulness of favoring the introduction of a European population. I confess that I consider such a remedy, if it could be applied, so dangerous that I would be tempted to return to laws that prevented the purchase of lands in India. It is necessary to start from the same point from which you start yourself: one can only hold India with the consent, at least tacit, of the Indians. Now, I have always noticed that wherever one introduced, not European authorities, but a European population, in the midst of the imperfectly civilized populations of the rest of the world, the real and pretended superiority of the former over the latter has accustomed them to feeling in a way so harmful to individual interests and so mortifying to the self-respect of the indigenous people that more anger resulted from that than from any political oppression. If that is true of almost all the European peoples, how much more reason is there for it to be true of the English people—the most adroit in exploiting for its own profit the advantages of each country, the least pliant, the most disposed to hold itself apart, and (one can say it because this defect is intimately tied to great qualities) the haughtiest of all the European peoples. When I think of all you have done for your Indian army—of the rigidity of the established regulations, of the raise in pay and pensions, and of all of the pleasant things that you have accorded the indigenous soldiers—I find that no army of this nature has ever been better, or even as splendidly, treated as that which has just committed the horrors with which we are acquainted. But, at the same time, although I have not been in India, I venture to assert that never has the European officer lived more removed from the Asiatic soldier than has yours, never more *closed* within himself, that never has less *camaraderie* ruled among comrades in arms, even among people whom the epaulet appears to bring closer together, but between whom civilization and race put such a great difference, that the one perceived at every instant not only that he was not the equal to but that he was not even of *the same nature* as the other. When one looks in depth for the true cause of the revolt of your Indian army, I am convinced that you will find it there. One will be able to group many secondary causes around this principal cause, but either I am seriously mistaken or one will arrive at this: I believe that the horrible events in India are not in any way an uprising against oppression. It is the revolt of barbarism against pride.

I am ashamed of the length of this letter, even more ashamed of the way in which it is scrawled, which makes it almost illegible. I tell you nothing of our affairs. You understand that the abominable assault[25] that has just taken place can gladden the friends of despotism, but that it can only fill the true partisans of liberty with sadness. It is they who will pay for the crimes of assassins, and the only peril to the government at this moment is in abusing the strength that such an event gives it and losing its advantage through violence.

Do you have news of Senior? Where must one write him?

Give me news of the Grotes. Tell me precisely when you will come to Paris. I count on being in that city in the first week of March.

Remember us especially to Madame Reeve and extend great affections to Mlle. Hope. Finally believe as always in my sentiments of sincere affection.

P.S. I perceive, on rereading, that I omitted speaking to you of the matter which, nonetheless, occupies me the most with regard to India: that is the result of the current fighting. Am I mistaken in thinking that things seem to be more serious than was earlier believed to be the case? My impression is perhaps badly founded, but your position now seems to me to be more distressing than I thought it was before the taking of Delhi. I was sure that that city would be taken and I was hoping that after its fall, the whole insurrection would be brought down with the same blow. It seems to me that now, the end is no longer in sight. Before one had only to make war against an army. One would say at present that it is against a population. Is this an error?

25. The January 14, 1858, attempt by Felice Orsini and others to assassinate Napoleon III. They failed, but their bombs killed eight and wounded over a hundred.

I just now received from Marseilles a letter from Senior.
They are in good health.

100. *To Gustave de Beaumont*

Tocqueville, February 27, 1858

I had been wanting to write to you for a long time and at
length, my dear friend, but I was prevented from doing so
first of all by a rather violent flu. When it was finished, I
found myself overwhelmed by things to do, which had accu-
mulated while I was ill. When these things were done, I was
overtaken again by the same little illness, and it still has hold
of me, not enough to make me truly ill, but in a manner
which assures that all application is difficult. I do not have a
fever. I sleep and I eat almost as well as when healthy; but I
have a tight throat and a general malaise which forces me to
remain in my room, which is very hard on a man like me
who was accustomed to staying in the fresh air five or six
hours every day. I hope and I believe that this painful condition will pass when the weather changes. For a month we
have had, doubtless as you have, an icy north wind, which
parches the earth and human throats in an extraordinary manner. Never, I believe, has more arid weather been seen. The
farmers are asking for water, but as doubtless somewhere else
someone is asking for dryness, these contradictory wishes
have little effect on providence.

What I shall tell you right away, before passing to other
subjects, is the joy the news you gave us about Antonin
brought us.[26] We expected much of him, but this surpasses all
reasonable expectations. I do not doubt now that he will
emerge among the first and have his choice of service. I assure
you that we rejoice with all our hearts at your satisfaction.
Our tender affection for your household would assuredly suf-

26. Beaumont reported that his son Antonin was in fine health, in excellent
spirits, and in good academic standing at Saint-Cyr.

fice to make your son's success very agreeable to us. We find
in it, moreover, that sort of moral pleasure that the spectacle
of good conduct bearing its natural fruits gives, of sacrifices
having their legitimate recompense: the honest leading to the
useful. Why does the world present so few spectacles of this
kind?

I do not need to tell you how much your last letter interested me, and how much I agree with you on the greater part
of the things you said in it and, among others, on the value of
liberty. Like you, I have never been more profoundly convinced that it alone can give to human societies in general, to
the individuals who compose them in particular, all the prosperity and all the grandeur of which our species is capable.
Each day drives me more deeply into this belief: my observations as I live, the recollections of history, contemporary
events, foreign nations, our own, all concur in giving to these
opinions of our youth the character of an absolute conviction.
That liberty is the necessary condition without which there
has never been a truly great and virile nation, that for me is
itself conclusive evidence. I have, on this point, a faith that I
would very much like to have on many others. But how difficult it is to establish liberty solidly among people who have
lost the practice of it, and even the correct notion of it! What
greater impotence than that of institutions, when ideas and
mores do not nourish them! I have always believed that the
endeavor of making France a free nation (in the true sense of
the word), that this endeavor, to which, for our small part,
we have consecrated our lives, I have always believed, I say,
that this endeavor was noble and bold. I find it to be bolder
every day, but at the same time to be nobler, so that, if I
could be reborn, I would prefer to risk myself completely in
this daring adventure than to bend under the necessity of being a servant. Will others be happier than we have been? I do
not know. But I am convinced that, in our day, we will not
see a free society in France, at least what we understand by
that word. That does not mean that we will not see a revolu-

tion there. There is nothing set, I assure you. An unforeseen circumstance, a new turn of affairs, any accident whatever can lead to extraordinary events that would force each to come out of his hole. That is what I referred to in my last letter, and not to the establishment of a regular liberty. Nothing can make us free, for a long time to come, for the best of reasons, which is that we do not seriously want to be free. That is, after all, the very core of the difficulty. It is not that I am one of those who say that we are a decrepit and corrupt nation, destined forever to servitude. Those who fear that it will be thus, and those who hope for it, those who, in this view, point out the vices of the Roman Empire, those who delight in the idea that we are going to reproduce that image on a small scale, all those people, as I see it, are living in books and not in the reality of their time. We are not a decrepit nation, but a nation tired and frightened of anarchy. We lack the healthy and lofty notion of liberty, but we deserve better than our current fate. We are not yet ripe for the regular and definitive establishment of despotism, and the government will become aware of this, if it ever has the misfortune of founding itself solidly enough to discourage conspiracies, to make the anarchist parties put down their arms, and to tame them to the point that they seem to disappear from the scene. It will then be completely astonished, in the midst of its triumph, to find a layer of Frondeurs[27] and opponents underneath the thick layer of fawners who seem today to cover the entire ground of France. Sometimes I think that the only chance that remains for seeing the lively taste for liberty reborn in France is in the tranquil and, on the surface, final establishment of despotism. Notice the mechanism of all our revolutions; it can be described very exactly today: the experience of these last seventy years has proved that the people *alone* cannot make a revolution; as long as this necessary element of revolutions is

27. The Fronde was an unsuccessful rebellion in the seventeenth century against a very young Louis XIV. The Frondeurs were generally members of the nobility trying to gain power from the king and the bourgeoisie.

isolated, it is powerless. It becomes irresistible only at the moment when one part of the enlightened classes comes to unite with it, and such men lend it their moral support or their material cooperation only at the moment when they no longer fear it. From this one can conclude that it has been at the very moment when each of our governments in the last sixty years has appeared the strongest that it began to be stricken by the malady that made it perish. The Restoration began to die the day no one any longer spoke of killing it; hence the July government. It will doubtless be the same for the current government. Antonin will tell one day if I am wrong.

Please forgive all this chattering by a sick man who is beginning to grow well again and who is amusing himself by chatting without constraint, but also with little usefulness.

I just put in the mail *La Revue des Deux-Mondes* of the 1st of January and the *Edinburgh Review* of the same date. *La Revue des Deux-Mondes* did not seem to me to contain anything outstanding. It contains a sequel to the maritime stories of Jurien de la Gravière. You will find yet two more of them in the following reviews. The work is serious and has interested me. It gives precious insights into the old French navy and even into the old society. The author does not lack a good eye and, except for some little sentimental and ridiculous anecdotes, his work can be read, in my opinion, pleasurably and even profitably. The last article, which you do not know, contains a picture of the cadets of noble family, in the Old Regime, that would not dishonor a master.

I particularly recommend that you read the article in the *Edinburgh Review* on India. It is by Reeve. It is one of the best he has done, and I know of nothing that gives in so few words so many correct and important notions on that country. The article on Pitt is by G. Lewis. It is interesting and is altogether Lewis, exact, colorless, and cold, as interesting and as true as an engraved portrait can be, in which the features are reproduced and the soul is lacking.

Have you read in the first number of the *La Revue des Deux-*

Mondes that I have sent you, the novel, or rather the fragment of the *Memoirs* by M. Gaschon, so-called de Molènes? What an ignoble and coarse picture of vicious and musty old men! The whole thing mixed with stinking pretensions and vanity! In previous articles, the same author had made tirades in favor of religion and full of the most superb disdain for the unbelieving. What strikes me in the literature of the day (if that can be called literature) is seeing on the one hand a sort of religious affectation and on the other a profound sinking into the material. Never, I believe, has coarser and more vulgar sensualism reigned in novels than today, and this is not one of the least troublesome signs of the spirit of the times. You know that this Gaschon (the most unbearable fop that can be imagined) passed, several years ago, for Madame de Rémusat's lover. That was told in the art tribe as incontestable, although perhaps it was not true.

I am stopping, because it is necessary to end a letter, for I have a hundred things to say. I am nevertheless adding as always a word on the railroad, which it appears quite certain will be put into circulation next July. I impress this fact on your memory.

I was counting on leaving for Paris in the first week of March. But I think I will not pull myself out of here before the 15th of next month, at the earliest.

Farewell. I embrace you with all my heart. A thousand affectionate remembrances to Madame de Beaumont.

P.S. I was forgetting the most important thing: Senior just traveled with his wife through the Orient. He is, at the moment, in the South of France. He just wrote to tell me that he was going to return to Paris and was counting on being at Tours about the 13th of next month. He asked me for your address in order to write you and tell you how much pleasure it would give him for you to see him in Tours. Although it is only a matter of Tours, I found the request for your address suspect; as a consequence, I answered him without giving it to

him. I said, it is true, that I would inform you when he
would be passing through. But I added that I thought that at
that time you would have left to go to Auvergne to sell
wood.

101. To Pierre Freslon

Tocqueville, March 16, 1858

Your letters, my dear friend, are truly one of the great pleasures of our solitude. I know that only conversation with you
could be worth even more. I hope to be able to enjoy it in a
fortnight. . . .

The other day I made a visit that greatly resembled the excursions Cuvier[28] made into the antediluvian world. I have
been to see a man who is ninety-six years old, and is as sharp
mentally as you and I. He is an old Benedictine, a man of
letters and of spirit who, without having renounced either his
station or his belief, had nonetheless *fallen,* as was said under
the Restoration, into the principles of the Revolution. He
mingled with the men of thought and action who appeared
immediately before or at the beginning of that Revolution.
Today he lives very retired some leagues from me. I have
been to see him. I found him seated before a little fire, and
surrounded by thick classical volumes that he was studying
thoroughly as if he were beginning his education. Picture to
yourself what it is to find oneself before a man who lived for
twenty-seven years under the old monarchy, who was older
in 1789 than I was in 1830, who attended the first proceedings
of the Estates General and followed the workings of the Constituent Assembly as an already mature man. I found this old
man yet more extraordinary than his age. This man's mind
has assuredly been conserved in a well-sealed jar, like those
fruits that keep their freshness when they are put away
sheltered from contact with external air. I have always noticed

28. Georges Cuvier (1769–1832), the famous French naturalist.

that in France the quantity of intellectual and moral warmth is in inverse proportion to the number of years. One is colder the younger one is, and temperature seems to rise with age. Men like you and me already seem to be very ridiculous enthusiasts to eighteen-year-old sages. According to this law my centenarian should have been completely aflame. And so he was when he was speaking of the hopes of '89 and the great cause of liberty. I assure you that it would have been difficult to make him admit that we now enjoy the institutions that those who made the Revolution desired. I asked him if he found France much changed with respect to morals. "Ah! Monsieur," he answered me, "I think I am dreaming when I recall the condition of minds in my youth, the vivacity, the sincerity of opinions, the respect for oneself and for public opinion, the disinterestedness in political passion. Ah! Monsieur," he added, while shaking my hand with the effusion and grandiloquence of the 18th century, "then people had a cause; now they have only interests. There were ties between men then; there are none any more. It is very sad, Monsieur, to outlive one's country!"

Farewell, believe in my keen and sincere friendship.

102. To Louis de Kergorlay

Tocqueville, May 16, 1858

I was very much annoyed to have left Paris, my dear friend, without having seen you. I had had Mathilde ask you to come one day about ten o'clock, so we could chat while we lunched together, before I left for my work. I was obliged to leave before you could put this plan into action. The three times I went to see you, you were out. I repeat that I regretted that we could not chat at least once really in depth and, of all things, after such a long separation and before another separation that may also be long, because I absolutely do not know how our summer and autumn will go. I had wanted to take my wife to the waters in order to try to cure the pain in her liver that torments her. But I am beginning to despair of being able to take her from here; she has such a horror of long trips and such a passionate love of the kind of life we lead in our retreat. Since Mrs. Belam is very well at the moment, and since the difficulty of our taking lodgings at the château of Chamarande is becoming greater and greater, nothing absolutely obliges us to leave. Marie therefore seems to me to want strongly to stay at Tocqueville, at least until the month of October, and I think that in the end I will accede to her on this point. So, you see that, if you do not have an opportunity to come to Tocqueville, we have a chance of going a rather long time more without seeing each other again.

I did not find Mathilde to be ill during the visit I made to her. It seems she sometimes has pains and illnesses. But her appearance does not indicate anything serious. I was glad for her and for you. Your two youngest children, whom I saw on the same occasion, seem to me to be flourishing.

Of the things I had wanted to chat with you about, my work was of the first order.[29] I am beginning to be a little anxious about it. I am sure I do not have to write a long book; but with the manner in which I have set about studying the facts and preparing myself for the final drafting, I fear I will never finish. Unfortunately, I do not know what discipline I should adopt to limit myself in my research. Between reading everything and reading nothing, I do not see any middle point. Now, the *literature* of the Revolution, as the Germans were saying, is so immense that a lifetime could go by in trying to know even superficially everything it contains. You know that it is less the facts that I am looking for in this reading than the traces of the movement of ideas and sentiments. It is that above all that I want to paint; the successive

29. Tocqueville is referring to a book on the French Revolution, which he never completed, a sequel to *The Old Regime and the French Revolution*.

changes that were made in the social state, in the institutions, in the mind and in the mores of the French as the Revolution progressed, that is my subject. For seeing it well, I have up to now found only one way; that is to live, in some manner, each moment of the Revolution with the contemporaries by reading, not what has been said of them or what they said of themselves since, but what they themselves were saying then, and, as much as possible, by discovering what they were really thinking. The minor writings of the time, private correspondence . . . are even more effective in reaching this goal than the debates of the assemblies. By the route I am taking, I am reaching the goal I am setting for myself, which is to place myself successively in the midst of the time. But the process is so slow that I often despair of it. Yet, is there any other?

There is besides something special in this malady of the French Revolution that I feel without being able to describe it well or to analyze its causes. It is a *virus* of a new and unknown kind. There were violent revolutions in the world, but the immoderate, violent, radical, desperate, audacious, almost mad, and nonetheless powerful and effective character of these revolutionaries is without precedent, it seems to me, in the great social agitations of past centuries. From whence came this new race? What produced it? What made it so effective? What is perpetuating it? For we are still faced with the same men, although the circumstances are different, and they have founded a family in the whole civilized world. My mind is worn out with forming a clear notion of this object and with looking for ways of painting it well. Independent of everything that is accounted for in the French Revolution, there is something unaccounted for in its spirit and its acts. I sense where the unknown object is, but try as I may, I cannot raise the veil that covers it. I feel this object as if through a strange body, preventing me from either touching it well or seeing it.

I learned our old friend Malartic lost his sister. When this happened, I wanted to write him. But I do not know his address. If you know it, send it to me.

I embrace you with all my heart. All the best from Marie to you and yours.

103. To Arthur de Gobineau

Tocqueville, September 16, 1858

It is not because your letter before last was not satisfactory to me, my dear friend, that I had not answered it. I was thinking that I would be leaving any day for Paris, and my principle is that it is only necessary to write people with whom one cannot chat. Indeed, I was in Paris two weeks ago. But I only spent forty-eight hours there. I went there, above all, to consult my doctor, as I have been dissatisfied with my health for three months. He found me sufficiently ill to order me to leave again right away to carry out in the country a treatment that would have been difficult and inconvenient to follow alone in the inn. I count on returning to Paris, and this time for a long while, toward the 8th of next month. I still hope to find you there and, if this happens, I will take real joy in it, because I have a great friendship for you, despite the quarrels that you accuse me, with some reason, of provoking with you. This bad habit on my part unfortunately does not date from yesterday, and I fear it has become a rather chronic ailment. I am very attached to you; I have esteem and affection for you. But there are, between our temperaments, differences and even oppositions that produce what you not wrongly complain of. I like men; it is very agreeable to be able to esteem them, and I know nothing sweeter than the sentiment of admiration, when it is possible. When I can neither esteem nor admire my fellow men, which happens very often to me, I confess, I like at least to seek amidst their vices some good sentiments that can be found mixed with the vices, and I take pleasure in fastening my sight on the small white points that can be observed on the black background of the picture. As for you, either naturally or as a consequence

of the painful struggles to which your youth was coura-
geously surrendered, you have become habituated to living
with the contempt that humanity in general and your country
in particular inspire in you. How do you expect, for example,
for me not to be a little impatient when I hear you say that
our nation has never taken things except on the small and pal-
try side and has not produced minds out of the ordinary, if
not perhaps that ignoble Rabelais in whose works I have never
found one louis d'or except after having turned over, to great
disgust, a pile of filth? As if several of the great things of this
world were not done by us? As if it were not we, especially,
who for three hundred years, through an uninterrupted succession of great writers, have most stirred the human mind,
have most pushed, animated, precipitated it in all the civilized
world, for good or for evil, that can be discussed, but powerfully, who doubts it? I know of no foreigner, unless perhaps
some cad of a German professor, who holds the opinion about
France that you, a Frenchman, hold of it. I am not saying this
to you to wage war on you, but as an example of what makes
me, all the while liking you immensely, unable to prevent
myself from quarreling with you. I find likewise that in the
same letter you are, in the same way, unjust toward your contemporaries. In what period of their lives have MM. Thiers,
Villemain, even Cousin,[30] despite being a little ridiculous in
his selection of subjects, done better than in their latest works?

30. Victor Cousin (1792–1867), a historian and, more importantly, the un-
disputed leader of French philosophy in the mid-nineteenth century. As a philosopher, Cousin was an eclectic, believing that the empiricism of Locke or
Condillac led to materialism and atheism, and hence needed to be supple-
mented by the notion that man's mind is active (Kant, Schelling) as well as
passive. Here he hoped to leave room for the spiritual and religious part of
man. In a later philosophical work, *Du vrai, du beau, et du bien* (1853), Cousin
sought to combine the empiricism of Locke, the rationalism of Plato, and the
romanticism of the heart.
Cousin was also famous for his work in the history of philosophy, such as
his *Cours de l'histoire de la philosophie* (1829), a book that also delves into the
philosophy of history. As a political thinker, Cousin defended the liberalism
fashionable under the July Monarchy.

And as for their intrinsic value, what historian is more celebrated today in Europe than M. Thiers, what more brilliant
mind is there than Villemain, what better writer than Cousin?
Lamartine, does he not incontestably remain the greatest poet
of the epoch, although now he no longer writes anything but
detestable verses and prose that is equal to the verse? What is
unfortunately true and very sad is that these men, who are not
of great genius but assuredly of great talent, are becoming old
men and are not being replaced by anyone. In the generations
placed beneath those who are fifty or sixty years old, that is to
say those who, after having been people of spirit, are gradually becoming old fools, what man, I am not saying of some
talent, but of real luster, of great renown is making himself
known? The old novelists themselves, the old vaudevillians
like Scribe who are assuredly not Molière or Lesage, but who
were read passionately in all the civilized world, are not being
replaced by men who seem to have the least chance in the
world of making the noise that those made. That is what sad-
dens me and what disturbs me, because the situation is new
and consequently it is still impossible to foresee how long it
will last. It results, I believe, in part from the extreme fatigue
of souls and from the clouds that fill and weaken all minds. It
requires strong hatreds, ardent loves, great hopes, and powerful convictions to set human intelligence in motion, and, for
the moment, people believe strongly in nothing, they love
nothing, they hate nothing, and they hope for nothing except
to profit at the stock exchange. But France has not had, up to
now, a temperament that permits it to stay sunk so long in
the taste for well-being, and I always hope that the same
movement, if it must come, which will raise it up again, will
reanimate its literary life.

It would be very difficult for me to say why and how
I have been led to relate all that to you. This is a real
lecture at full speed. Do not respond, since we are soon going
to see each other again after this long absence and speak of
all that and of a thousand other things. A thousand affections

from the heart. Do not fail to remember us to Mme. de Gobineau.

104. To Gustave de Beaumont

Cannes, March 4, 1859

My dear friend, I know nothing that has ever grieved me so much as what I am going to say to you: *I ask you to come.* Here we are all alone. Hippolyte having made off; Edouard, who is in Nice, about to do the same. Here we are falling into solitude, just when our strength is returning, as our intellectual and physical activity is reawakening. If ever you could do something good for us, it is now. Nonetheless, I would not have wrenched you this way from the delightful life you are leading, in order to throw you into the kind of cistern we are in, without having a reason which I can tell only you, but which will show you the *urgency* of the relief: my wife's state of mind makes me *fear,* my friend.[31] She is suffering, suffering, more than she had been for a month: it is apparent she is coming to the last extremity of her physical and *mental* strength; that this condition engenders ideas in her soul, feelings, sorrows, and fears, which in the end could lead her mind I know not where. You know Marie. Reason itself, up to the point at which it seems that suddenly the reins hang loose. Moreover, our servants, especially Auguste, are in a state of semi-illness which brings about a slackness of service, now when it is necessary to increase one's ardor and one's zeal a hundredfold. What can I say to you, my friend, if not this: COME. COME, as fast as you can. *You alone* can put us back on the field. Your cheerfulness, your courage, your liveliness,

31. Beaumont relates that at one time during Marie's illness, the doctor ordered her to remain in complete darkness in order to treat an eye illness. Because Tocqueville needed sunshine for his illness, they were in effect separated until he could bear it no longer. He returned, saying: "Dear Marie, the sunshine ceases to do me good if, to enjoy it, I must give up seeing you."

the complete knowledge you have of us and our affairs, will
make easy for you what would be impracticable for someone
else. Come. I know that what I am asking of you is an immense proof of friendship. I know it; but I know to whom
I am addressing myself. *Two* weeks here will suffice grandly.
You understand that it is no longer necessary to mention the
inn. Let me treat you like a brother; have you not been a
thousand times more in a thousand situations! The room in
which Hippolyte lived will be ready for you. Do not answer.
Come. Do not be too vexed with the man who is imposing
such a cruel tax on you; but think rather of the unfortunate
man, of the friend of more than thirty years, who fears all
sorts of misfortunes, if you do not come to his aid. It is best
to reach Marseilles by a train that only takes 19 hours to go
from Marseilles to Paris. Once in Marseilles, take the Nice
stage coach. There is one every day. This will bring you to
Cannes in 23 hours. There, since you will have a little trunk,
take a cabriolet, which, for 40 sous, I think, will bring you to
my place. We are three-quarters of a league from town.
Come. May Madame de Beaumont pardon us or rather I am
sure she has already pardoned us. I embrace you from the
depth of my soul.[32]

32. Despite the fact that he mentions only his wife's illness, Tocqueville's
own physical condition proved to be more serious. He died April 16, 1859; his
wife died December 22, 1864.

APPENDIX A

BIOGRAPHICAL SKETCHES OF TOCQUEVILLE'S CORRESPONDENTS

Ampère, Jean-Jacques (1800–1864). Son of André Marie Ampère, the famous physicist. Jean-Jacques Ampère was a philologist, literary critic, and professor of the history of French literature. Among other works, he published *De l'histoire de la poésie* (1830) and *Histoire romaine à Rome,* 4 vols. (1861–1864).

Beaumont, Gustave de (1802–1866). Tocqueville's closest and most loyal friend. Beaumont and Tocqueville met in 1827 when both were serving as *juge-auditeurs* in the court of Versailles. After the Revolution of 1830, they both took the oath to support the July Monarchy, but since this was a very sensitive issue to their aristocratic families and friends, they managed to secure an official mission to study the penitentiary system in the United States. In 1831–1832, they made their extraordinary journey to the United States and duly completed their observations on the United States' prison system in *Du système pénitentiaire aux Etats-Unis et de son application en France* (1833).

After this, each turned to write about the United States, and in 1835, when Tocqueville published the first part of *Democracy in America,* Beaumont blended romance and fact in his *Marie, ou l'esclavage aux Etats-Unis: Tableau des moeurs américaines* in order to protest the practice of slavery in the United States. Once more, the two friends published together. In 1840 Tocqueville finished the second part of *Democracy in America;* in 1839, only a few months earlier, Beaumont had published an excellent historical and political analysis in his two volumes entitled *L'Irlande sociale, politique, et religieuse.* For his work, Beaumont became a member of the Academy of Moral and Political Sciences in 1842.

By 1839 the two friends were in the Chamber of Deputies together, working together in the left opposition on such issues as prison reform, extension of the suffrage, an end to slavery in French colonies, and a more coherent policy toward Algeria. Under the Second Republic, both were elected to the Constituent Assembly and Legislative Assembly, but Beaumont was first appointed ambassador to London and then, after Tocqueville became minister of foreign affairs, Beaumont was appointed ambassador to Vienna. During the coup of December 2, 1851, they were arrested together, and each subsequently retired from political life— Tocqueville to continue his intellectual work and Beaumont forced, out of economic necessity, to attend to financial matters.

With the exception of a rift between the two in 1844 caused by a quarrel concerning the newspaper *Le Commerce,* this friendship of thirty-two years must have been one of the deepest and most fruitful of this period in French history. Twice they made long and perilous journeys together, to North America and to Algeria, and both times Beaumont displayed a marvelous loyalty in nursing Tocqueville through serious illness. In political life, they worked together closely until they adopted one common position, and neither would publish anything without the other reading it closely and making suggestions and criticisms. In the final letter of this volume, Tocqueville makes a desperate plea to his friend for help and, characteristically, Beaumont rushed to be with his lifelong friend.

Chabrol, Ernest de (1803–1889). Chabrol, who received some of Tocqueville's most insightful letters written from the United States, shared an apartment in Versailles in 1828 with Tocqueville and Beaumont when they were all government officials. Chabrol continued to practice law and later was a banker.

Circourt, Adolphe de (1801–1879). A French writer, government official, and ambassador to a variety of European capitals during his long career. His many articles in the French press consistently supported the monarchy and the claims of the Bourbons. Madame de Circourt maintained one of the most famous salons in mid-nineteenth century Paris.

Clamorgan, Paul. While Tocqueville served in the Chamber of Deputies under the July Monarchy and in both the Constituent Assembly and Legislative Assembly under the Second Republic, Clamorgan was his key contact in the district of Valognes, which Tocqueville represented. Thus, Clamorgan informed Tocqueville of district problems and concerns and acted as something of an election organizer and public relations manager in Tocqueville's home district.

Corcelle, Claude-François de (called *Francisque* by Tocqueville) (1802–1892). One of Tocqueville's most loyal friends and during the July Monarchy a member of the Chamber of Deputies who allied himself with Tocqueville's independent but liberal position. During the Second Republic, he was elected both to the Constituent Assembly and the Legislative Assembly. Corcelle tended to be more enthusiastic about Catholicism and the Catholic church than did Tocqueville, and, unlike Tocqueville, Corcelle defended France's 1849 invasion of Rome for the purpose of restoring a repressive papacy.

Freslon, Pierre (1808–1867). A lawyer, a member of the Constituent Assembly elected in 1848, briefly minister of public instruction under the Second Republic, and finally general advocate in the Supreme Court of Appeal. His hostility to the Second Empire prompted him to resign, and he became Tocqueville's lawyer and frequent correspondent.

Gobineau, Joseph Arthur de, Count (1816–1882). French author and diplomat. During his diplomatic career, he was ambassador at various times to Bern, Hanover, Frankfurt, Teheran, Athens, Rio de Janeiro, and Stockholm. Gobineau is most famous for his *Essai sur l'inégalité des races humaines,* 4 vols. (1853–1855). In this book Gobineau offered the racist theory that the "white" race was superior both to the "black" and "yellow" races, but he used this argument to conclude that—with the intermingling of the races—European society was heading for decline and not the happy progress many in the nineteenth century predicted. Because he feared debilitation of the "white" race by mixing this race with the other two, he opposed both imperialism and any egalitarianism. In the end, he opposed nationalism and liberalism and hoped for an international aristocracy of great creativity and vigor. This idea emerges most clearly in his *La Renaissance* (1877). Gobineau also published some very successful literary works, particularly *Les Pléiades* (1874), and a two-volume *Histoire des Perses* (1869).

Grote, Harriet (1792–1878). A close friend of Tocqueville's since his 1835 journey to England. In 1850 she wrote a pamphlet entitled *The Case of the Poor Against the Rich, Fairly Stated by a Mutual Friend,* ardently defending the right to private property. In 1851, after Tocqueville wrote a long letter condemning Louis Napoleon's coup, she smuggled it out of France and published it in the *London Times.* She was married to George Grote, a well-known Utilitarian, author of *Essentials of Parliamentary Reform,* member of the House of Commons for a decade, and most famous for his *History of Greece,* 12 vols. (1846–1856).

Hatherton, Lord Edward John Littleton (1791–1863). Member of Parliament from 1812 to 1835, where he was a strong advocate of the rights of Catholics. In 1833 he became secretary in charge of Irish affairs in the ministry of Earl Grey. Here he clashed unsuccessfully with the more dynamic Daniel O'Connell.

Kergorlay, Louis de (1804–1880). Tocqueville's oldest friend and a distant cousin. From earliest childhood Tocqueville and Kergorlay were fast friends; their parents lived on the same street in Paris, and in La Manche their châteaux were not far apart. Both went to the lycée in Metz, but Tocqueville went into law while Kergorlay pursued a career in the military. In 1830, Kergorlay distinguished himself in the French campaign against Algiers, but Kergorlay was an ardent Legitimist who refused to take the oath to Louis Philippe and resigned from military service. All his life he clung to Legitimist principles, disliking the house of Orléans, the crass bourgeoisie running the July Monarchy, and any republic.

In 1832, Kergorlay became involved in the Duchess de Berry's bold but outlandish plan to land a force in Marseilles, gather a popular army, and sweep the Bourbons back into power. The plan failed, and Kergorlay was arrested and accused of treason. Tocqueville, who had taken the oath to Louis Philippe and whose political principles were emphatically not those of Kergorlay, rushed to defend him, and after an impassioned defense, Kergorlay was acquitted.

After this incident, Kergorlay felt embittered toward a world that no longer recognized his most cherished principles, and he protested by means of inaction. He did write occasional articles, and he was pressed by financial necessity to become involved in industrial affairs, but he had no energy for the broader political and intellectual worlds in which his friend was making such a mark. Tocqueville occasionally wrote to Beaumont that Kergorlay's inaction was disappointing because he always believed Kergorlay to have such immense potential. Finally, in the 1850s, when Tocqueville himself was confined to political inaction, Tocqueville discussed his ideas for *The Old Regime and the French Revolution* with Kergorlay at great length because Kergorlay could still clarify and stimulate Tocqueville's ideas in an extraordinary manner. In 1871, Kergorlay was elected to the National Assembly where he supported the Legitimist party.

Mandat-Grancey, Jeanne-Rachel de Cordoüe de, Countess. One of
Tocqueville's cousins and earliest acquaintances. Like Tocqueville, the countess was a great-grandchild of Lamoignon de
Malesherbes, the famous eighteenth-century statesman and
lawyer.

Mill, John Stuart (1806–1873). Mill was, of course, nineteenth-
century England's most famous philosopher, economist, and
political philosopher, writing such works as *A System of Logic*
(1843), *Principles of Political Economy* (1848), *On Liberty*
(1859), *Considerations on Representative Government* (1861),
Utilitarianism (1863), and *The Subjection of Women* (1869).
    Mill and Tocqueville met on Tocqueville's second journey
to England in 1835. In that same year, Mill reviewed the first
part of Tocqueville's *Democracy in America* in the *London Review,* proclaiming Tocqueville the Montesquieu of the nineteenth century. In 1836, Mill persuaded Tocqueville to write
an article entitled "Political and Social Condition of France"
for the *London and Westminster Review.* After the second part
of *Democracy in America* appeared in 1840, Mill reviewed it
with great enthusiasm in the *Edinburgh Review* and privately
wrote to Tocqueville that he "had changed the face of political philosophy." After 1843, the correspondence between
Mill and Tocqueville tapered off dramatically—possibly because they were never close friends, possibly because of
Mill's increasing attention to Harriet Taylor, possibly because some letters have been lost, but quite likely because,
between 1840 and 1842, Tocqueville and Mill exchanged
some tense words reflecting the political quarrels between
France and England.

Mottley, Mary (1799–1864). Tocqueville's wife, who was living
in Versailles in 1828 with her aunt when Tocqueville met
her. Mottley was English, from a family with ties to the
Royal Navy, and was older than Tocqueville, not very
wealthy, and certainly without a distinguished family.
Tocqueville's family and some of his friends opposed this
marriage to this poor foreigner, and, perhaps because of this
or perhaps because she devoted herself to Tocqueville with a

spiteful possessiveness, she was never fully welcomed into his family. Tocqueville himself found her to be a source of happiness, strength, and intellectual stimulation, and Beaumont seemed to care for her a great deal.

Radnor, William Pleydell-Bouverie, third Earl of (1779–1869). An eminent Whig statesman, an economic liberal whose views were closely linked to those of his friend William Cobbett, and a central figure in the English aristocracy. Both in the House of Commons and later in the House of Lords (after he succeeded to the title of Radnor in 1828), he was a strong advocate of parliamentary reform, an increase in social legislation, and the protection of citizens from government coercion. When Tocqueville visited England in 1833, he concluded his journey with a stay at Lord Radnor's Longford Castle. Here Tocqueville noted how the English aristocracy dominated local government.

Reeve, Henry (1813–1895). A writer, editor, and Tocqueville's English translator. Reeve, who seemed to travel in Europe's highest literary circles, became friends with Tocqueville in 1835 in Madame de Circourt's salon. In that year, Reeve translated the first part of *Democracy in America,* and in 1840 he translated the second part.

Reeve began his career as an editor with the *British and Foreign Quarterly Review,* then joined the staff of the *London Times,* and eventually took over the editorship of the *Edinburgh Review* from Sir George Cornewall Lewis. Reeve seemed to inspire great respect, friendship, and trust. He was frequently entrusted with private negotiations between the governments of England and France, and men such as Lord Hatherton relied on Reeve's discretion in editing their letters and personal papers.

Royer-Collard, Pierre-Paul (1763–1845). Probably the most influential French statesman under the Bourbon Restoration. Royer-Collard was the leader of the so-called Doctrinaires, an ill-defined group that supported a king, a hereditary nobility, and a legislature dominated by men of great property.

To Royer-Collard, this seemed to be a common sense compromise between the absolutist aspirations of most royalists and the republican notions of 1789. At the center of this political compromise stood the Charter of 1814, a document that took steps toward defending equality before the law, freedom of speech and religion, and the inviolability of property. Said Royer-Collard: "The principles of the Charter are the *eternal* principles of reason and justice."

Royer-Collard served in the Chamber of Deputies from 1815 to 1839. In his later years, under the July Monarchy, he shared Tocqueville's discouragement, but under the Restoration he was the Chamber's central figure and sometime president. With considerable courage and with long discourses of powerful eloquence, he sought to preserve what he considered to be a fair balance between the royalty, the aristocracy (Chambers of Peers), and the middle class (Chamber of Deputies). As a result, he often found himself in the opposition, opposing the monarchists, who threatened the lower chamber, and similarly opposing turmoil from below.

Between 1811 and 1814, Royer-Collard was a professor of philosophy at the Sorbonne. Here he introduced into France the philosophy of Thomas Reid. Royer-Collard rejected the sensationalism of Etienne de Condillac, contending instead that we are influenced greatly by sensations but that our minds must actively organize sense experience. He also rejected the traditionalism of Joseph de Maistre and the Catholic church, arguing instead that one need not yield to the judgments of authority because the individual has a direct common sense that understands right and wrong, as well as true and false. In politics, as well as in philosophy, he sought to use common sense (something that leads almost to a natural law position) in order to find a compromise between conflicting and opposing positions.

Sedgwick, Theodore (1811–1859). An American author, lawyer, and diplomat. Tocqueville met Sedgwick in the United States, and in 1833–1834, while Tocqueville was writing the first volume of *Democracy in America,* Sedgwick was an attaché to the U.S. legation in Paris. As a result, Sedgwick was very helpful in the writing of *Democracy in America* because Tocqueville could talk at length with an American who knew the constitutional and legal system of the United States so completely.

Senior, Nassau William (1790–1864). English economist, lawyer, and professor of political economy at Oxford from 1825 to 1830 and from 1847 to 1852. Senior was a member of the Poor Law Inquiry Commission of 1832 and in 1861 a member of the commission inquiring into the state of English education. He was most famous, however, for his tracts on political economy that defended a laissez-faire system and asserted that the desire for wealth was the sole motivation in all economic activity. Senior published many of his Oxford lectures and contributed frequently to the *Edinburgh Review* and the *London Review*. His most important book was probably *An Outline of the Science of Political Economy* (1836).

Stoffels, Charles (1808–1886). Younger brother of Tocqueville's lifelong friend Eugène Stoffels.

Stoffels, Eugène (1805–1852). Next to Kergorlay, Stoffels was Tocqueville's oldest friend, one whom he met at the lycée at Metz when Tocqueville was about fourteen years old. Stoffels later became a public official at Metz and wrote an occasional article on education and political economy. Even though Tocqueville moved in entirely different circles, he still maintained fairly close contact with Stoffels; for example, Kergorlay, Beaumont, and Stoffels were the first to hear of Tocqueville's plans for writing *The Old Regime and the French Revolution*.

Swetchine, Anne-Sophie Soymonov (1782–1857). A Russian mystic who, because of the influence of Joseph de Maistre, joined the Catholic church and moved to Paris. Here she established one of the nineteenth century's most remarkable salons, one famous for its courtesy, its intellectual vigor, and above all, its religious enthusiasm. Her home even had a private chapel attached. In 1860, M. de Falloux published her *Life and Works*.

Tocqueville, Louis-Edouard Clérel de, Viscount (1800–1874). The second of Tocqueville's two older brothers, Edouard was a member of the military guard for Charles X, but, of course, he resigned from the army after the Revolution of 1830. After his military career, Edouard took a great interest in agricultural matters, administering his own estate and writing several manuscripts on agricultural problems. He also participated extensively in local government—founding the Agricultural Institute in Beauvais, becoming vice-president of his local General Council, and eventually becoming mayor of Baugy.

Tocqueville, François-Hippolyte Clérel de, Count (1797–1877). Tocqueville's oldest brother, Hippolyte was in the military under the Restoration, was disenchanted with the July Monarchy, took an oath of allegiance to the Second Empire, and late in his life was a deputy and then a senator under the Third Republic from 1871 to 1877.

Tocqueville, Hubert de (1832–1864). Tocqueville's nephew, the second oldest child of his brother Edouard. With Tocqueville's advice and guidance, Hubert entered the diplomatic service as an assistant to the ambassador to Berlin, before his very early death.

Tocqueville, Louise-Madeleine-Marguerite Le Pelletier de Rosanbo de, Countess (1771–1836). Tocqueville's mother, granddaughter of Lamoignon de Malesherbes, and daughter of Louis Le Pelletier de Rosanbo. Tocqueville spoke infrequently of his mother, and we know comparatively little about her. We do know that she was imprisoned in 1793 with her husband, watched her grandfather and her parents led to their deaths in the Revolution, was saved herself only by Robespierre's fall, and was apparently quite shaken by these events.

Her husband, and Tocqueville's father, was *Hervé-Louis-François-Bonaventure Clérel, Count de Tocqueville* (1772–1856). In 1789, Hervé de Tocqueville supported the initial reforms of the French Revolution and criticized those who were emigrating. By 1792, he himself emigrated only to return and fight with the army supporting Louis XVI. In 1793 he was imprisoned and narrowly escaped death, but in 1794 he was declared a friend of the Revolution. Under the Restoration he served as a prefect in several *départements,* including Versailles, and was named a peer of France in 1827. After retiring from politics, he published two major works: *Histoire philosophique du règne de Louis XV* (1847) and *Coup d'oeil sur le règne de Louis XVI* (1850).

APPENDIX B

CHRONOLOGY

Tocqueville's Life		*Major Events in France*	
1805	Born in Paris July 29. Great-grandson of Lamoignon de Malesherbes, the famous eighteenth-century statesman and defender of Louis XVI.	1804–14	Napoleon I, emperor of France.
1812–23	Tutored by the Abbé Lesueur, his father's former tutor and an important moral and religious influence in Tocqueville's life. Attends the lycée in Metz.	1814	Louis XVIII, brother of Louis XVI, assumes the throne and restores the Bourbon regime.
			June 14 Acceptance of the Charter that established a hereditary monarchy, a Chamber of Peers, and a Chamber of Deputies, the last elected by a very limited suffrage.
		1815	*March 1* Napoleon's One Hundred Days.
			June 8 Act of the Congress of Vienna, restoring monarchies in Austria, Prussia,

Tocqueville's Life		*Major Events in France*
		and Spain.
		June 18 The Battle of Waterloo.
1823–27	Studies law in Paris.	1820–24 Louis XVIII and his royalist allies pressure the bourgeoisie and threaten the Charter by: (1) changing the electoral law and giving more power to landed proprietors and less to the commercial classes, (2) legislation designed to regulate the press and to limit personal liberties, and (3) dismissing liberal professors.
		1824 Charles X succeeds Louis XVIII.
		1825 The royalists continue to press for conservative change: (1) a law taxing the bourgeoisie in order to pay the ancient nobility for land seized during the Revolution, and (2) more power to the Catholic church.
1826–27	Travels in Italy and Sicily with his brother Edouard. Writes *Voyage en Sicile*.	
1827–30	Serves as *juge-auditeur* in the courts at Versailles.	1827–30 Charles X in continual conflict with his more liberal Chamber of Deputies.
1828	Begins attending Guizot's lectures on the history of Europe and the philosophy of history. Meets and becomes engaged to the Englishwoman Mary Mottley.	
		1830 *July 5* The French capture Algiers.
		July 26 "July Ordinances" announced: rigid control over the press, another dissolution of the Chamber, and a further revision of electoral laws to give more power to the royalists.

Tocqueville's Life	*Major Events in France*
	July 26–30 July Revolution.
	July 30 Lafayette, having declined the position of president of a new republic, hails Louis Philippe (Duke d'Orléans) as a new constitutional monarch. Liberal deputies, such as Thiers, fear a more radical government and eagerly turn to the new king, Louis Philippe.
1830 Reluctantly swears allegiance to King Louis Philippe and the July Monarchy.	
	1830–36 Agitation by radical republicans and members of the laboring classes, who were dissatisfied with the July Monarchy, its very limited franchise, and its lack of social legislation.
1831–32 Journeys to the United States with Gustave de Beaumont, ostensibly to study American penitentiaries, but actually to see American democracy. From May 1831 to February 1832, they travel as far north as Quebec, as far west as Lake Michigan and Memphis, and as far south as New Orleans.	1831 Insurrection at Lyons. 1831–32 Prime Minister Casimir Périer restores some order to France.
1833 Tocqueville and Beaumont publish *Du système pénitentiaire aux Etats-Unis et son application en France*. Tocqueville takes his first trip to England.	1833 Guizot's Primary Education Law extends education to more children but strengthens the position of the church in education. 1834 Working class rebellions in Paris and Lyons.
1835 Publishes the first part of *Democracy in America*. Takes his second trip to England and also visits Ireland.	1835 September Laws designed: (1) to curtail the press severely and (2) to speed the convictions of the insurgents.

Tocqueville's Life		*Major Events in France*	
1836	*October 26* Marries Mary Mottley. As a favor to John Stuart Mill, writes an article for the *London and Westminster Review* entitled "Political and Social Condition of France." Travels to Switzerland.	1836	Thiers as prime minister.
		1836–39	Molé as prime minister.
1837	Loses his election to the Chamber of Deputies.		
1838	Elected to the Academy of Moral and Political Sciences.		
1839	Elected to the Chamber of Deputies from Valognes (Normandy), near the château of Tocqueville. Will be reelected for the duration of the July Monarchy. Delivers a report to the Chamber of Deputies urging the abolition of slavery in French colonies, a report later reprinted by abolitionist groups in the United States.		
1840	Publishes the second part of *Democracy in America*.	1840	Thiers as prime minister. *July 15* Treaty of London: England, Russia, Prussia, and Austria join to oppose France and Egypt, France's ally in the Middle East.
		1840–48	Guizot as prime minister—the central figure defending the status quo.
1841	Elected to the French Academy. Travels with Beaumont to Algeria.		

Tocqueville's Life		*Major Events in France*	
1842	Elected to the General Council of La Manche. Later will become president of the General Council, a position in local government he always cherished.	1842–46	Tensions between France and England continue partially because of a quarrel over interests in Spain.
	Speech to the Chamber of Deputies criticizing the growing self-interest and lack of public participation in French politics.		
1841–43	Works on a study of India (*L'Inde*).		
1843	Delivers a report to the Chamber of Deputies urging prison reform.		
1844–45	Becomes the leading force behind a progressive newspaper, *Le Commerce,* which berates the opposition for not offering a clear alternative to Guizot, defends freedom of the press and the Catholic church's right to open schools, proposes programs to alleviate the new urban poverty, pushes for an extension of the franchise, and criticizes the growing atomization and indifference of society.		
1846	Writes *Notice sur Cherbourg,* a history of the city.	1846–47	Economic depression.
	A second trip to Algeria, this time with his wife.		

Tocqueville's Life		*Major Events in France*	
1847	Report to the Chamber of Deputies on Algeria, urging colonization but also just and honorable dealings with the local population.	1847–48	Banquet campaigns. Thiers and Barrot, as opposition leaders to Guizot's ministry, hold a long series of banquets across the country proposing: (1) an extension of the suffrage and (2) an end to corruption in government. This was to culminate in a large banquet in France on February 22, 1848, but the banquet was canceled.
1848	*January 27* Famous speech to the Chamber warning of approaching rebellion: "I think that we are slumbering on a volcano."		
		1848	*February 22* The 1848 Revolution begins, February 22–24. Demonstrations lead first to Guizot's resignation, then to the abdication of Louis Philippe, and finally to a provisional government headed by Lamartine.
			February 26 National workshops established, roughly corresponding to ideas of Louis Blanc.
1848	*April 23* Elected to the Constituent Assembly.		*April 23* Elections for the Constituent Assembly of the Second Republic. The Paris radicals find to their great surprise that the Assembly has about 80 radicals, 500 moderate republicans, and 300 royalists.
	June Chosen for the legislative committee designated to write a new constitution.		
	June 23–26 Helps coordinate resistance to the working-class rebellion.		*June 23–26* The June Days: bloody street fighting between the Parisian working class and an army supporting the propertied classes.
			July–August General Cavaignac, who put down

Tocqueville's Life		Major Events in France
		the revolt, becomes tempo-rary dictator and issues harsh laws curbing free-dom of the press and free-dom of association.
December 10 Votes for Cavaignac for president.		*December 10* Louis Napo-leon, nephew of Napoleon I, sweeps the presidential election.
	1849	*April-June* France intervenes militarily to overthrow the Roman republic and restore a repressive papacy.
1849	*May 13* Elected to new Legislative Assembly.	*May 13* Elections for new Legislative Assembly.
	June 2 Appointed by Louis Napoleon to be minister of foreign affairs.	*June 2* Barrot as prime minister.
		June 13 Ledru-Rollin at-tempts a poorly planned revolt.
	October 31 Resigns as min-ister of foreign affairs.	*October 31* Barrot's cabinet resigns.
1850–51	Writes *Recollections*, an analysis of the period 1848–1851 in the form of per-sonal memoirs.	1850	*March 15* Falloux Law, a concession to the Catholic majority in the Legislative Assembly. Extends Cath-olic influence in secondary education.
		May 31 An end to universal manhood suffrage.
	1851	*July 15* Proposal to revise Constitution and to allow President Louis Napoleon to run for reelection is defeated.
1851	*December 2* Tocqueville and other members of the As-sembly oppose the coup. Tocqueville is arrested and held for one day.	*December 2* Louis Napo-leon's coup d'état.
	December 11 At some risk, Tocqueville smuggles out a letter to be printed anony-mously in the *London Times,* denouncing the coup.	

Tocqueville's Life		*Major Events in France*
	1852	*February 17* Repressive measures against the press.
		December 2 Second Empire established with Napoleon III as emperor.
1853	Begins to study documents in the archives at Tours in preparation for his study of the Old Regime.	1853–60	Napoleon III uses powers of the state to promote commerce: banking reform, government loans, development of railroads and shipping, etc. Also some legislation to provide modest improvement in the conditions of the working class. Finally, a public works program, highlighted by Baron Haussmann's widening of the boulevards of Paris.
1854	Travels to Germany to study feudalism and why the Revolution surfaced in France instead of somewhere else in Europe.	1854	France declares war on Russia in the Crimea.
		1855	Paris International Exposition boasting of economic and technological progress of France.
1856	Publishes *The Old Regime and the French Revolution,* the first part of a more comprehensive study of the Revolution that he intended to finish later.	1856	Crimean War ends.
1857	Journeys to England to study documents on the French Revolution. The English navy puts a warship at his disposal for his return to France.		
1859	*April 16* Dies at Cannes.		
		1860–70	A moderate liberalization of Napoleon III's empire.

APPENDIX C

SOURCES FOR THE TEXTS

For over three decades the Commission nationale pour l'édition des oeuvres d'Alexis de Tocqueville in Paris has been steadily publishing the definitive edition of Tocqueville's complete works. At present the Commission nationale has under its control the largest collection of Tocqueville's books, papers, and letters, and these are unavailable for purposes of research. Fortunately, the Commission nationale has published a great many of Tocqueville's letters in the multivolume work still being published under the direction of J. P. Mayer (*Oeuvres complètes* [Paris: Gallimard, 1951–]). Our volume of translated letters could not have been completed without these important publications, and in the following list when the source of a letter is indicated, we refer to this edition as *Oeuvres* (M).

Another edition of Tocqueville's "complete" works appeared over a century ago. This edition was published by Madame de Tocqueville and edited by Gustave de Beaumont (*Oeuvres complètes d'Alexis de Tocqueville* [Paris: Michel Lévy Frères, 1860–1866]). In this edition, Beaumont included three volumes of Tocqueville's letters, but to protect living contemporaries and for a variety of other reasons, Beaumont deleted some key passages and changed the style occasionally—besides making some errors of transcription. Many of the passages deleted by Beaumont cannot be restored by the Commission nationale. As a result, Beaumont's edition is unreliable but still extremely valuable for two reasons. First, it presently provides our only source of letters to important people in Tocqueville's life, and, second, the degree to which Beaumont distorted his friend's letters has been occasionally exaggerated. For example, a comparison between certain letters to Kergorlay in Beaumont's edition and the same letters in the definitive edition published in *Oeuvres* (M) reveals important differences, but nothing so serious that it alters Tocqueville's basic meaning. Whereas we would of course prefer to use the letters in *Oeuvres* (M), we have been compelled to use letters from Beaumont's edition about one-fifth of the time. In the following list of sources, we refer to this edition as *Oeuvres* (B).

About a dozen letters come from other sources, the most important of which is the Beinecke Rare Book and Manuscript Library at Yale University. This library has the finest collection of papers relating to Tocqueville's journey to America, and we have incorporated four important letters written from America and available to scholars at the moment only from the Tocqueville Manuscripts Collection at Yale University.

Primary Sources

LETTERS

1. *Oeuvres* (B), V.
2. *Oeuvres* (M), XIII, pt. 1.
3. *Oeuvres* (M), XIII, pt. 1.
4. *Oeuvres* (M), XIII, pt. 1.
5. *Oeuvres* (M), VIII, pt. 1.
6. Beinecke Rare Book and Manuscript Library, Yale University Tocqueville Manuscripts Collection.
7. Beinecke Rare Book and Manuscript Library, Yale University Tocqueville Manuscripts Collection.
8. *Oeuvres* (M), XIII, pt. 1.
9. Beinecke Rare Book and Manuscript Library, Yale University Tocqueville Manuscripts Collection.
10. *Oeuvres* (B), VII.
11. Beinecke Rare Book and

Manuscript Library, Yale
University Tocqueville
Manuscripts Collection.

12. *Oeuvres* (B), VII.
13. *Oeuvres* (M), VIII, pt. 1.
14. *Oeuvres* (B), V.
15. *Oeuvres* (M), VIII, pt. 1.
16. *Oeuvres* (B), VII.
17. *Oeuvres* (M), XIII, pt. 1.
18. *Oeuvres* (M), XIII, pt. 1.
19. *Oeuvres* (M), XIII, pt. 1.
20. *Oeuvres* (B), VI.
21. *Oeuvres* (B), V.
22. *Oeuvres* (M), VI, pt. 1.
23. *Oeuvres* (M), XIII, pt. 1.
24. *Oeuvres* (M), VIII, pt. 1.
25. *Oeuvres* (B), VI.
26. *Oeuvres* (M), XI.
27. *Oeuvres* (B), V.
28. *Oeuvres* (M), VI, pt. 1.
29. *Oeuvres* (M), XI.
30. *Oeuvres* (M), VIII, pt. 1.
31. *Oeuvres* (M), VIII, pt. 1.
32. *Oeuvres* (M), VIII, pt. 1.
33. *Alexis de Tocqueville als Abge-
    ordneter: Briefe an seinen Wahl-
    agenten Paul Clamorgan,
    1837–1851* (Hamburg: Ernst
    Hauswedell & Co., 1972);
    hereafter referred to as *Alexis
    de Tocqueville als Abgeord-
    neter.*
34. *Oeuvres* (M), VIII, pt. 1.
35. *Alexis de Tocqueville als
    Abgeordneter.*
36. *Oeuvres* (M), VI, pt. 1.
37. *Oeuvres* (M), VIII, pt. 1.
38. *Oeuvres* (M), XI.
39. *Oeuvres* (B), VI.
40. *Oeuvres* (M), VI, pt. 1.
41. *Oeuvres* (M), XI.
42. *Oeuvres* (M), XI.

43. *Alexis de Tocqueville als
    Abgeordneter.*
44. *Oeuvres* (M), VIII, pt. 1.
45. *Oeuvres* (M), VIII, pt. 1.
46. *Oeuvres* (M), VIII, pt. 1.
47. *Oeuvres* (M), VIII, pt. 1.
48. *Oeuvres* (M), VIII, pt. 1.
49. *Oeuvres* (M), VIII, pt. 1.
50. *Oeuvres* (M), VIII, pt. 1.
51. *Alexis de Tocqueville als
    Abgeordneter.*
52. *Oeuvres* (B), VII.
53. *Oeuvres* (M), XIII, pt. 2.
54. *Alexis de Tocqueville als
    Abgeordneter.*
55. *Oeuvres* (B), VI; bracketed
    text from *Correspondence . . .
    Senior.*
56. *Oeuvres* (M), VIII, pt. 2.
57. *Oeuvres* (B), VI.
58. *Alexis de Tocqueville als
    Abgeordneter.*
59. *Oeuvres* (B), V.
60. *Oeuvres* (M), VIII, pt. 2.
61. *Alexis de Tocqueville als
    Abgeordneter.*
62. *Oeuvres* (M), VIII, pt. 2.
63. *Oeuvres* (M), VIII, pt. 2.
64. *Oeuvres* (M), VIII, pt. 2.
65. *Oeuvres* (M), IX.
66. *Oeuvres* (M), VIII, pt. 2.
67. *Oeuvres* (B), VI.
68. *Oeuvres* (M), XIII, pt. 2.
69. *Oeuvres* (M), VIII, pt. 2.
70. *London Times,* December 11,
    1851, p. 5; also in Alexis de
    Tocqueville, *Memoir, Letters,
    and Remains* (Boston: Tick-
    nor & Fields, 1862), vol. 2.
71. *Oeuvres* (M), VI, pt. 1.
72. *Oeuvres* (M), VIII, pt. 3.
73. *Oeuvres* (M), VIII, pt. 3.

74. *Oeuvres* (B), VI.
75. *Oeuvres* (B), VI.
76. *Oeuvres* (M), IX.
77. *Oeuvres* (B), VI.
78. *Oeuvres* (M), IX.
79. *Oeuvres* (M), VIII, pt. 3.
80. *Oeuvres* (M), VIII, pt. 3.
81. Richmond Laurin Hawkins, ed., *Newly Discovered French Letters of the Seventeenth, Eighteenth, and Nineteenth Centuries* (Cambridge, Mass.: Harvard University Press, 1933; rpt. New York: Kraus Reprint Corporation, 1966).
82. *Oeuvres* (M), VIII, pt. 3.
83. *Oeuvres* (M), VIII, pt. 3.
84. *Oeuvres* (B), VI.
85. *Oeuvres* (M), VIII, pt. 3.

86. *Oeuvres* (M), VIII, pt. 3.
87. *Oeuvres* (B), VI.
88. *Oeuvres* (M), VIII, pt. 3.
89. *Oeuvres* (M), VIII, pt. 3.
90. *Oeuvres* (B), VI.
91. *Oeuvres* (B), VII.
92. *Oeuvres* (M), IX.
93. *Oeuvres* (B), VI.
94. *Oeuvres* (B), VII.
95. *Oeuvres* (M), VIII, pt. 3.
96. *Oeuvres* (B), VI.
97. *Oeuvres* (M), XIII, pt. 2.
98. *Oeuvres* (B), VI.
99. *Oeuvres* (M), VI, pt. 1.
100. *Oeuvres* (M), VIII, pt. 3.
101. *Oeuvres* (B), VI.
102. *Oeuvres* (M), XIII, pt. 2.
103. *Oeuvres* (M), IX.
104. *Oeuvres* (M), VIII, pt. 3.

Secondary Sources

The editor has used information about people and events taken from general histories of the period, encyclopedias, and reference works of all kinds. Some of the most important of these sources should be acknowledged. The many editors of *Oeuvres* (M) have constituted one important source in providing biographical information about some of the less famous people to whom Tocqueville refers. Other important sources include but are not limited to the following.

Allison, John M. *Thiers and the French Monarchy*. Boston and New York: Houghton Mifflin, 1926.
Arnaud, René. *The Second Republic and Napoleon III*. Translated by E. F. Buckley. London: William Heinemann Ltd., 1930.
Chanoine, G.-A. Simon. *Histoire généalogique des Clérel seigneurs de Rampan, Tocqueville*. Caen: Imprimerie Ozanne, 1954.

Cobban, Alfred. *A History of Modern France.* Vol. 2, 1799–1871. Baltimore: Penguin Books, 1961.

Drescher, Seymour. *Tocqueville and England.* Cambridge, Mass.: Harvard University Press, 1964.

Johnson, Douglas. *Guizot: Aspects of French History, 1787–1874.* Toronto: University of Toronto Press, 1963.

Langer, William L. *Political and Social Upheaval, 1832–1852.* New York: Harper & Row, 1969.

Lucas-Dubreton, J. *The Restoration and the July Monarchy.* Translated by E. F. Buckley. London: William Heinemann Ltd., 1929.

Mayer, J. P. *Alexis de Tocqueville: A Biographical Study in Political Science.* Gloucester, Mass.: Peter Smith, 1966.

Palmer, R. R., and Joel Colton. *A History of the Modern World.* 6th ed. New York: Knopf, 1984.

Wolf, John B. *France: 1815 to the Present.* New York: Prentice-Hall, 1940.

Wright, Gordon. *France in Modern Times: 1760 to the Present.* Chicago: Rand-McNally, 1960.

Tocqueville's Works Mentioned in the Text

VOLUMES USED FROM THE MAYER EDITION (*Oeuvres* [M])

VI, pt. 1. *Correspondance anglaise: Correspondance d'Alexis de Tocqueville avec Henry Reeve et John Stuart Mill.* Edited and annotated by J. P. Mayer and Gustave Rudler. 1954.

VIII, 3 pts. *Correspondance d'Alexis de Tocqueville et de Gustave de Beaumont.* Edited and annotated by André Jardin. 1967.

IX. *Correspondance d'Alexis de Tocqueville et d'Arthur de Gobineau.* Edited and annotated by Maurice Degros. 1959.

XI. *Correspondance d'Alexis de Tocqueville avec Pierre-Paul Royer-Collard et avec Jean-Jacques Ampère.* Edited and annotated by André Jardin. 1970.

XIII, 2 pts. *Correspondance d'Alexis de Tocqueville et de Louis de Kergorlay.* Edited and annotated by André Jardin and Jean-Alain Lesourd. 1977.

VOLUMES USED FROM THE BEAUMONT EDITION (*Oeuvres* [B])

V–VI. *Oeuvres et correspondance inédites.* Edited by Gustave de Beaumont. 1861.

VII. *Nouvelle correspondance entièrement inédite d'Alexis de Tocqueville.* Edited by Gustave de Beaumont. 1866.

OTHER

Alexis de Tocqueville als Abgeordneter: Briefe an seinen Wahlagenten Paul Clamorgan, 1837–1851. Hamburg: Ernst Hauswedell & Co., 1972.

Correspondence and Conversations of Alexis de Tocqueville with Nassau William Senior, from 1834 to 1859. Edited by M. C. M. Simpson. 2d ed. New York: Augustus M. Kelley, 1968. Reprint of earlier edition: London: Henry S. King, 1872, which was translated by Senior's daughter, the wife of M. C. M. Simpson.

Democracy in America. 2 vols. Translated by Henry Reeve, Francis Bowen, and Phillips Bradley. New York: Vintage Books, 1945. The first part of *De la démocratie en Amérique* (2 vols.) appeared in France in 1835; the second part (2 more vols.) appeared in 1840 (Paris: Charles Gosselin). Henry Reeve translated the first part into English in 1835 and the second part in 1840.

L'Inde, in *Oeuvres* (M), III, *Ecrits et discours politiques.* 1962.

Memoir, Letters, and Remains. Translated by Mrs. M. C. M. Simpson. Boston: Ticknor & Fields, 1862.

The Old Regime and the French Revolution. Translated by Stuart Gilbert. Garden City, N.Y.: Doubleday & Co., 1955. Originally *L'Ancien régime et la Révolution* (Paris: Michel Lévy Frères, 1856).

On the Penitentiary System in the United States and Its Application in France. Written with Gustave de Beaumont. Translated by Francis Lieber. Carbondale: Southern Illinois University Press, 1964. Tocqueville and Beaumont published *Du système pénitentiaire aux Etats-Unis et son application en France* in 1833 (Paris: H. Fournier Jeune).

"Political and Social Condition of France." *London and Westminster Review,* April 1836.

Recollections. Edited by J. P. Mayer and A. P. Kerr. Translated by George Lawrence. Garden City, N.Y.: Doubleday & Co., 1971. *Souvenirs,* the French title, was first published in 1893 (Paris: C. Lévy), but with serious omissions. The first edition to restore most of the most important passages appeared in 1942 (Paris: Gallimard). The definitive French edition appeared in 1964 in *Oeuvres* (M), XII. Information from the editors was occasionally helpful.

Tocqueville and Beaumont on Social Reform. Edited and translated by Seymour Drescher. New York: Harper & Row, 1968. This includes selections of papers and speeches by Tocqueville and Beaumont, some of which appear in *Oeuvres* (B) and in *Oeuvres* (M).

INDEX

on railway, 286; tries to avert war, 287n; plans to go to Orient, 313; and English alliance, 317; and peace, 319; assassination attempt on, 364
National, Le, 241
Nemours, Duke de, 240–41
New Orleans, 69
Newport, 43
New York, 43–44
Nicholas I, 286n, 316n, 319

O'Connell, Daniel, 120, 167–68
Old Regime and the French Revolution, The, 228, 229; Tocqueville conceives of writing, 252–58, 265; Montesquieu as model, 257; preparation for, 285, 291, 295–97; plan of, 293; theme of, 296; research in Germany on, 305–6, 307–8; concluding, 322; ideas contrary to those of contemporaries, 325–27; during proof preparation of, 327–28, 329–31; laboriousness in writing, 331; published, 332; Tocqueville contemplates sequel to, 372–73
On the Penitentiary System in the United States and Its Application in France (Du Système pénitentiare aux Etats-Unis et son application en France), 74, 77–78
Ordre, L', 248
Orleanists, 260n, 263, 271n
Orsini, Felice, 364n
Ottoman Empire. *See* Turkey

Palmerston, Henry John Temple, Viscount, 186n, 266n, 286, 309n
Paris, 30; demonstrations in, 45n; concessions to, 100n; fortification of, 164, 185; as threat to stable republic, 203; fighting in, 212–14; government may need to flee, 213; people of prosperous, 290; as place for fellowship, 340–41

Parties, political: exploitation of ideas, 81; Tocqueville has none, 115, 257, 269; peace and war, 151–52, 156; do not represent country, 151; need for men independent of, 151–52; Tocqueville's distaste for, 154–56; lack of liberal, 156; conservative, 165; spirit of, 183–84; violent, 200; rivalries of disappear, 201; end of in 1848, 210–11; revolutionary versus moderate in Germany, 230–32; leaders of humiliated, 235; failure to unify, 267; despotism as reaction against, 346–47
Pays, Le, 241
Peel, Sir Robert, 115, 120n
Périer, Casimir-Pierre, 44, 44–45n, 80n
Périer, Joseph, 275–76
Persia, 348
Philosophy: how to mix with history, 256–57; must look to moral effect, 303; as romance for soul, 320–21
Piedmont, 56n, 222n
Pitt, William, 361
Plato, 109–10, 112, 130, 131
Plutarch, 124–25, 129–30
Politics: and moral principle, 81, 146; as career, 119, 210; sterility of, 135; indifference toward in July Monarchy, 138–39; and local interests, 143; suffer from lack of public life, 144; lack of passion in, 152–53; need for action in, 154–55; love of free institutions center of Tocqueville's, 158; public indifference to as game, 181–82; described in class terms, 198; Tocqueville's isolation from, 229; no indifference toward during revolution, 247; of eighteenth century, 330
Protestantism, 48–53, 109n
Prussia, 143n, 190, 218, 227, 230–31n, 231, 233, 305. *See also* Germany
Puritans, 192

Designer: Sandy Drooker
Compositor: Huron Valley Graphics, Inc.
Printer: Vail-Ballou Press
Binder: Vail-Ballou Press
Text: 10/13 Bembo
Display: Yale and Bembo